STOP!

This is the back of the book.
You wouldn't want to spoil a great ending!

This book is printed "manga-style," in the authentic Japanese right-to-left format. Since none of the artwork has been flipped or altered, readers get to experience the story just as the creator intended. You've been asking for it, so TOKYOPOP® delivered: authentic, hot-off-the-press, and far more fun!

DIRECTIONS

If this is your first time reading manga-style, here's a quick guide to help you understand how it works.

It's easy... just start in the top right panel and follow the numbers. Have fun, and look for more 100% authentic manga from TOKYOPOP®!

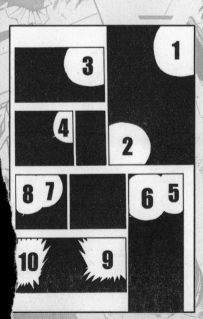

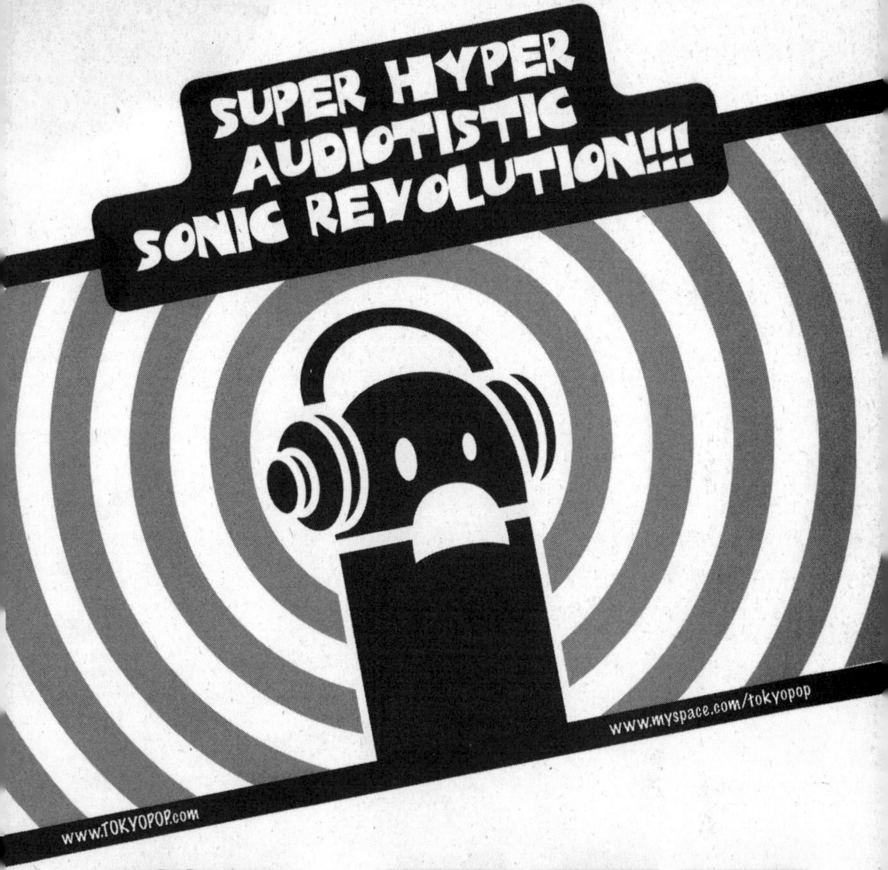
SUPER HYPER
AUDIOTISTIC
SONIC REVOLUTION!!!
www.myspace.com/tokyopop
www.TOKYOPOP.com

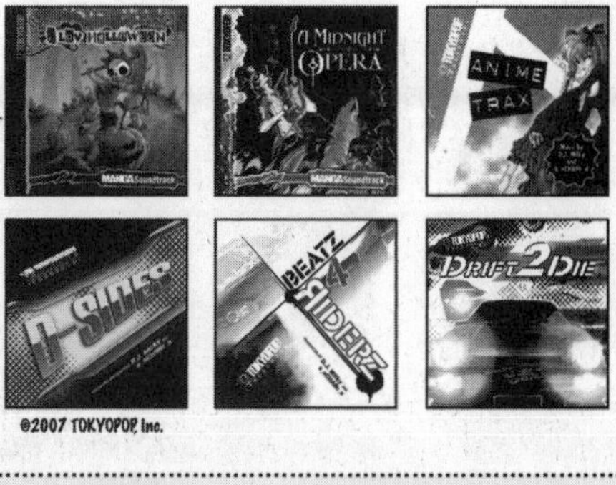
I LUV HALLOWEEN
A MIDNIGHT OPERA
ANIME TRAX
B-SIDES
BEATZ 4 RIDERZ
DRIFT 2 DIE

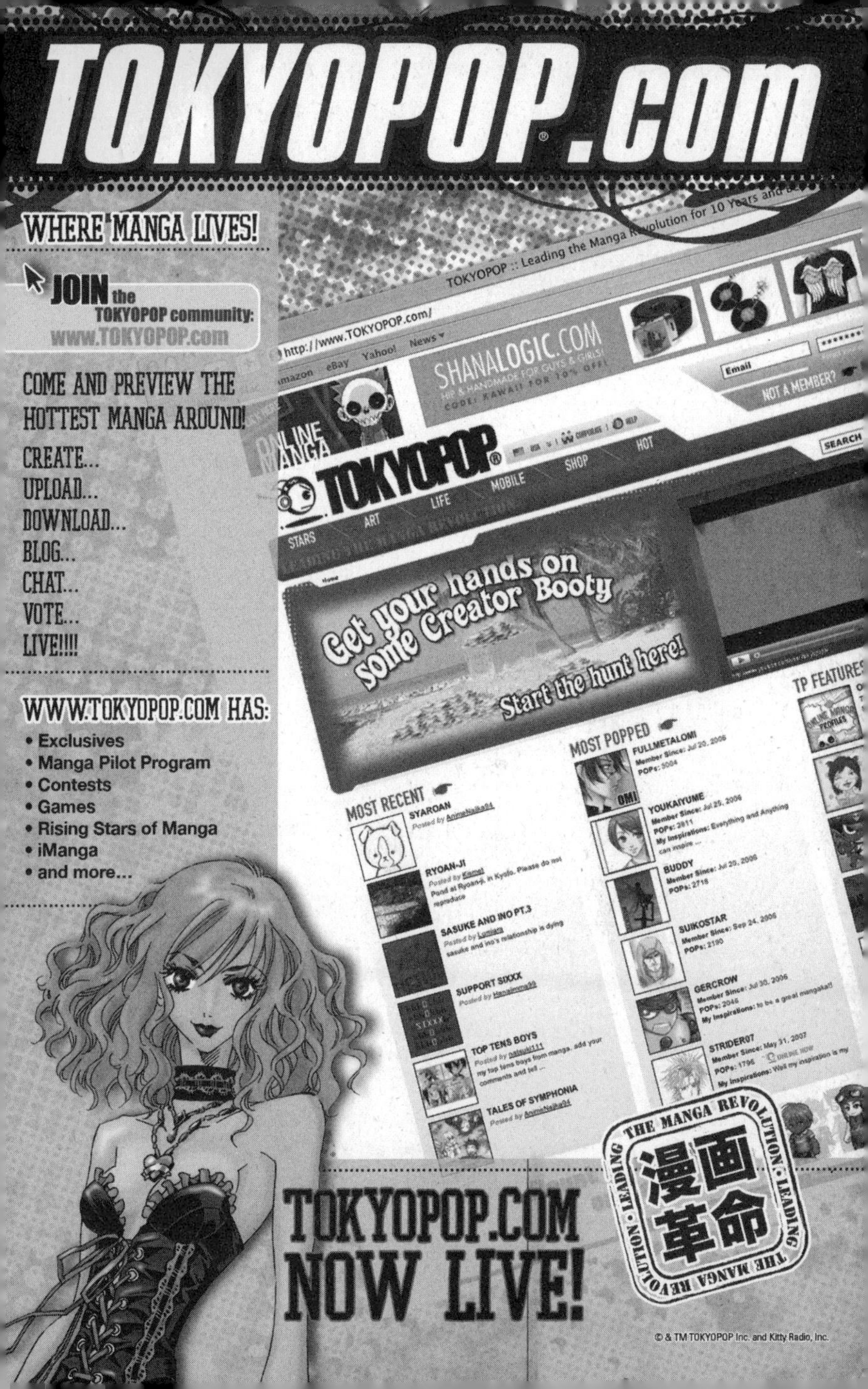

TOKYOPOP.com
WHERE MANGA LIVES!
JOIN the TOKYOPOP community: www.TOKYOPOP.com
COME AND PREVIEW THE HOTTEST MANGA AROUND!
CREATE...
UPLOAD...
DOWNLOAD...
BLOG...
CHAT...
VOTE...
LIVE!!!!
WWW.TOKYOPOP.COM HAS:
• Exclusives
• Manga Pilot Program
• Contests
• Games
• Rising Stars of Manga
• iManga
• and more...
TOKYOPOP :: Leading the Manga Revolution for 10 Years and B
http://www.TOKYOPOP.com/
SHANALOGIC.COM
ONLINE MANGA
TOKYOPOP
STARS
ART
LIFE
MOBILE
SHOP
HOT
SEARCH
Get your hands on some Creator Booty
Start the hunt here!
MOST POPPED
MOST RECENT
TP FEATURES
TOKYOPOP.COM NOW LIVE!
THE MANGA REVOLUTION • LEADING THE MANGA REVOLUTION • LEADING
漫画革命
© & TM TOKYOPOP Inc. and Kitty Radio, Inc.

A GUIDE TO THE HISTORICAL ERA OF *PEACE MAKER*

SO FAR NANAE CHRONO'S *PEACE MAKER* HAS FOCUSED ON *RONIN*, BUT THIS VOLUME TURNS AN EYE TOWARDS THE NINJA (CALLED *SHINOBI* IN THE JAPANESE). THE INSPIRATION FOR THESE MASTERS OF REDIRECTION CAN BE TRACED TO SUN TZU'S *ART OF WAR*, WHICH PREACHES WEAKENING OF THE ENEMY FIRST AND BATTLE ONLY AS A FINISHING STROKE. DECEPTIVE WARRIORS WHO IMPERSONATED ENEMY TROOPS, SPIED BEHIND ENEMY LINES OR SCALED IMPENETRABLE CASTLE WALLS UNDER COVER OF NIGHT ARE AS OLD AS SAMURAI CULTURE ITSELF, THE NINJA ALWAYS PLAYING SHADOW TO THE SPARKLING FACADE OF THE HONORABLE SAMURAI. MANY OF THE HISTORICAL ACCOUNTS OF THE NINJA COME FROM BEFORE AND DURING THE SENGOKU PERIOD ("WARRING STATES PERIOD;" 1336-1603). DURING THIS TIME, MERCENARY WARRIORS FROM THE IGA PROVINCE, SAID TO BE THE HOMELAND OF THE NINJA, PROVIDED JAPAN'S QUIBBLING *DAIMYO* (FEUDAL LORDS) WITH SPECIAL FORCES WHO COULD ENGAGE IN BEHIND-THE-SCENES ACTIONS THE WAY LARGE ARMIES OR HONORABLE SAMURAI COULD NOT.

THE MODERN MYTH OF THE NINJA WAS PROPAGATED BY THE JAPANESE THEMSELVES EARLY ON. UNDER THE TOKUGAWA SHOGUNATE (1603-1868), A PERIOD OF RELATIVE PEACE FELL OVER THE COUNTRY, AND A FLOURISHING OF TALL TALES ABOUT THE OLDEN DAYS, INCLUDING NINJA WHO COULD TURN INVISIBLE, TRANSFORM INTO ANIMALS OR WERE OTHERWISE ENDOWED WITH FANTASTICAL POWERS LEAPT TO LIFE IN KABUKI THEATRE AND WOODBLOCK PRINTS. MUCH LIKE ROBIN HOOD, BRUTAL MEN LIKE ISHIKAWA GOEMON WERE RE-IMAGINED AS CULTURAL HEROES. THE MYTH OF THE SUPERHUMAN NINJA CONTINUES TODAY IN VIDEO GAMES, MOVIES AND MANGA. NOT WANTING TO MISS OUT, EVEN IGA BOASTS A NINJA HOUSE FOR TOURISTS, AND NAGANO HAS ITS OWN NINJA VILLAGE THEME PARK!

YAMAZAKI SUSUMU AND THE UNKNOWN *KUNOICHI* (FEMALE NINJA) ARE SHOWN USING SOME CLASSIC NINJA WEAPONS. ALTHOUGH THE HISTORICAL ACCURACY OF THROWING STARS IS DEBATABLE, OTHER *SHURIKEN* SUCH AS DARTS OR KNIVES WOULD HAVE BEEN USED ALONGSIDE THE SHORT SWORD. *TETSU-BISHI* (CALTROPS) AND *SHUKO* (HAND CLAWS) WERE COMMON CONCEALED WEAPONRY TO BE EMPLOYED ALONGSIDE A KNOWLEDGE OF MEDICINES AND MARTIAL ARTS. THE *KUSARI-GAMA*, OR SICKLE WITH CHAIN, WAS AN ADAPTED PEASANT TOOL THAT ALLOWED NINJA TO GO UNDERCOVER AS GARDENERS (REPORTEDLY THE TOKUGAWA PALACE GUARDS) AND NEVER BE SUSPECTED. BUT THE MOST IMPORTANT NINJA TOOL WAS DISGUISE. ALTHOUGH THERE ARE HISTORICAL ILLUSTRATIONS OF THE STEREOTYPICAL BLACK-CLAD NINJA ASSASSIN, THE TASKS FACING REAL NINJA OFTEN REQUIRED THE NINJA TO DRESS AS SOMEONE TO BE TRUSTED. THIS TECHNIQUE IS USED TO GREAT EFFECT BY THE YAMAZAKI SIBLINGS IN THEIR INVESTIGATION OF MASUYA. IF A KUNOICHI WERE TO BE FOUND OUT, THE *NEKO-TE* (IRON FINGERNAILS) WERE A FAVORED WEAPON. AYUMU USES A SIMPLIFIED VERSION TO SHRED HER BINDINGS.

SADLY, THOUGH HISTORY RECORDS LITTLE ABOUT THE NINJA, IT IS CLEAR THAT THE FATE AWAITING MOST WAS AN EARLY DEATH.

-HOPE DONOVAN

In the Next

PEACE MAKER
ピースメーカー

In battle bloody
Revenge is executed.
But At what price vengeance?

Coming Soon!

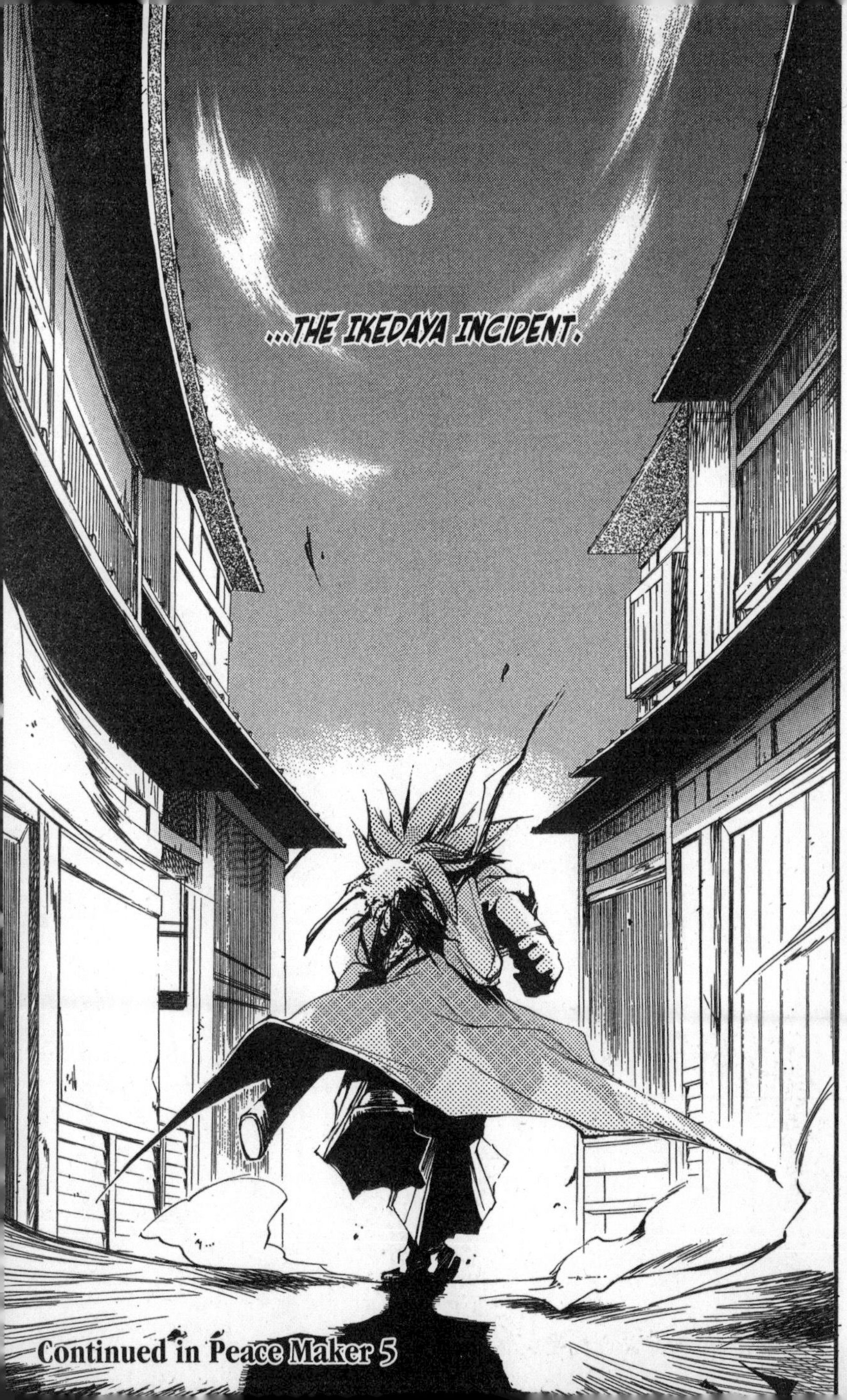
...THE IKEDAYA INCIDENT.

Continued in Peace Maker 5

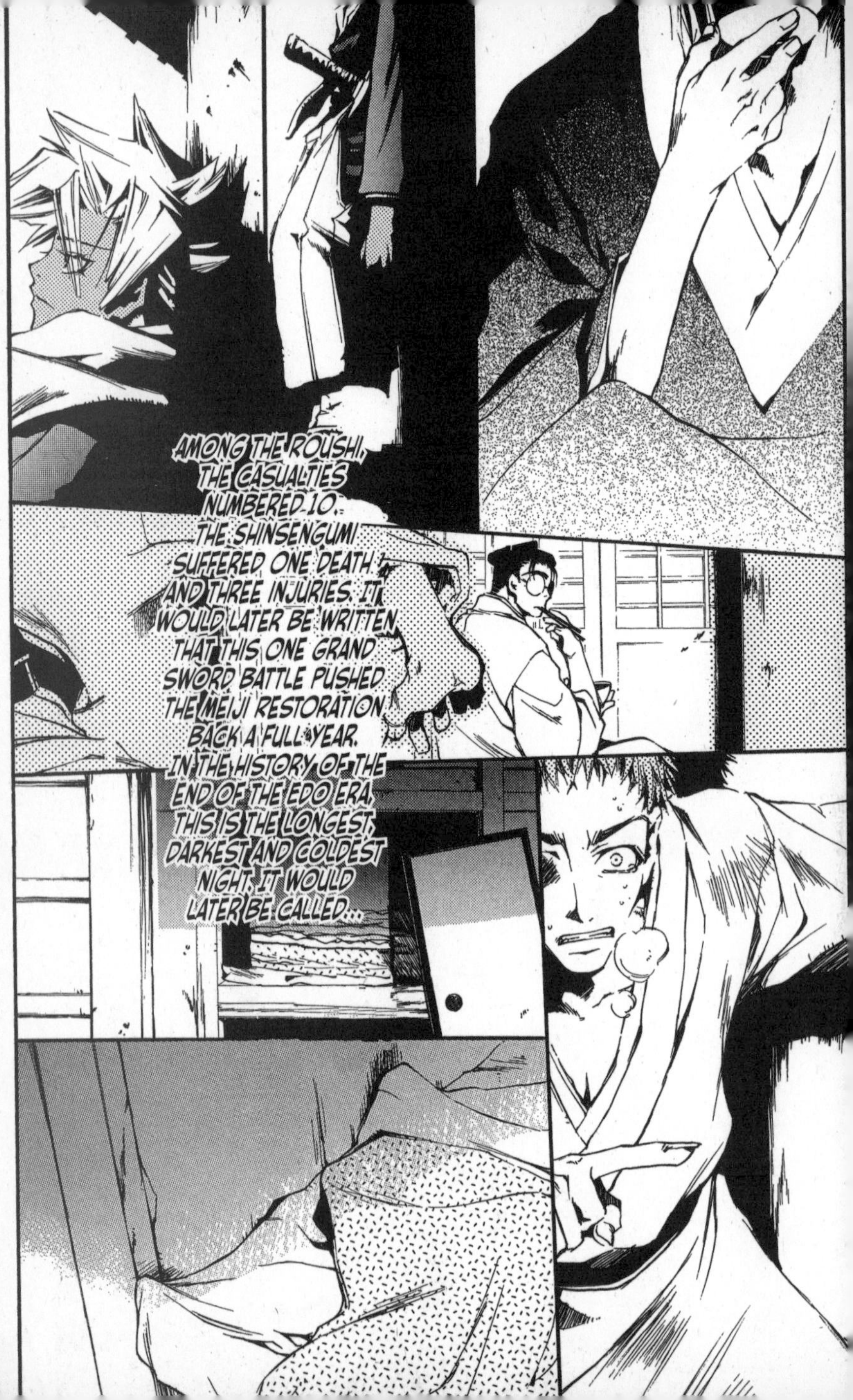
AMONG THE ROUSHI, THE CASUALTIES NUMBERED 10. THE SHINSENGUMI SUFFERED ONE DEATH AND THREE INJURIES. IT WOULD LATER BE WRITTEN THAT THIS ONE GRAND SWORD BATTLE PUSHED THE MEIJI RESTORATION BACK A FULL YEAR. IN THE HISTORY OF THE END OF THE EDO ERA, THIS IS THE LONGEST, DARKEST AND COLDEST NIGHT. IT WOULD LATER BE CALLED...

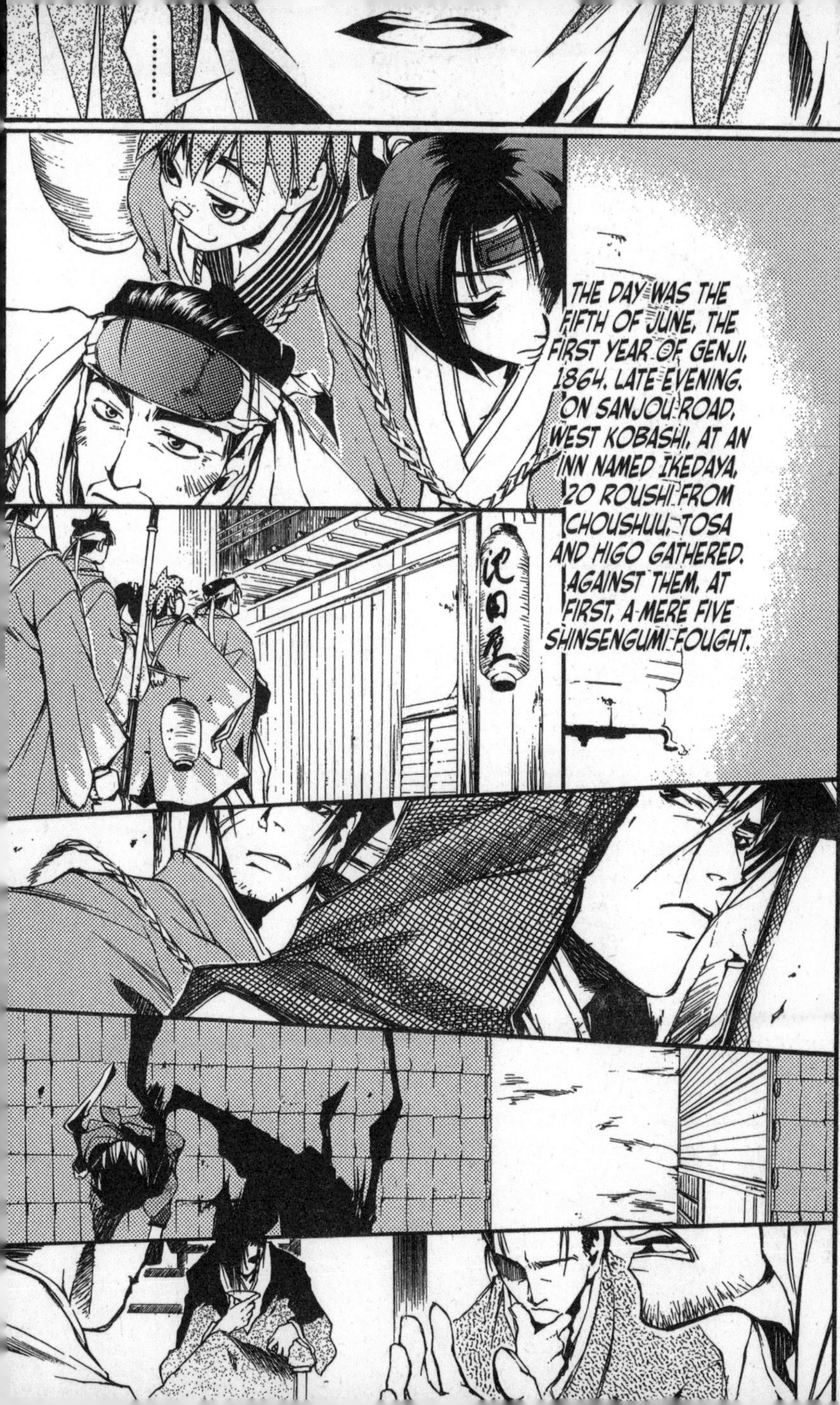
THE DAY WAS THE FIFTH OF JUNE, THE FIRST YEAR OF GENJI, 1864. LATE EVENING. ON SANJOU ROAD, WEST KOBASHI, AT AN INN NAMED IKEDAYA, 20 ROUSHI FROM CHOUSHUU, TOSA AND HIGO GATHERED. AGAINST THEM, AT FIRST, A MERE FIVE SHINSENGUMI FOUGHT.

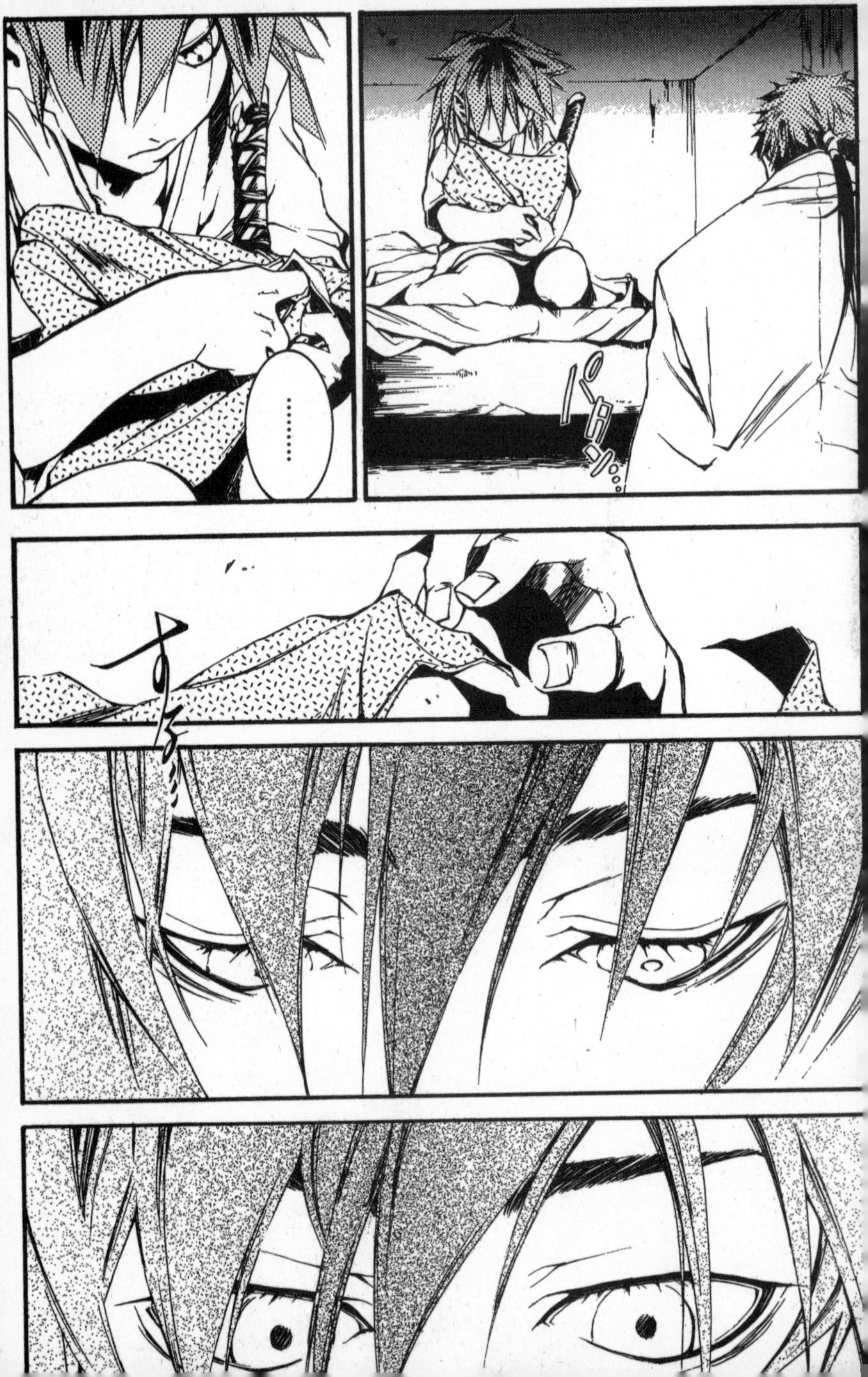

パタン…
……
する…

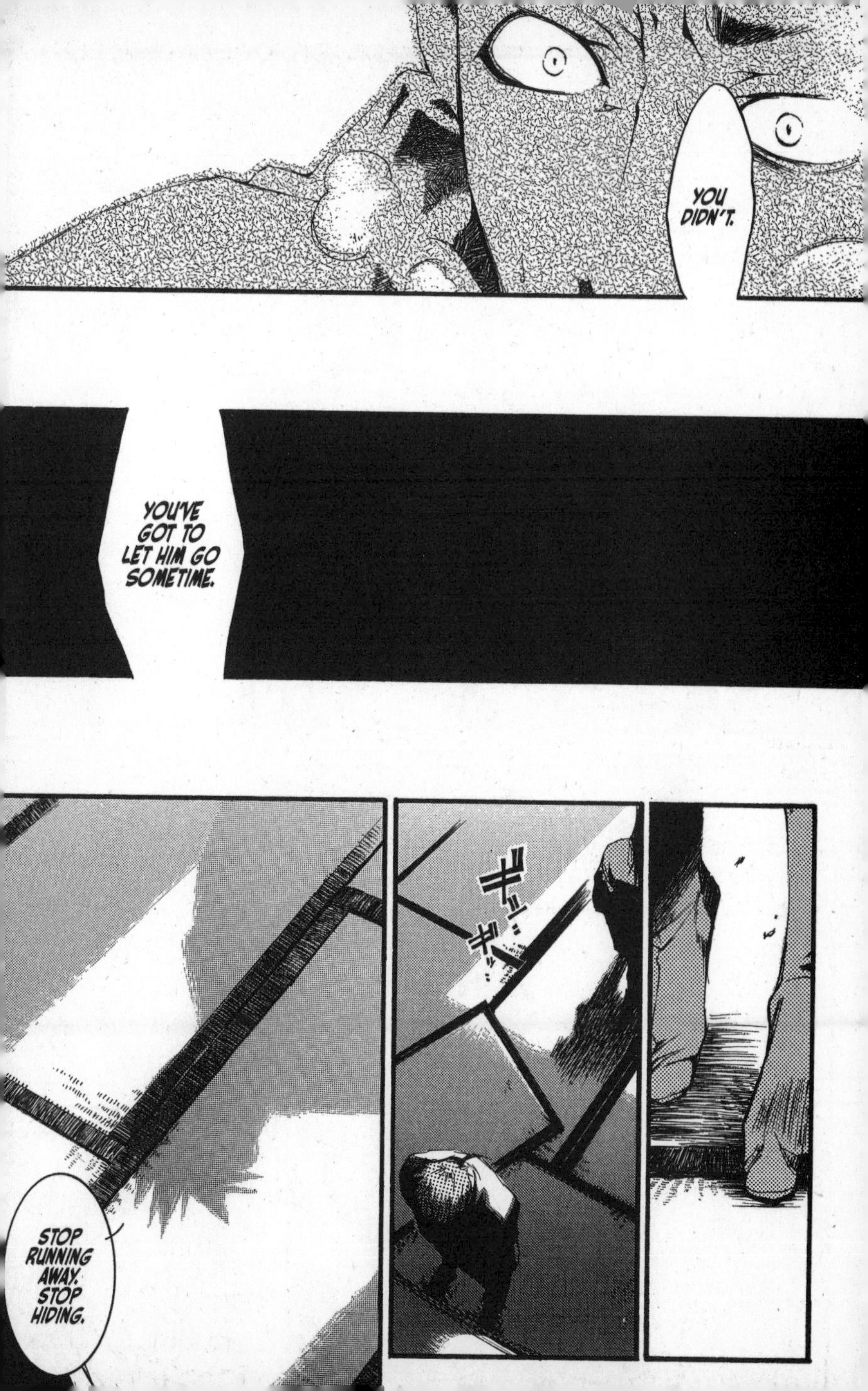
YOU DIDN'T.
YOU'VE GOT TO LET HIM GO SOMETIME.
ギッ
ギッ
STOP RUNNING AWAY. STOP HIDING.

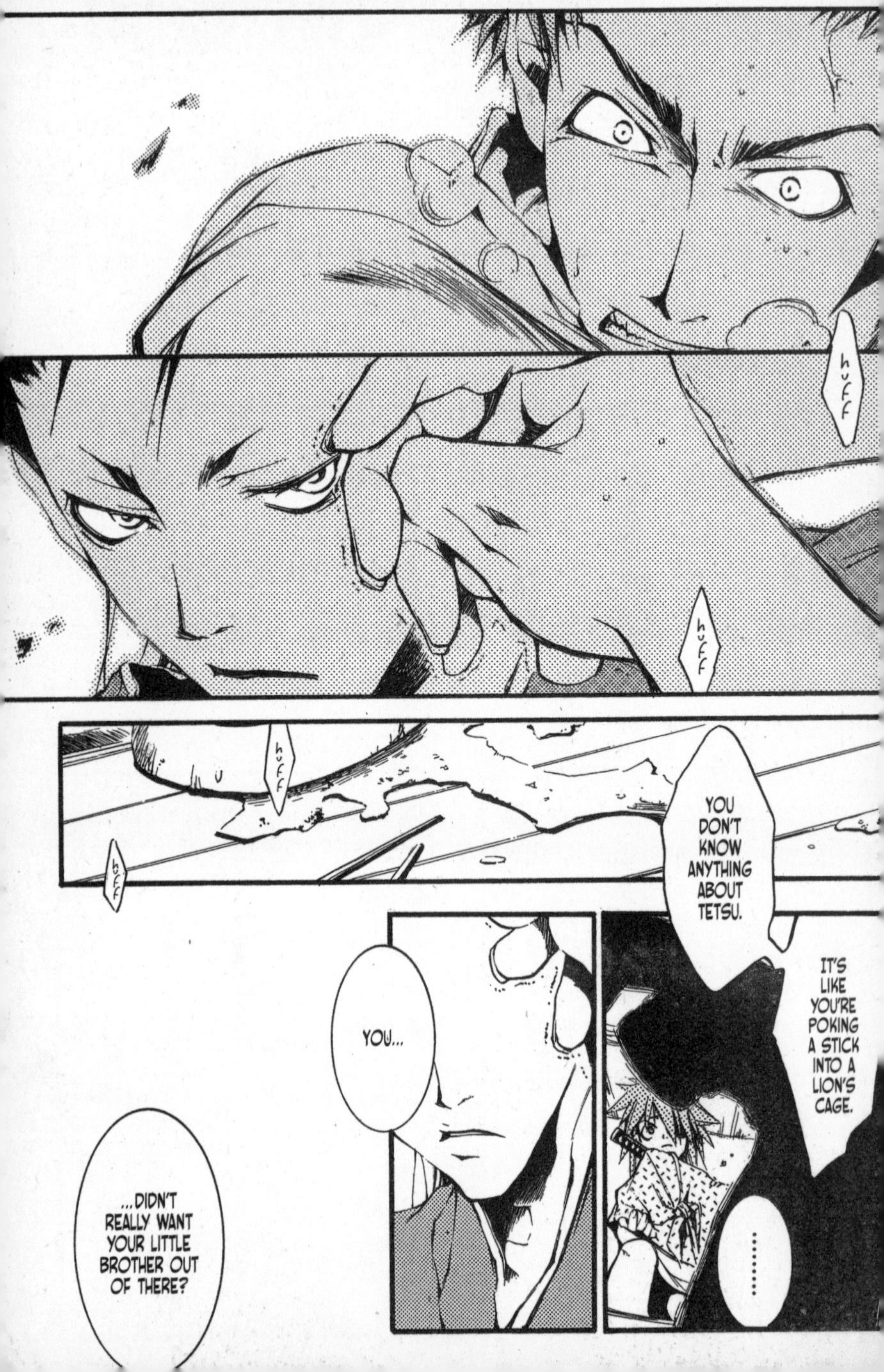
huff
huff
huff
huff
YOU DON'T KNOW ANYTHING ABOUT TETSU.
IT'S LIKE YOU'RE POKING A STICK INTO A LION'S CAGE.
....
YOU...
...DIDN'T REALLY WANT YOUR LITTLE BROTHER OUT OF THERE?

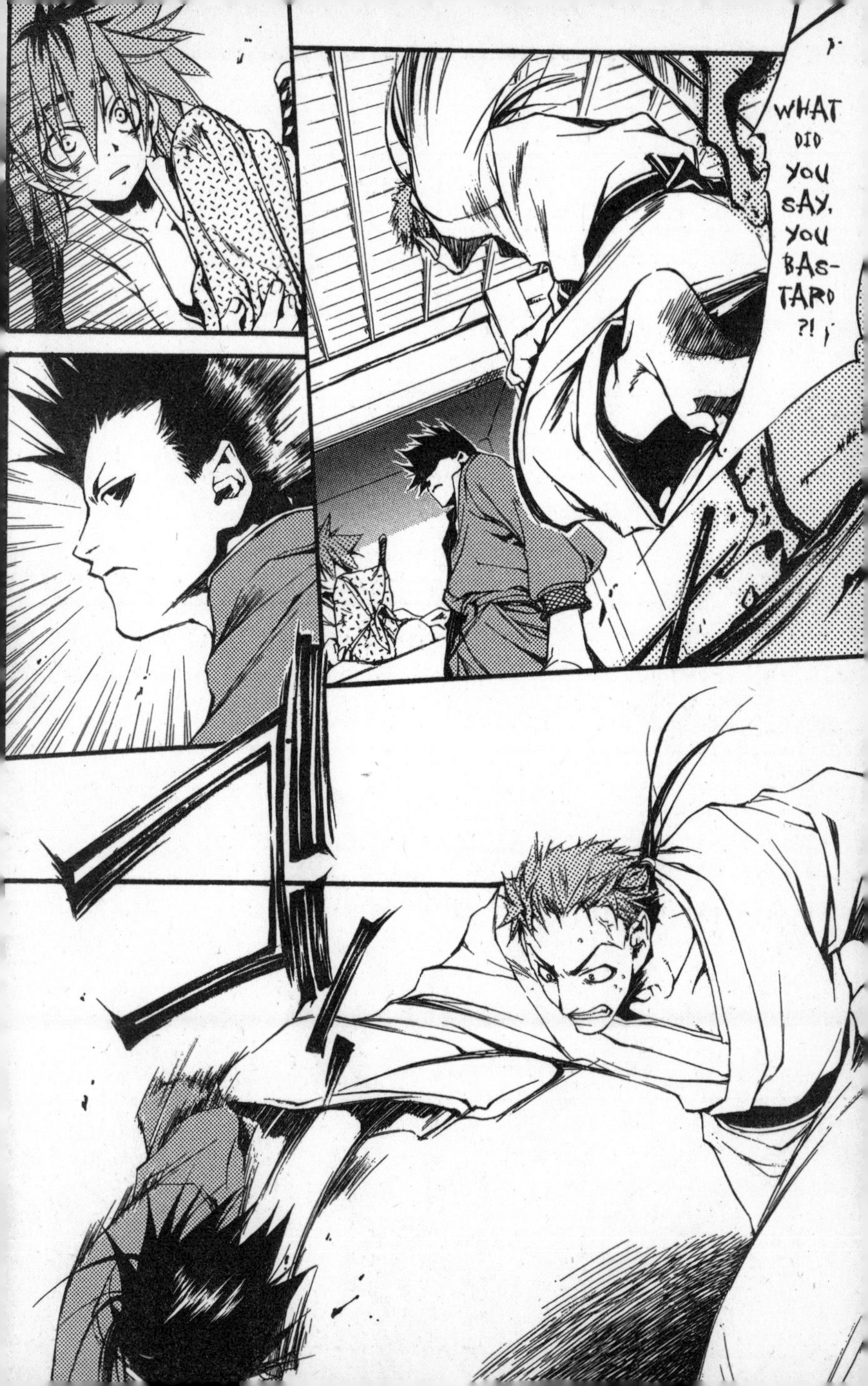
WHAT DID YOU SAY, YOU BAS-TARD?!

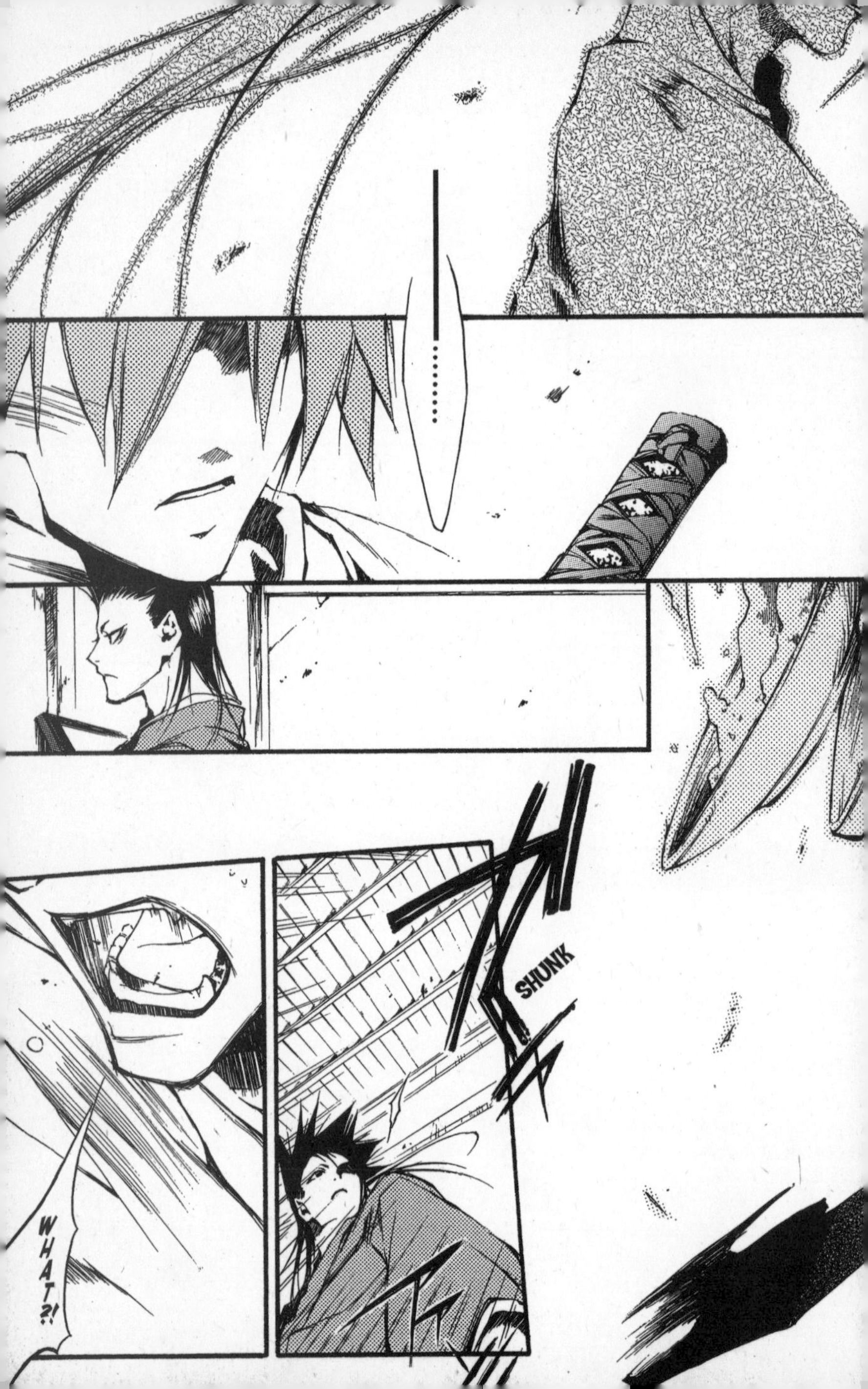
SHUNK
WHAT?!

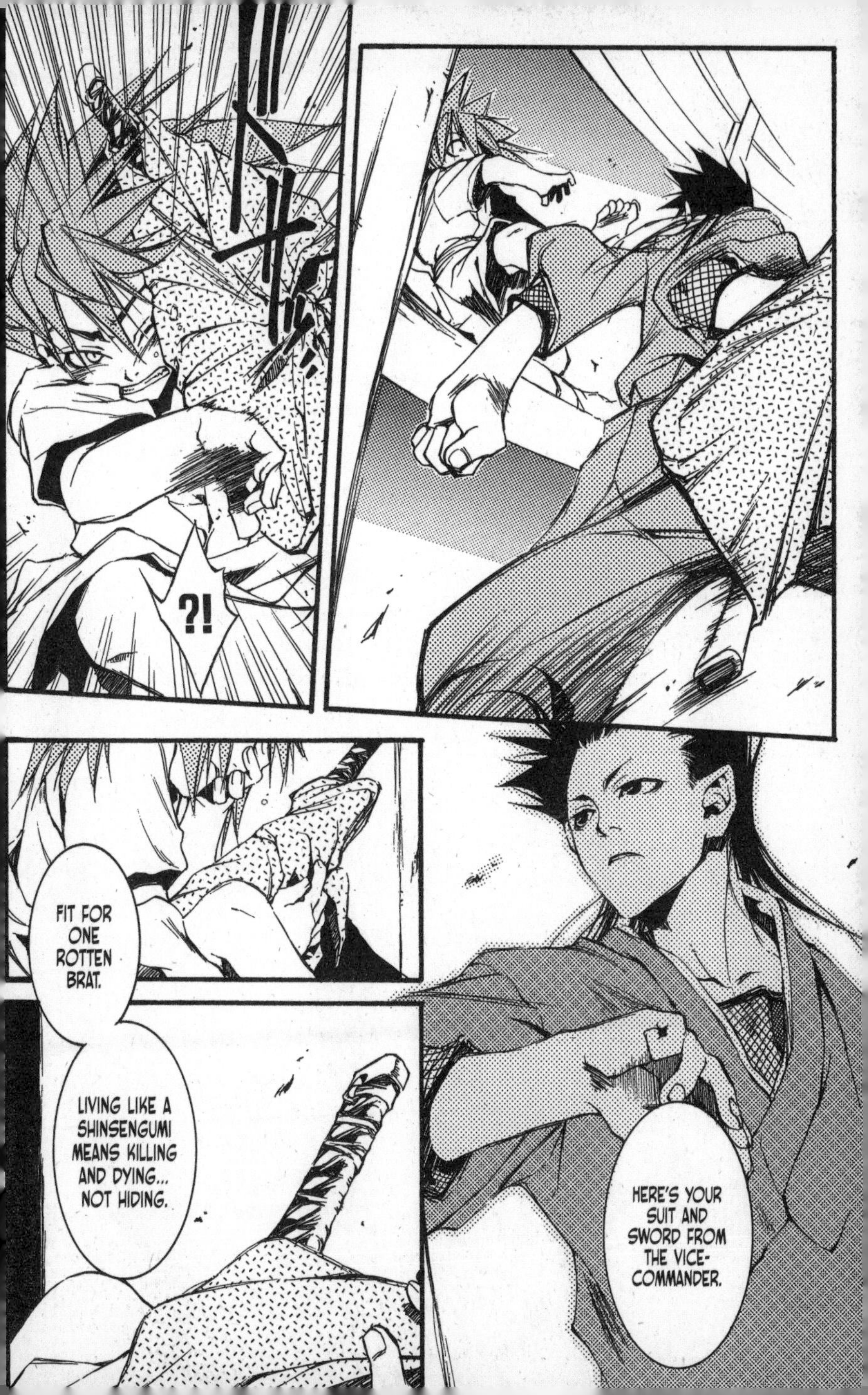
?!
HERE'S YOUR SUIT AND SWORD FROM THE VICE-COMMANDER.
FIT FOR ONE ROTTEN BRAT.
LIVING LIKE A SHINSENGUMI MEANS KILLING AND DYING... NOT HIDING.

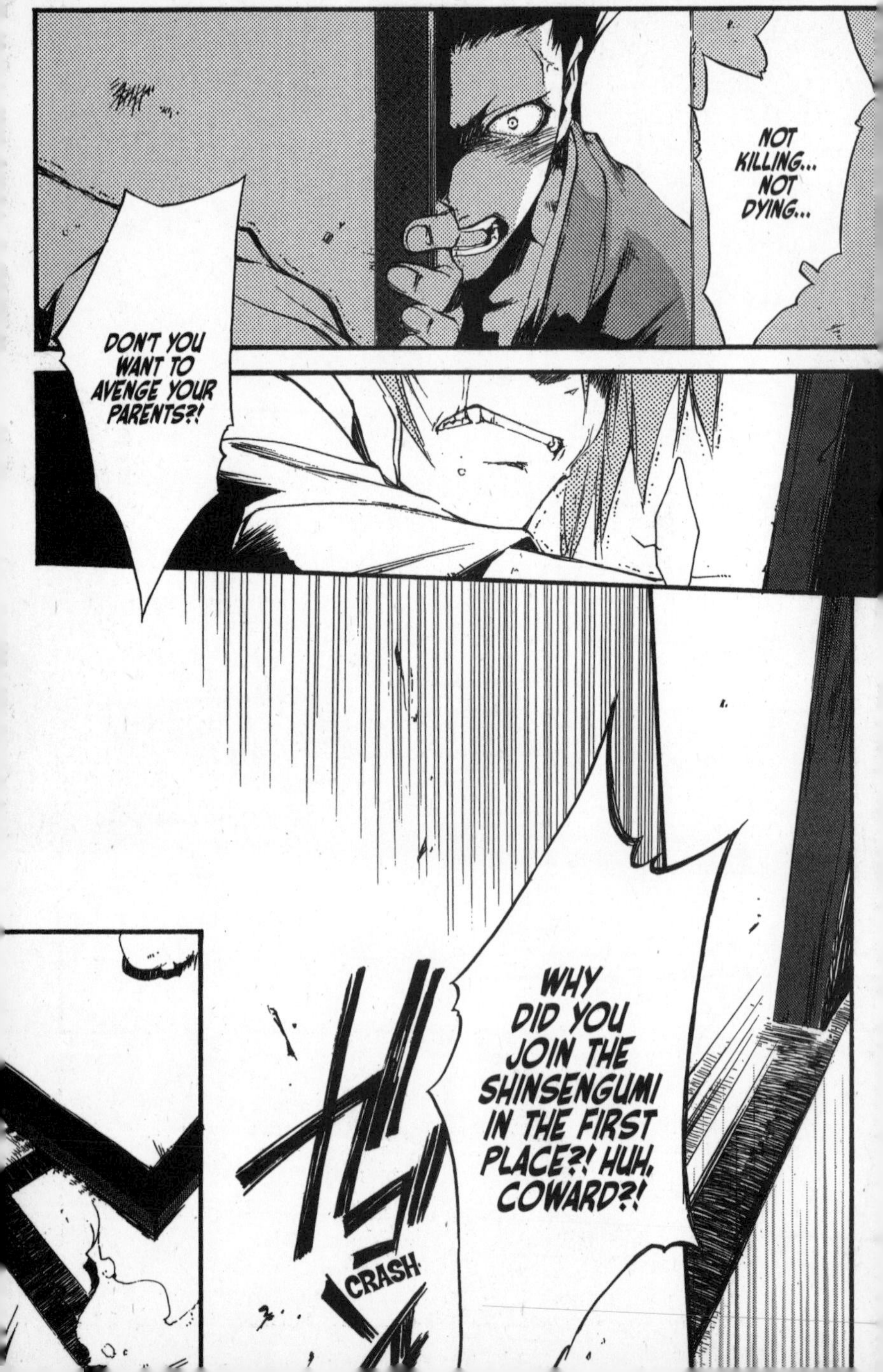
NOT KILLING... NOT DYING...
DON'T YOU WANT TO AVENGE YOUR PARENTS?!
WHY DID YOU JOIN THE SHINSENGUMI IN THE FIRST PLACE?! HUH, COWARD?!
CRASH

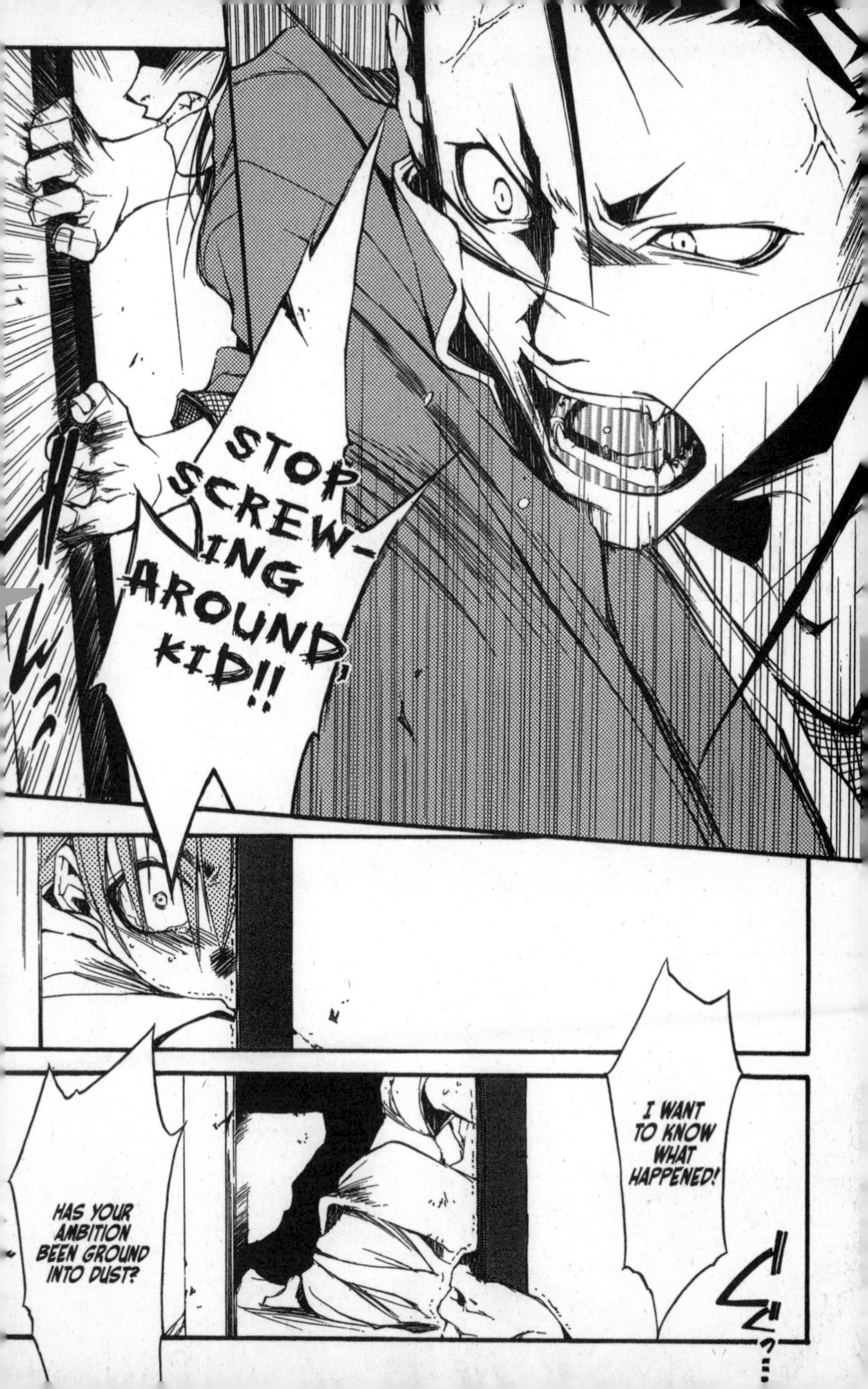
STOP SCREW-ING AROUND, KID!!
I WANT TO KNOW WHAT HAPPENED!
HAS YOUR AMBITION BEEN GROUND INTO DUST?

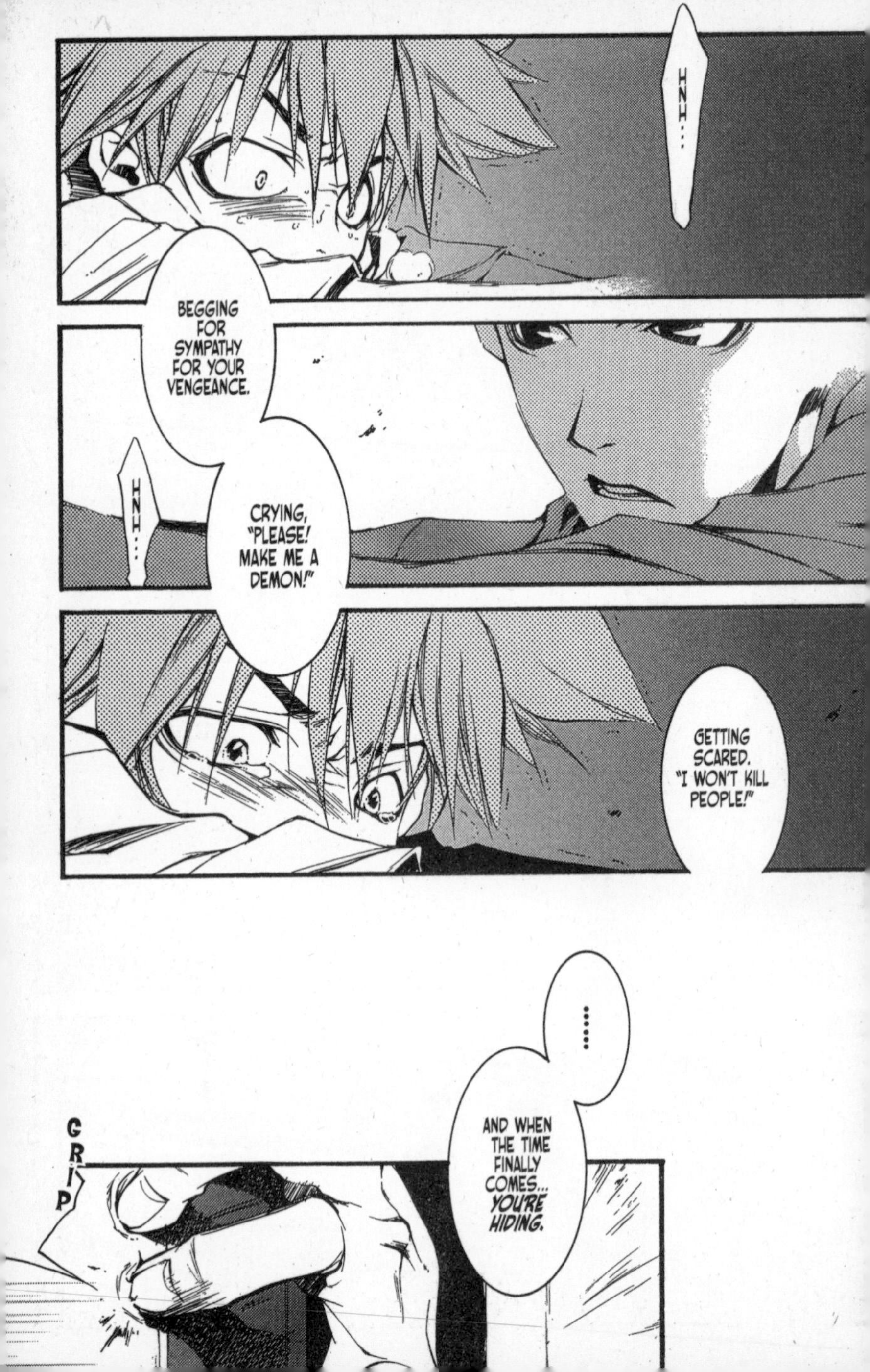
HNH...
BEGGING FOR SYMPATHY FOR YOUR VENGEANCE.
CRYING, "PLEASE! MAKE ME A DEMON!"
HNH...
GETTING SCARED. "I WON'T KILL PEOPLE!"
......
AND WHEN THE TIME FINALLY COMES... *YOU'RE HIDING.*
GRIP

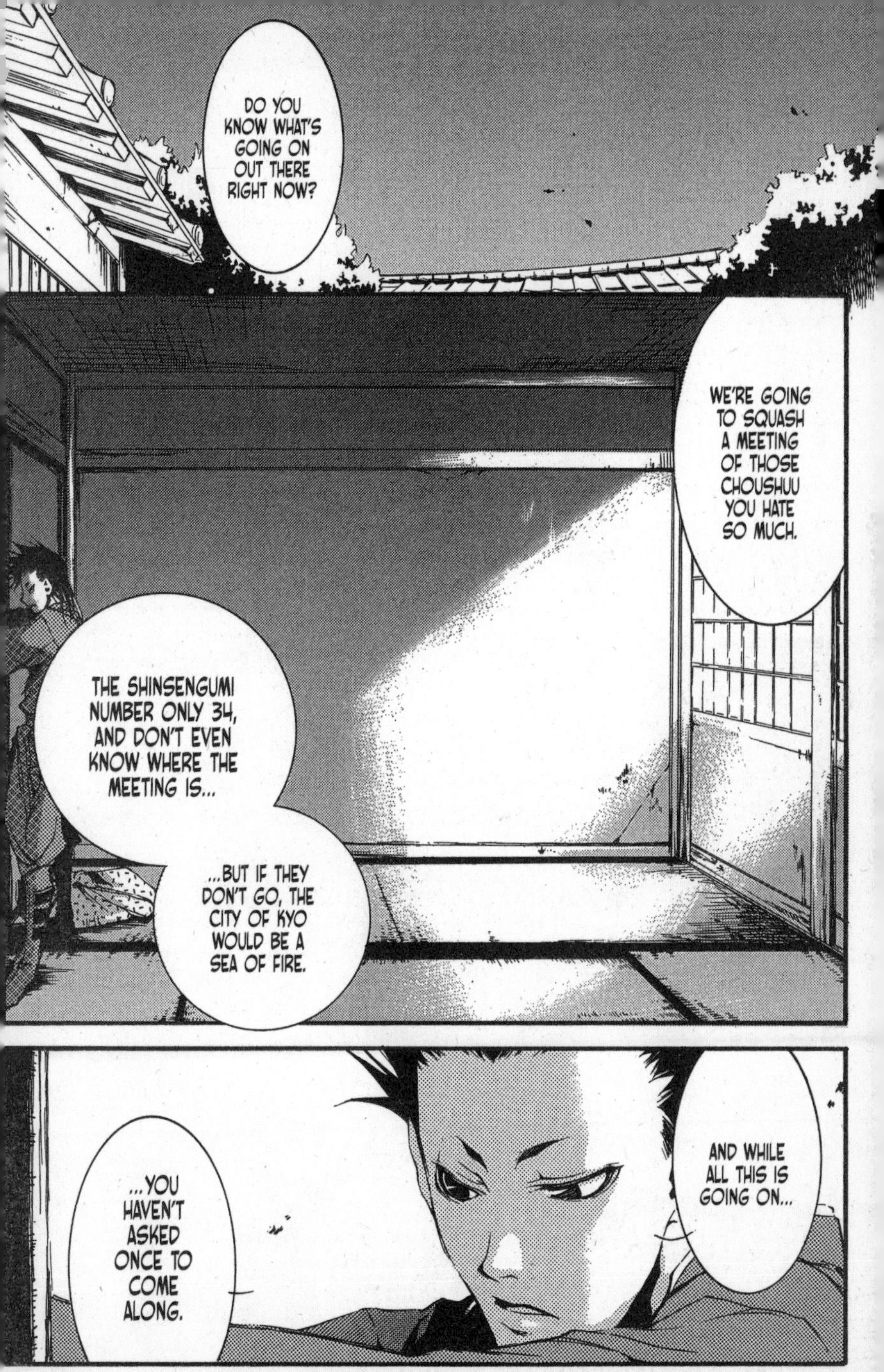
DO YOU KNOW WHAT'S GOING ON OUT THERE RIGHT NOW?
WE'RE GOING TO SQUASH A MEETING OF THOSE CHOUSHUU YOU HATE SO MUCH.
THE SHINSENGUMI NUMBER ONLY 34, AND DON'T EVEN KNOW WHERE THE MEETING IS...
...BUT IF THEY DON'T GO, THE CITY OF KYO WOULD BE A SEA OF FIRE.
AND WHILE ALL THIS IS GOING ON...
...YOU HAVEN'T ASKED ONCE TO COME ALONG.

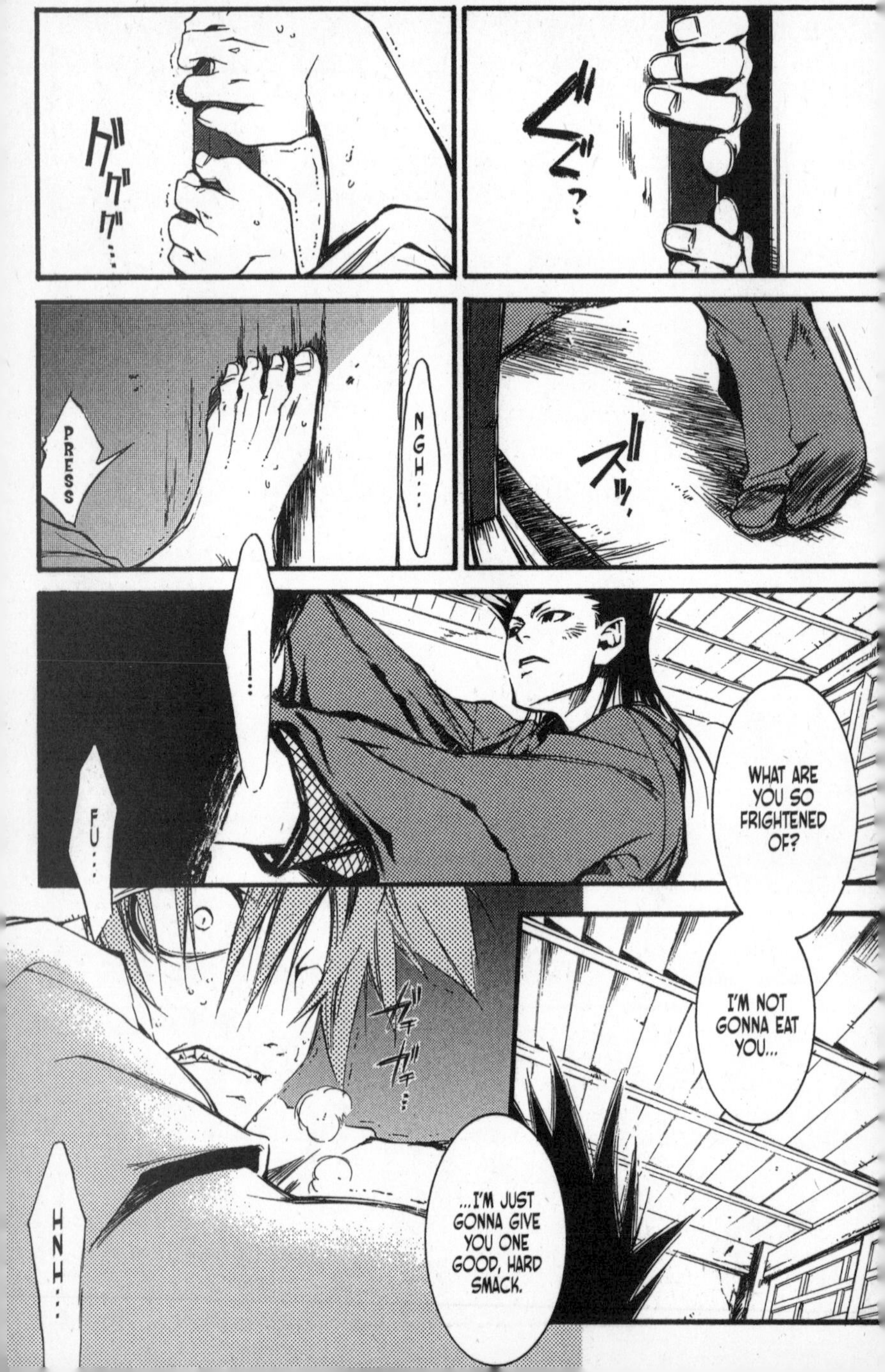
ぐぐっ…
グググ…
ズッ
NGH…
PRESS
!…
WHAT ARE YOU SO FRIGHTENED OF?
FU…
I'M NOT GONNA EAT YOU...
...I'M JUST GONNA GIVE YOU ONE GOOD, HARD SMACK.
ガチガチ…
HNH…

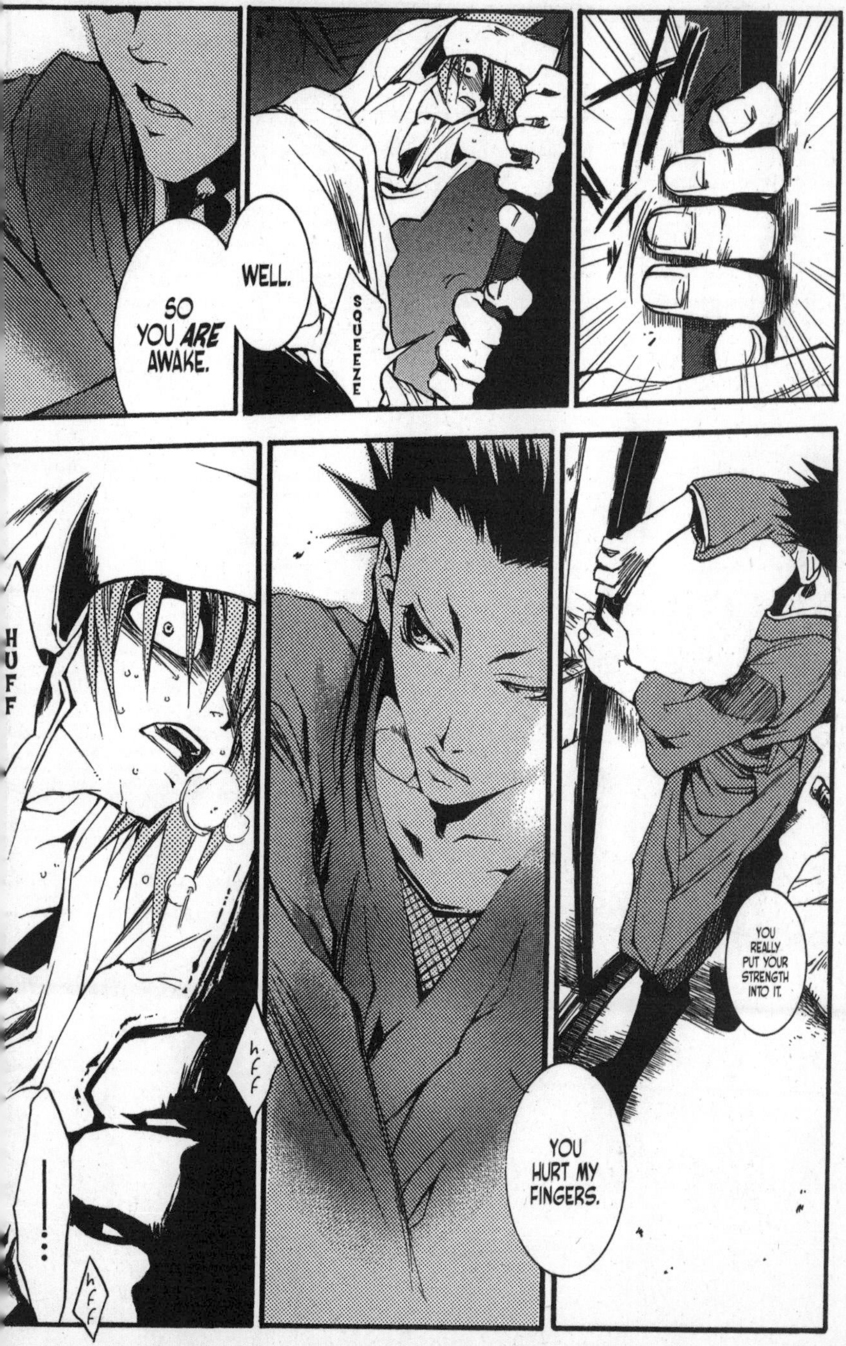
SQUEEZE
WELL.
SO YOU *ARE* AWAKE.
YOU REALLY PUT YOUR STRENGTH INTO IT.
YOU HURT MY FINGERS.
HUFF
hff
......
hff

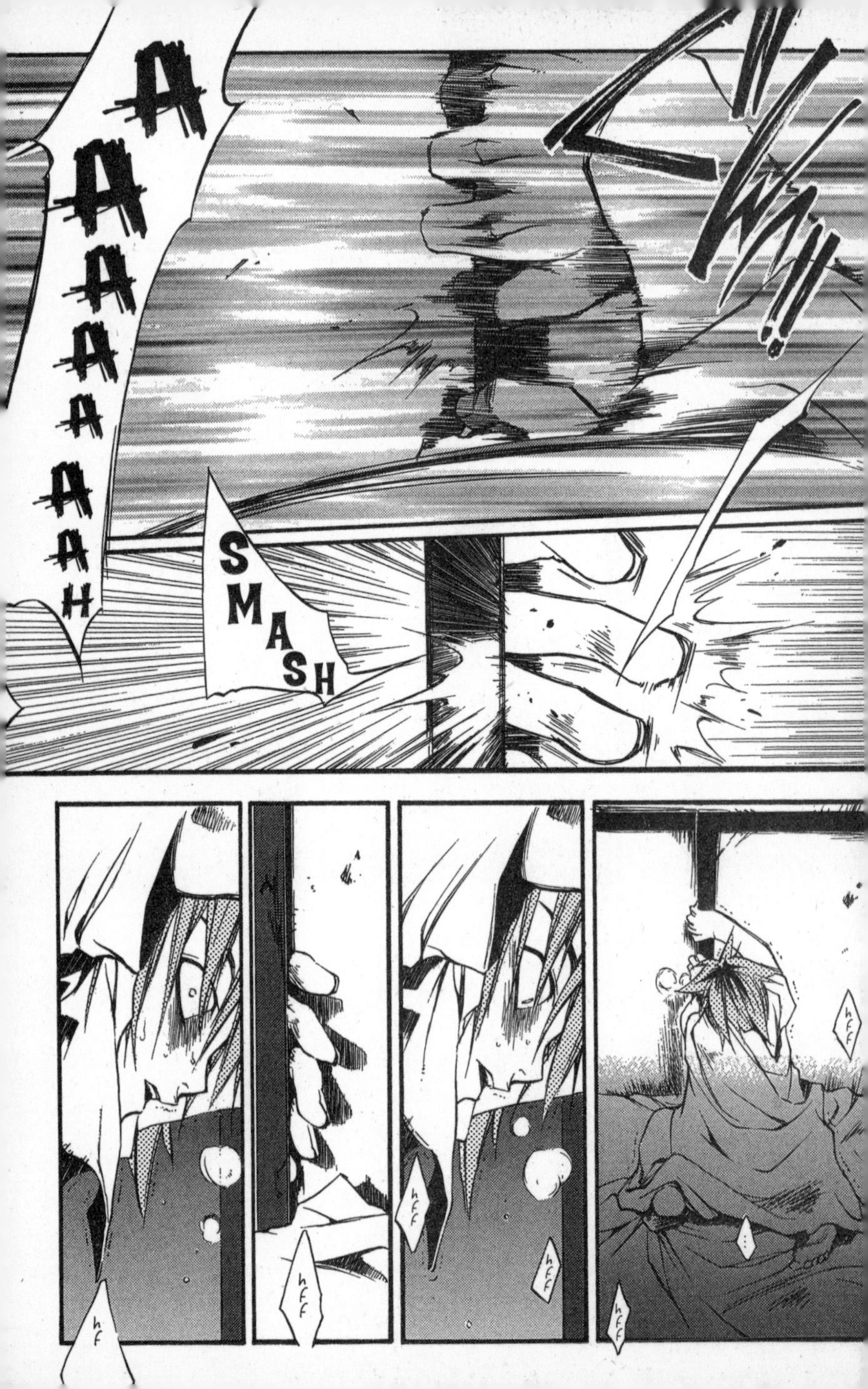
AAAAAAAH
SMASH
hff
...
hff
hff
hff
hff
hf

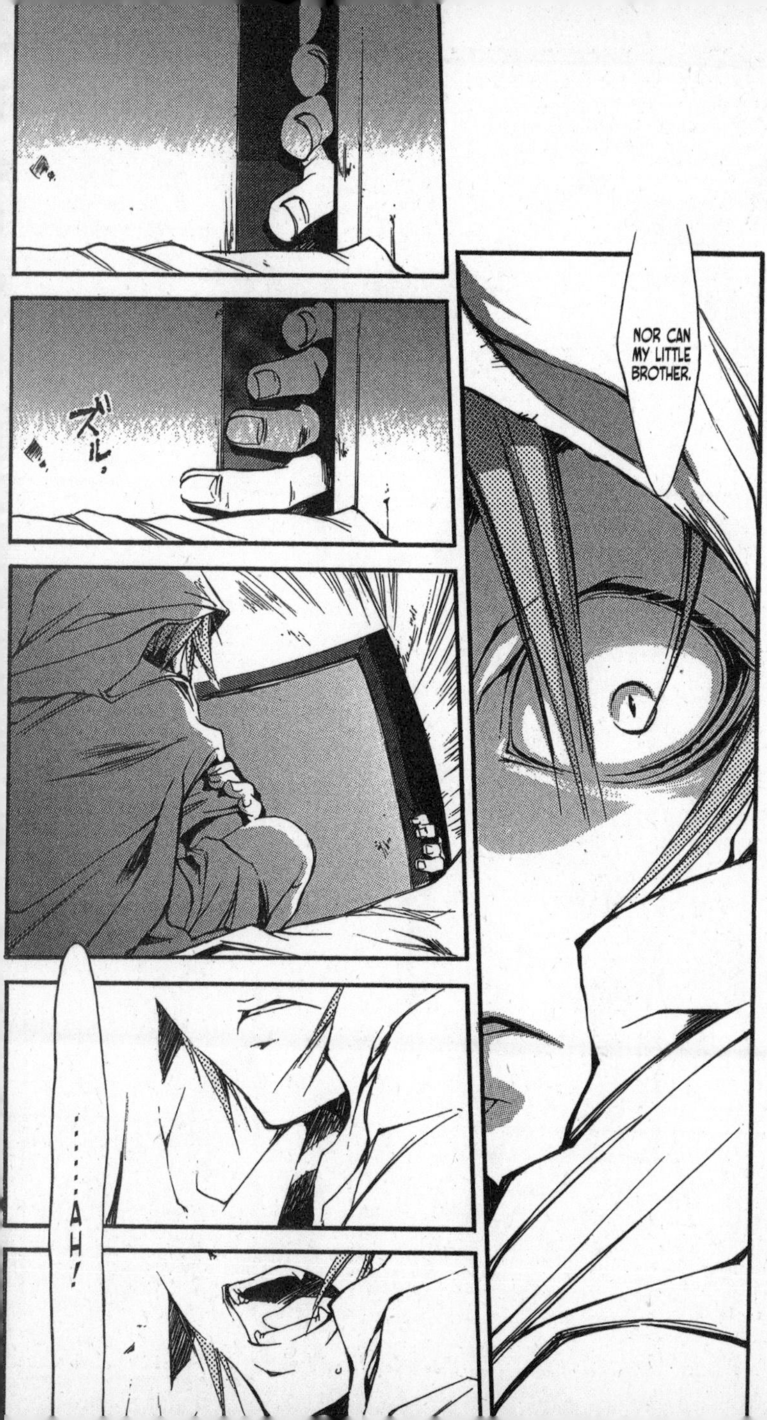
NOR CAN MY LITTLE BROTHER.
ズル
......AH!

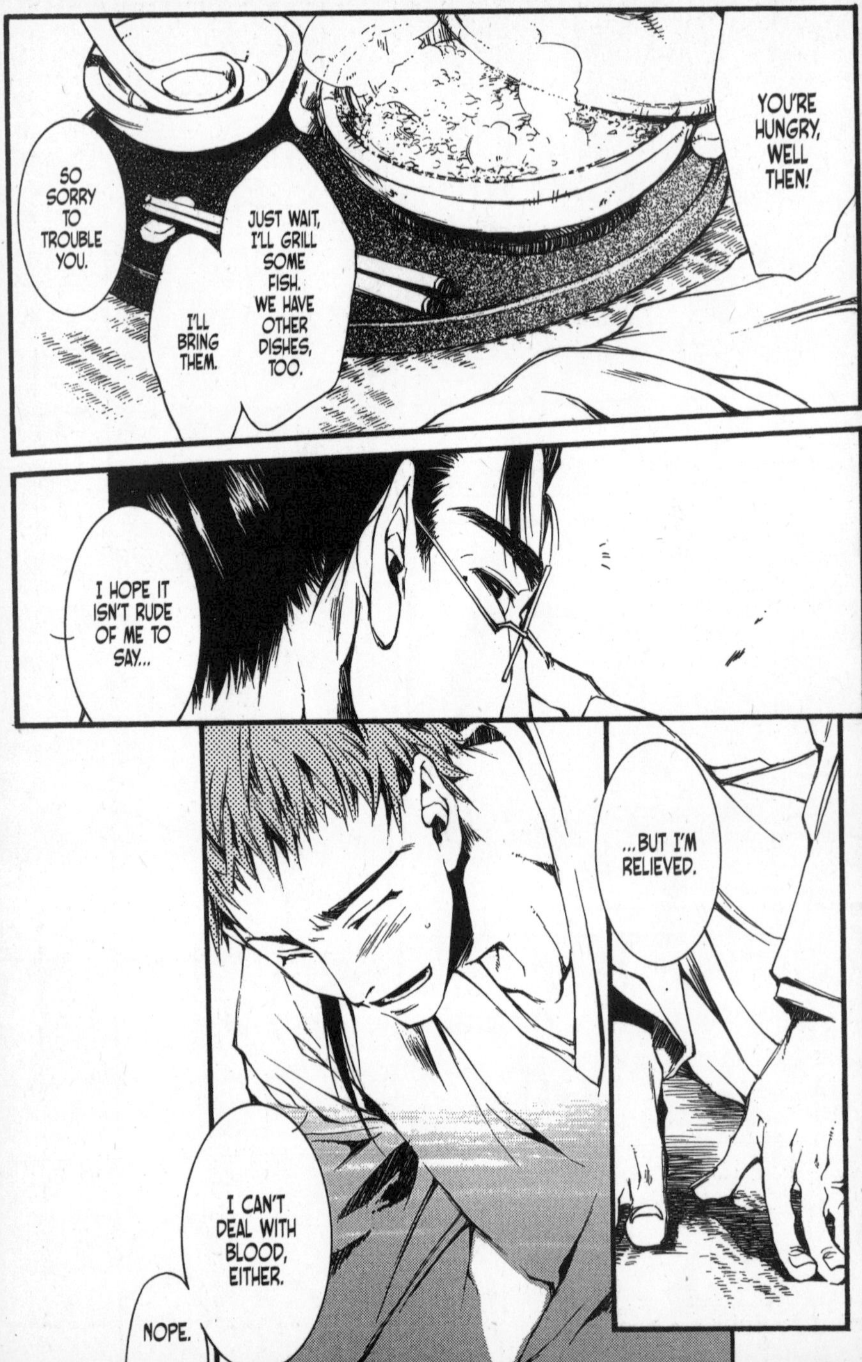
YOU'RE HUNGRY, WELL THEN!
JUST WAIT, I'LL GRILL SOME FISH. WE HAVE OTHER DISHES, TOO.
I'LL BRING THEM.
SO SORRY TO TROUBLE YOU.
I HOPE IT ISN'T RUDE OF ME TO SAY...
...BUT I'M RELIEVED.
I CAN'T DEAL WITH BLOOD, EITHER.
NOPE.

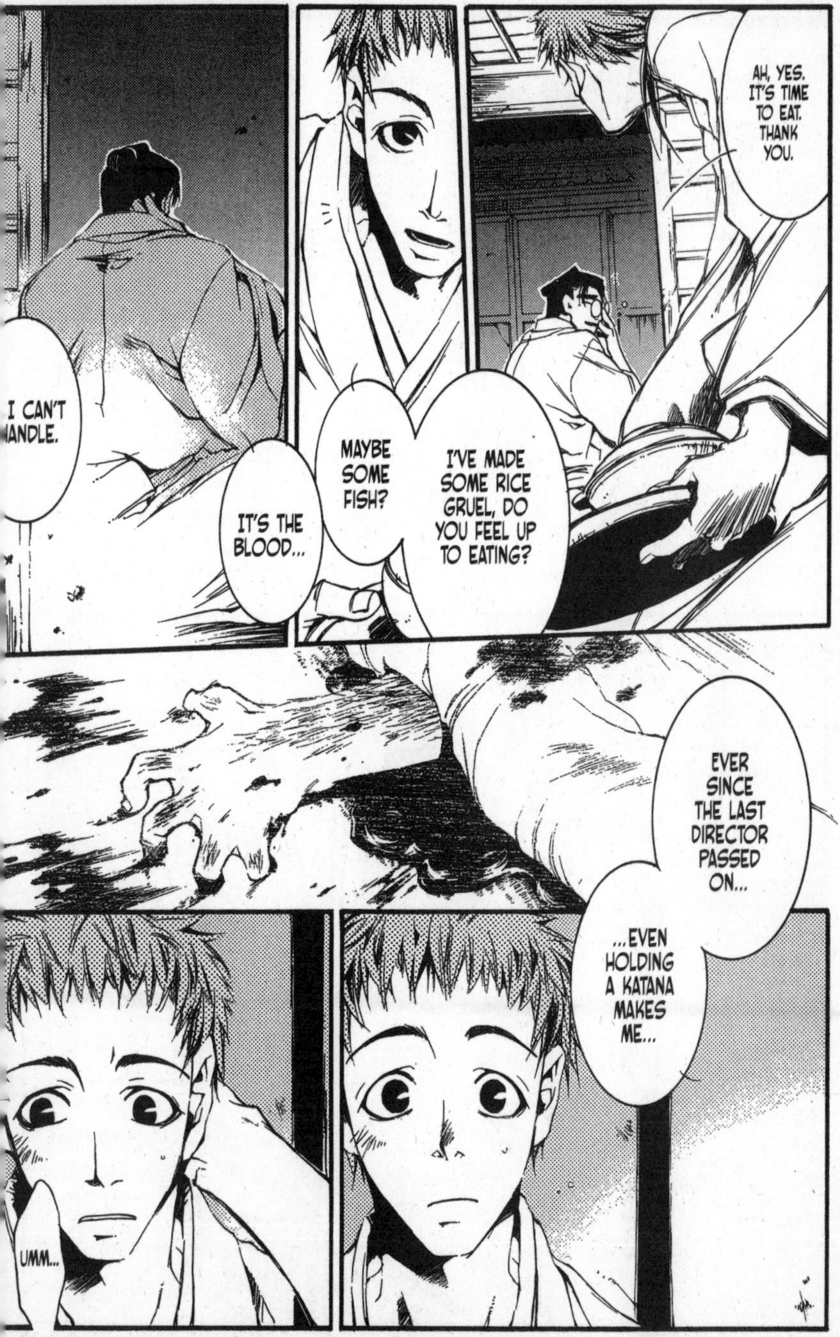
AH, YES. IT'S TIME TO EAT. THANK YOU.
I'VE MADE SOME RICE GRUEL, DO YOU FEEL UP TO EATING?
MAYBE SOME FISH?
IT'S THE BLOOD...
I CAN'T ANDLE.
EVER SINCE THE LAST DIRECTOR PASSED ON...
...EVEN HOLDING A KATANA MAKES ME...
UMM...

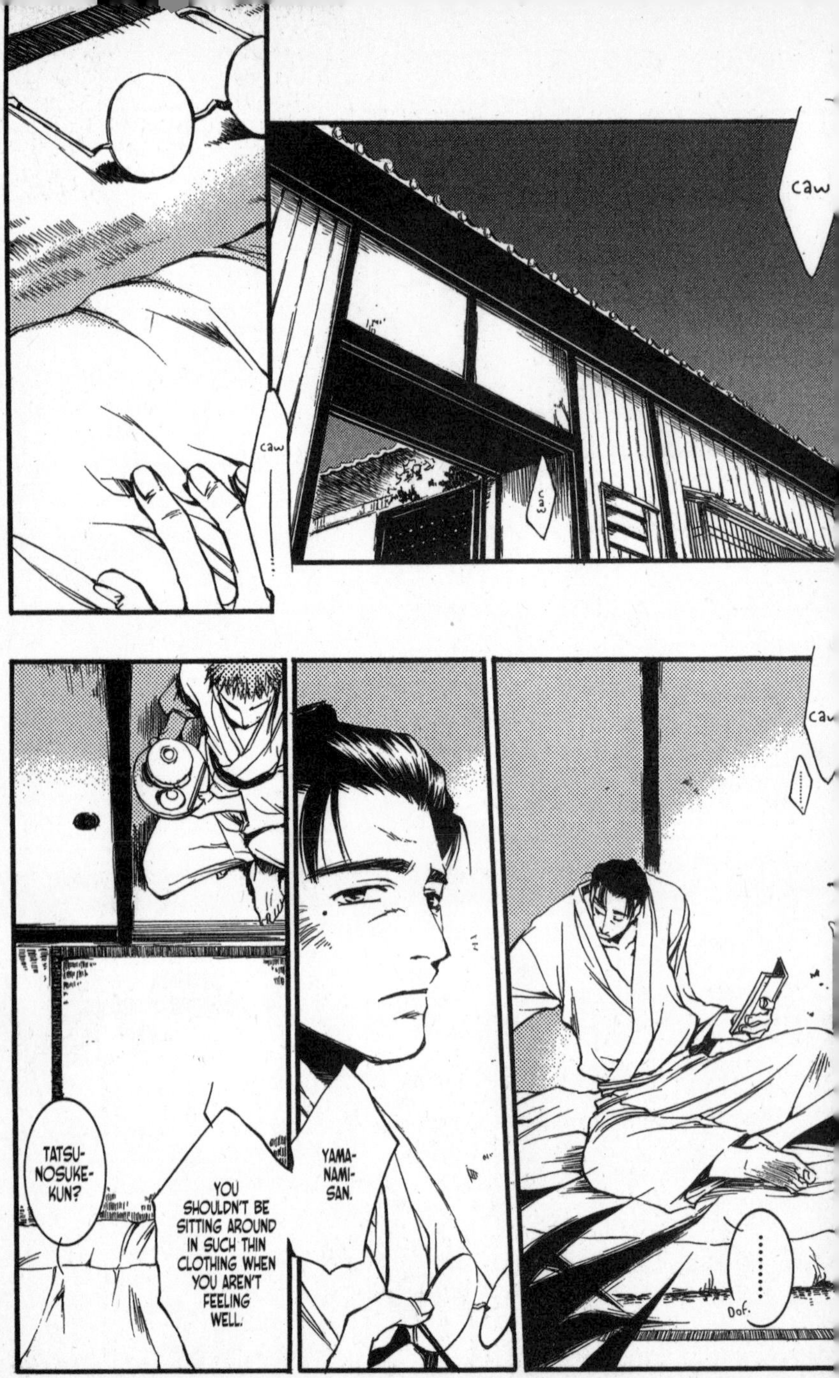
caw
caw
caw
caw
......
......
Dof.
YAMA-NAMI-SAN.
TATSU-NOSUKE-KUN?
YOU SHOULDN'T BE SITTING AROUND IN SUCH THIN CLOTHING WHEN YOU AREN'T FEELING WELL.

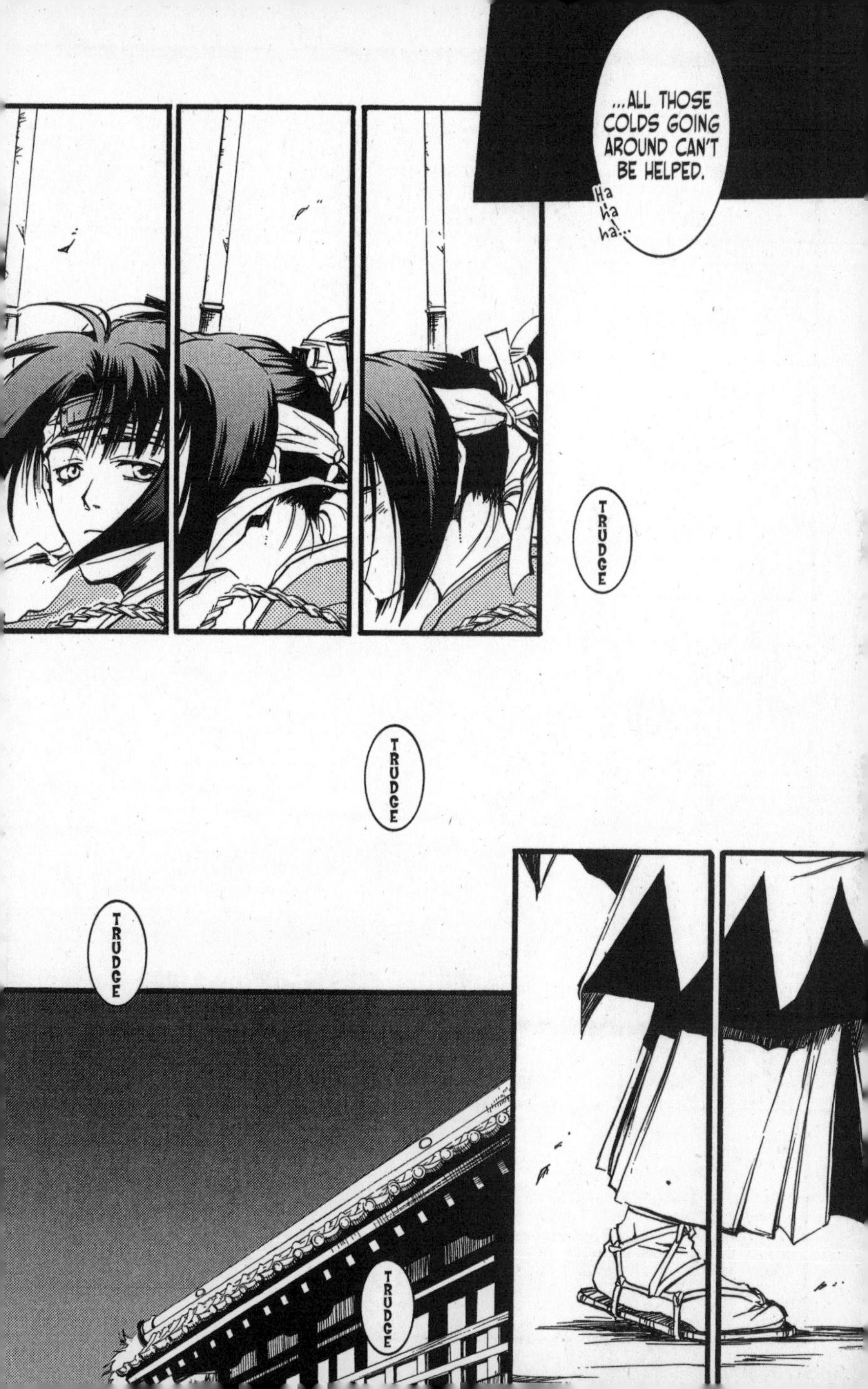
...ALL THOSE COLDS GOING AROUND CAN'T BE HELPED.
Ha ha ha...
TRUDGE
TRUDGE
TRUDGE
TRUDGE

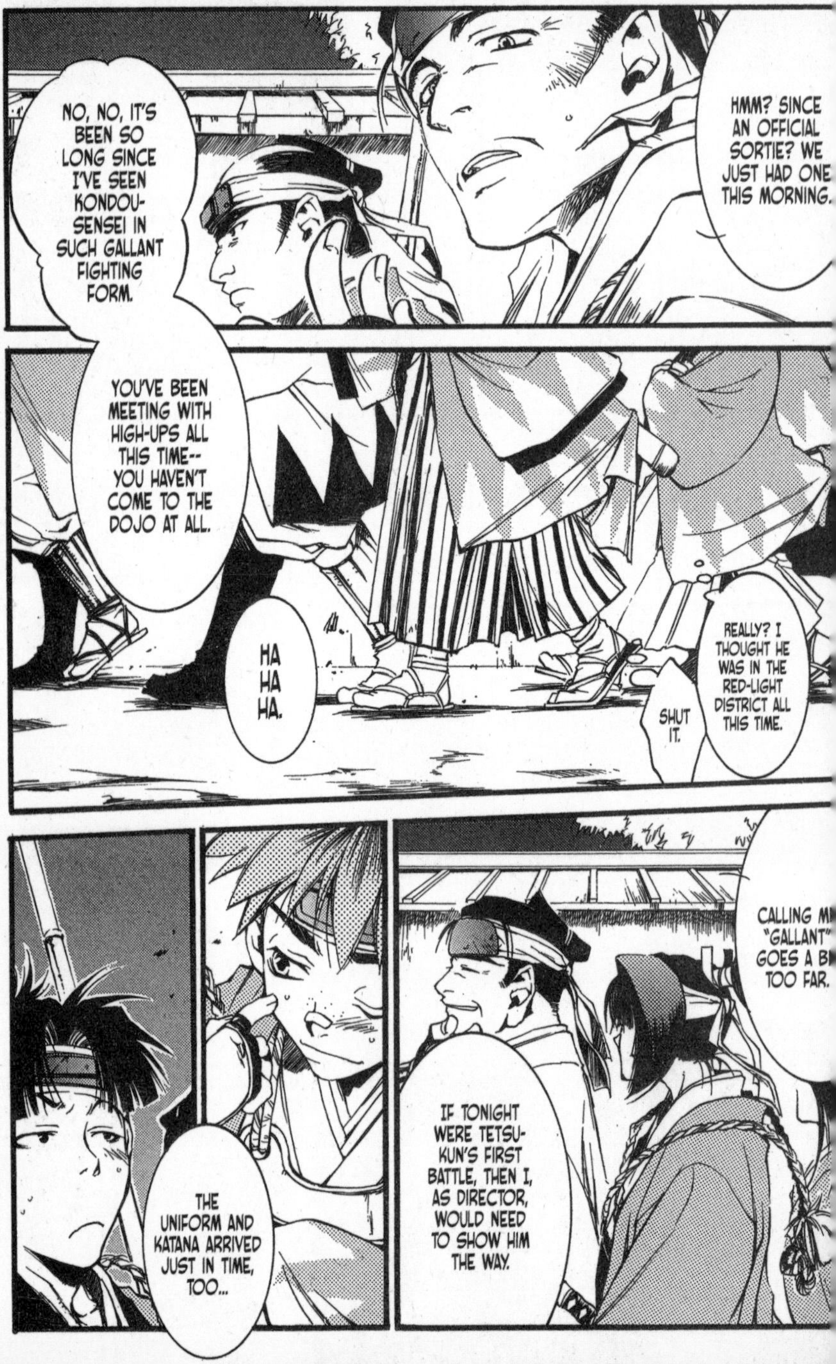
HMM? SINCE AN OFFICIAL SORTIE? WE JUST HAD ONE THIS MORNING.
NO, NO, IT'S BEEN SO LONG SINCE I'VE SEEN KONDOU-SENSEI IN SUCH GALLANT FIGHTING FORM.
YOU'VE BEEN MEETING WITH HIGH-UPS ALL THIS TIME--YOU HAVEN'T COME TO THE DOJO AT ALL.
HA HA HA.
REALLY? I THOUGHT HE WAS IN THE RED-LIGHT DISTRICT ALL THIS TIME.
SHUT IT.
CALLING M "GALLANT" GOES A B TOO FAR.
IF TONIGHT WERE TETSU-KUN'S FIRST BATTLE, THEN I, AS DIRECTOR, WOULD NEED TO SHOW HIM THE WAY.
THE UNIFORM AND KATANA ARRIVED JUST IN TIME, TOO...

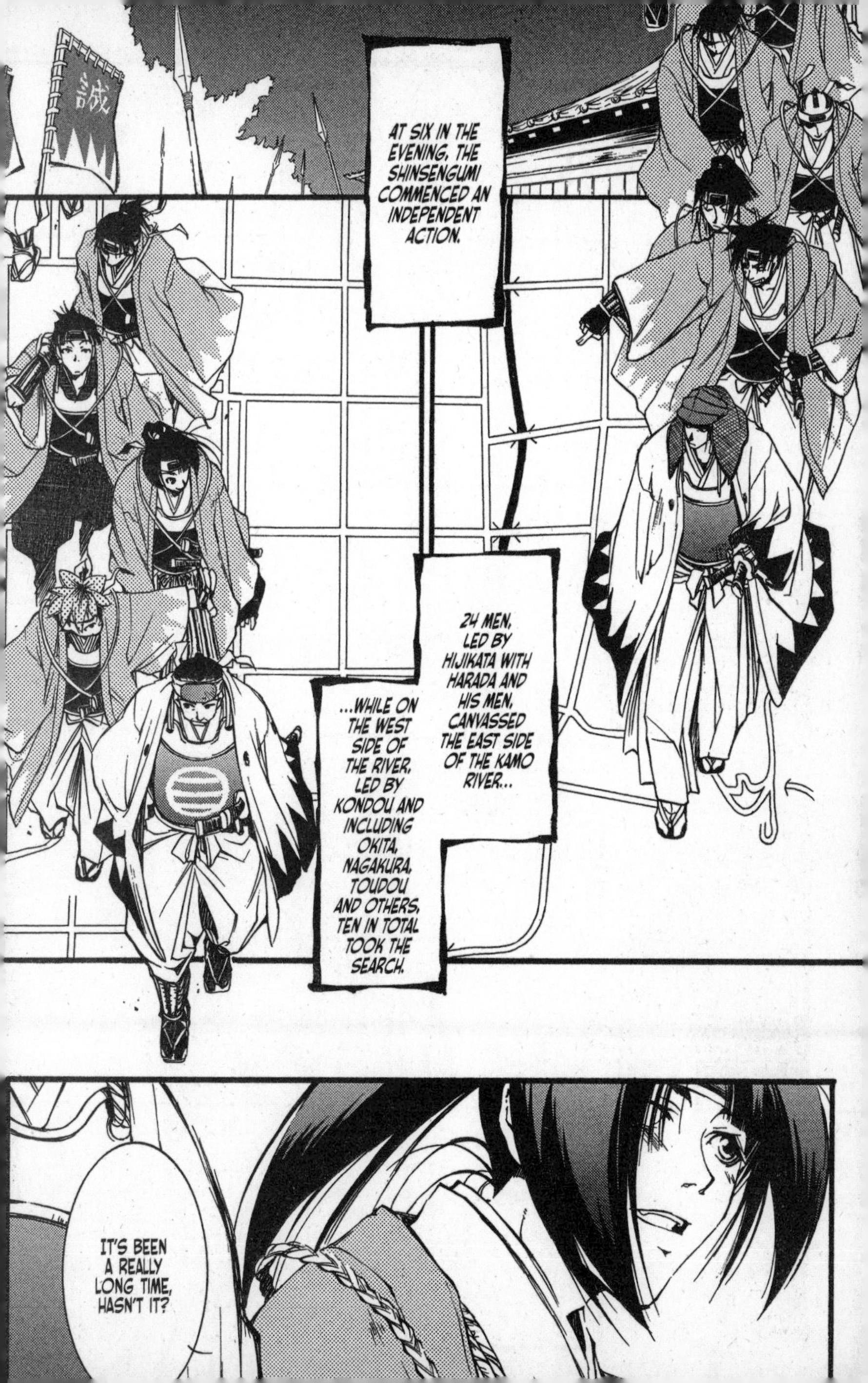

誠
AT SIX IN THE EVENING, THE SHINSENGUMI COMMENCED AN INDEPENDENT ACTION.
24 MEN, LED BY HIJIKATA WITH HARADA AND HIS MEN, CANVASSED THE EAST SIDE OF THE KAMO RIVER...
...WHILE ON THE WEST SIDE OF THE RIVER, LED BY KONDOU AND INCLUDING OKITA, NAGAKURA, TOUDOU AND OTHERS, TEN IN TOTAL TOOK THE SEARCH.
IT'S BEEN A REALLY LONG TIME, HASN'T IT?

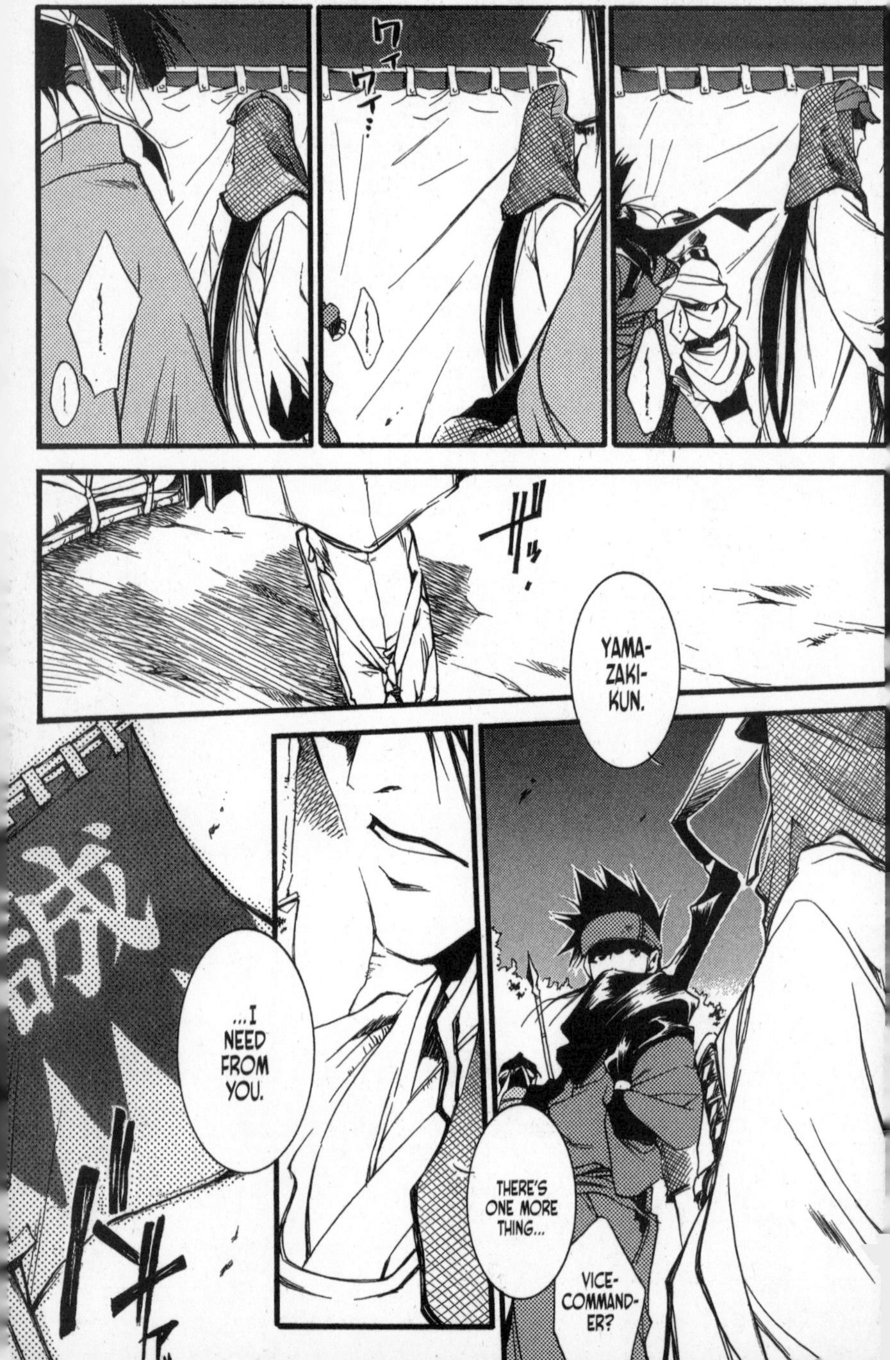
ワイワイ…
YAMA-ZAKI-KUN.
VICE-COMMANDER?
THERE'S ONE MORE THING...
...I NEED FROM YOU.

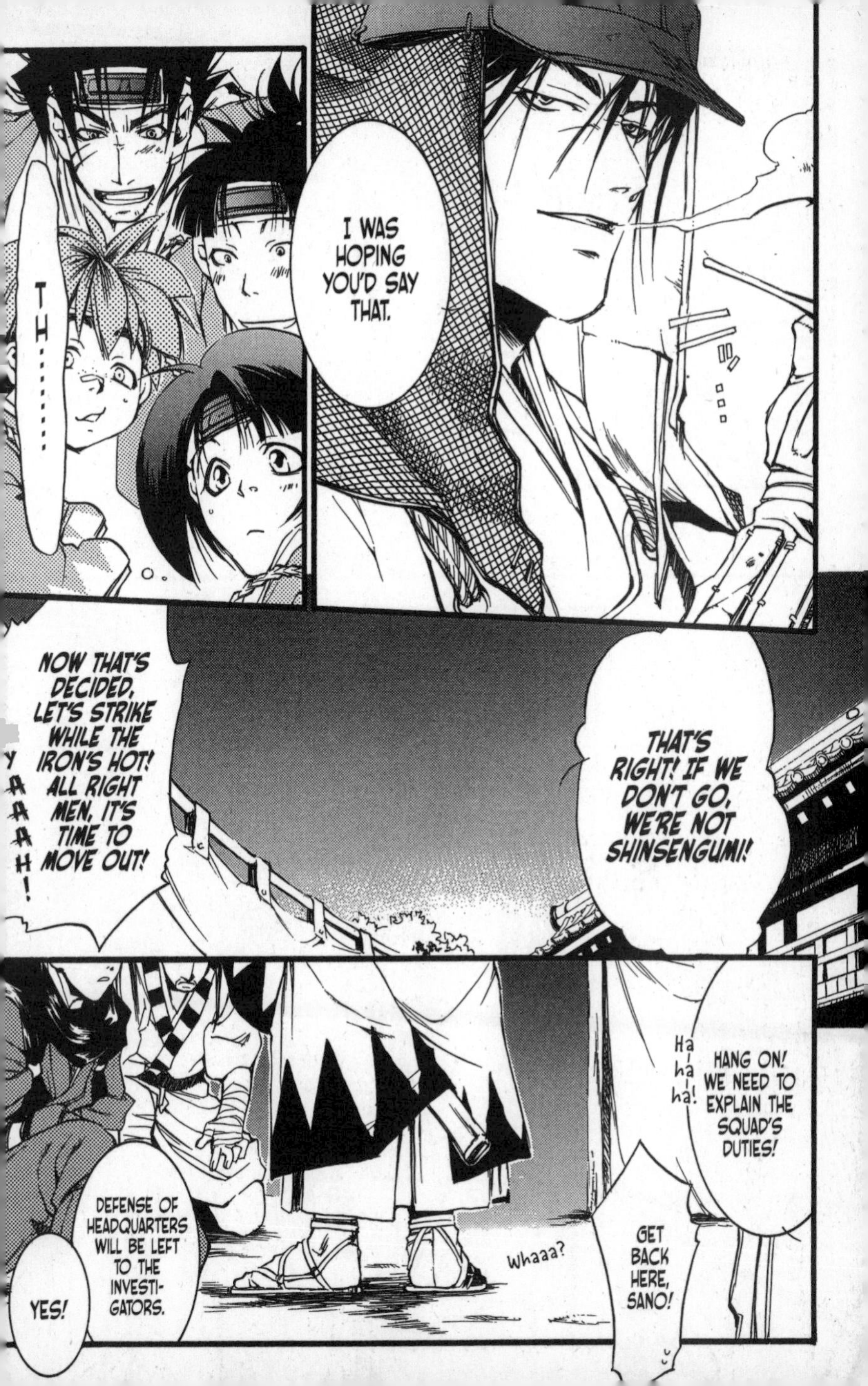
I WAS HOPING YOU'D SAY THAT.
TH......
THAT'S RIGHT! IF WE DON'T GO, WE'RE NOT SHINSENGUMI!
NOW THAT'S DECIDED, LET'S STRIKE WHILE THE IRON'S HOT! ALL RIGHT MEN, IT'S TIME TO MOVE OUT!
YAAAAH!
HANG ON! WE NEED TO EXPLAIN THE SQUAD'S DUTIES!
Ha ha ha!
GET BACK HERE, SANO!
Whaaa?
DEFENSE OF HEADQUARTERS WILL BE LEFT TO THE INVESTIGATORS.
YES!

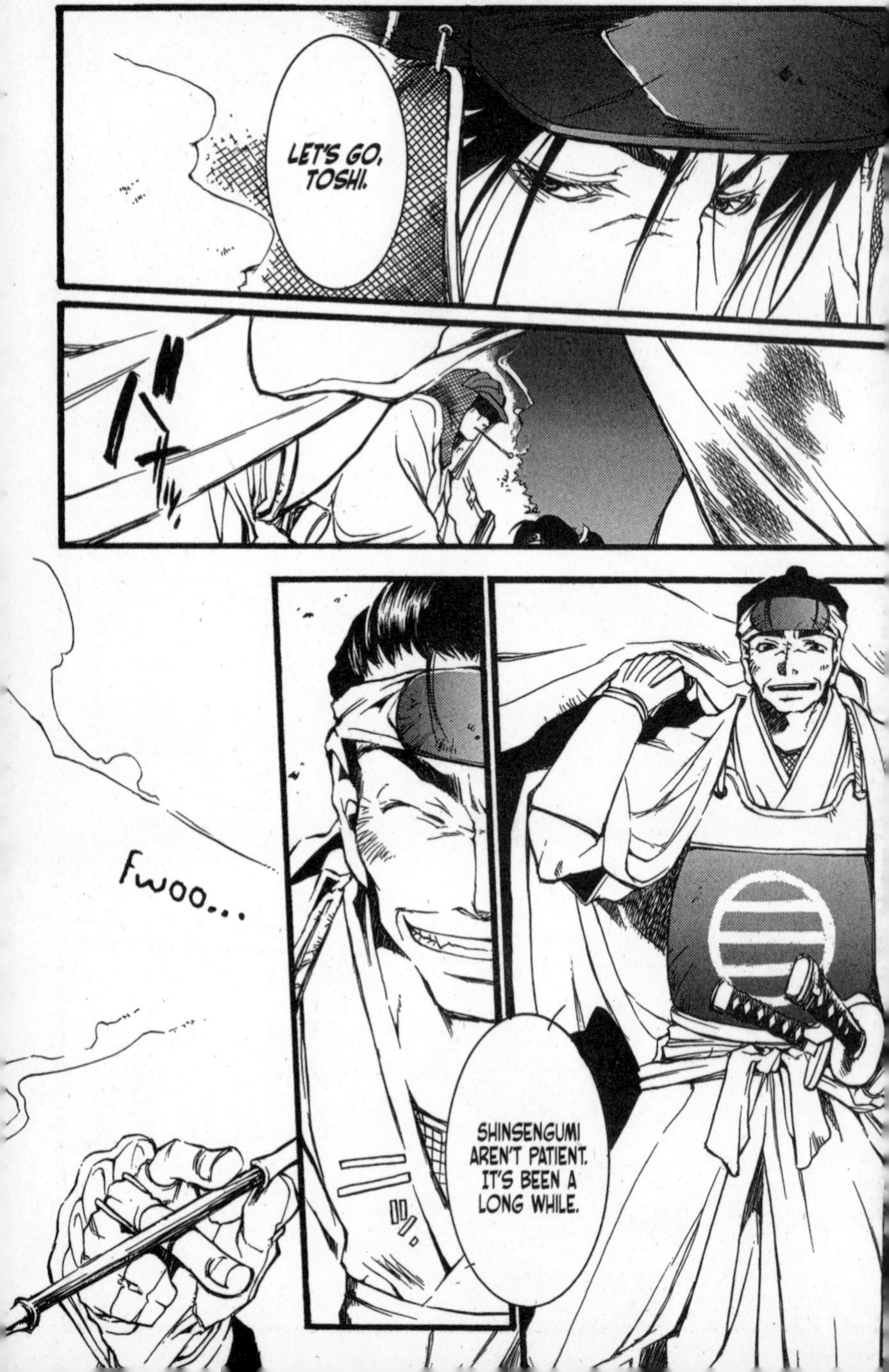
LET'S GO, TOSHI.
Fwoo...
SHINSENGUMI AREN'T PATIENT. IT'S BEEN A LONG WHILE.

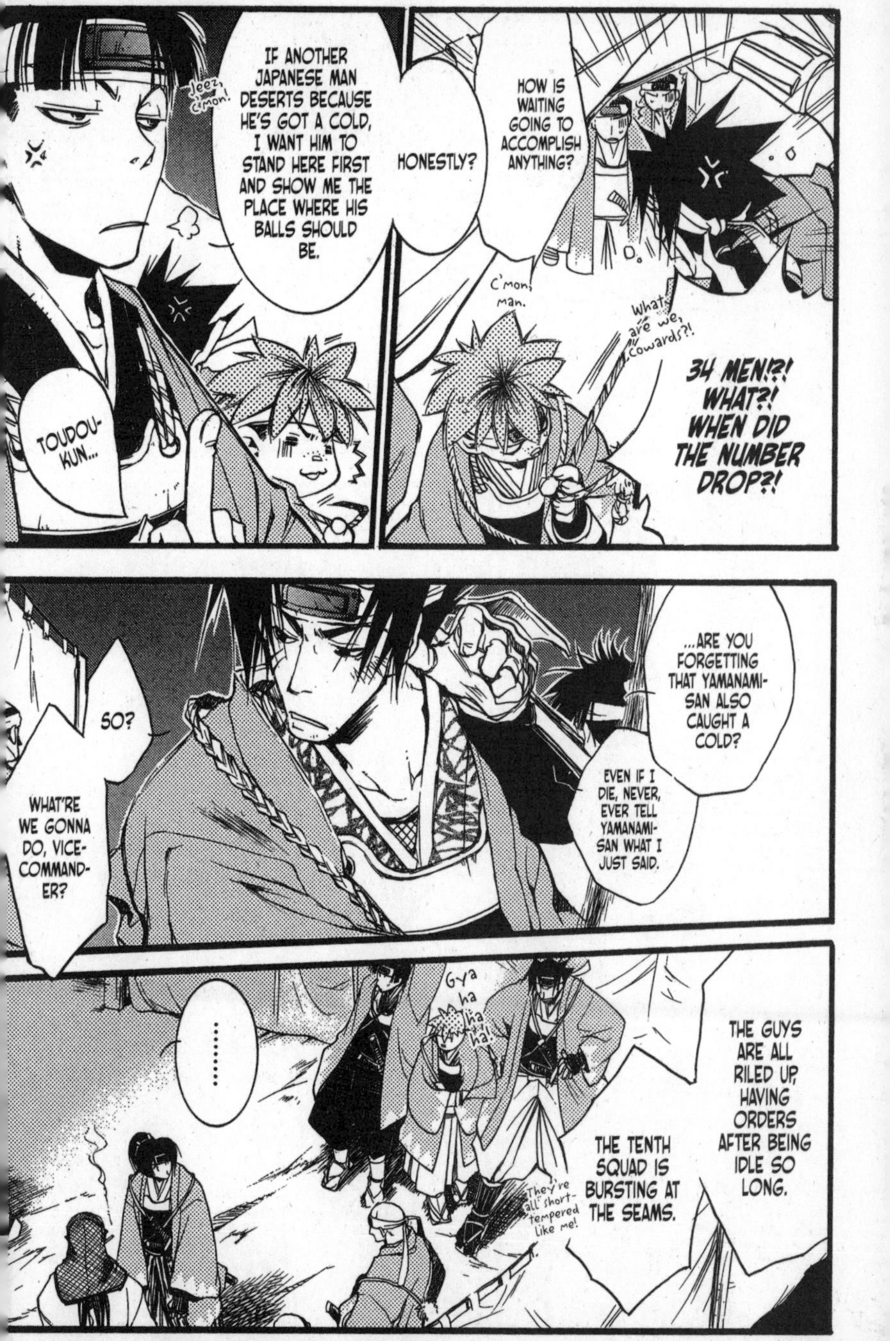
HOW IS WAITING GOING TO ACCOMPLISH ANYTHING?
HONESTLY?
34 MEN!?! WHAT?! WHEN DID THE NUMBER DROP?!
What, are we, cowards?!
C'mon, man.
IF ANOTHER JAPANESE MAN DESERTS BECAUSE HE'S GOT A COLD, I WANT HIM TO STAND HERE FIRST AND SHOW ME THE PLACE WHERE HIS BALLS SHOULD BE.
Jeez, c'mon!
TOUDOU-KUN...
...ARE YOU FORGETTING THAT YAMANAMI-SAN ALSO CAUGHT A COLD?
EVEN IF I DIE, NEVER, EVER TELL YAMANAMI-SAN WHAT I JUST SAID.
SO?
WHAT'RE WE GONNA DO, VICE-COMMANDER?
THE GUYS ARE ALL RILED UP, HAVING ORDERS AFTER BEING IDLE SO LONG.
THE TENTH SQUAD IS BURSTING AT THE SEAMS.
They're all short-tempered like me!
Gya ha ha ha ha!
....

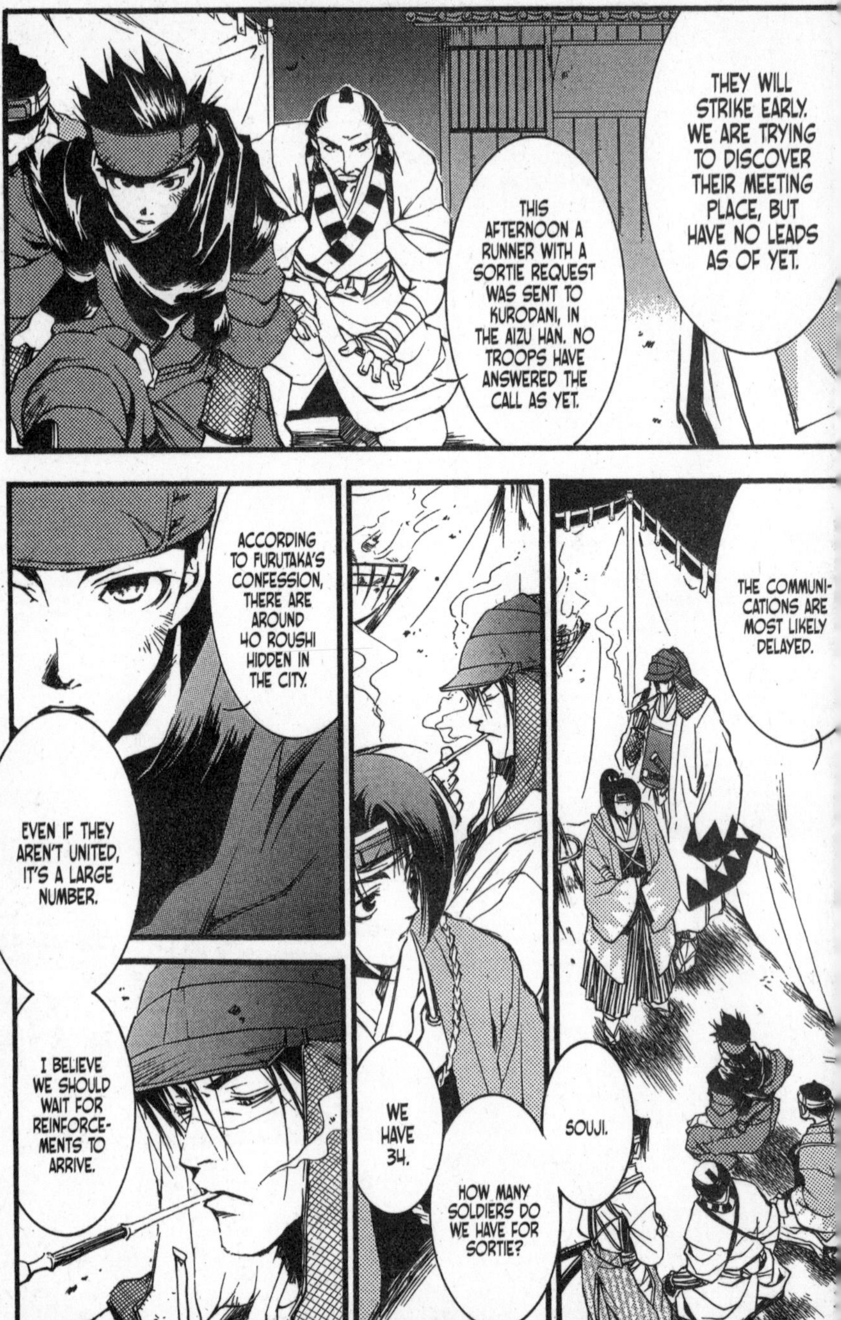
THEY WILL STRIKE EARLY. WE ARE TRYING TO DISCOVER THEIR MEETING PLACE, BUT HAVE NO LEADS AS OF YET.
THIS AFTERNOON A RUNNER WITH A SORTIE REQUEST WAS SENT TO KURODANI, IN THE AIZU HAN. NO TROOPS HAVE ANSWERED THE CALL AS YET.
THE COMMUNICATIONS ARE MOST LIKELY DELAYED.
SOUJI.
HOW MANY SOLDIERS DO WE HAVE FOR SORTIE?
WE HAVE 34.
ACCORDING TO FURUTAKA'S CONFESSION, THERE ARE AROUND 40 ROUSHI HIDDEN IN THE CITY.
EVEN IF THEY AREN'T UNITED, IT'S A LARGE NUMBER.
I BELIEVE WE SHOULD WAIT FOR REINFORCEMENTS TO ARRIVE.

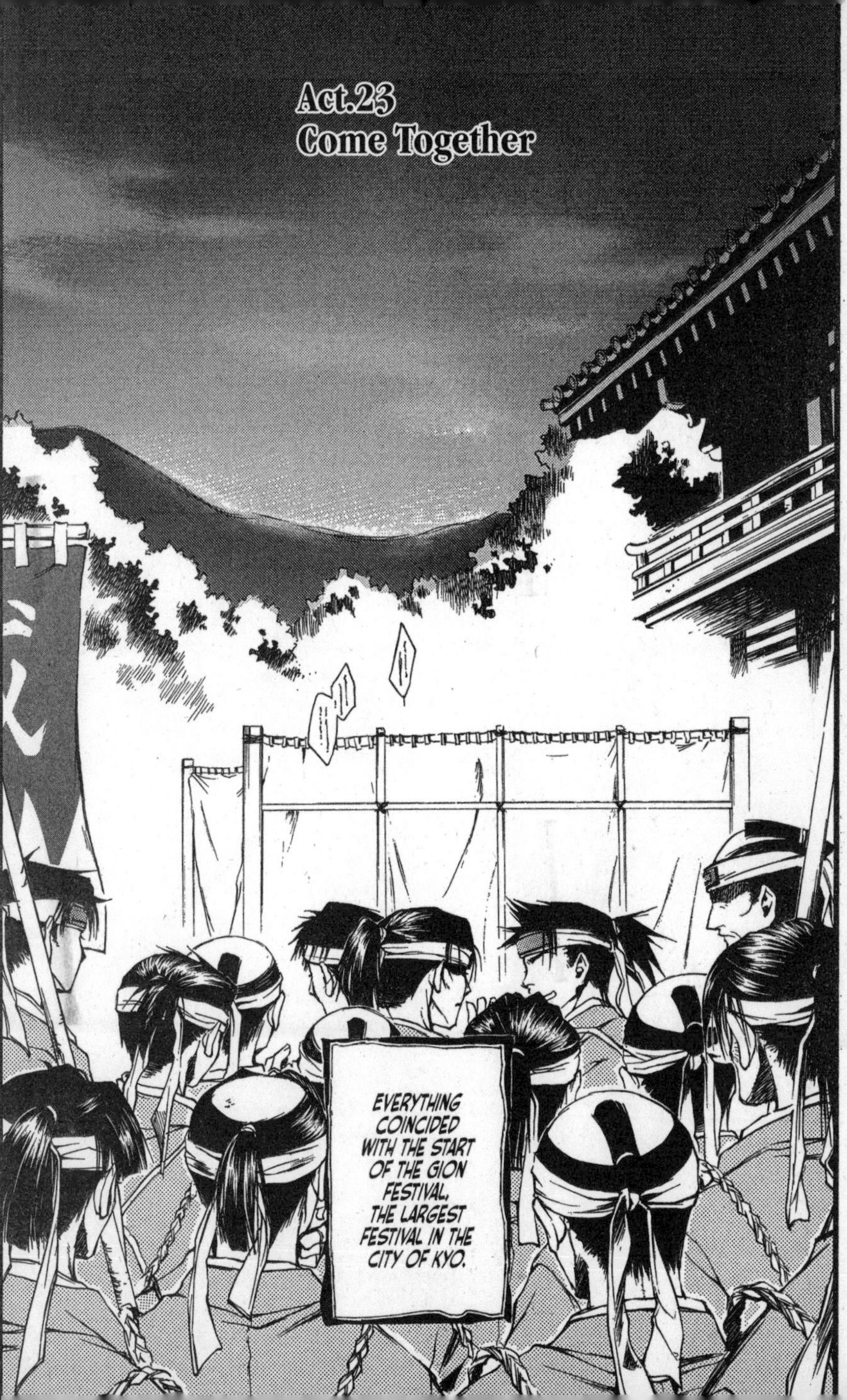
Act.23
Come Together
EVERYTHING COINCIDED WITH THE START OF THE GION FESTIVAL, THE LARGEST FESTIVAL IN THE CITY OF KYO.

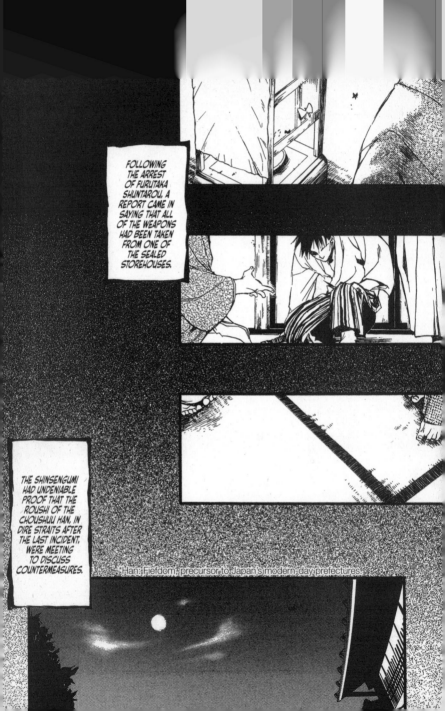

FOLLOWING THE ARREST OF FURUTAKA SHUNTAROU, A REPORT CAME IN SAYING THAT ALL OF THE WEAPONS HAD BEEN TAKEN FROM ONE OF THE SEALED STOREHOUSES.

THE SHINSENGUMI HAD UNDENIABLE PROOF THAT THE ROUSHI OF THE CHOUSHUU HAN, IN DIRE STRAITS AFTER THE LAST INCIDENT, WERE MEETING TO DISCUSS COUNTERMEASURES.

*Han: Fiefdom; precursor to Japan's modern-day prefectures.

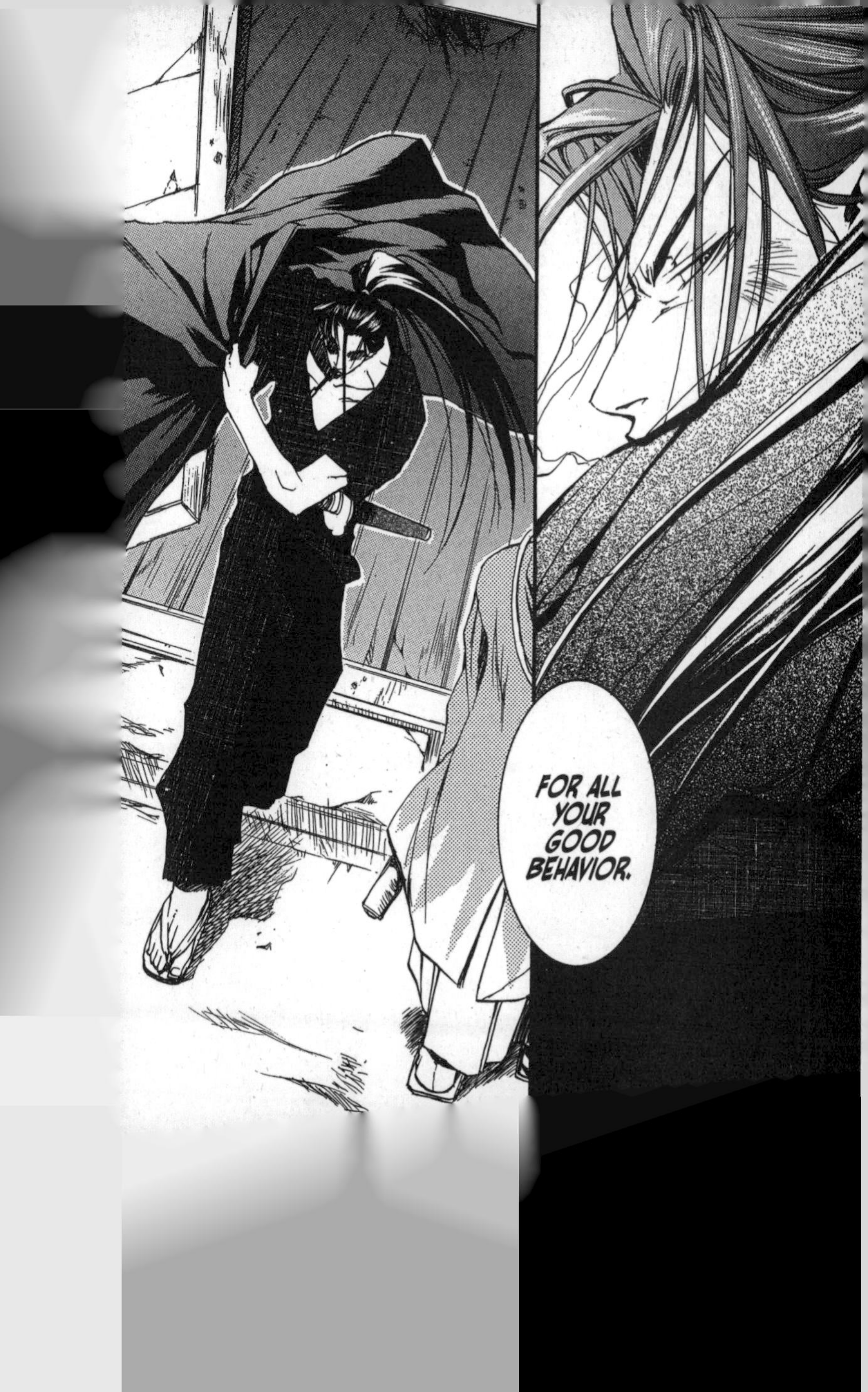
FOR ALL YOUR GOOD BEHAVIOR.

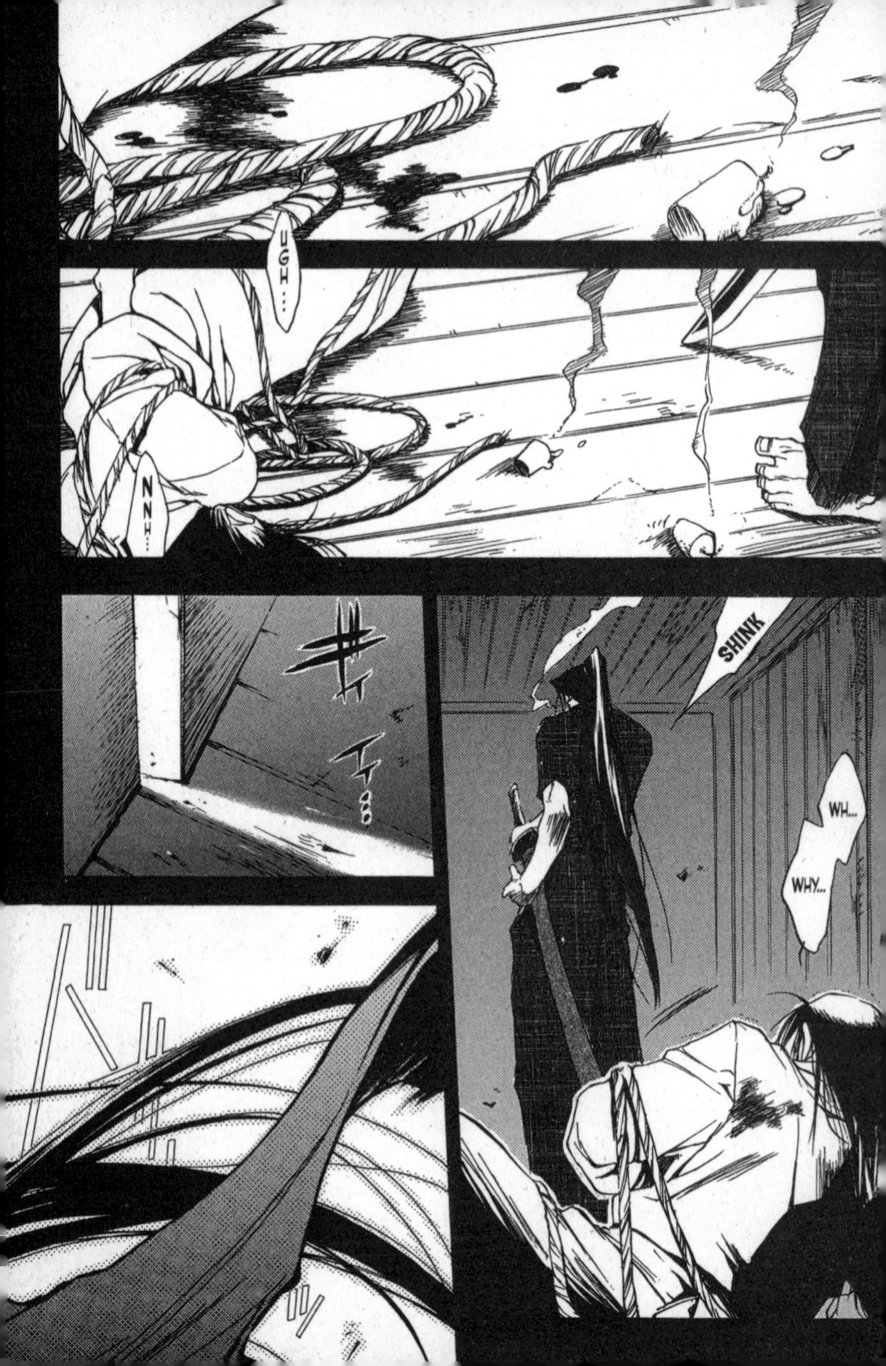
UGH...
NNH...
SHINK
WH...
WHY...

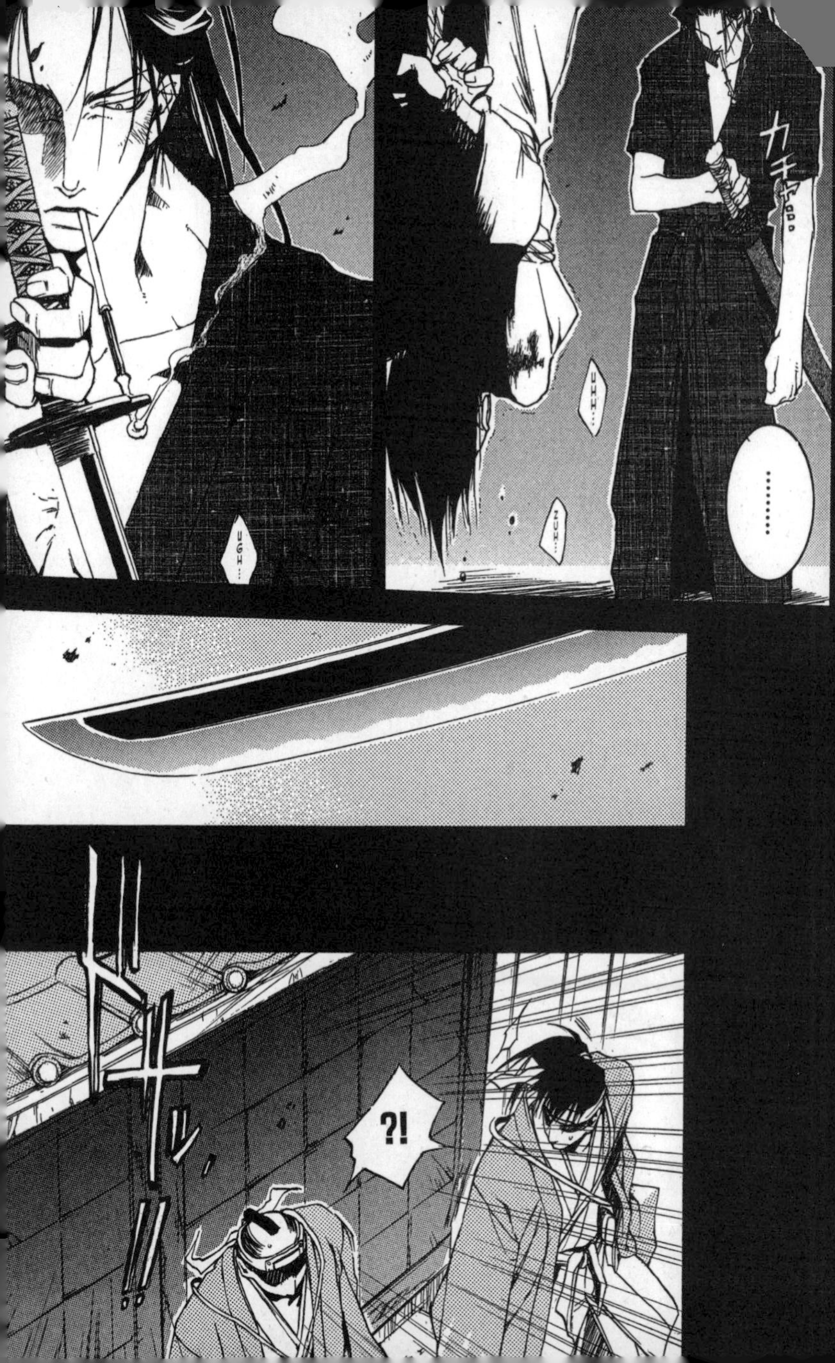
......
UHH...
ZUH...
UGH...
?!

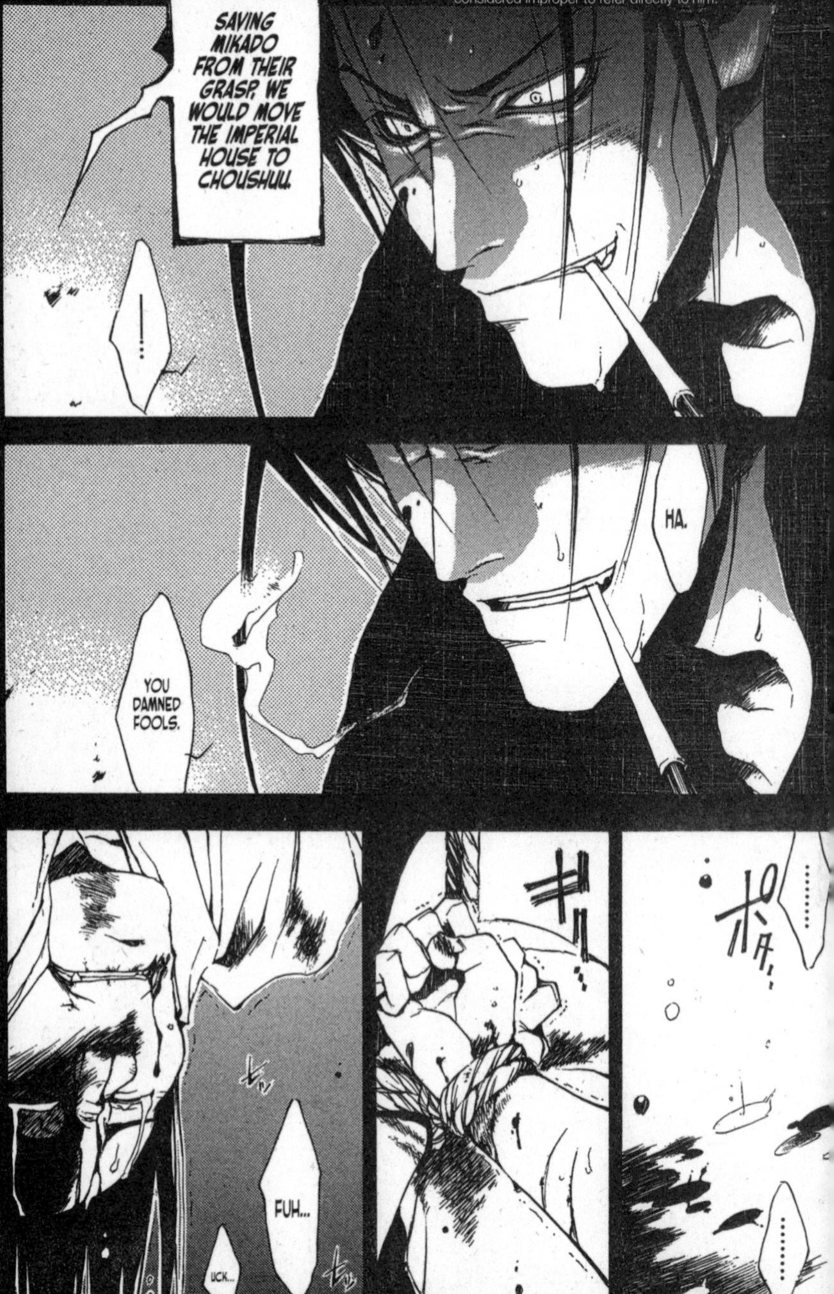
SAVING MIKADO FROM THEIR GRASP, WE WOULD MOVE THE IMPERIAL HOUSE TO CHOUSHUU.
HA.
YOU DAMNED FOOLS.
......
ポタ
......
ギリ
FUH...
UCK...

*Mikado: Another name for the Emporer, as it was considered improper to refer directly to him.

kugawa Shogunate.

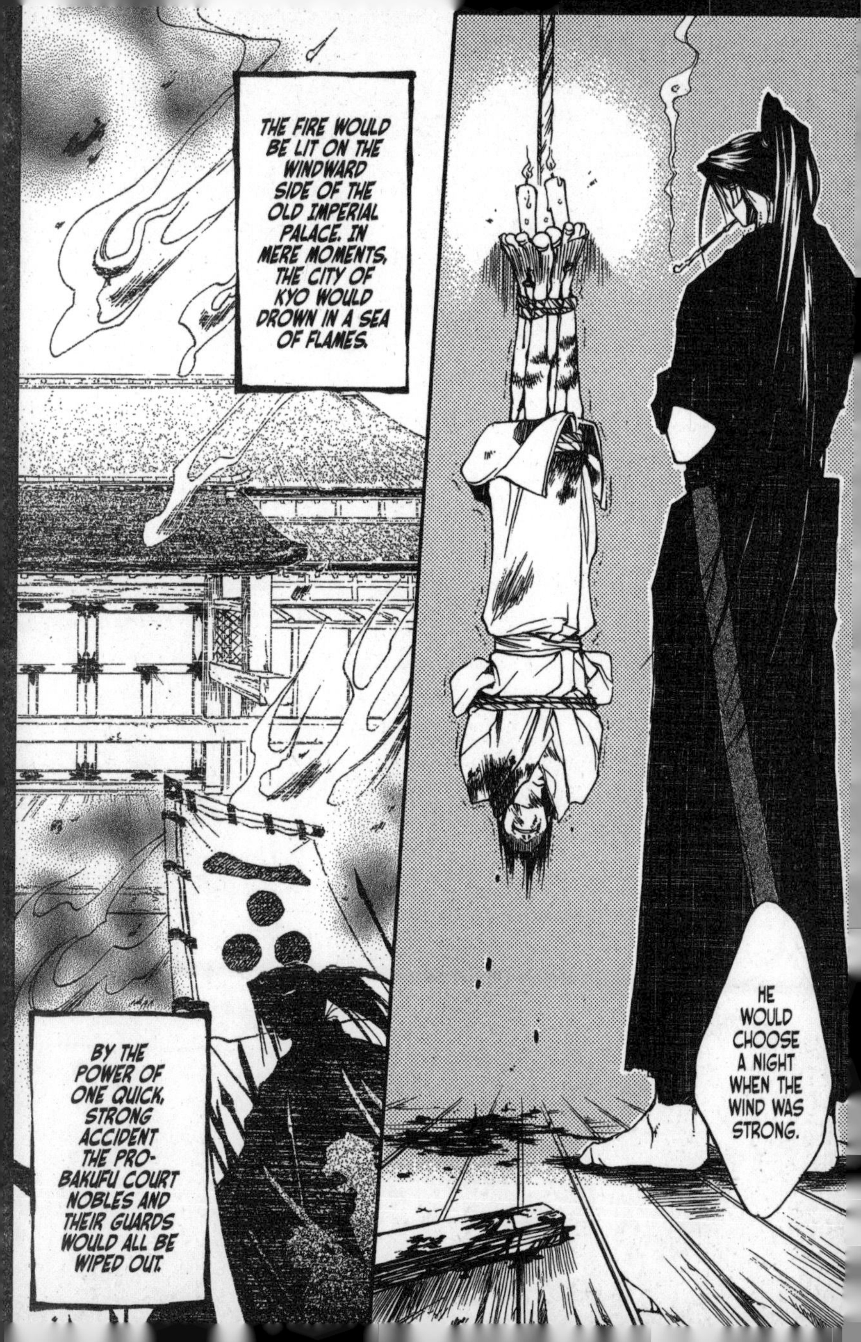

HE WOULD CHOOSE A NIGHT WHEN THE WIND WAS STRONG.
THE FIRE WOULD BE LIT ON THE WINDWARD SIDE OF THE OLD IMPERIAL PALACE. IN MERE MOMENTS, THE CITY OF KYO WOULD DROWN IN A SEA OF FLAMES.
BY THE POWER OF ONE QUICK, STRONG ACCIDENT THE PRO-BAKUFU COURT NOBLES AND THEIR GUARDS WOULD ALL BE WIPED OUT.

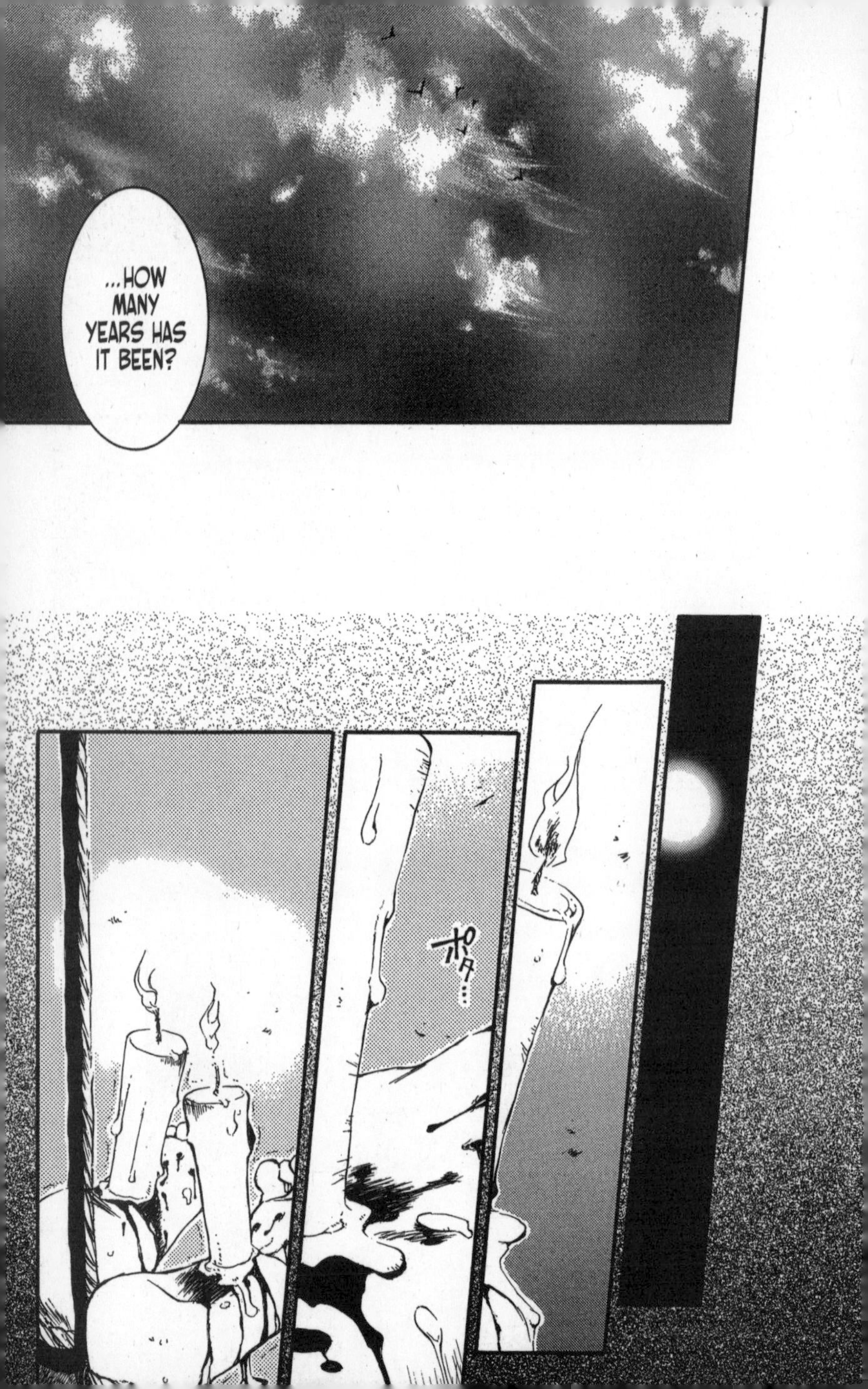
...HOW MANY YEARS HAS IT BEEN?
ポタ…

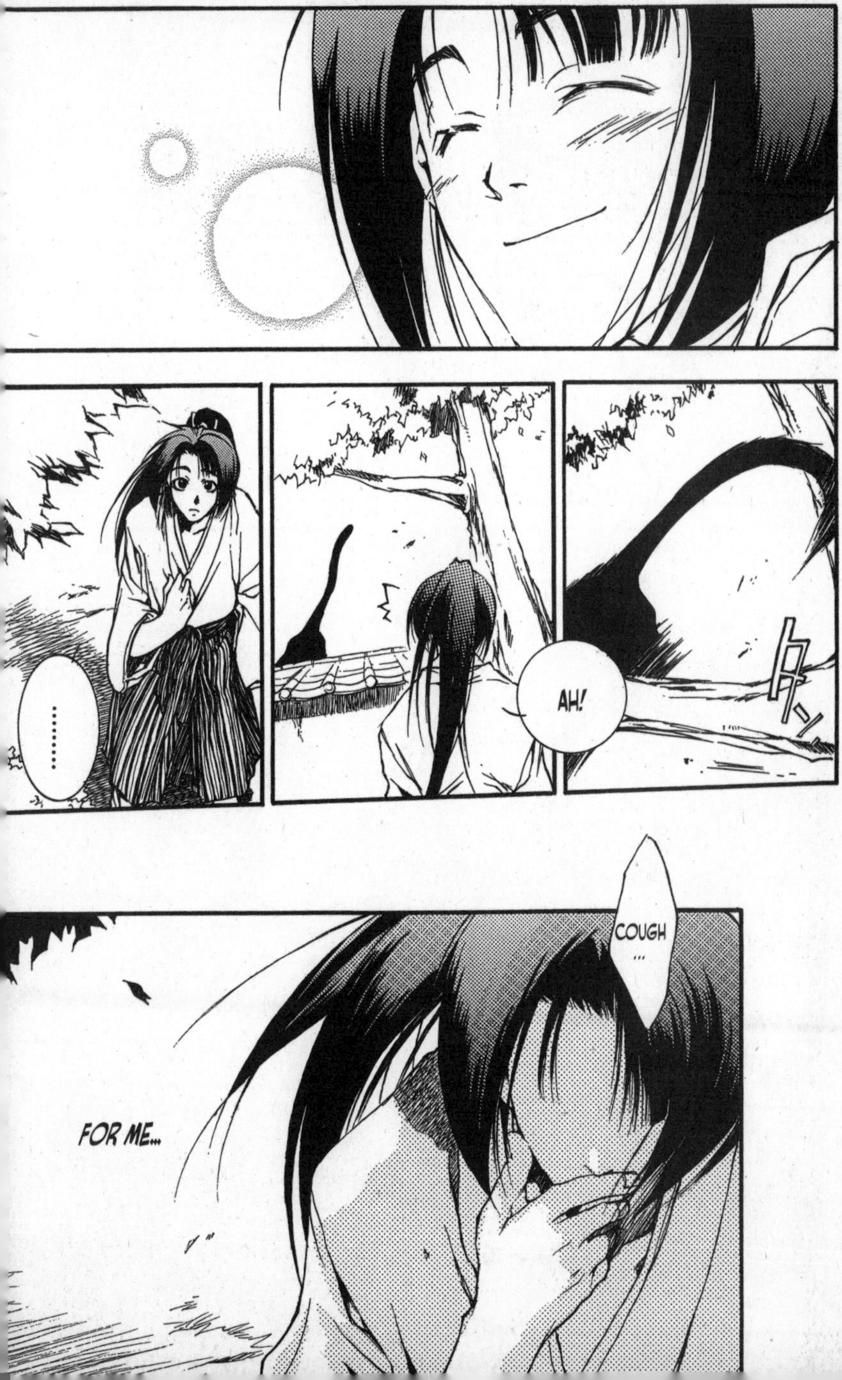
AH!
....
COUGH ...
FOR ME...

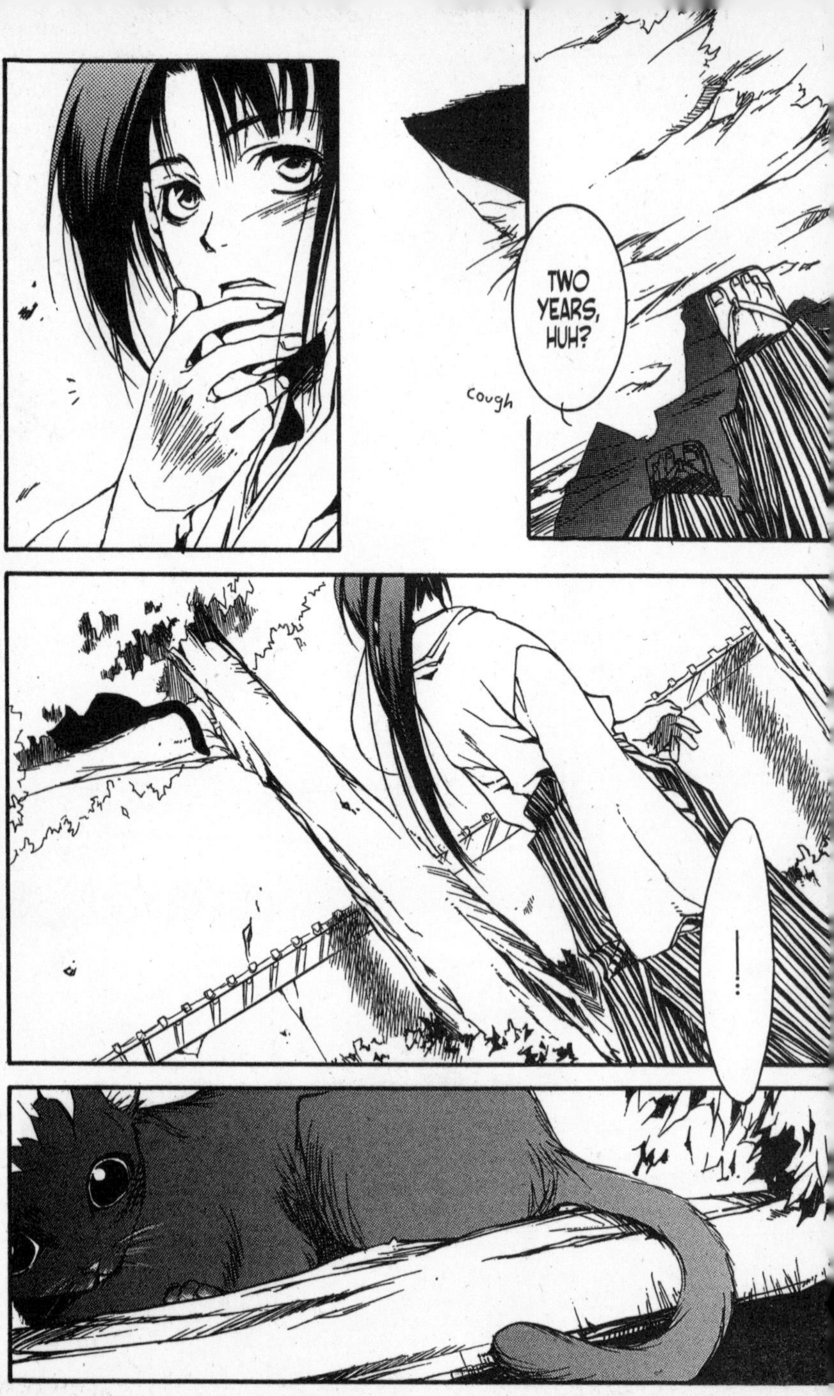
TWO YEARS, HUH?
cough
......!

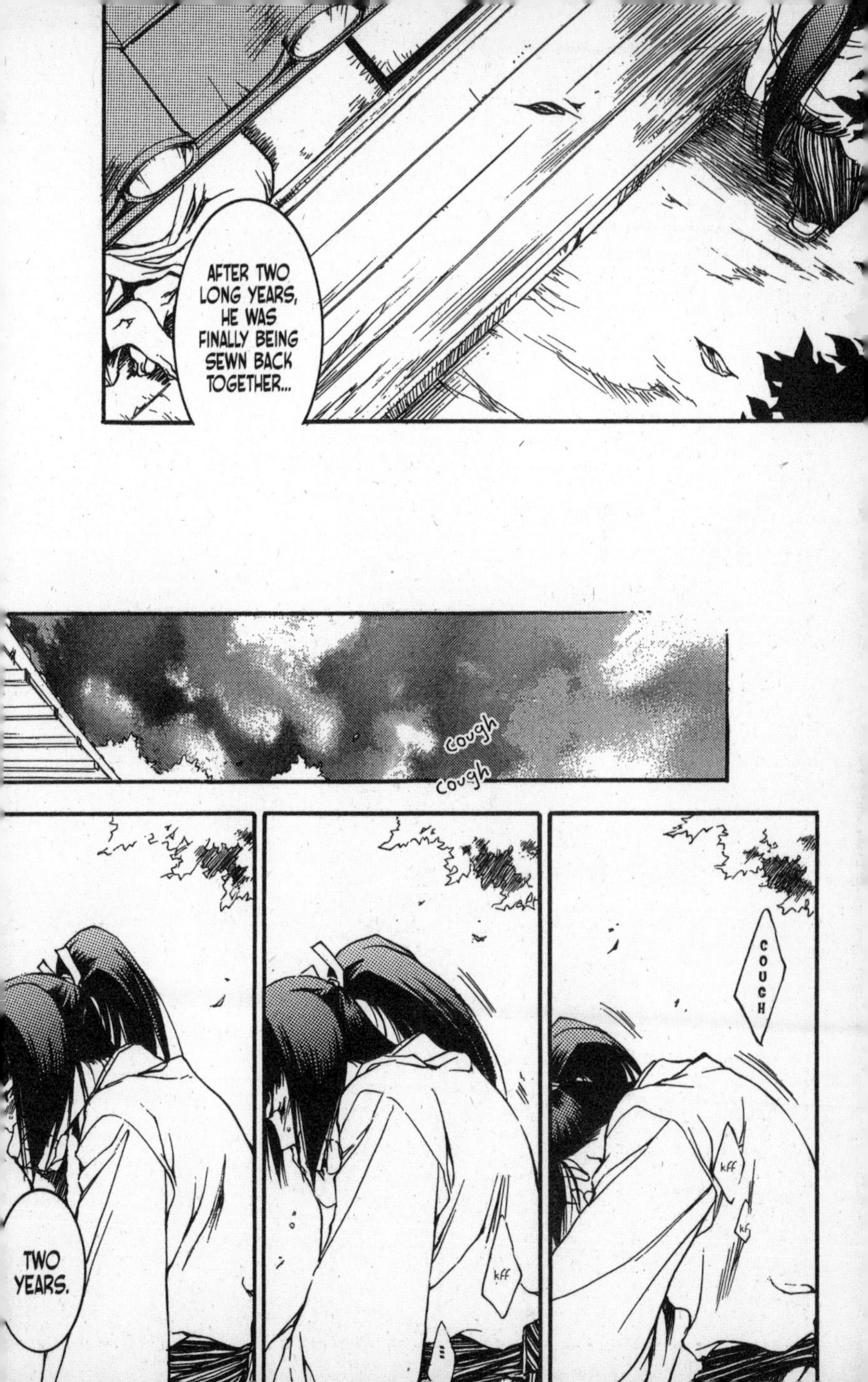
AFTER TWO LONG YEARS, HE WAS FINALLY BEING SEWN BACK TOGETHER...
cough
cough
COUGH
kff
kf
kff
TWO YEARS.

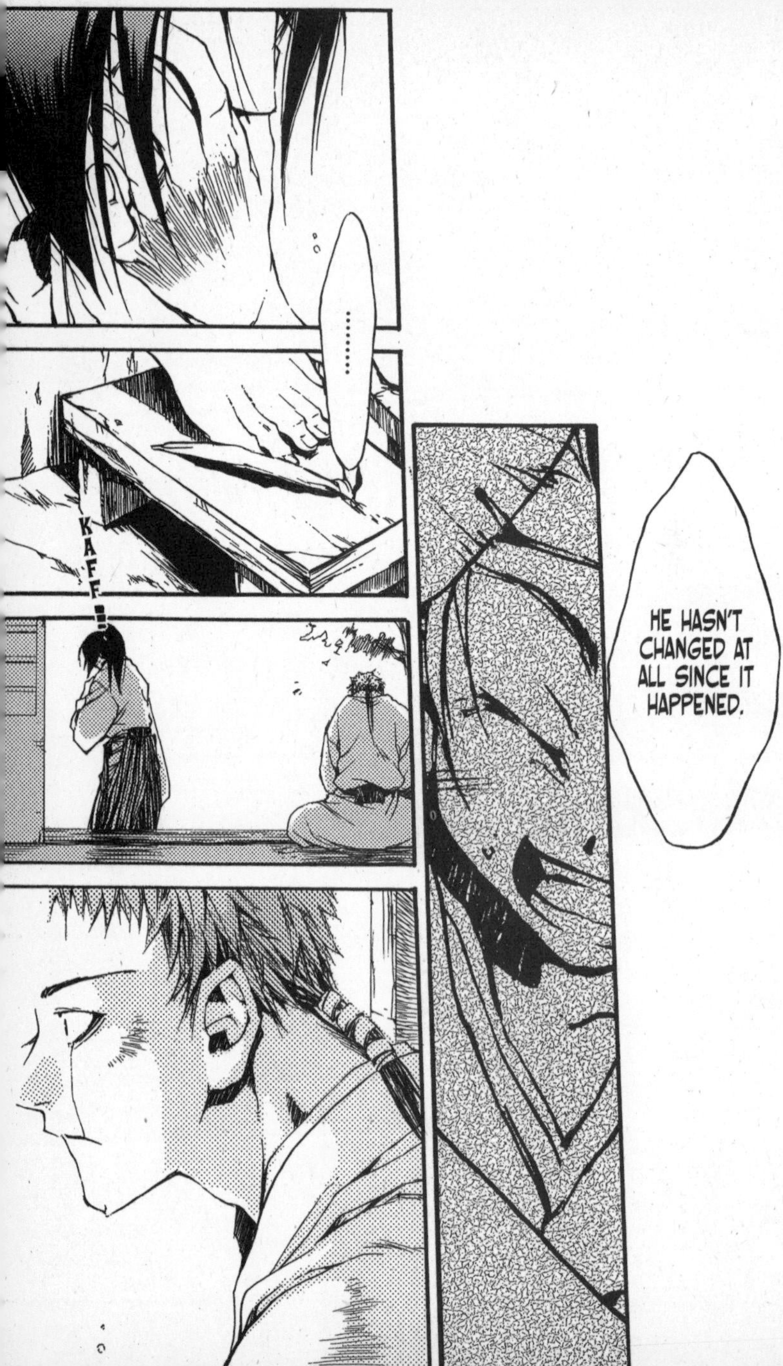
......
HE HASN'T CHANGED AT ALL SINCE IT HAPPENED.
KAFF

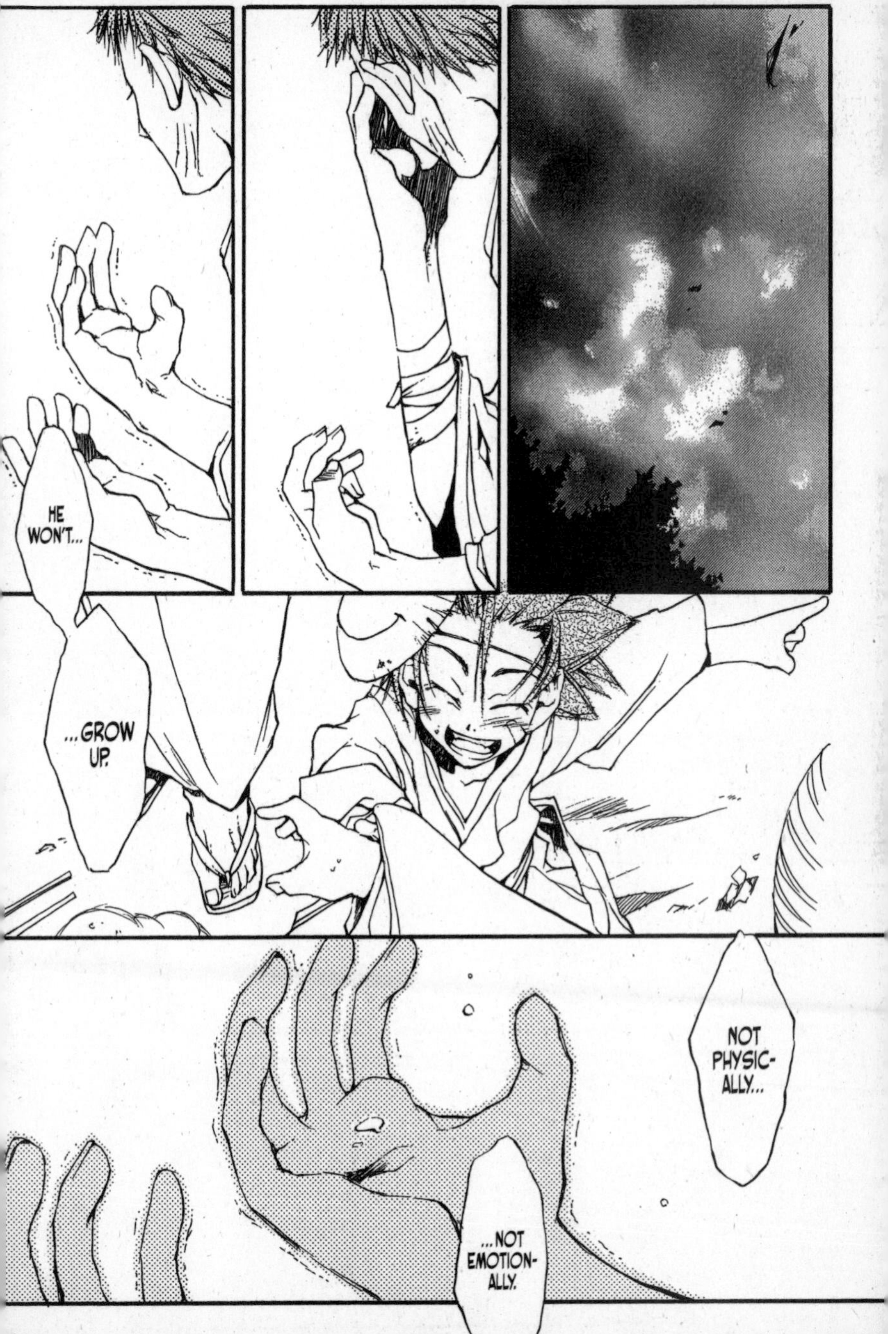
HE WON'T...
...GROW UP.
NOT PHYSIC-ALLY...
...NOT EMOTION-ALLY.

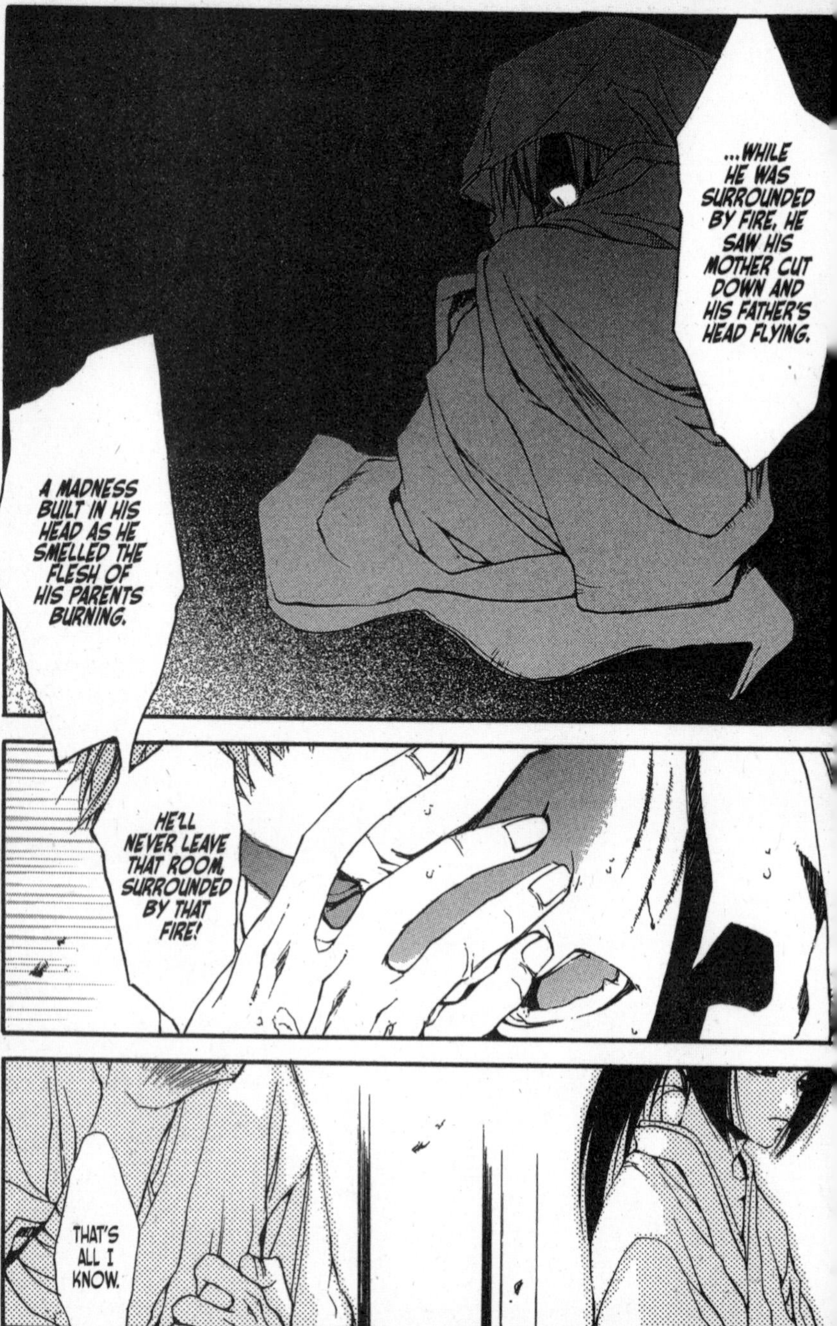
...WHILE HE WAS SURROUNDED BY FIRE, HE SAW HIS MOTHER CUT DOWN AND HIS FATHER'S HEAD FLYING.
A MADNESS BUILT IN HIS HEAD AS HE SMELLED THE FLESH OF HIS PARENTS BURNING.
HE'LL NEVER LEAVE THAT ROOM, SURROUNDED BY THAT FIRE!
THAT'S ALL I KNOW.

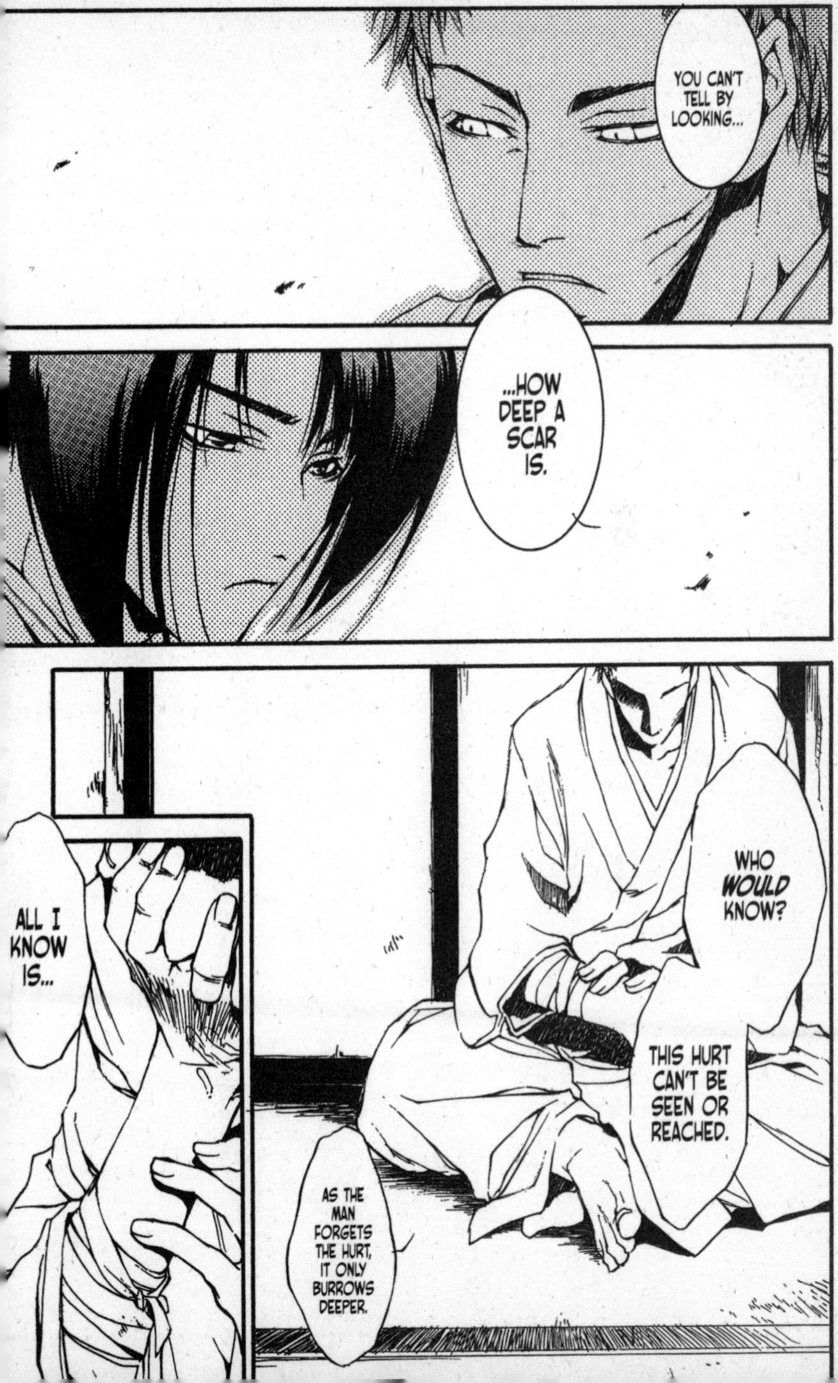
YOU CAN'T TELL BY LOOKING...
...HOW DEEP A SCAR IS.
WHO *WOULD* KNOW?
THIS HURT CAN'T BE SEEN OR REACHED.
AS THE MAN FORGETS THE HURT, IT ONLY BURROWS DEEPER.
ALL I KNOW IS...

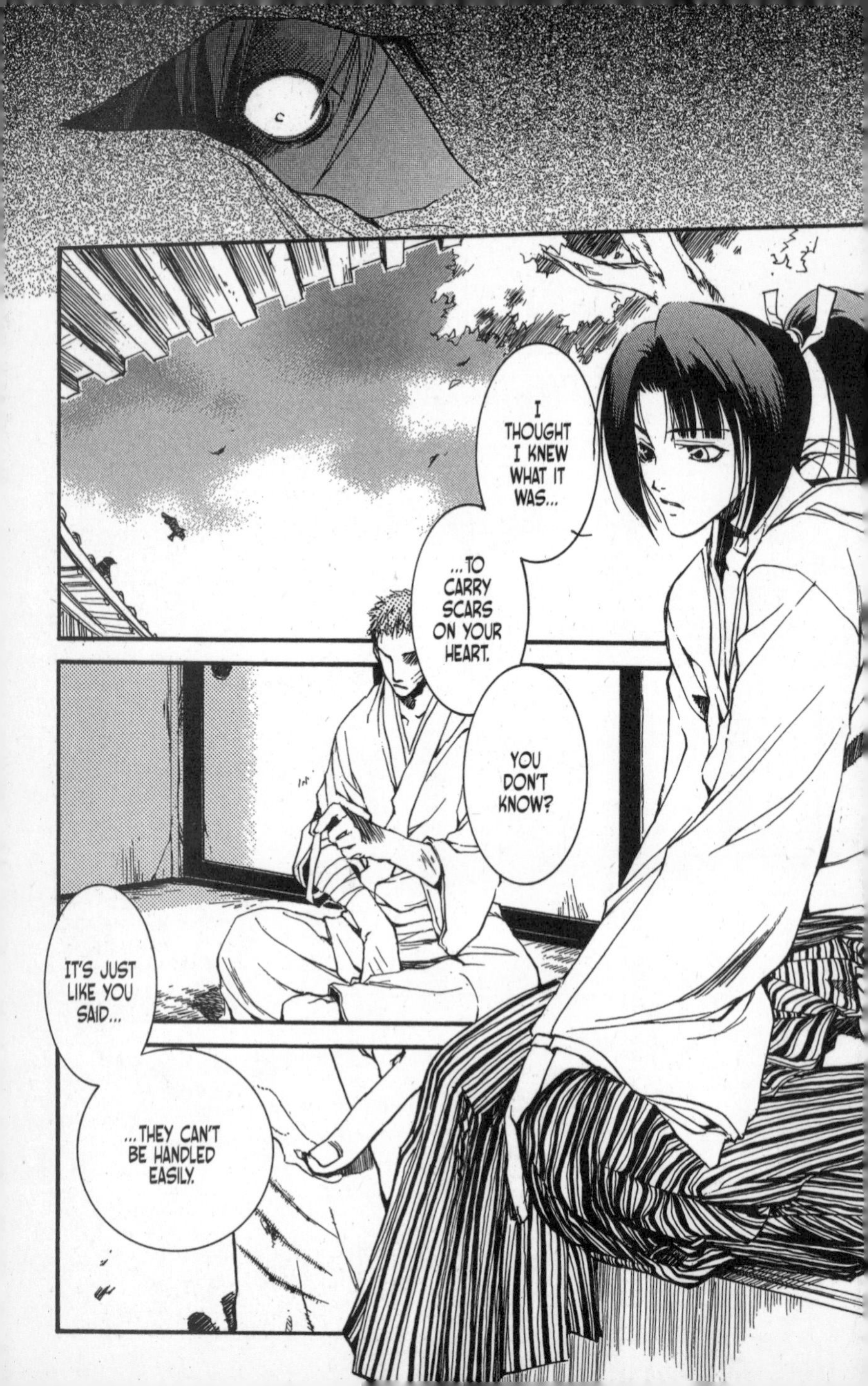
I THOUGHT I KNEW WHAT IT WAS...
...TO CARRY SCARS ON YOUR HEART.
YOU DON'T KNOW?
IT'S JUST LIKE YOU SAID...
...THEY CAN'T BE HANDLED EASILY.

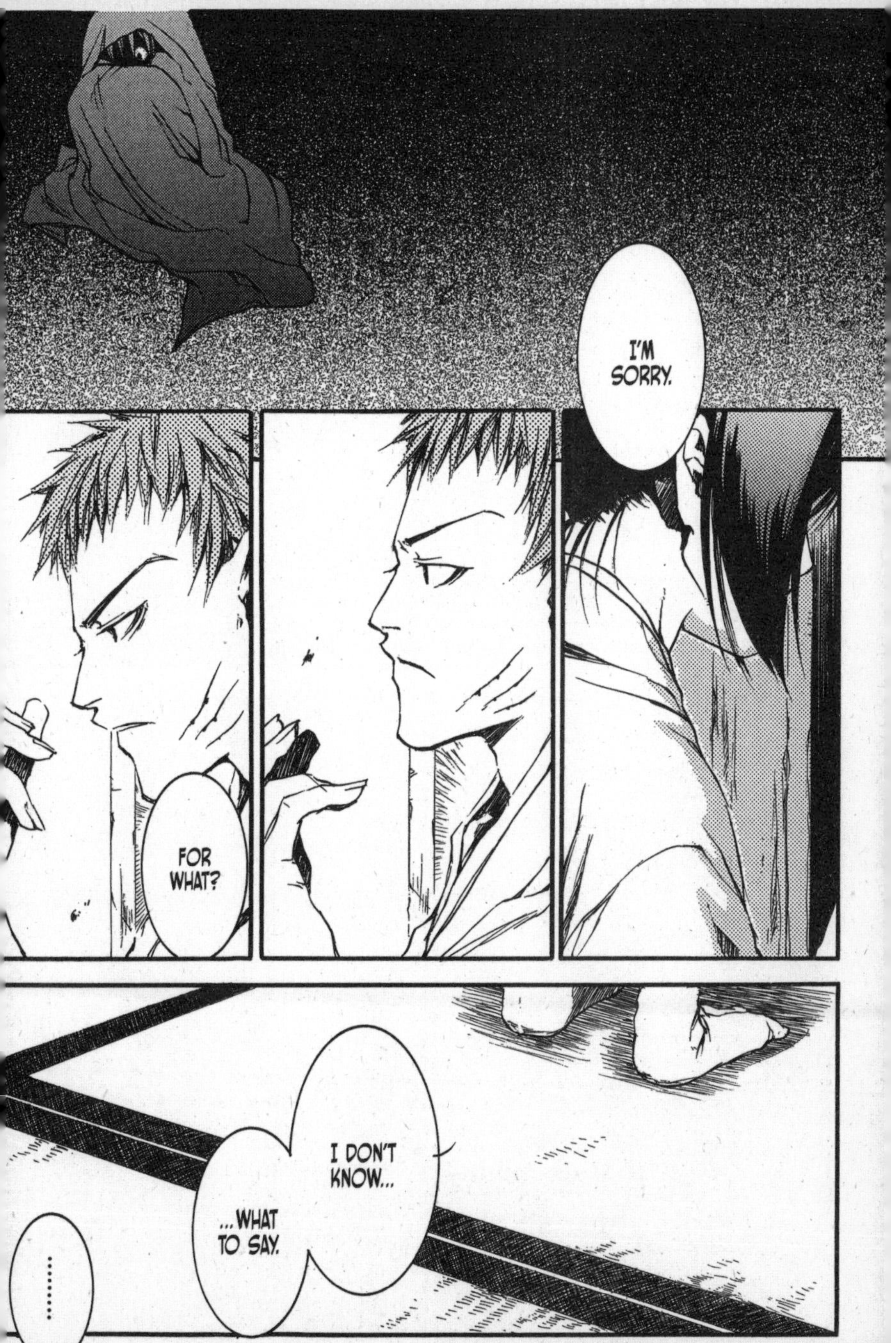
I'M SORRY.
FOR WHAT?
I DON'T KNOW...
...WHAT TO SAY.
....

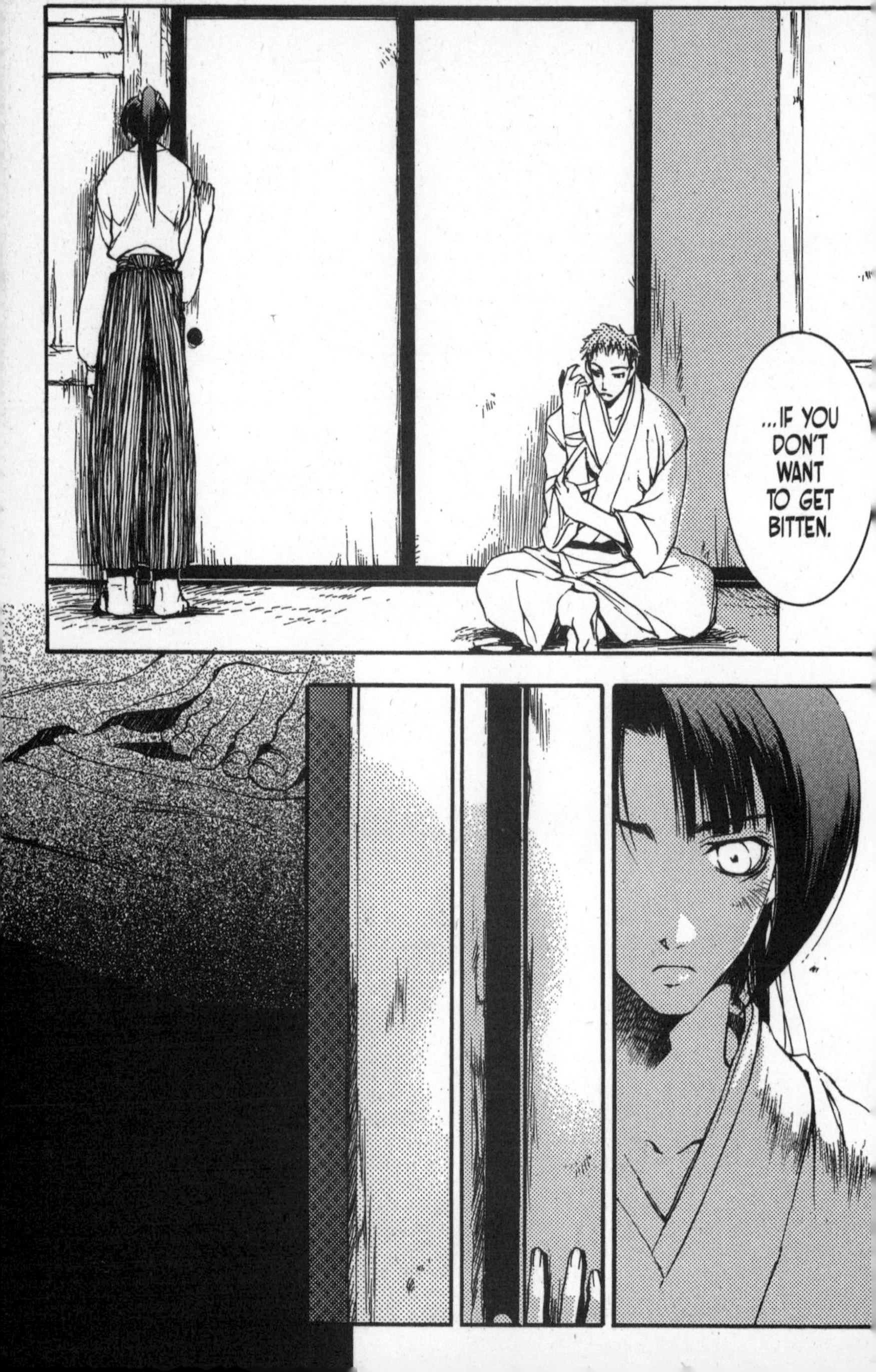
...IF YOU DON'T WANT TO GET BITTEN.

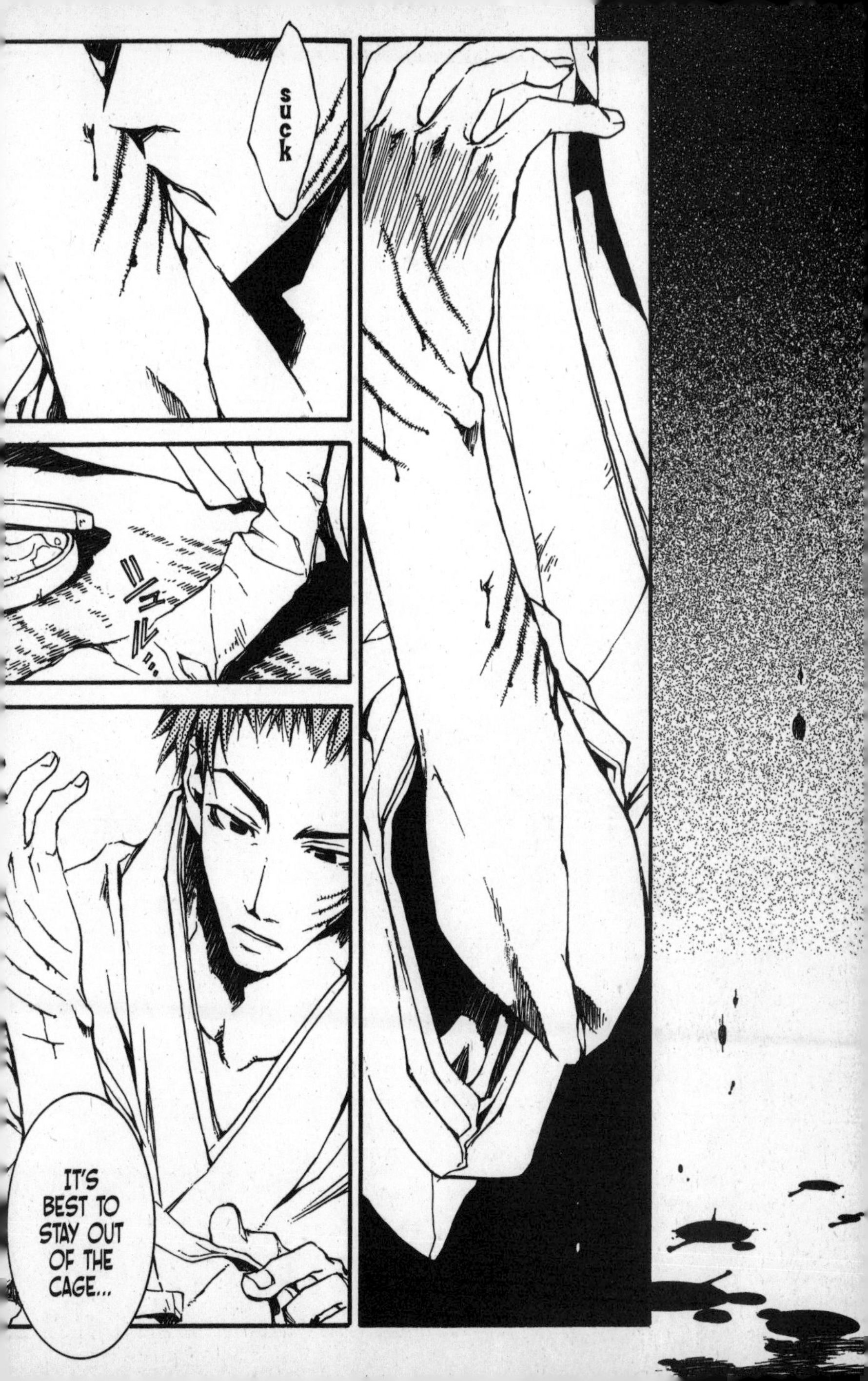
suck
シュル...
IT'S BEST TO STAY OUT OF THE CAGE...

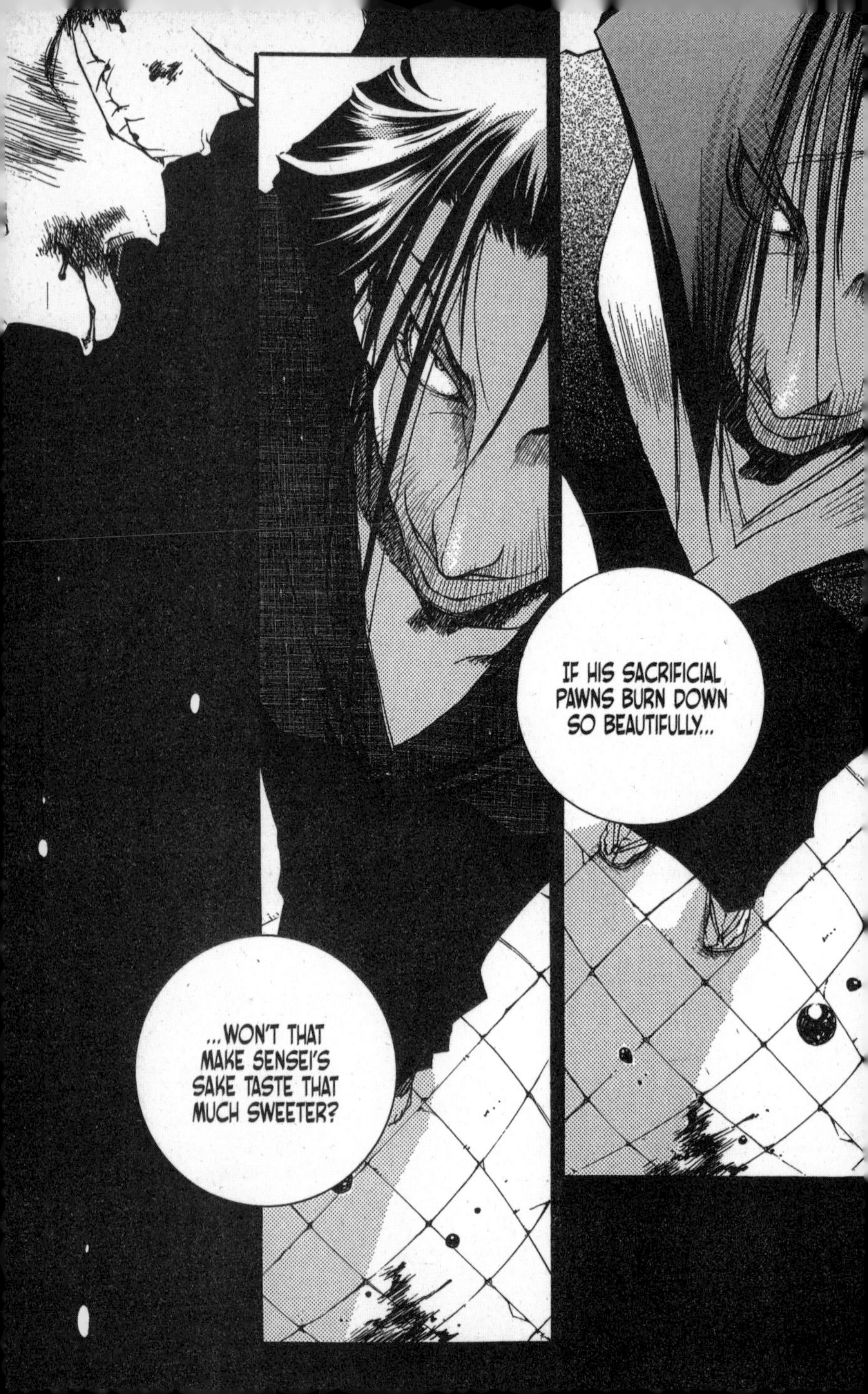
IF HIS SACRIFICIAL PAWNS BURN DOWN SO BEAUTIFULLY...
...WON'T THAT MAKE SENSEI'S SAKE TASTE THAT MUCH SWEETER?

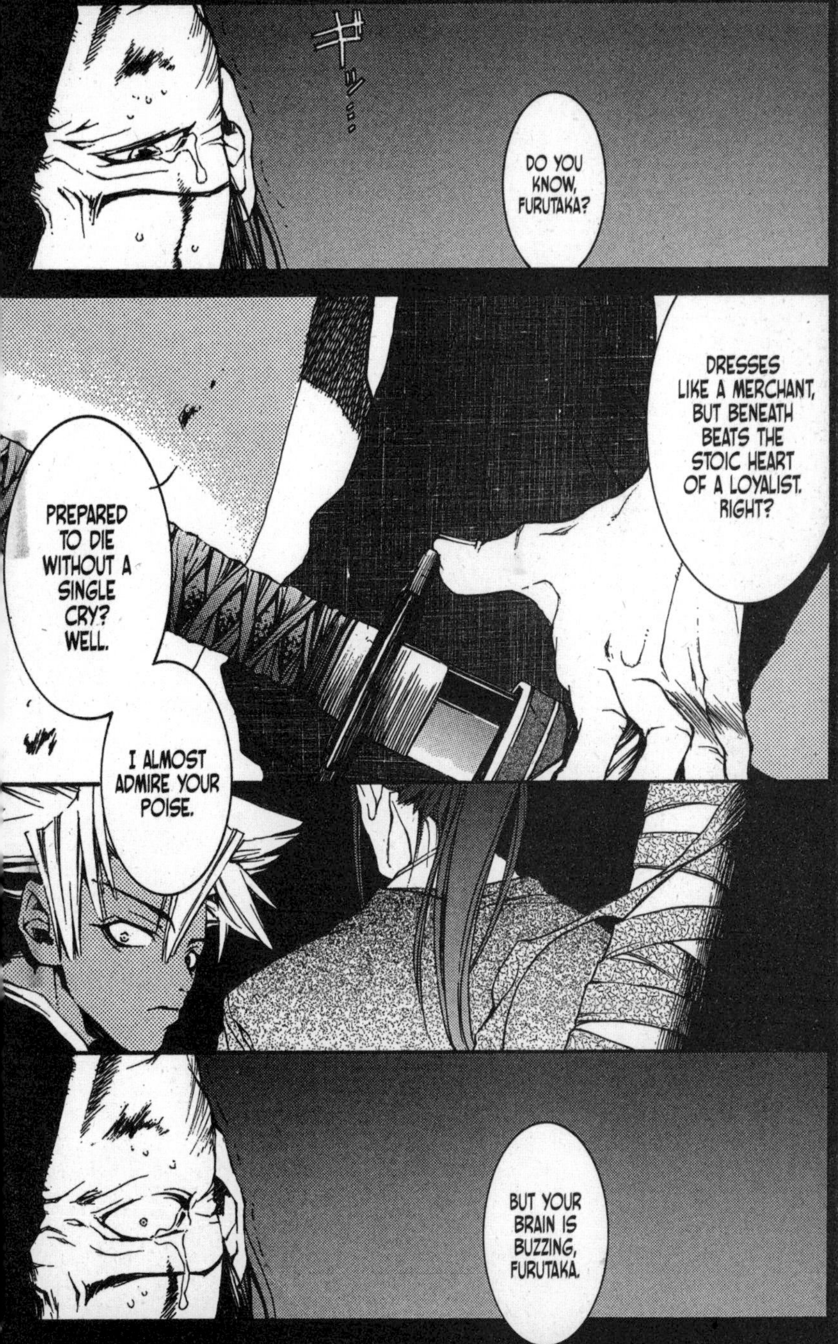
DO YOU KNOW, FURUTAKA?
DRESSES LIKE A MERCHANT, BUT BENEATH BEATS THE STOIC HEART OF A LOYALIST. RIGHT?
PREPARED TO DIE WITHOUT A SINGLE CRY? WELL.
I ALMOST ADMIRE YOUR POISE.
BUT YOUR BRAIN IS BUZZING, FURUTAKA.

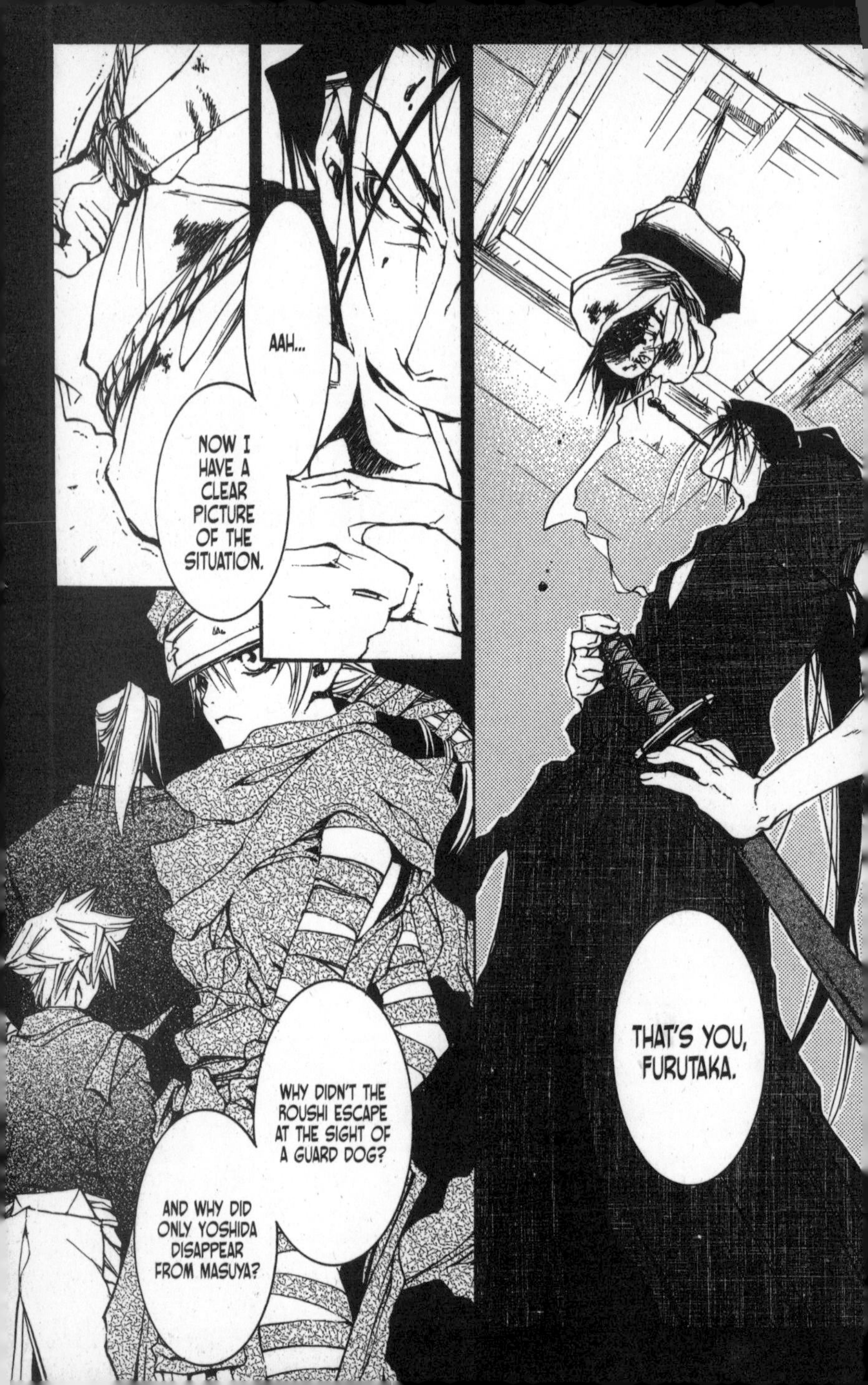
THAT'S YOU, FURUTAKA.
AAH...
NOW I HAVE A CLEAR PICTURE OF THE SITUATION.
WHY DIDN'T THE ROUSHI ESCAPE AT THE SIGHT OF A GUARD DOG?
AND WHY DID ONLY YOSHIDA DISAPPEAR FROM MASUYA?

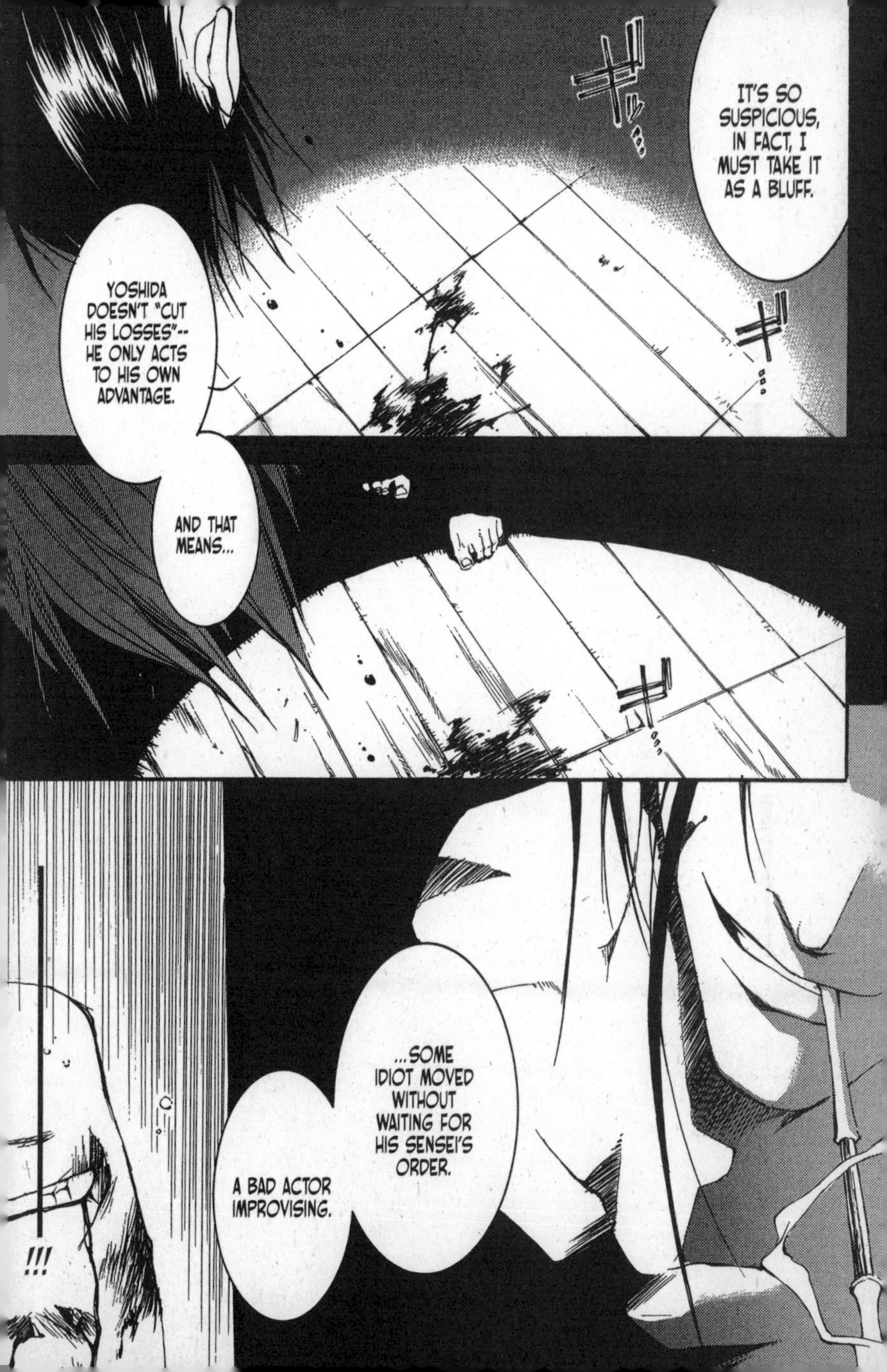
IT'S SO SUSPICIOUS, IN FACT, I MUST TAKE IT AS A BLUFF.
YOSHIDA DOESN'T "CUT HIS LOSSES"--HE ONLY ACTS TO HIS OWN ADVANTAGE.
AND THAT MEANS...
...SOME IDIOT MOVED WITHOUT WAITING FOR HIS SENSEI'S ORDER.
A BAD ACTOR IMPROVISING.
!!!

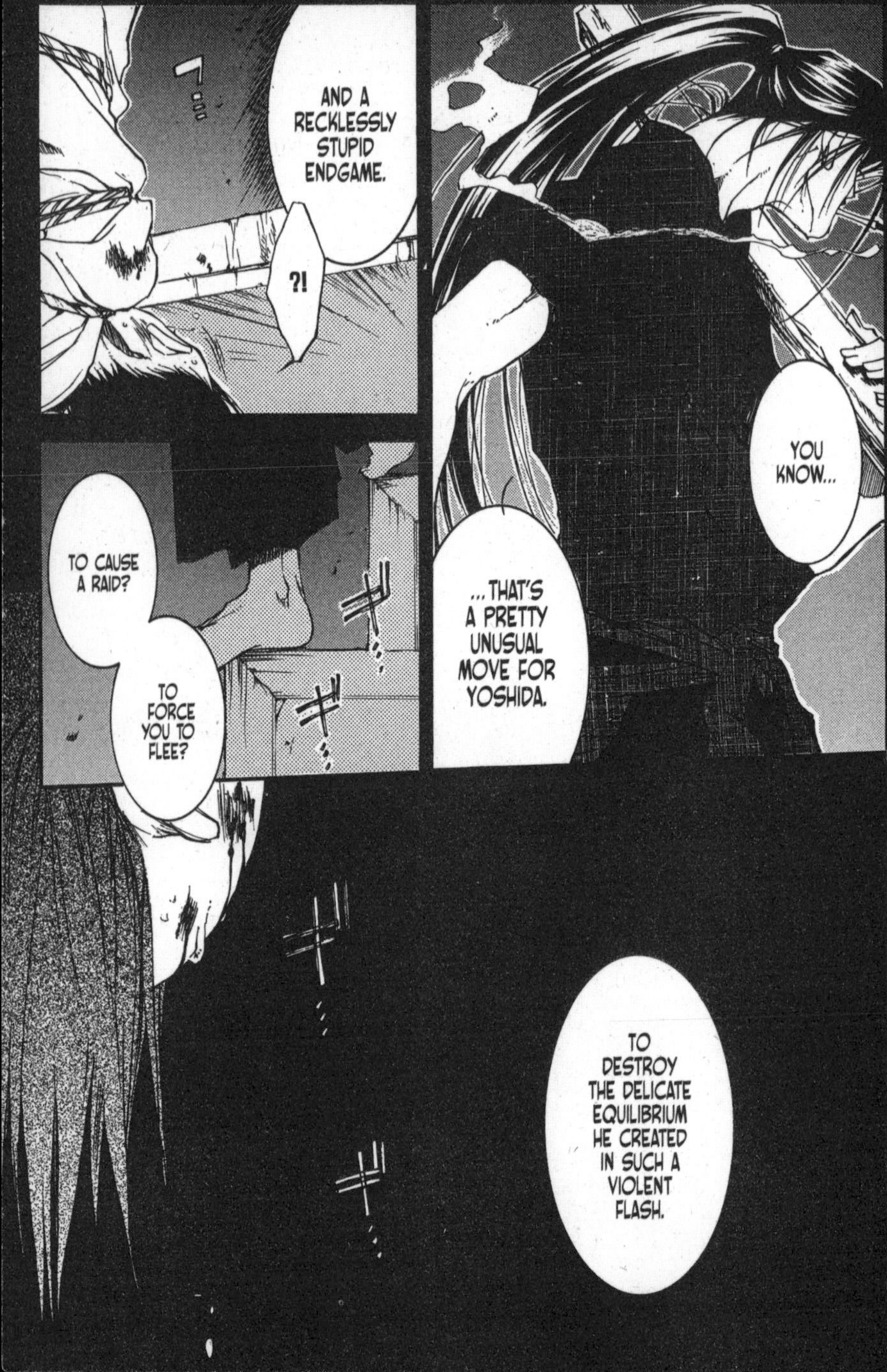
YOU KNOW...
...THAT'S A PRETTY UNUSUAL MOVE FOR YOSHIDA.
AND A RECKLESSLY STUPID ENDGAME.
?!
TO CAUSE A RAID?
TO FORCE YOU TO FLEE?
TO DESTROY THE DELICATE EQUILIBRIUM HE CREATED IN SUCH A VIOLENT FLASH.

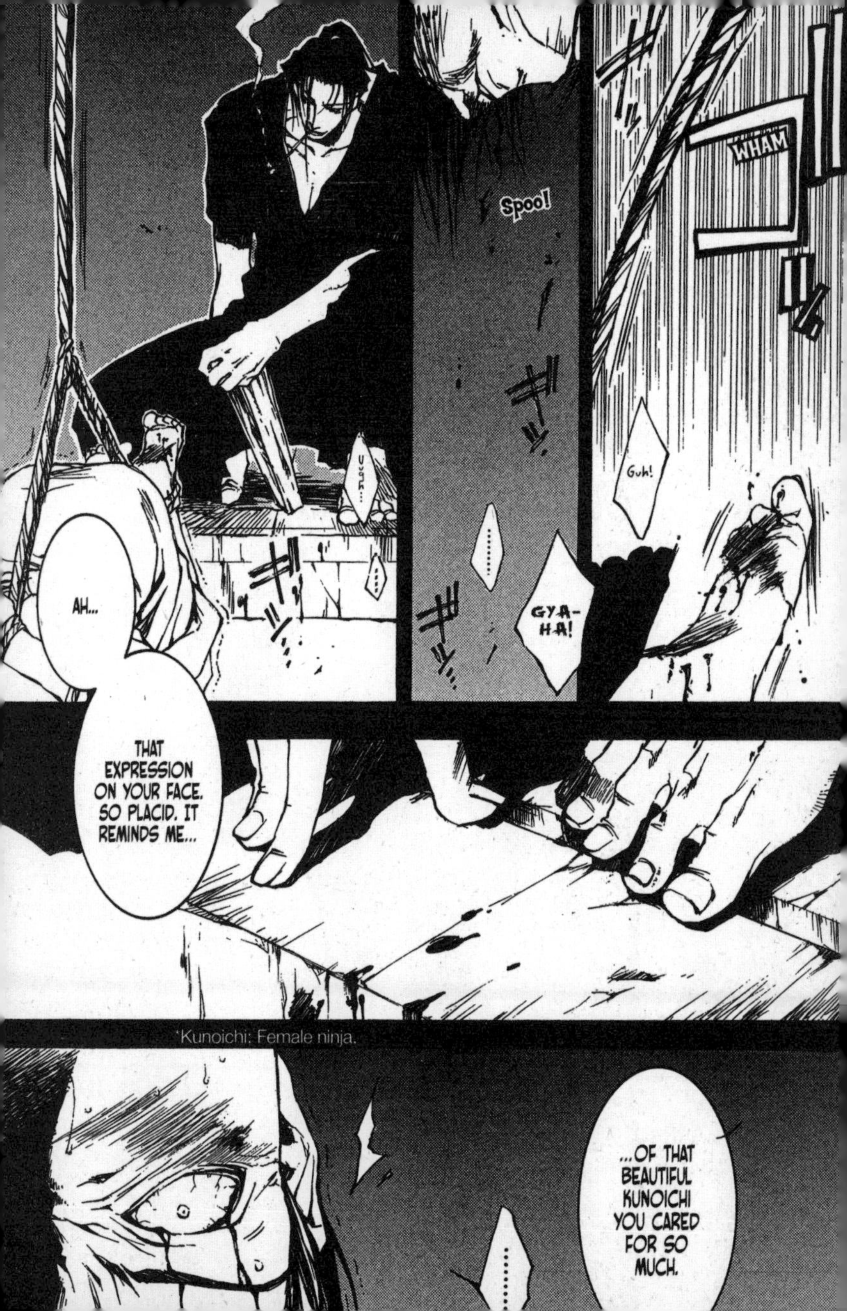
WHAM
Guh!
GYA-HA!
Spoo!
......
Ugh...
...
AH...
THAT EXPRESSION ON YOUR FACE. SO PLACID. IT REMINDS ME...
...OF THAT BEAUTIFUL KUNOICHI YOU CARED FOR SO MUCH.
......

*Kunoichi: Female ninja.

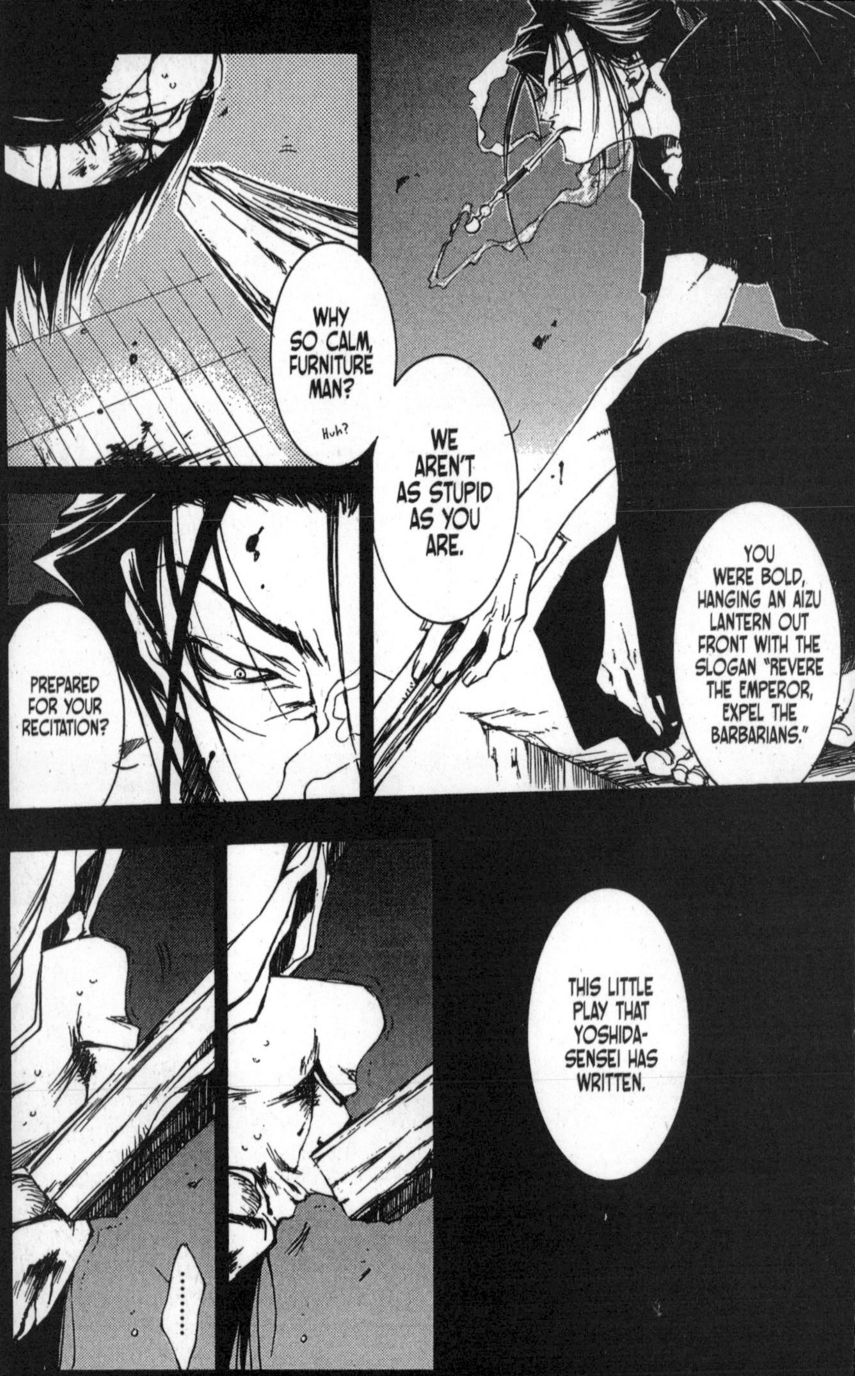
YOU WERE BOLD, HANGING AN AIZU LANTERN OUT FRONT WITH THE SLOGAN "REVERE THE EMPEROR, EXPEL THE BARBARIANS."
WHY SO CALM, FURNITURE MAN?
Huh?
WE AREN'T AS STUPID AS YOU ARE.
PREPARED FOR YOUR RECITATION?
THIS LITTLE PLAY THAT YOSHIDA-SENSEI HAS WRITTEN.
......

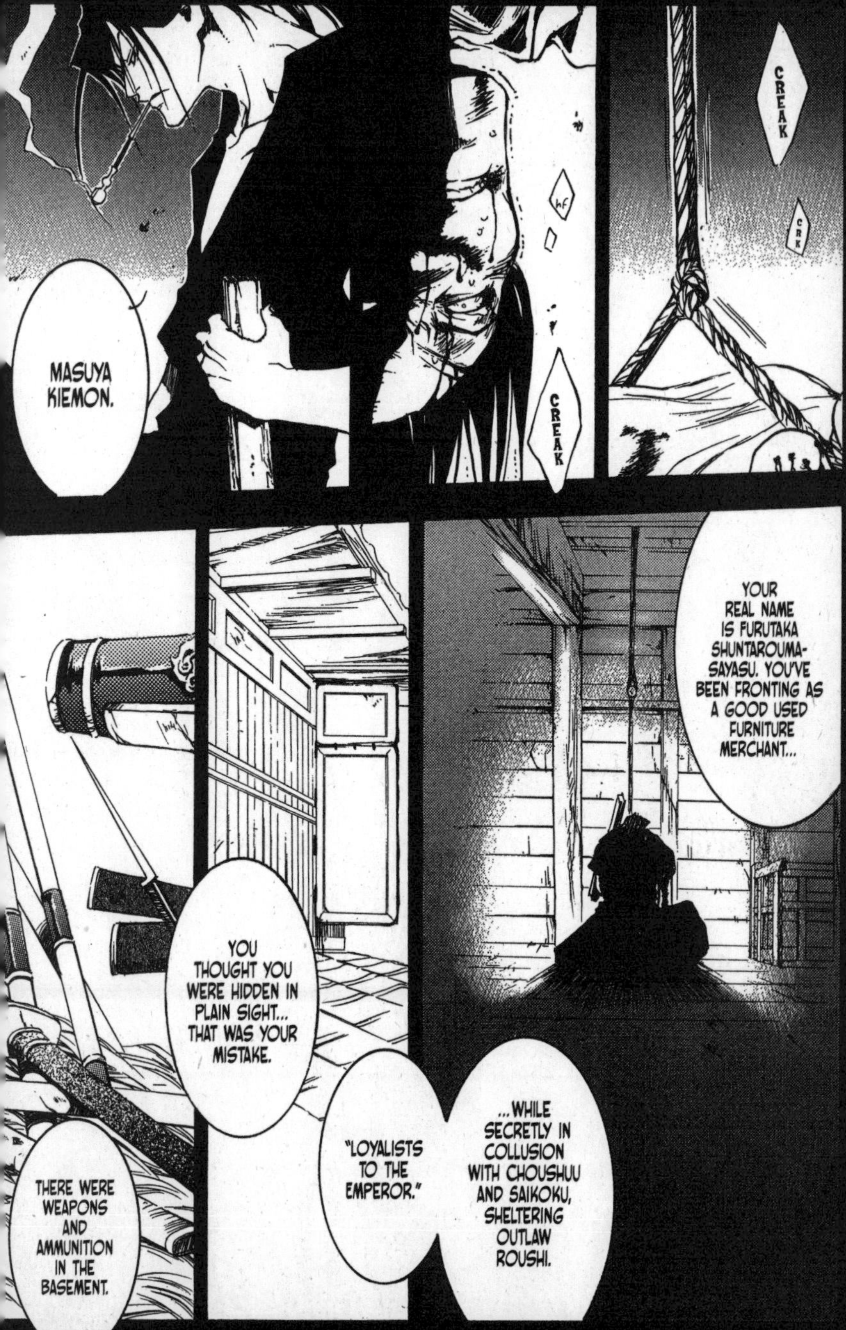
CREAK
CRK
hf
CREAK
MASUYA KIEMON.
YOUR REAL NAME IS FURUTAKA SHUNTAROUMA-SAYASU. YOU'VE BEEN FRONTING AS A GOOD USED FURNITURE MERCHANT...
...WHILE SECRETLY IN COLLUSION WITH CHOUSHUU AND SAIKOKU, SHELTERING OUTLAW ROUSHI.
"LOYALISTS TO THE EMPEROR."
YOU THOUGHT YOU WERE HIDDEN IN PLAIN SIGHT... THAT WAS YOUR MISTAKE.
THERE WERE WEAPONS AND AMMUNITION IN THE BASEMENT.

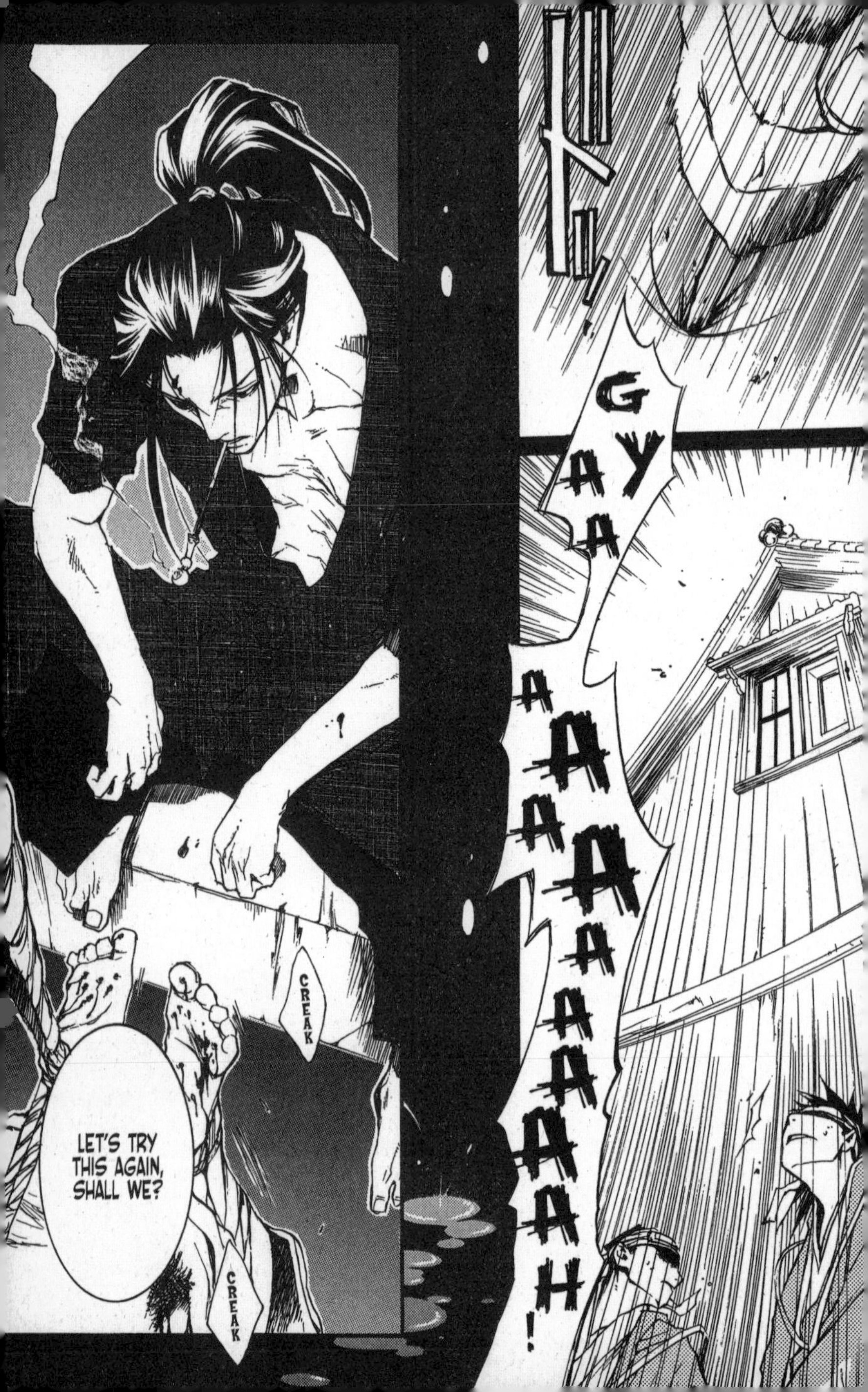
GYAAAAAAAAAAAH!
CREAK
LET'S TRY THIS AGAIN, SHALL WE?
CREAK

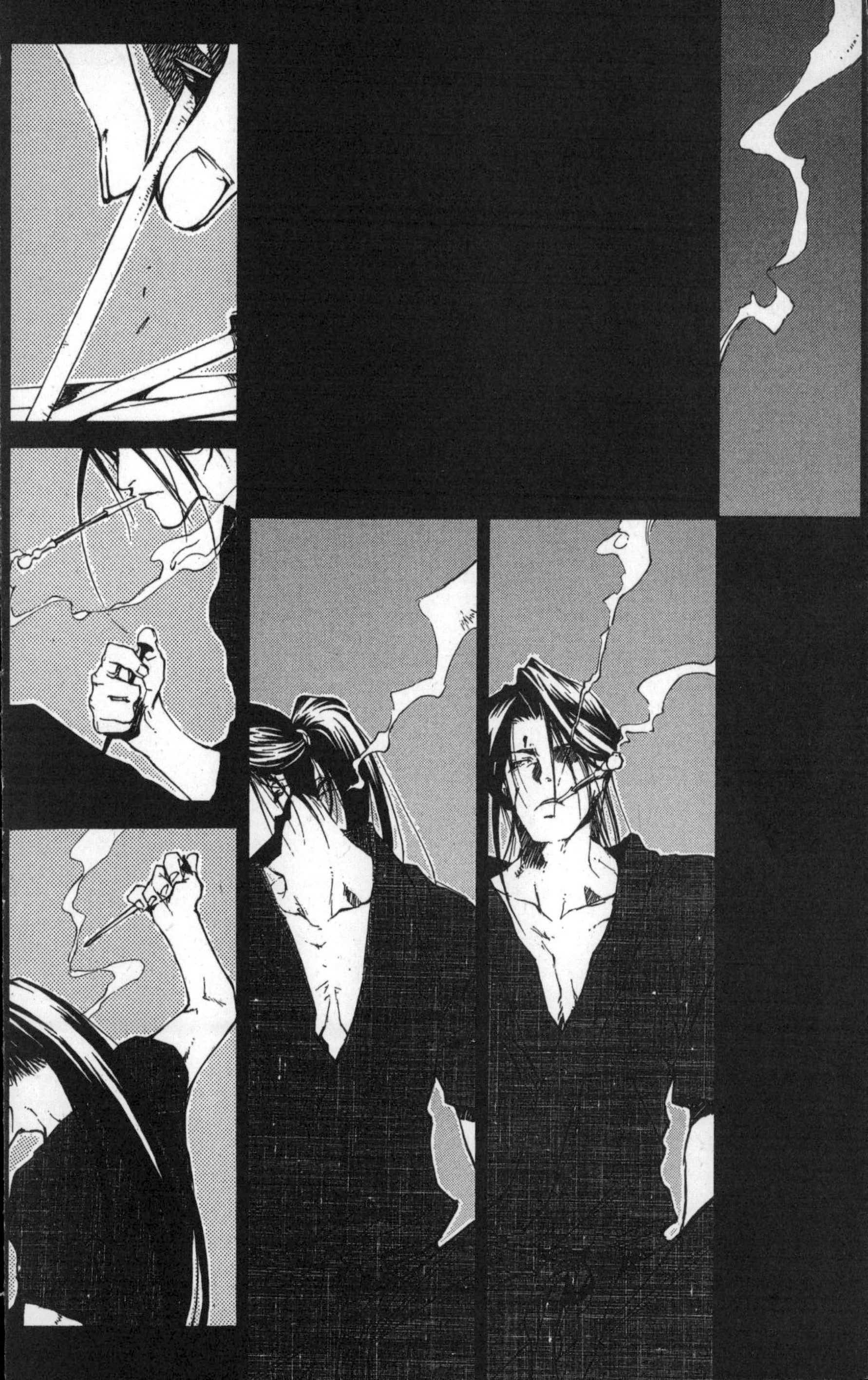

**Act.22
Misery**

AFTER TWO LONG YEARS, HE WAS FINALLY BEING SEWN BACK TOGETHER...

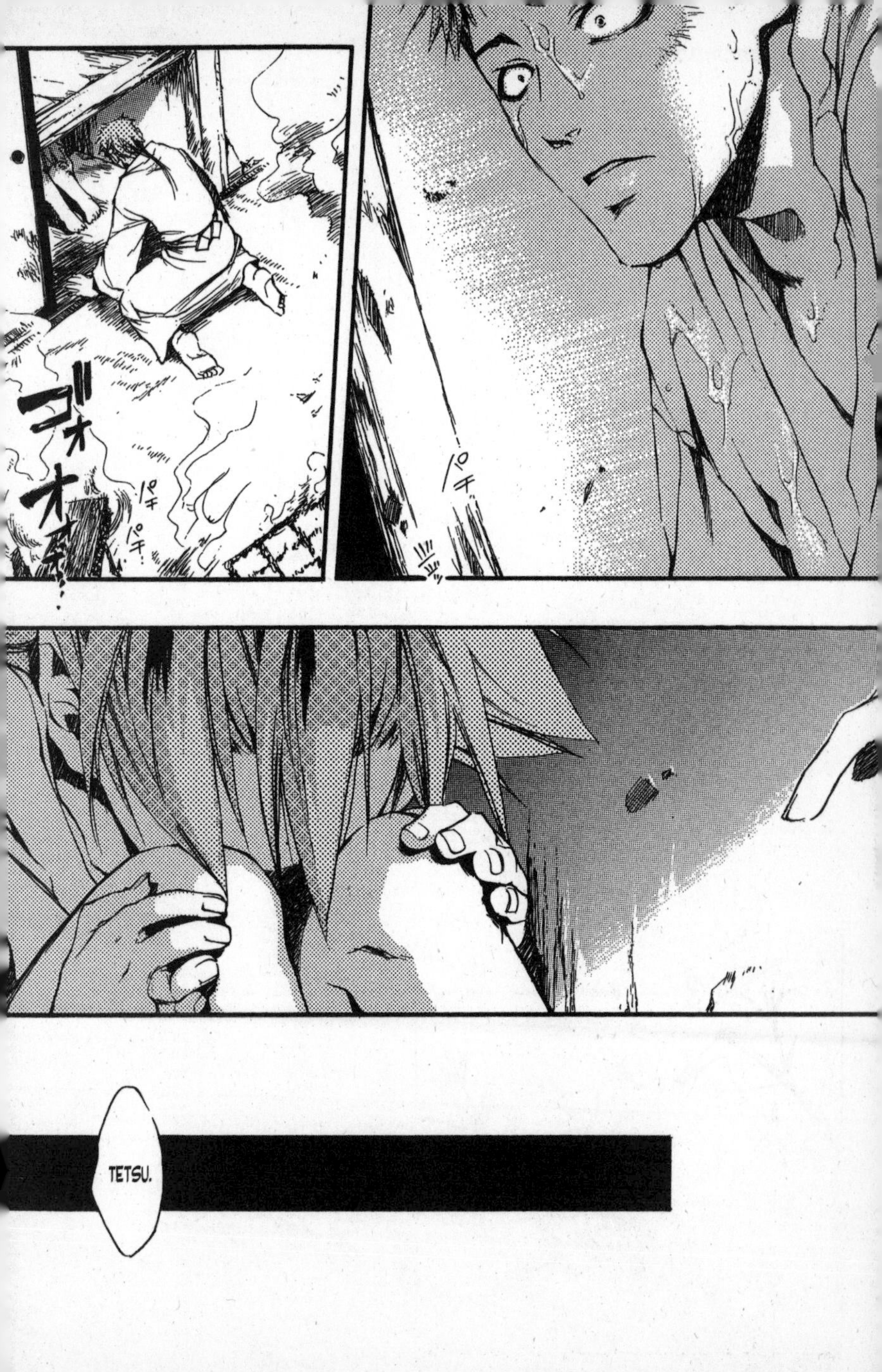
パチ…
パチ
パチ…
TETSU.

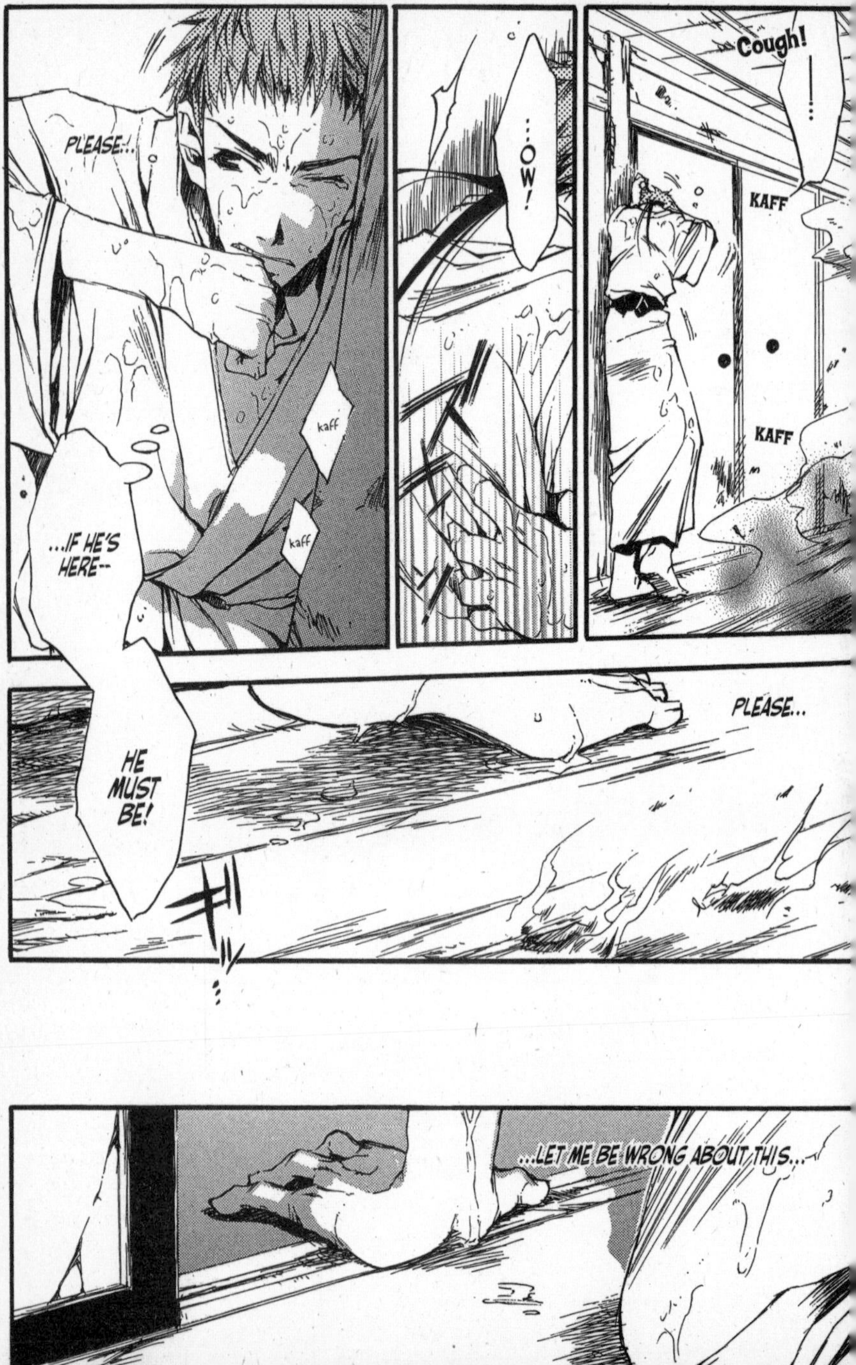
Cough!
—!
KAFF
KAFF
...OW!
PLEASE..!
kaff
kaff
...IF HE'S HERE--
HE MUST BE!
PLEASE...
...LET ME BE WRONG ABOUT THIS...

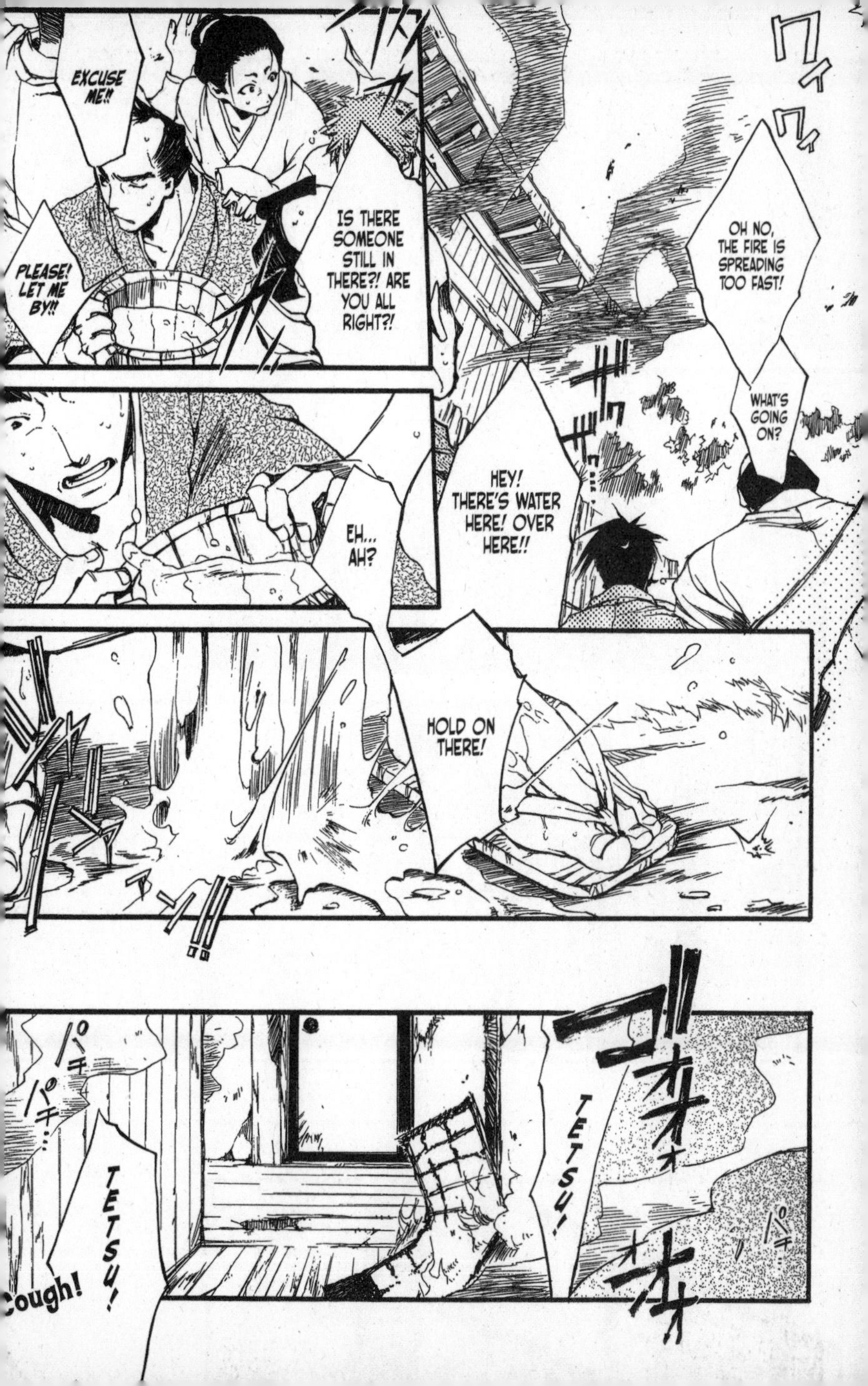
OH NO, THE FIRE IS SPREADING TOO FAST!
WHAT'S GOING ON?
HEY! THERE'S WATER HERE! OVER HERE!!
IS THERE SOMEONE STILL IN THERE?! ARE YOU ALL RIGHT?!
EXCUSE ME!!
PLEASE! LET ME BY!!
EH... AH?
HOLD ON THERE!
TETSU!
TETSU!
Cough!

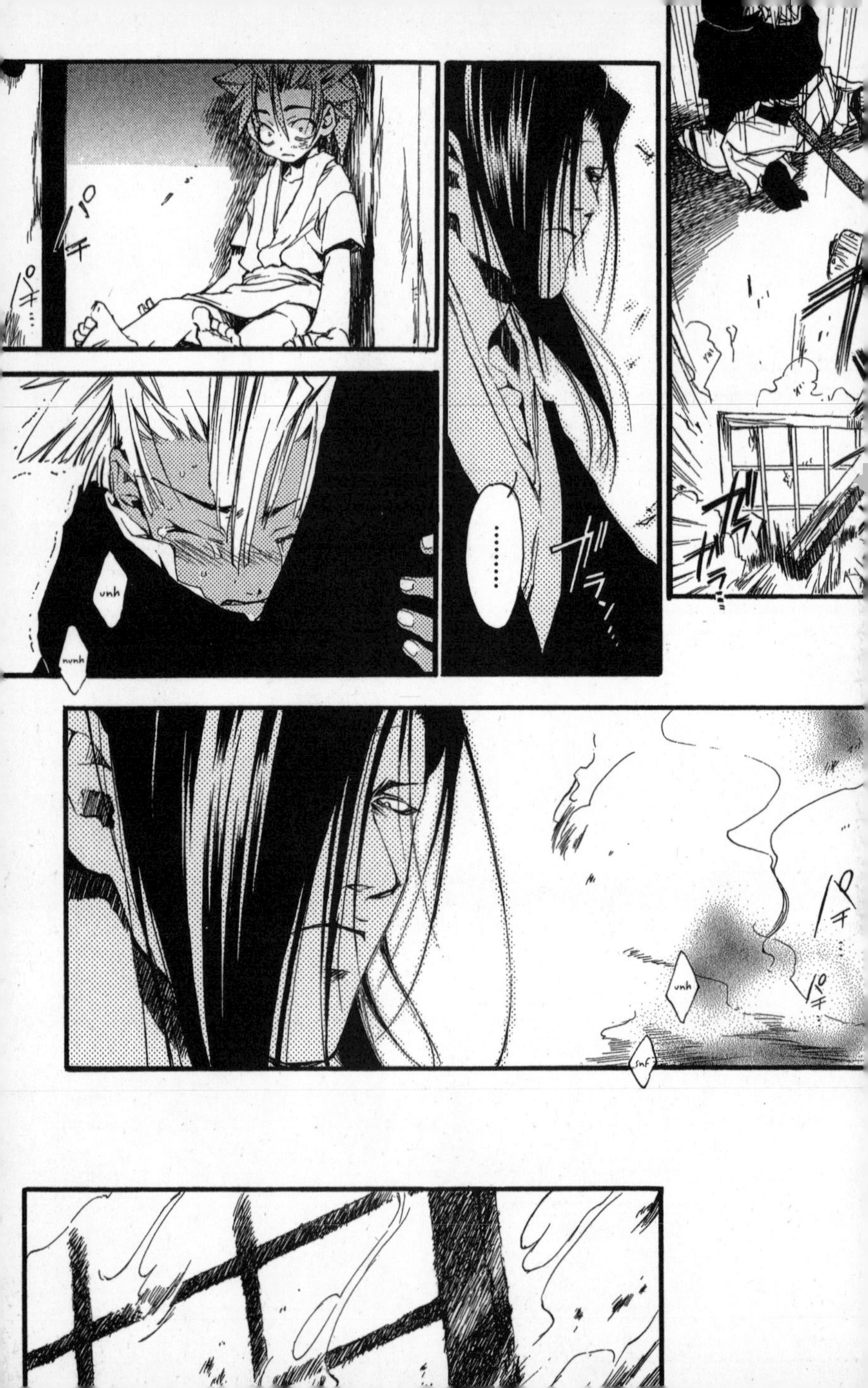
……
unh
nunh
unh
snf

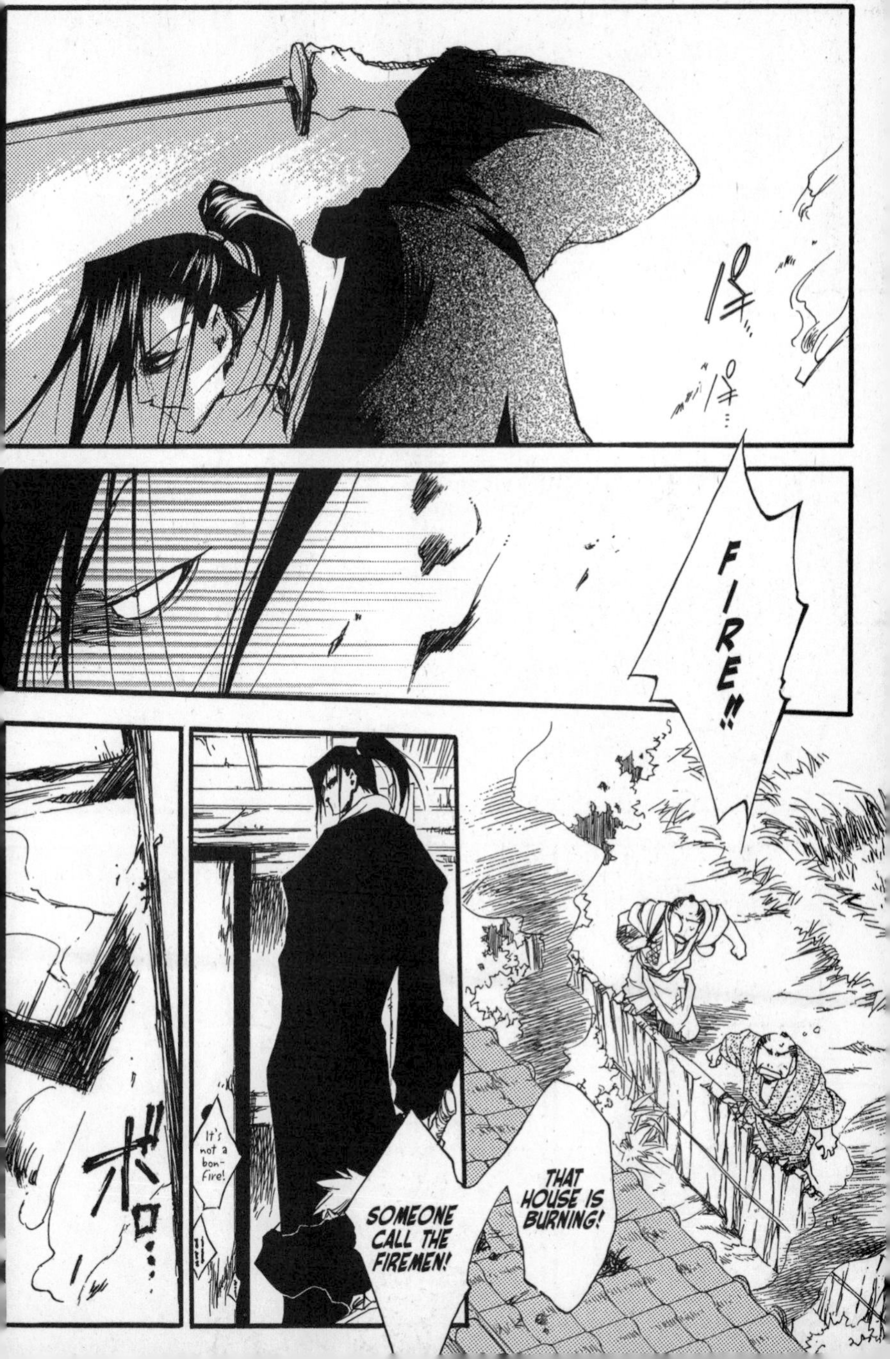
パチ…
パチ…
FIRE!!
THAT HOUSE IS BURNING!
SOMEONE CALL THE FIREMEN!
It's not a bon-fire!
ボロ…

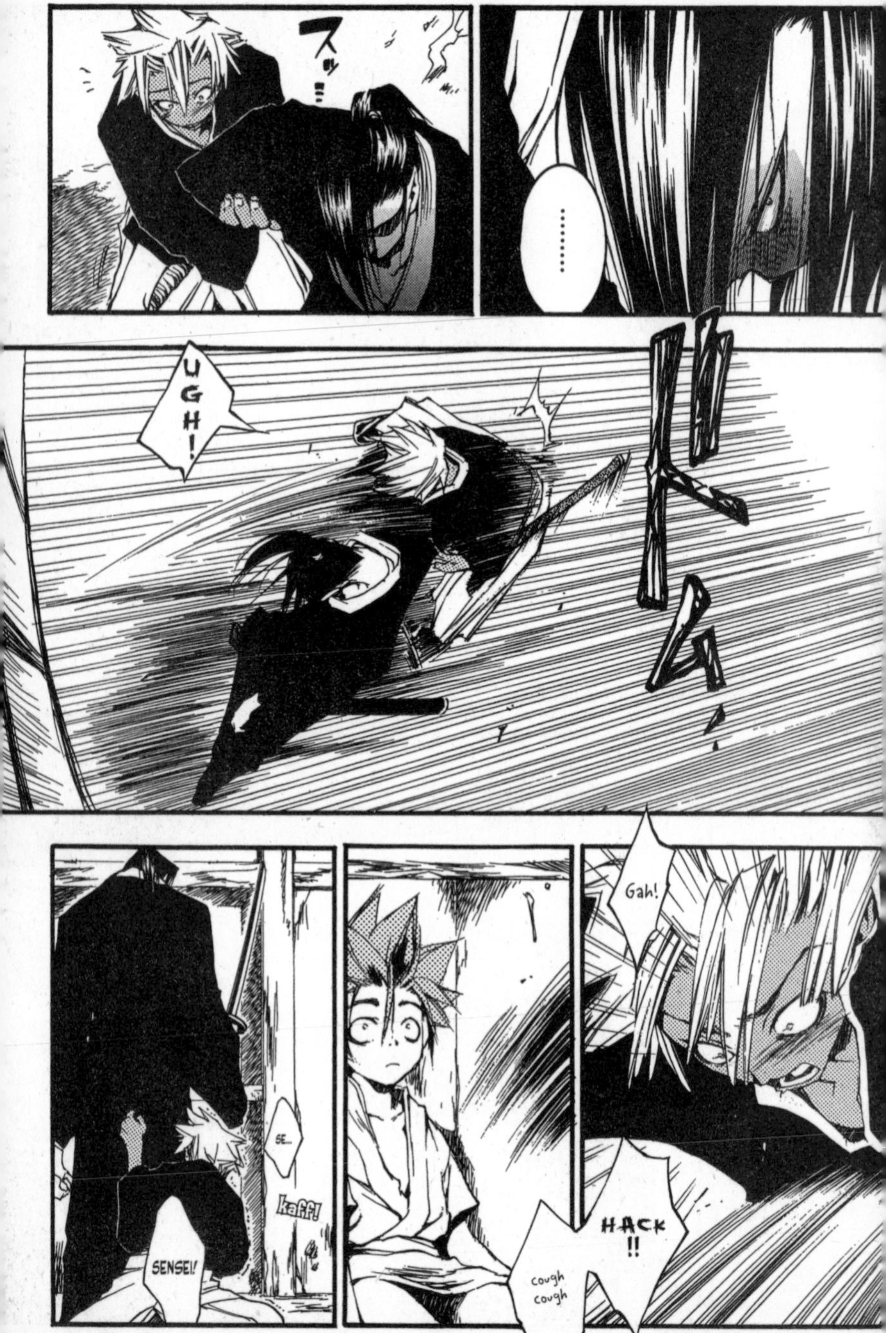
......
スッ
ドム!
UGH!
Gah!
HACK !!
cough cough
SE...
kaff!
SENSEI!

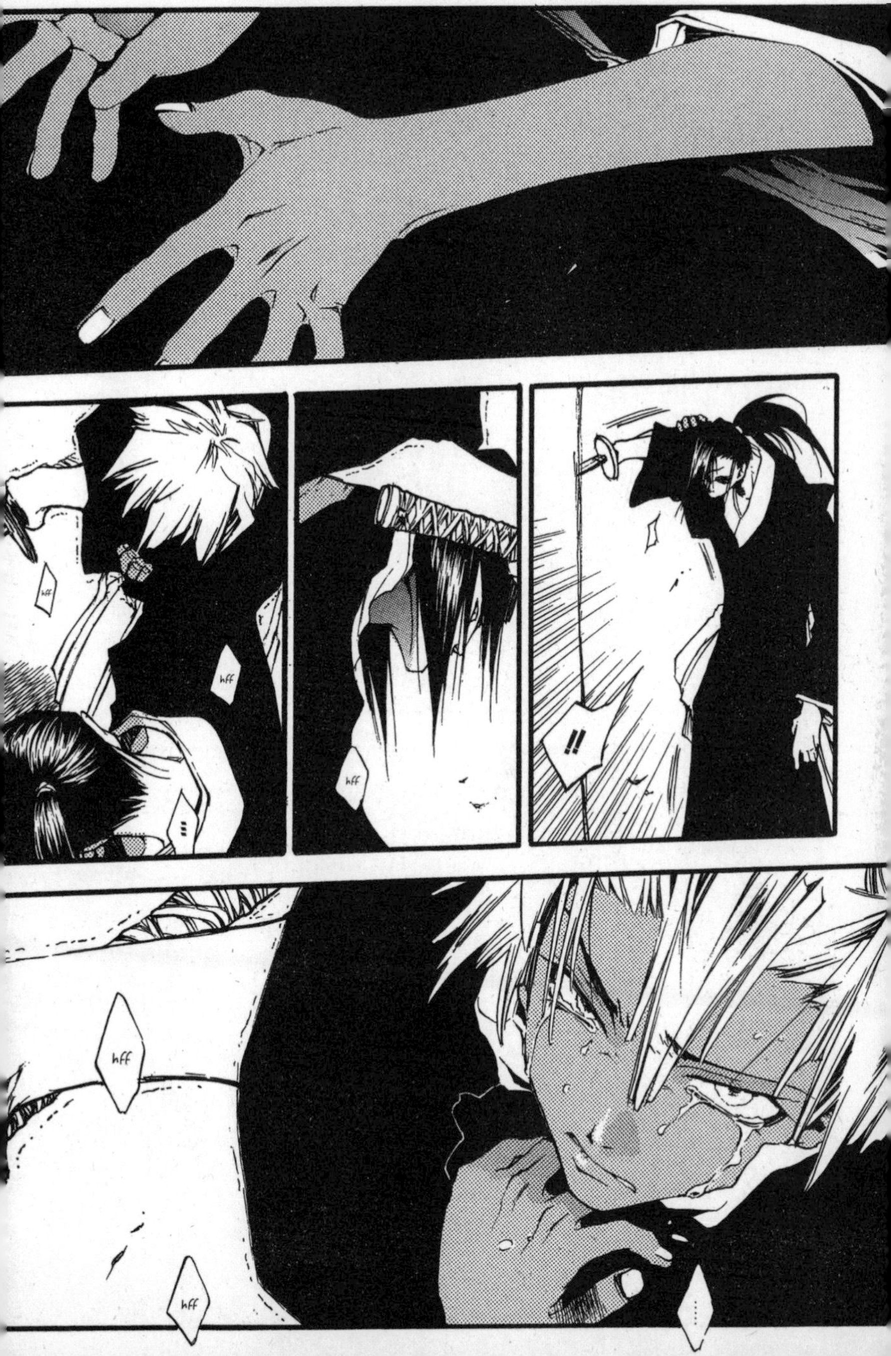
!!
hff
hff
hff
...
hff
hff
...

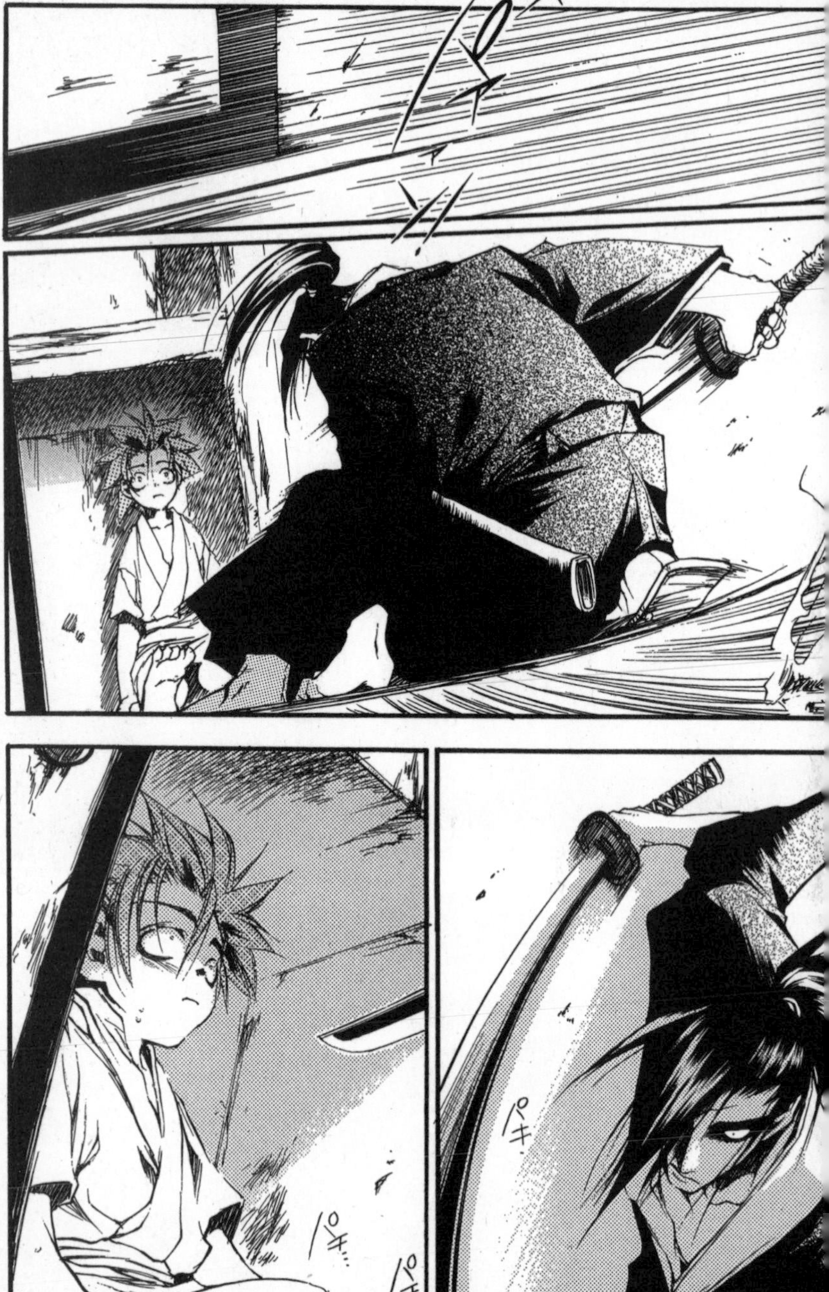
スパァァン!!
パキ
パキ…
パキ.

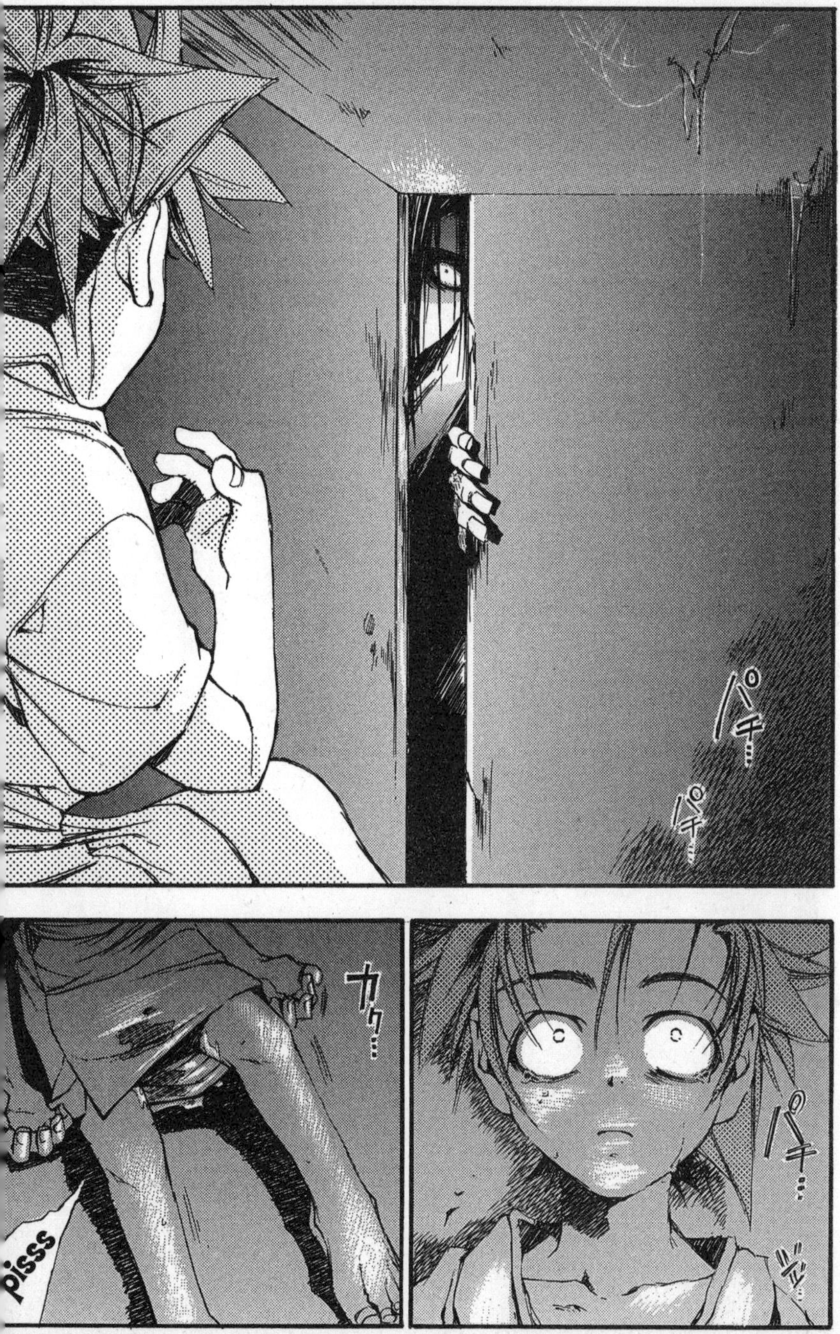
パチ…
パチ…
パチ…
ジュ…
カク…
pisss

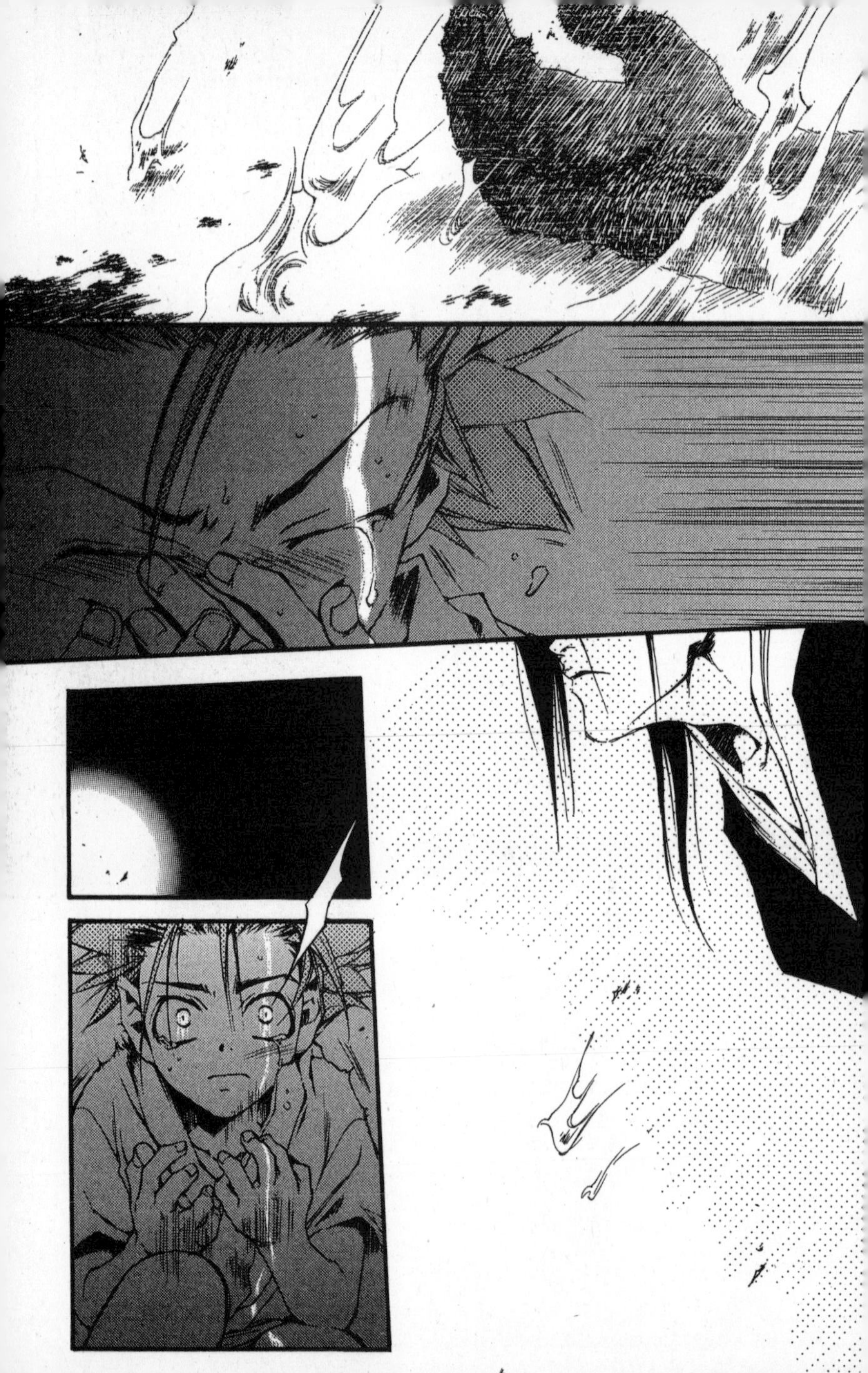

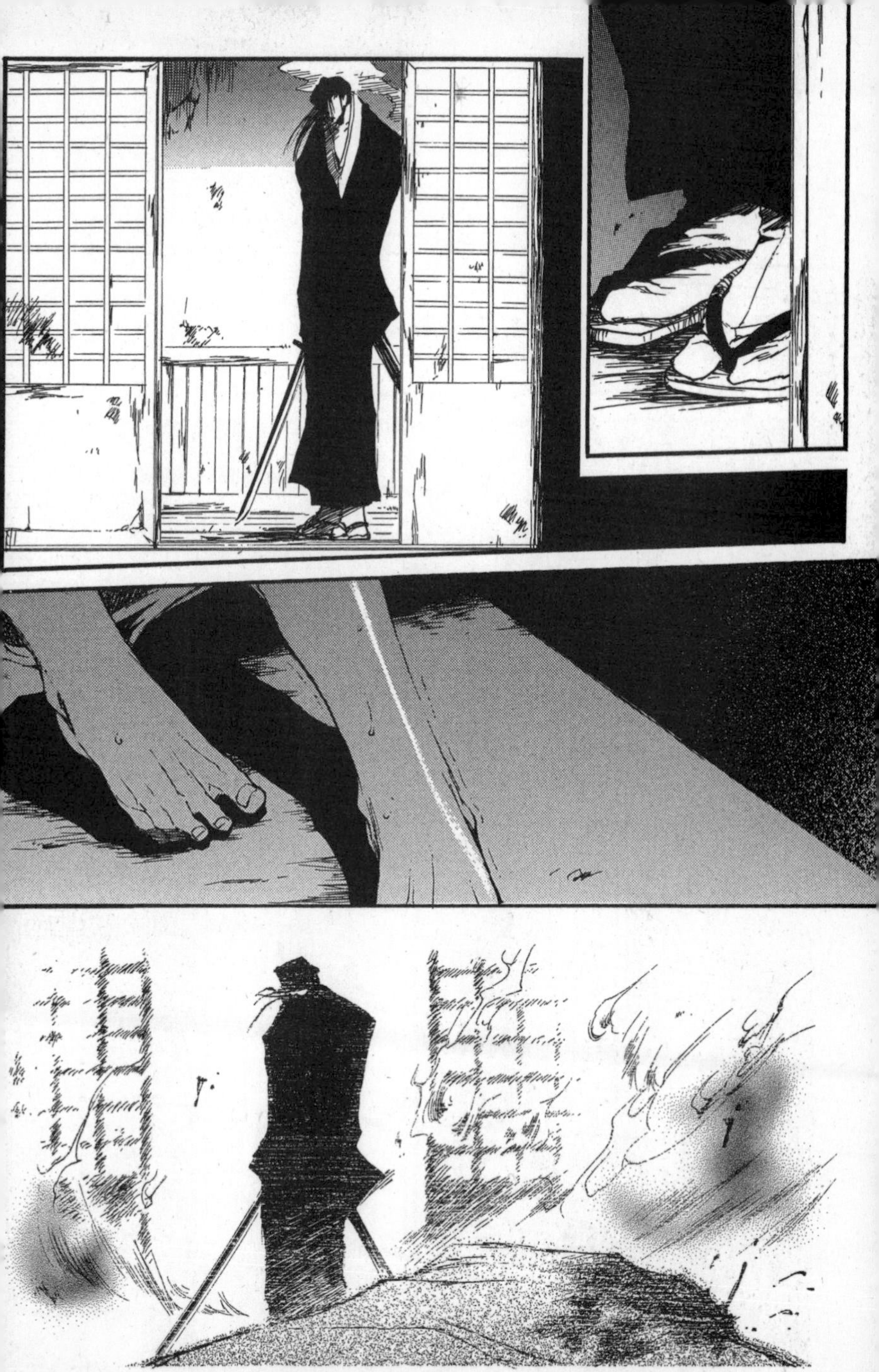

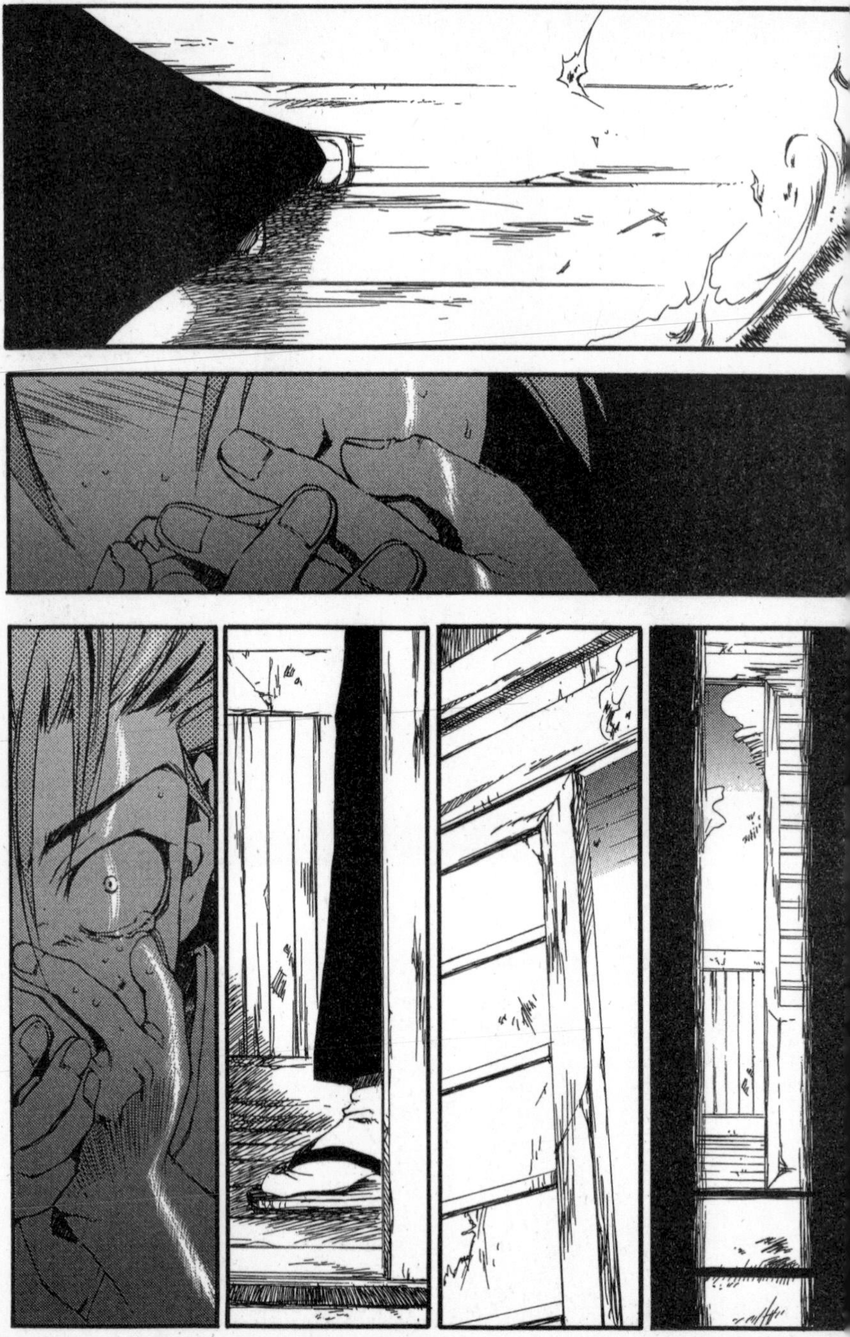

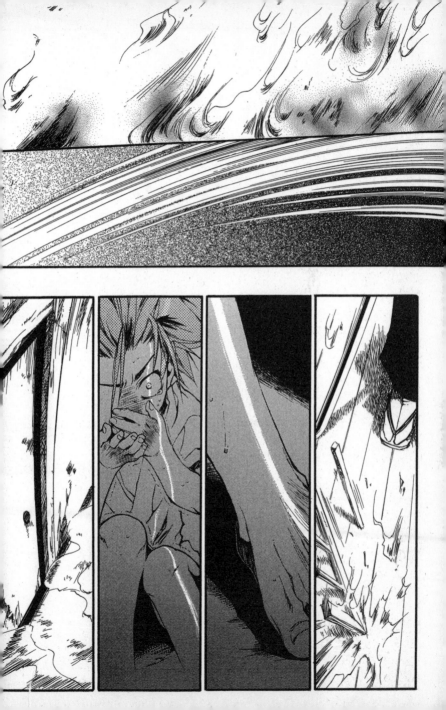

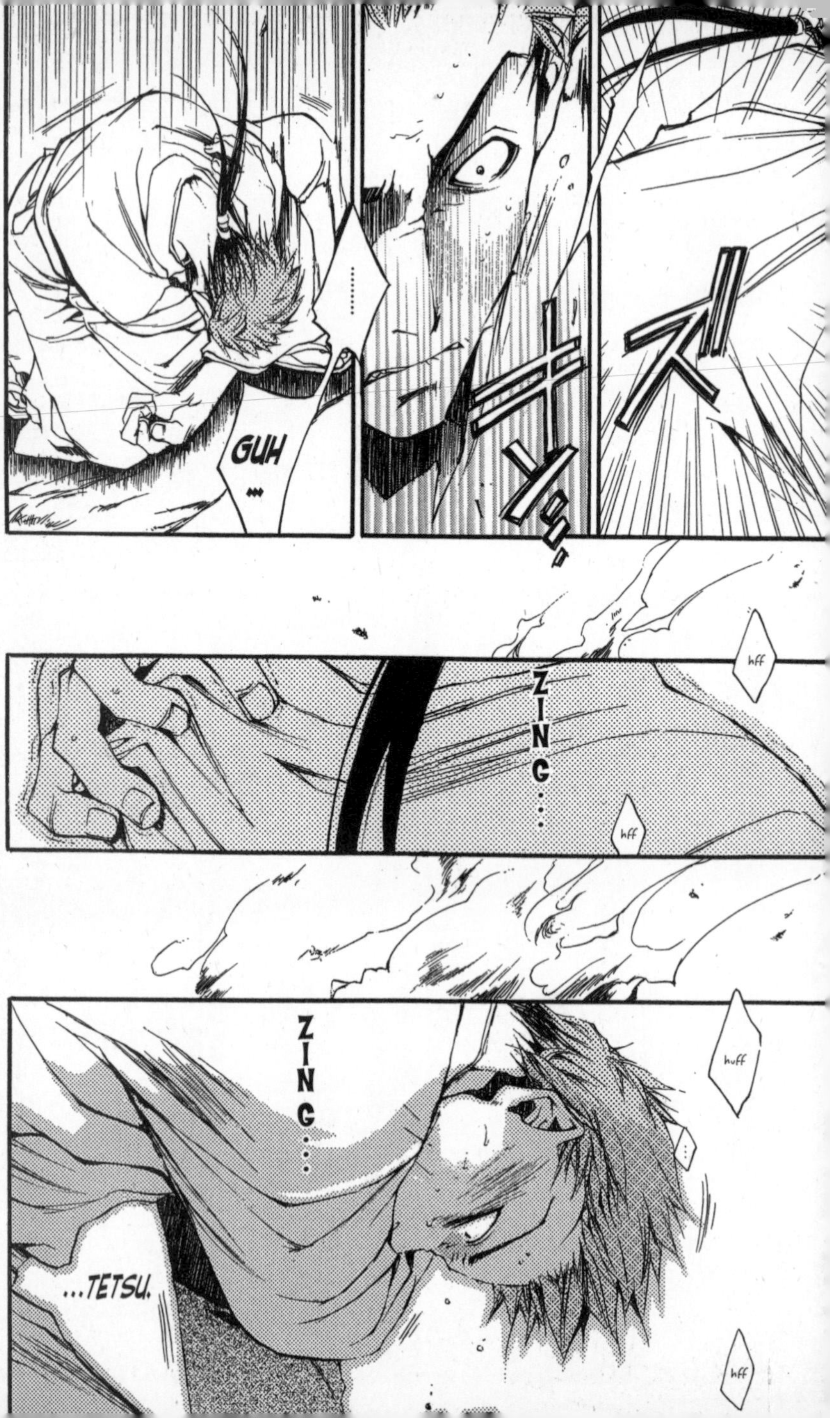

......
GUH ...
hff
ZING....
hff
huff
ZING...
...
...TETSU.
hff

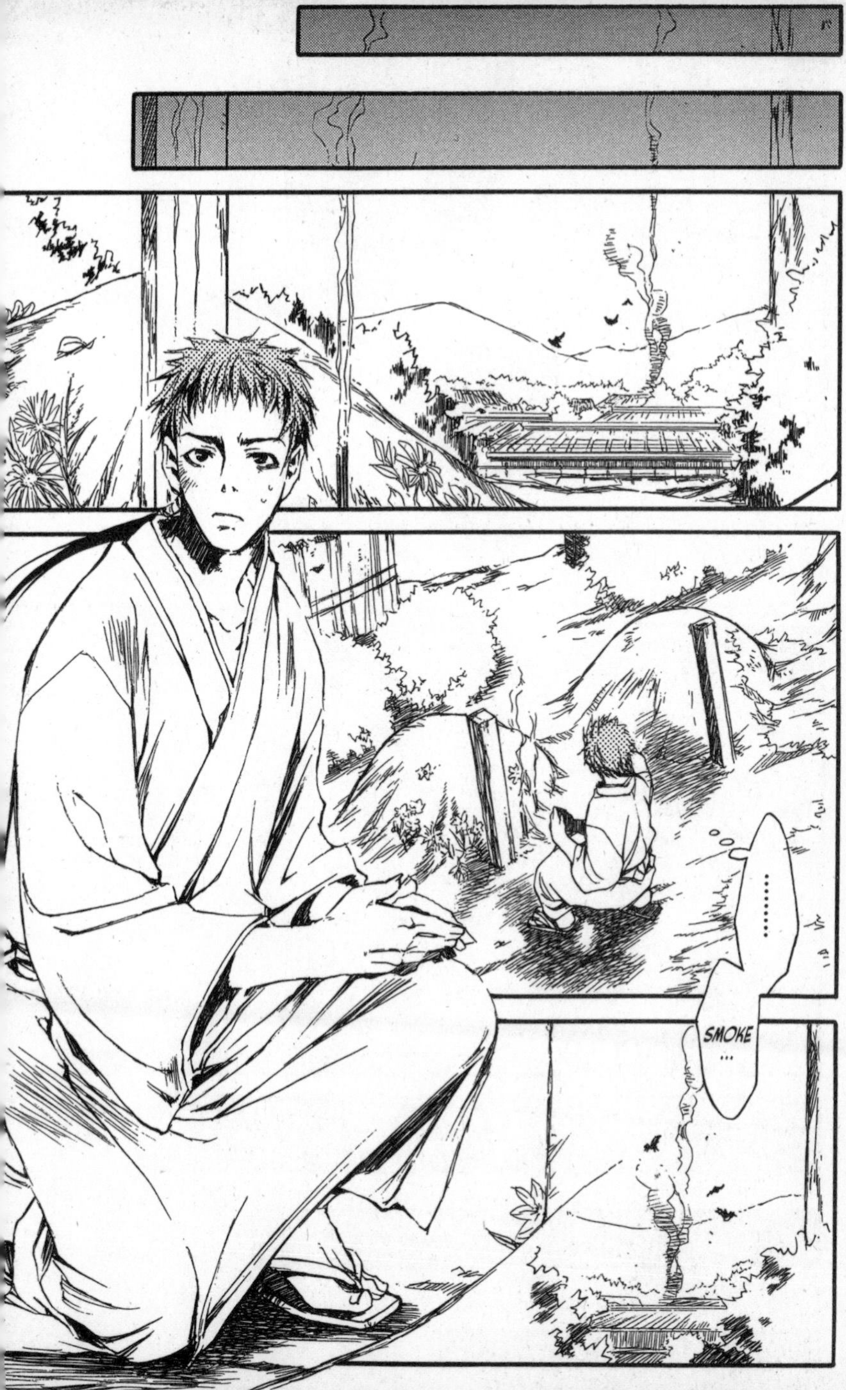
......
SMOKE
...

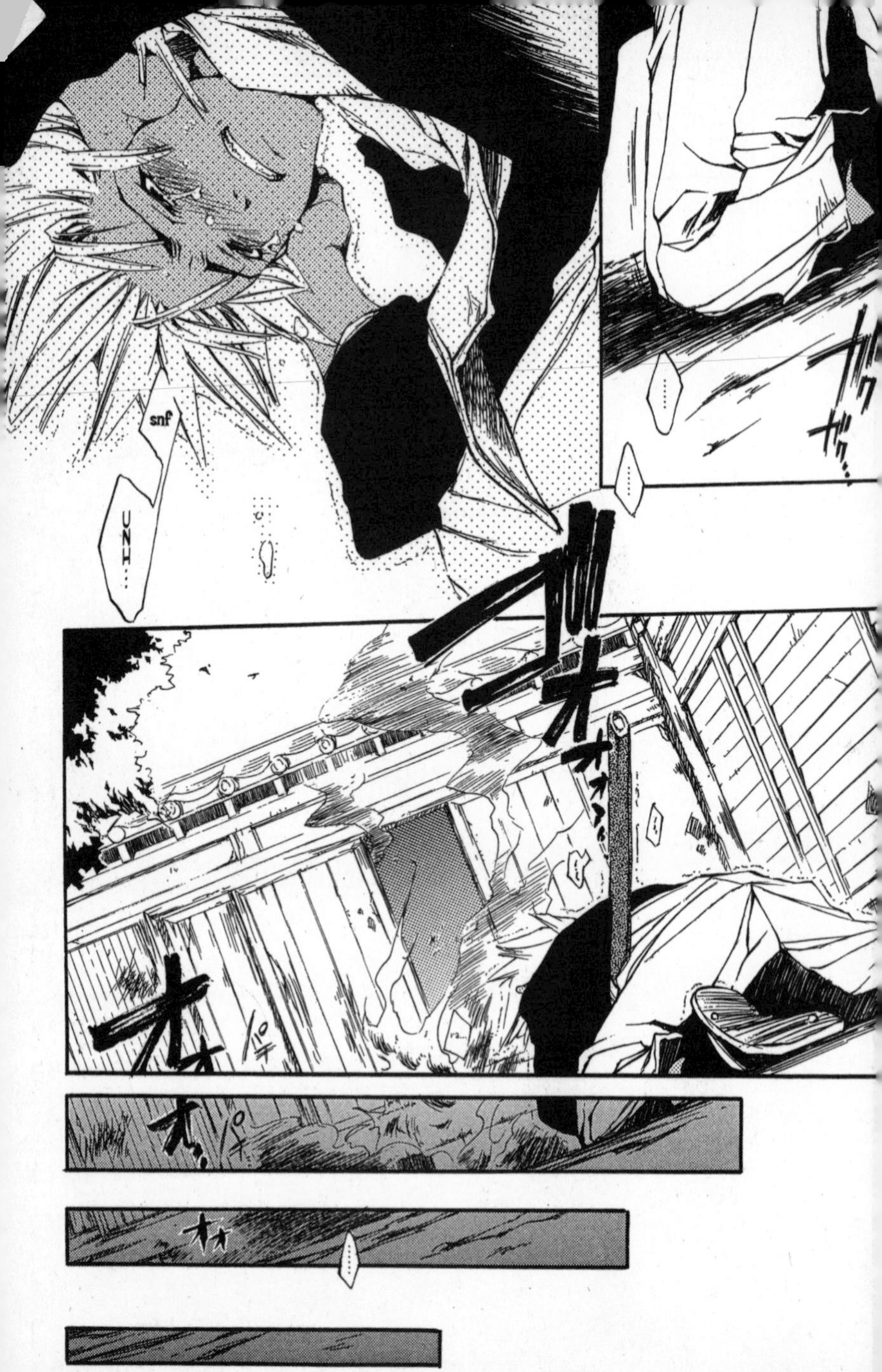

......
......
snf
UNH...
......

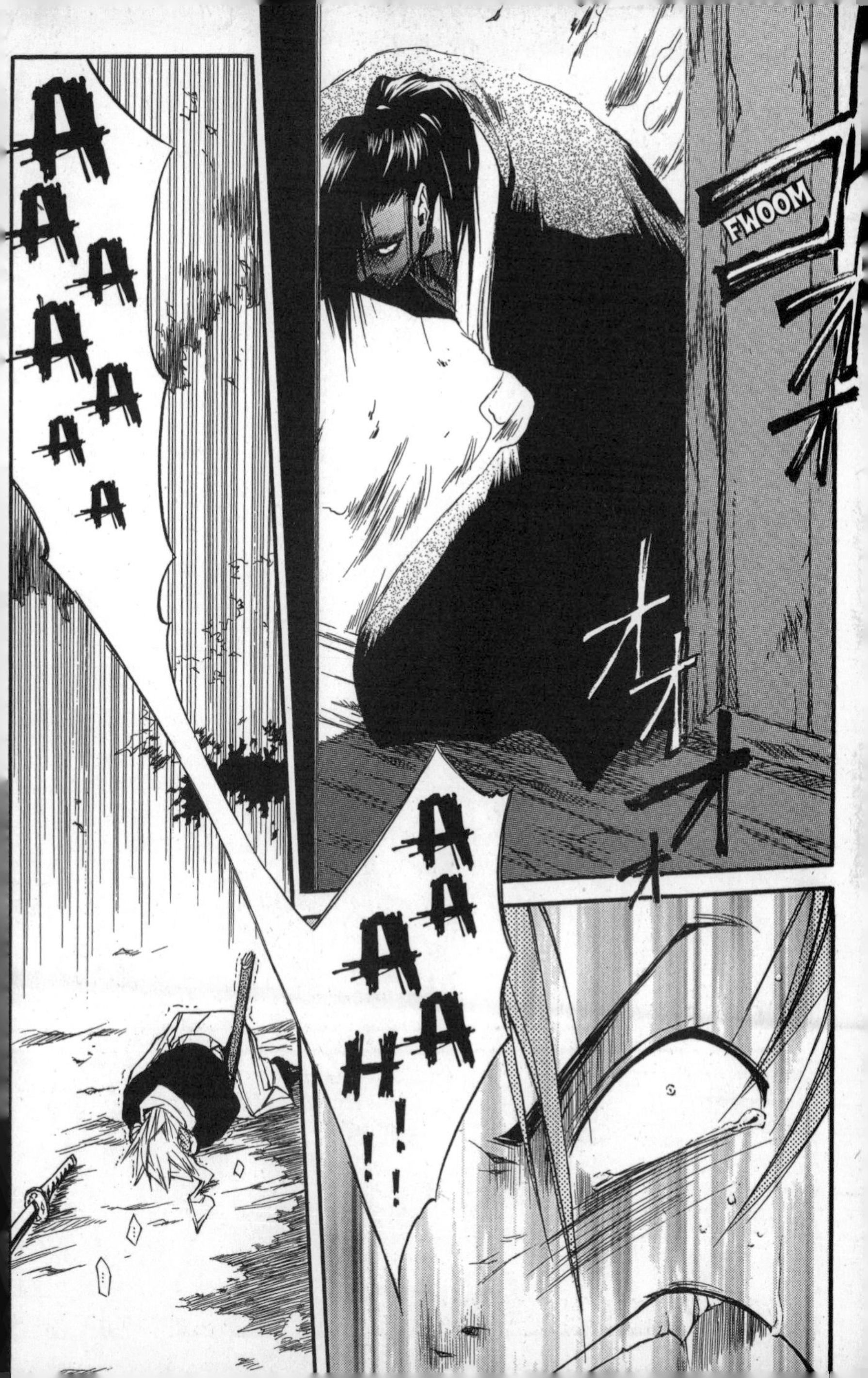
FWOOM
AAAAAAA
AAAAH!!

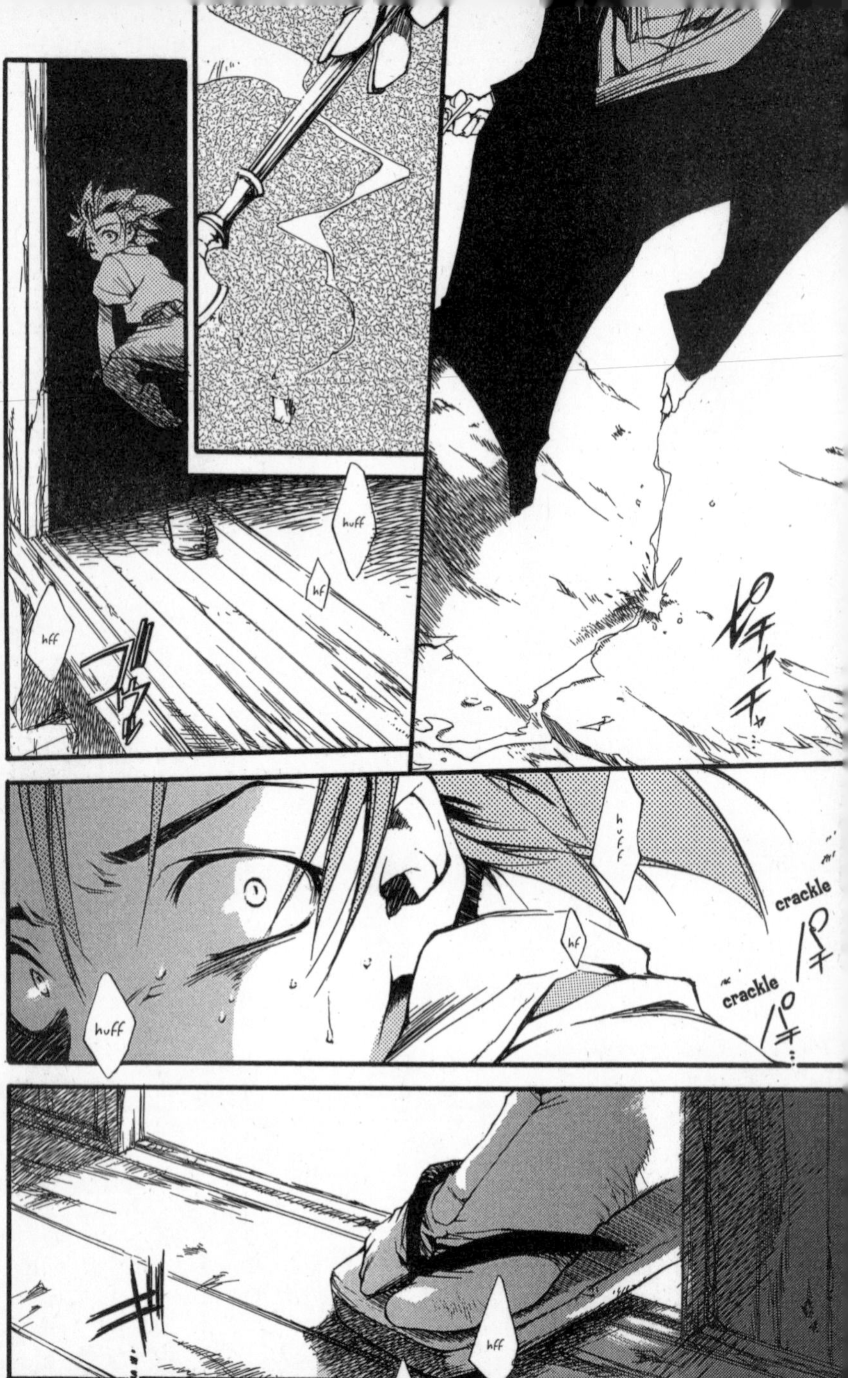
huff
hf
huff
huff
crackle
パチ
hf
crackle
パチ…
huff
hff
…

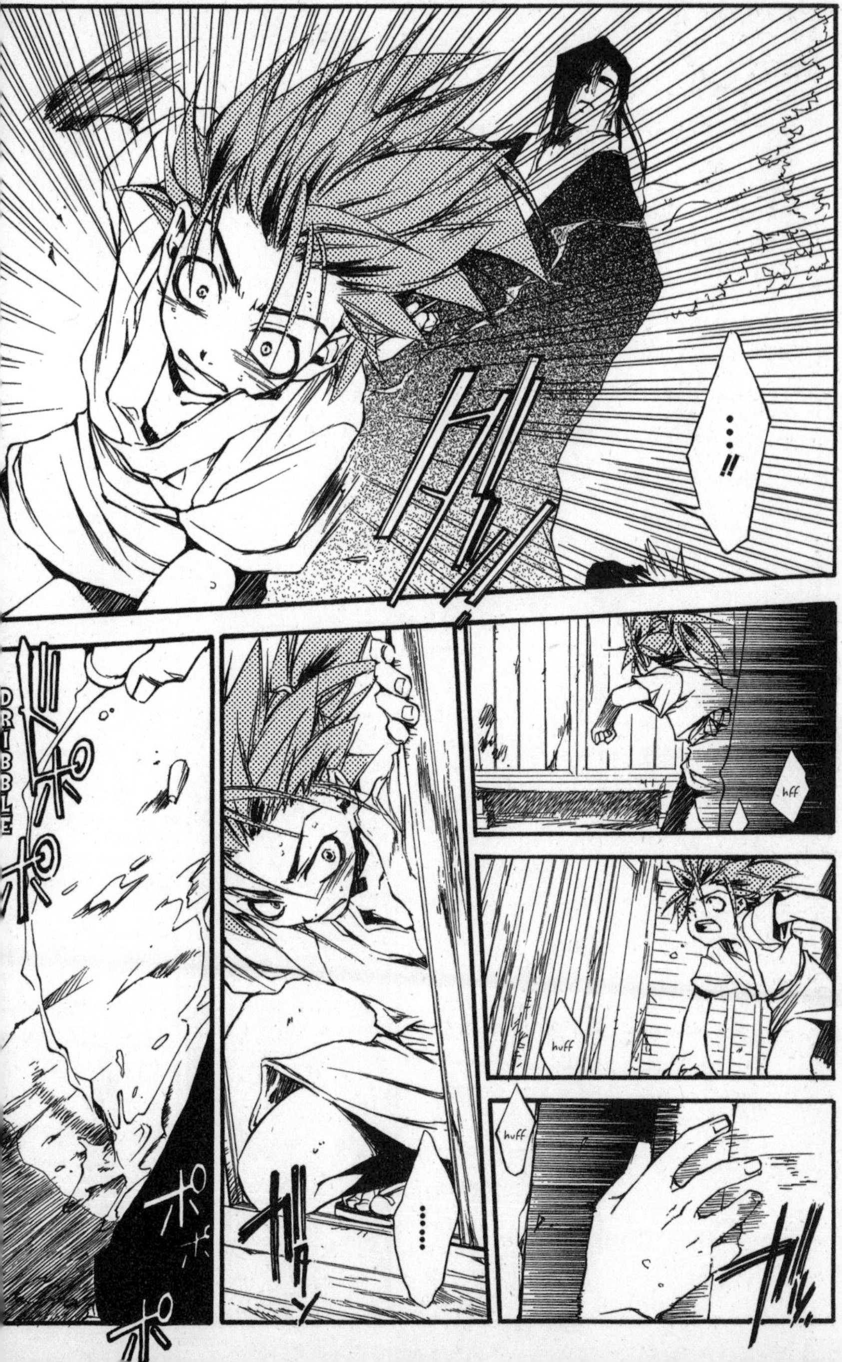
...!!
huff
huff
huff
......
DRIBBLE

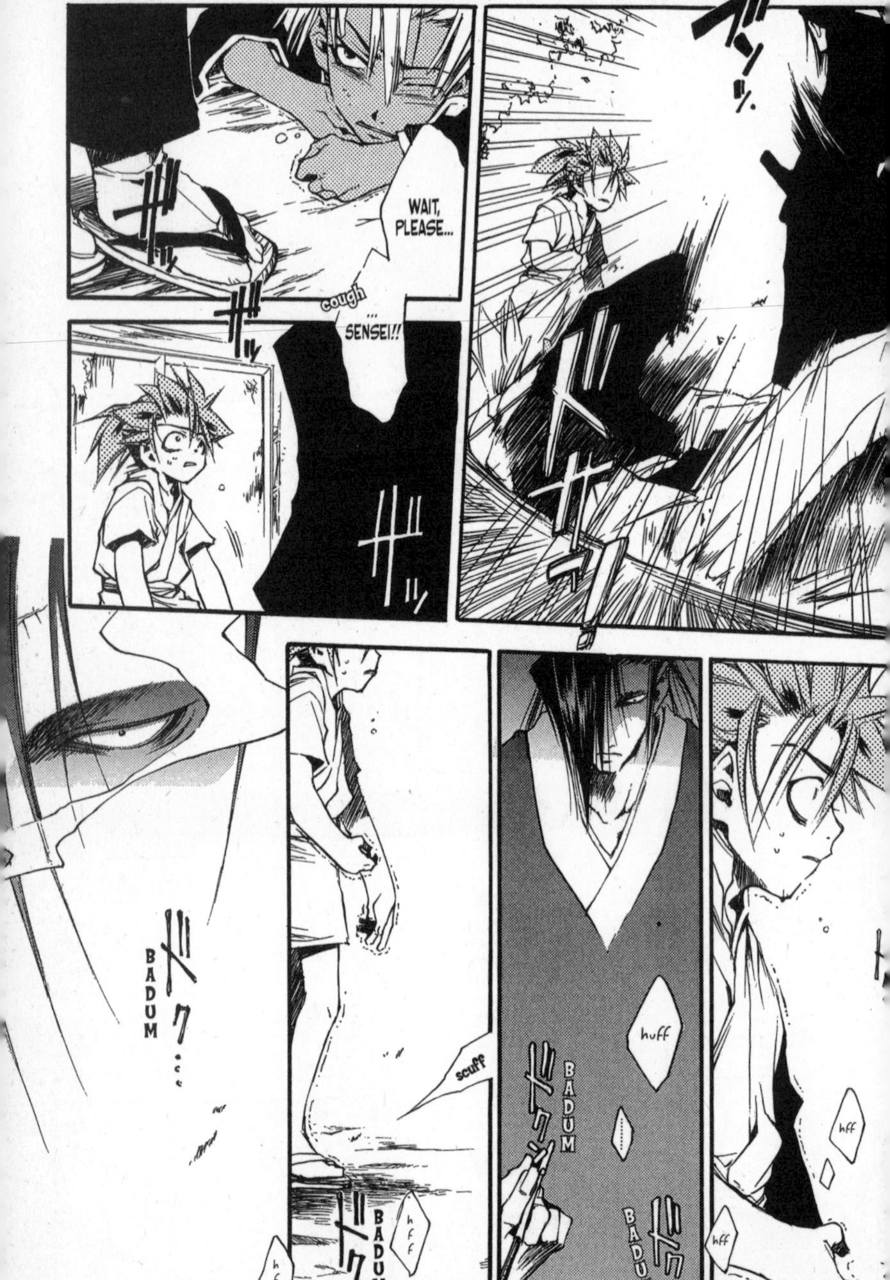

WAIT, PLEASE...
cough
...SENSEI!!
hff
hff
huff
...
BADUM
BADUM
scuff
BADUM
hff
hff
BADUM

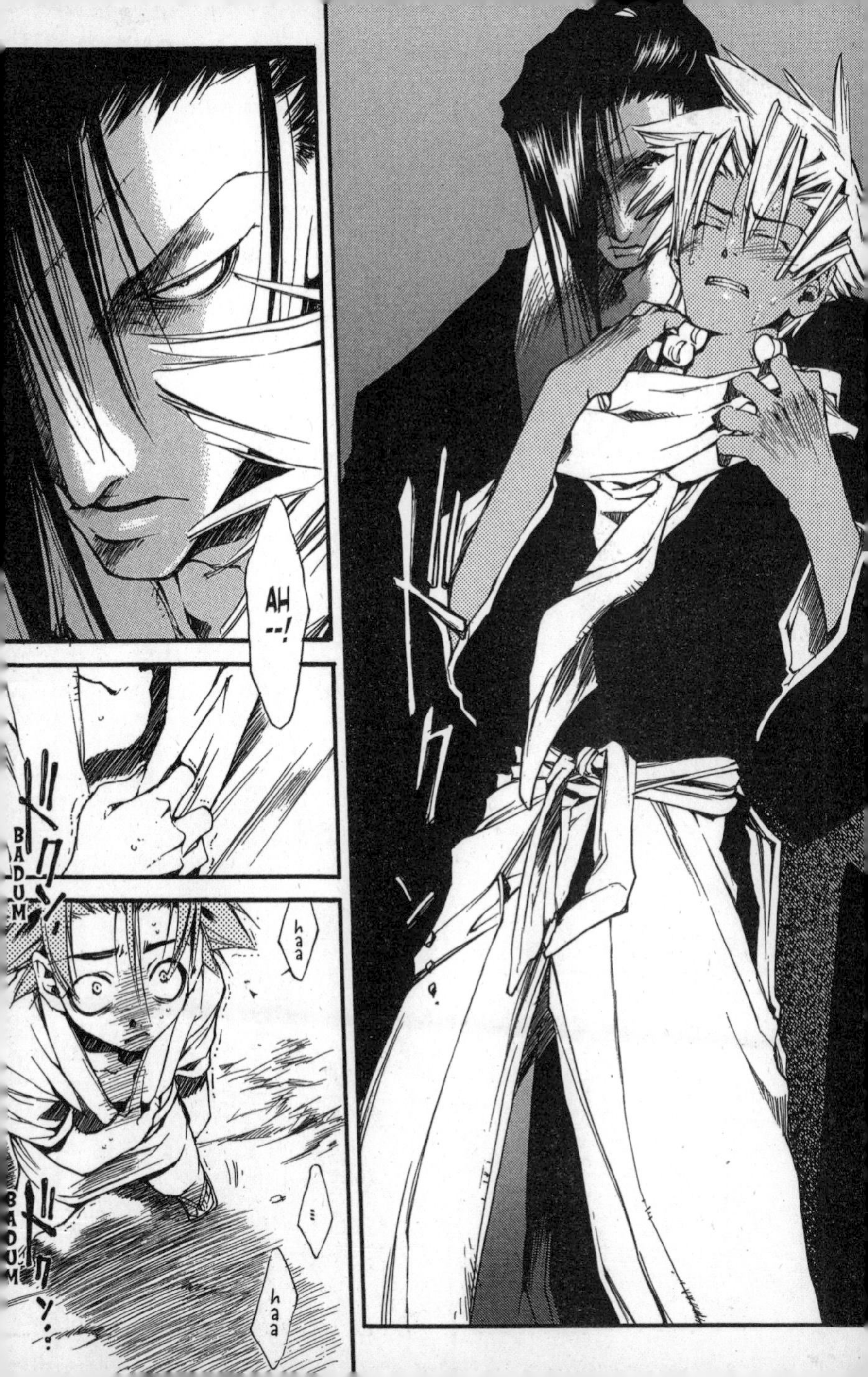
AH --!
BADUM
haa
...
BADUM
haa

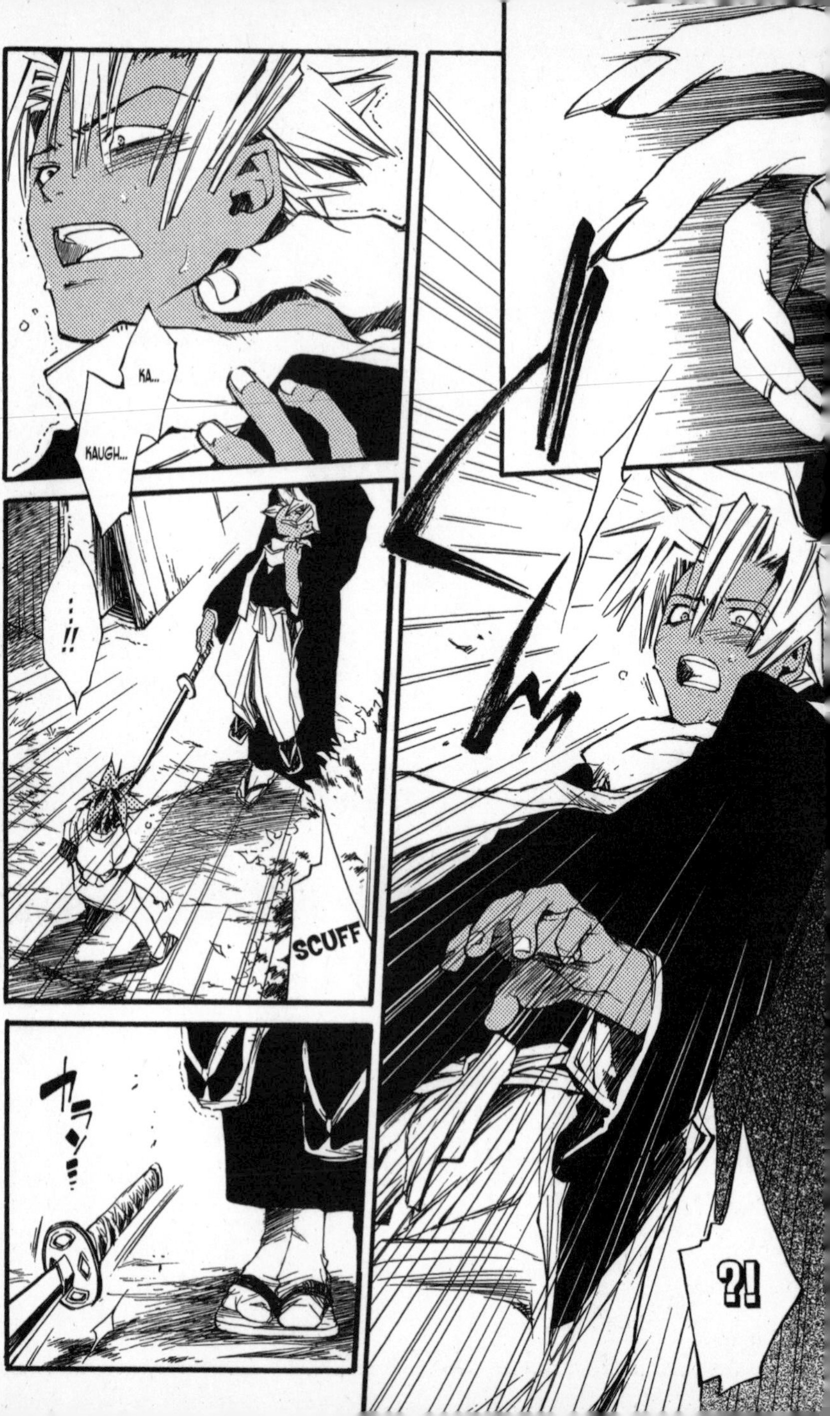
?!
KA...
KAUGH...
...!!
SCUFF
カラン

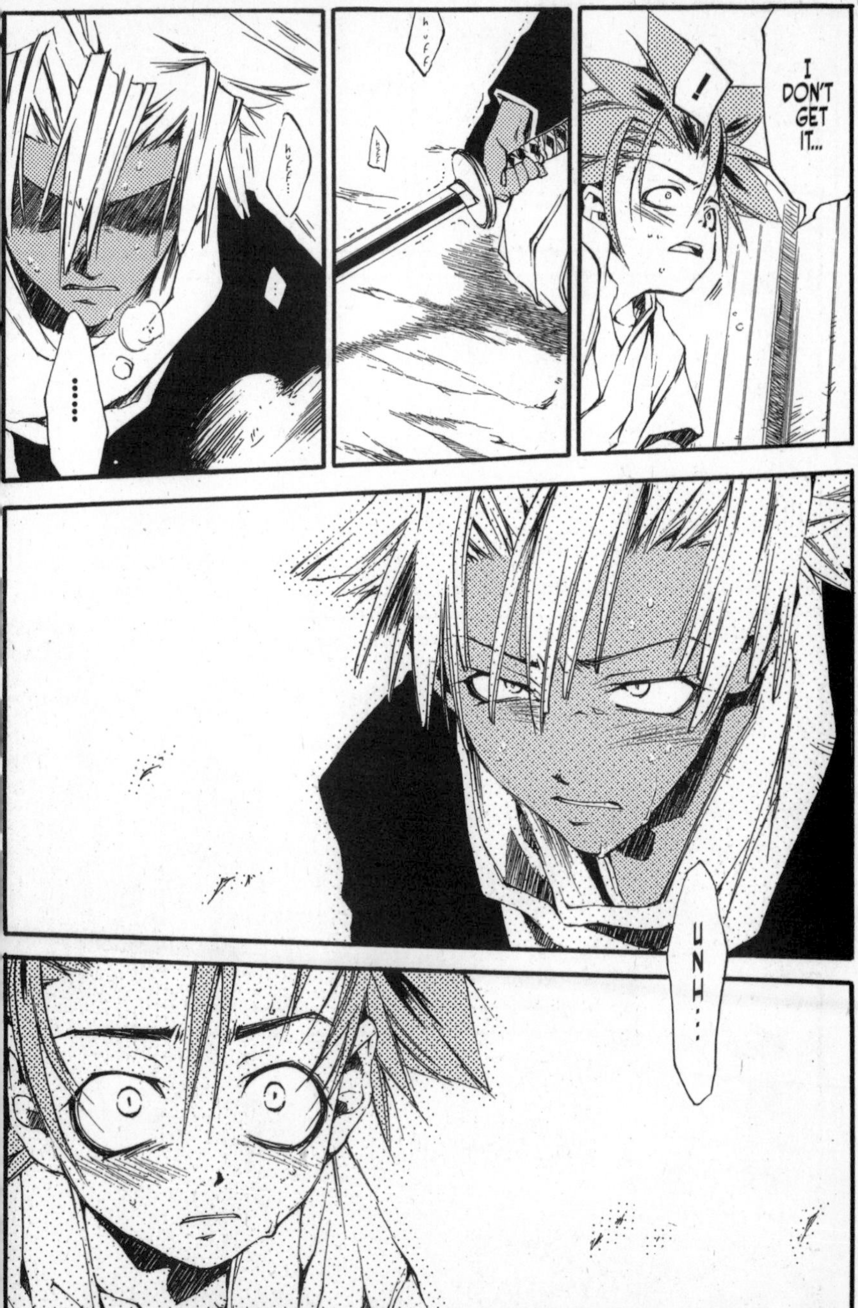
!
I DON'T GET IT...
huff
huff
huff...
......
UNH...

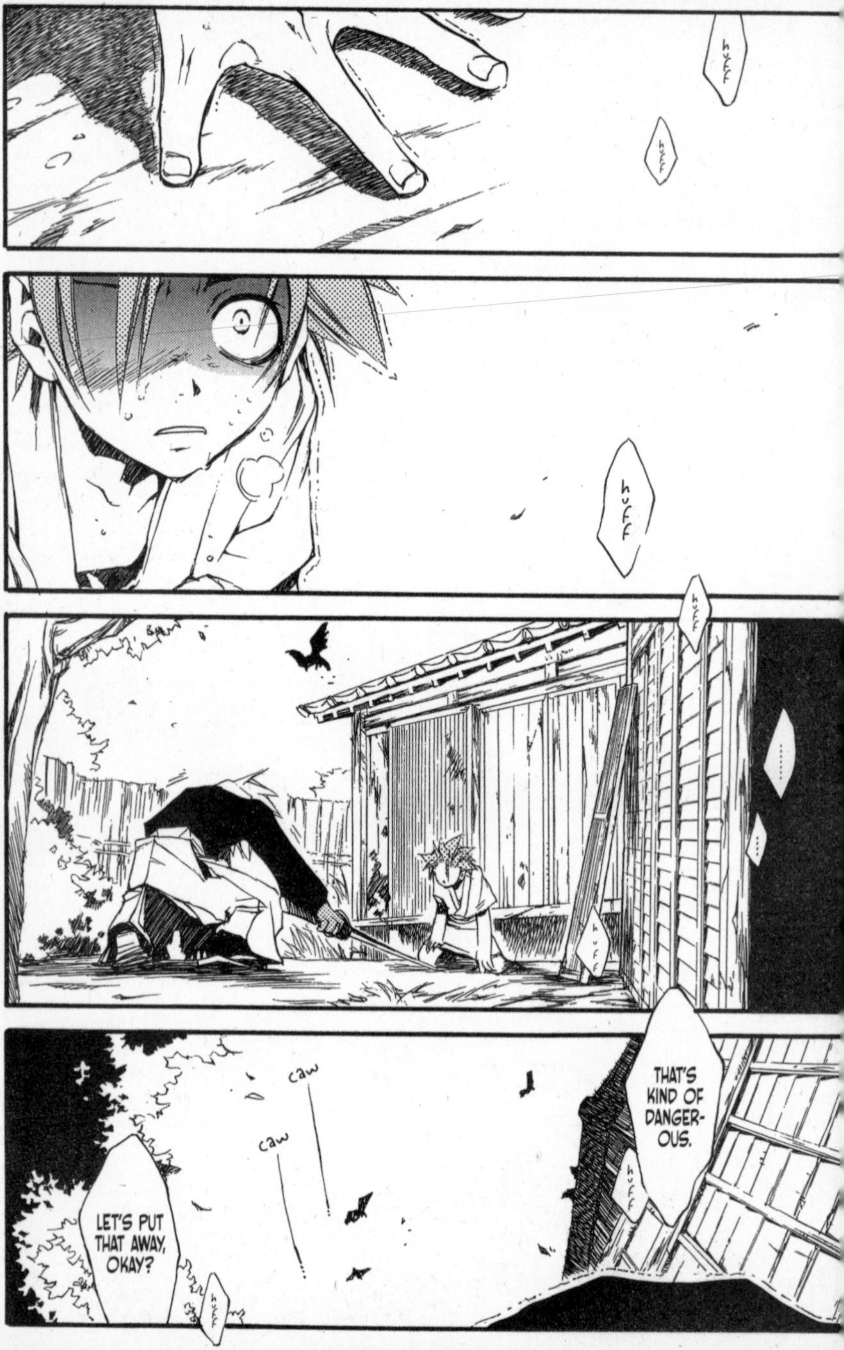

huff
huff
huff
huff
......
...
huff
THAT'S KIND OF DANGER-OUS.
huff
caw
caw
LET'S PUT THAT AWAY, OKAY?
huff

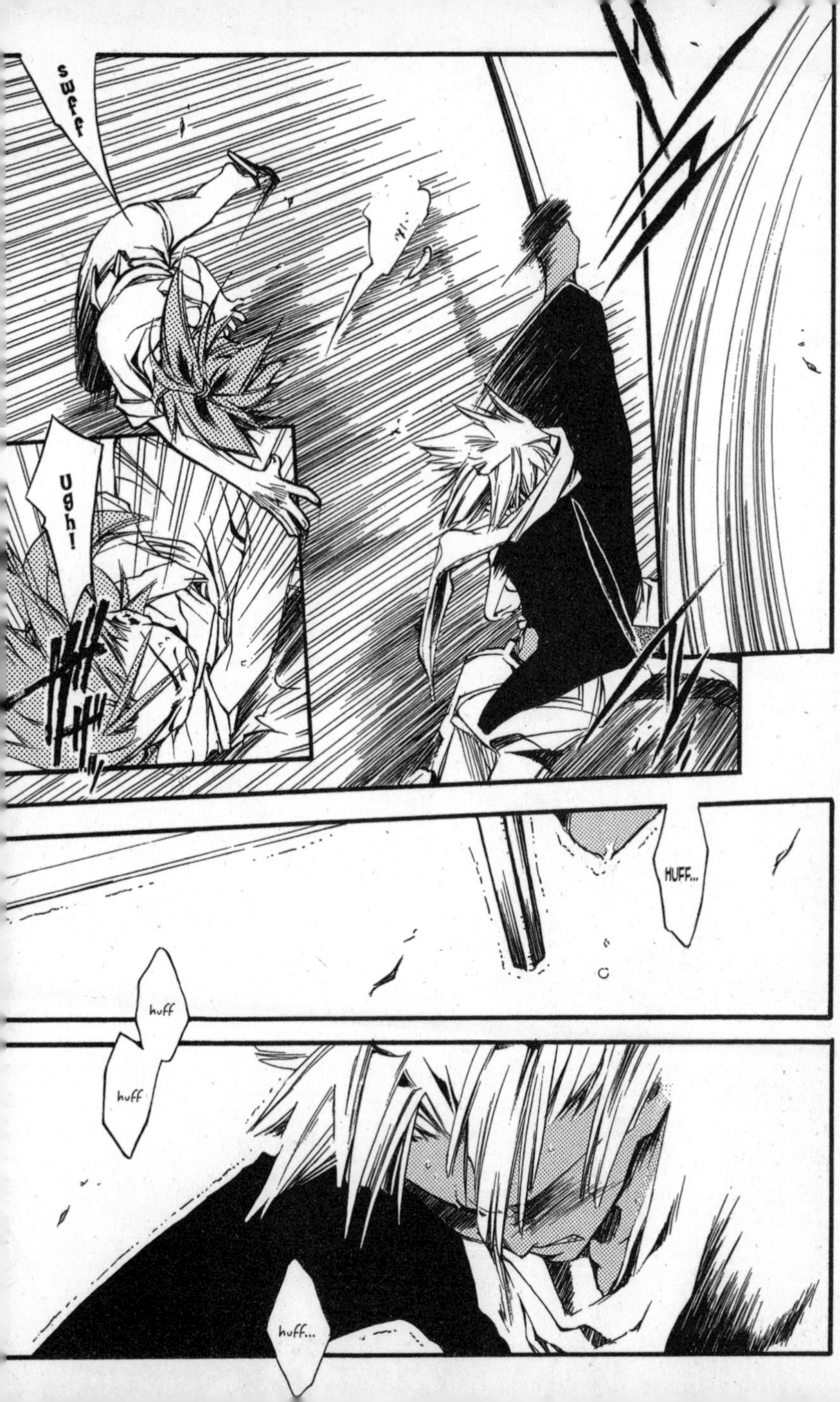
swfff
Ugh!
HUFF...
huff
huff
huff...

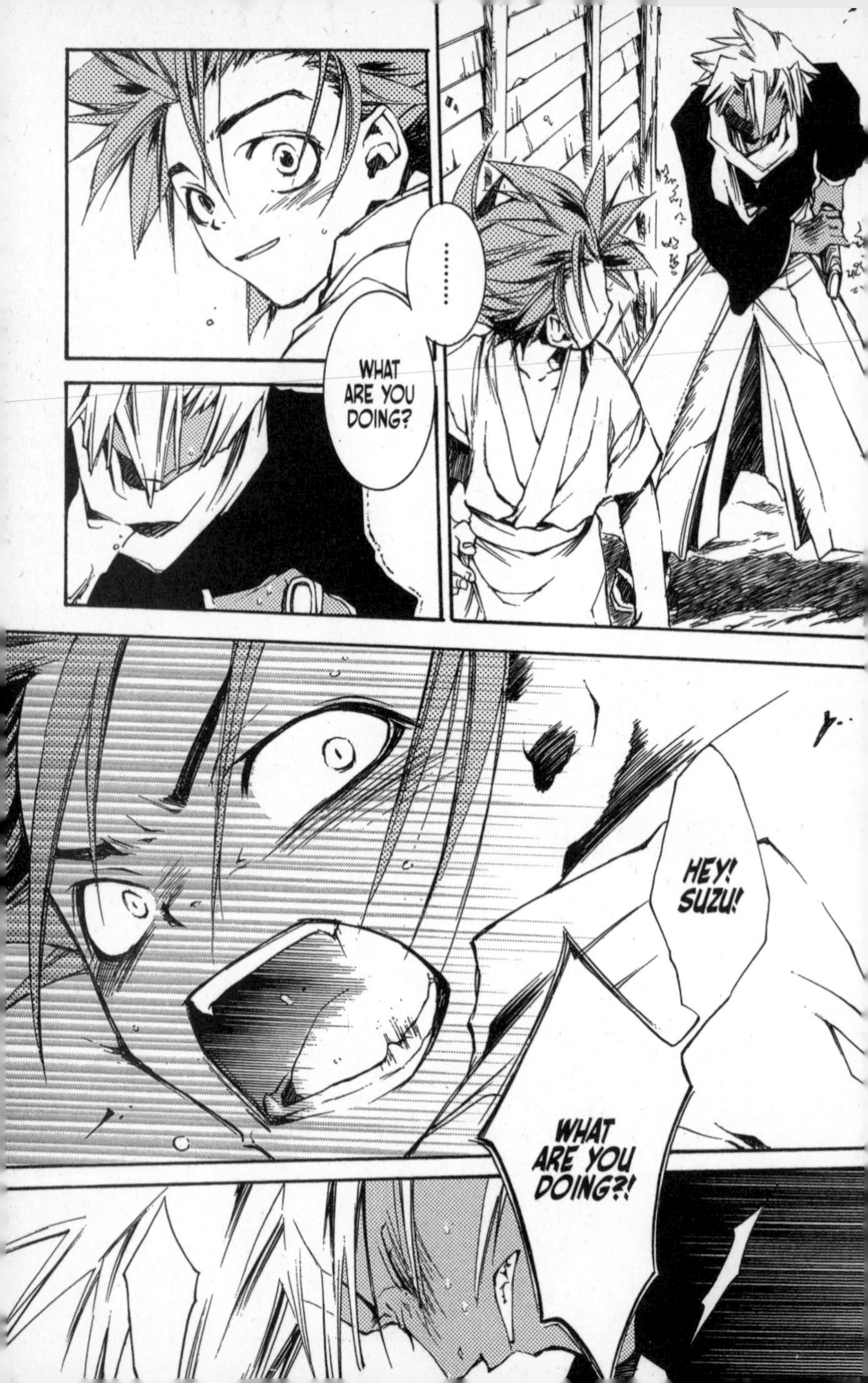
......
WHAT ARE YOU DOING?
HEY! SUZU!
WHAT ARE YOU DOING?!

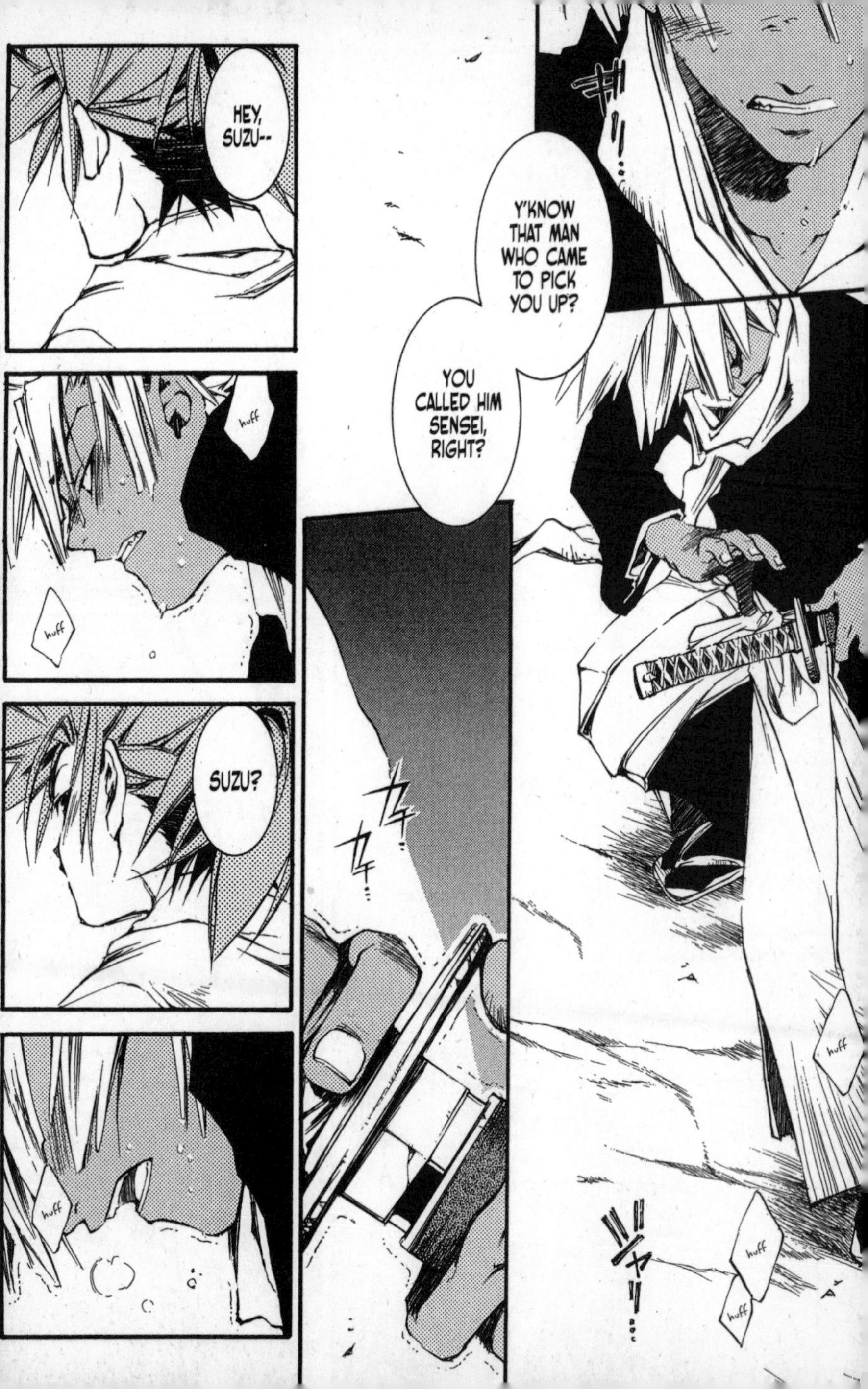
Y'KNOW THAT MAN WHO CAME TO PICK YOU UP?
YOU CALLED HIM SENSEI, RIGHT?
huff
huff
huff
HEY, SUZU--
huff
huff
SUZU?
huff

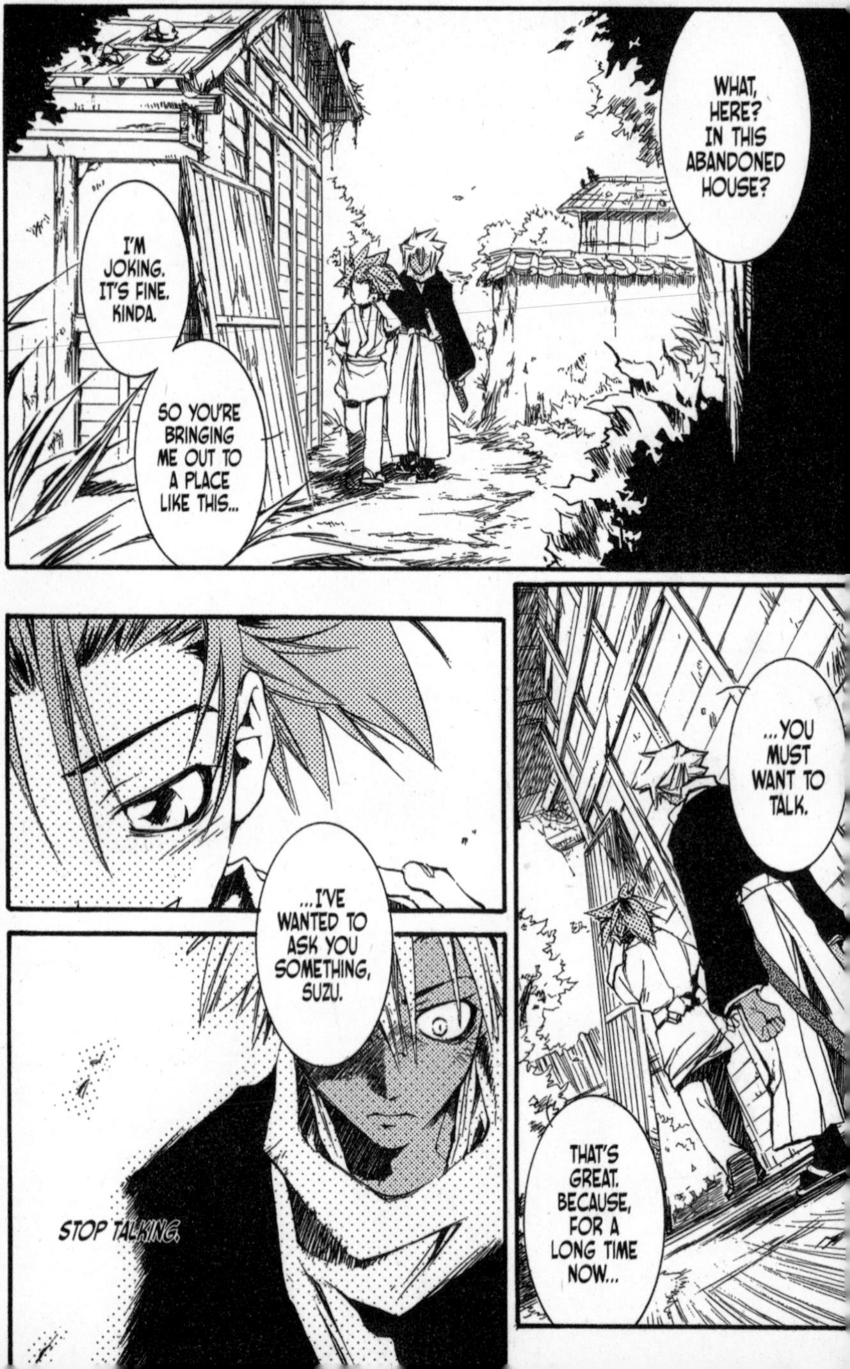
WHAT, HERE? IN THIS ABANDONED HOUSE?
SO YOU'RE BRINGING ME OUT TO A PLACE LIKE THIS...
I'M JOKING. IT'S FINE. KINDA.
...YOU MUST WANT TO TALK.
THAT'S GREAT. BECAUSE, FOR A LONG TIME NOW...
...I'VE WANTED TO ASK YOU SOMETHING, SUZU.
STOP TALKING.

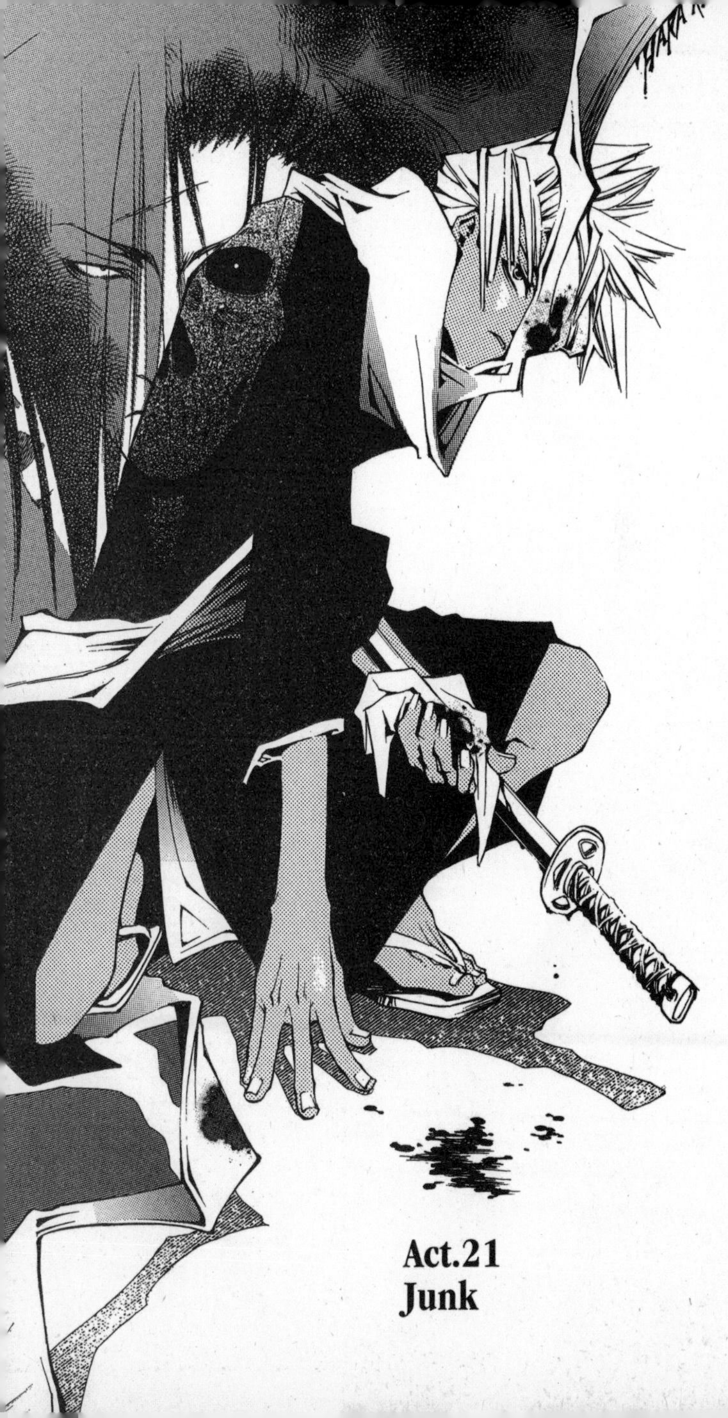
HARA

Act.21 Junk

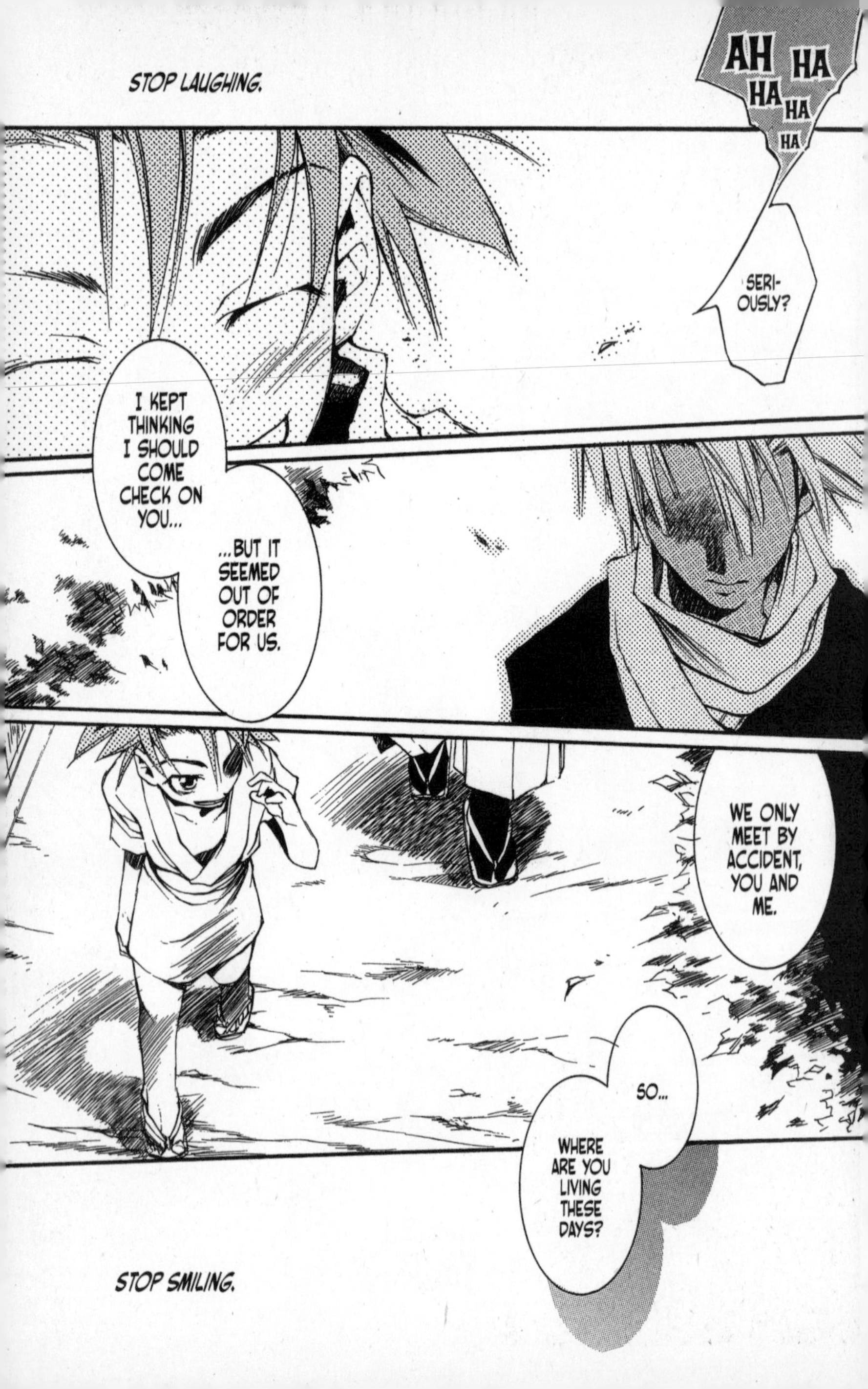
AH HA HA HA HA
STOP LAUGHING.
SERI-OUSLY?
I KEPT THINKING I SHOULD COME CHECK ON YOU...
...BUT IT SEEMED OUT OF ORDER FOR US.
WE ONLY MEET BY ACCIDENT, YOU AND ME.
SO...
WHERE ARE YOU LIVING THESE DAYS?
STOP SMILING.

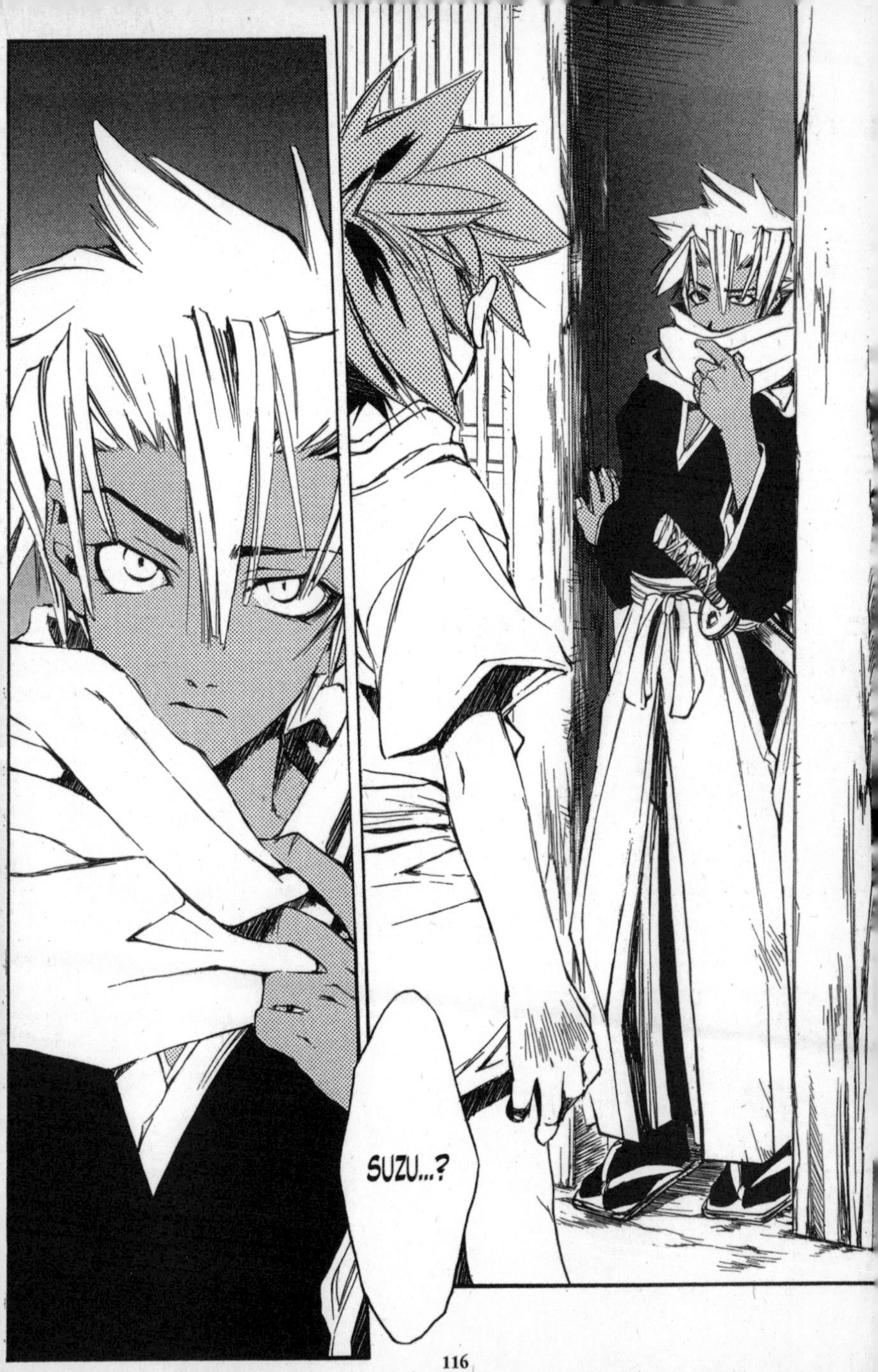
SUZU...?

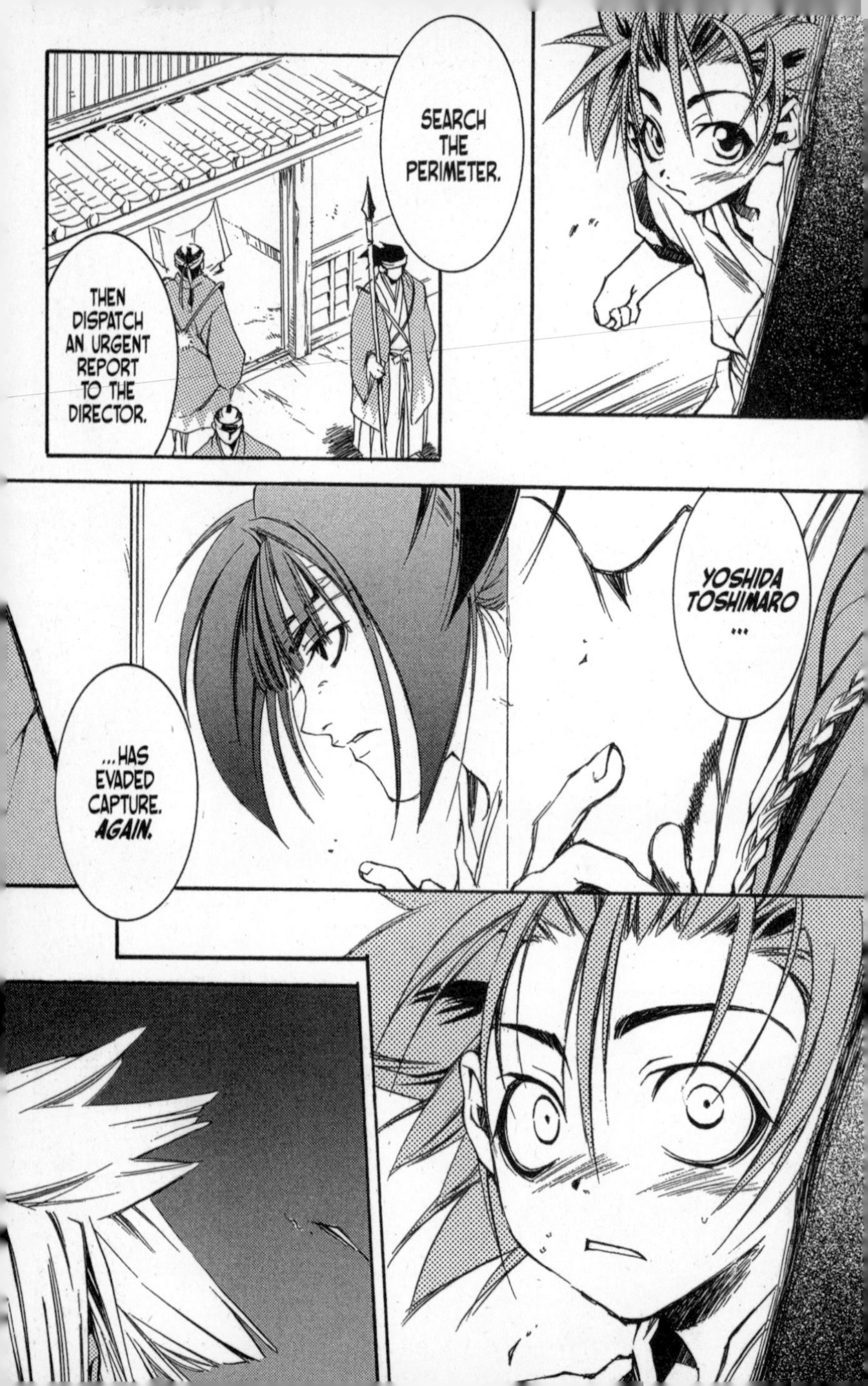
SEARCH THE PERIMETER.
THEN DISPATCH AN URGENT REPORT TO THE DIRECTOR.
YOSHIDA TOSHIMARO ...
...HAS EVADED CAPTURE. AGAIN.

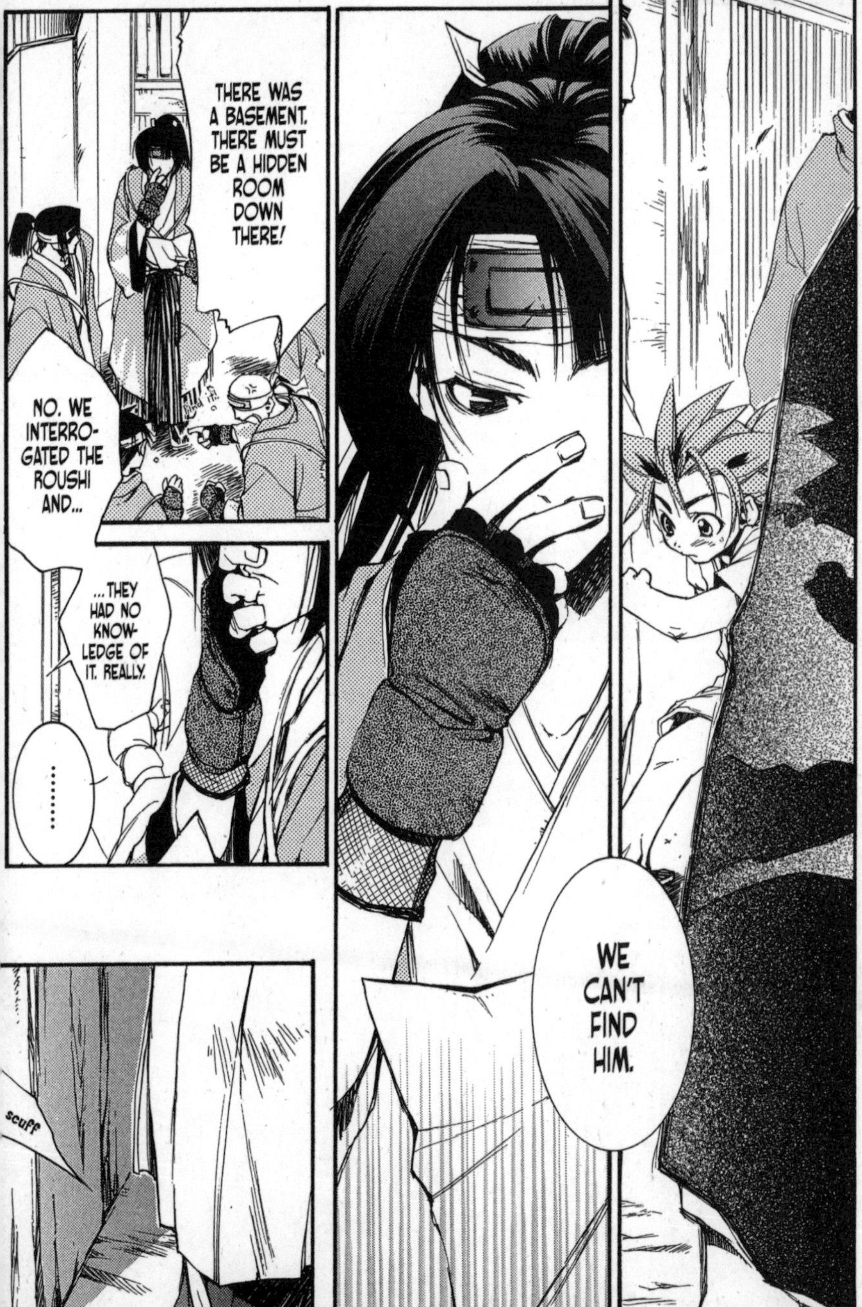
WE CAN'T FIND HIM.
THERE WAS A BASEMENT. THERE MUST BE A HIDDEN ROOM DOWN THERE!
NO. WE INTERRO-GATED THE ROUSHI AND...
...THEY HAD NO KNOW-LEDGE OF IT. REALLY.
......
scuff

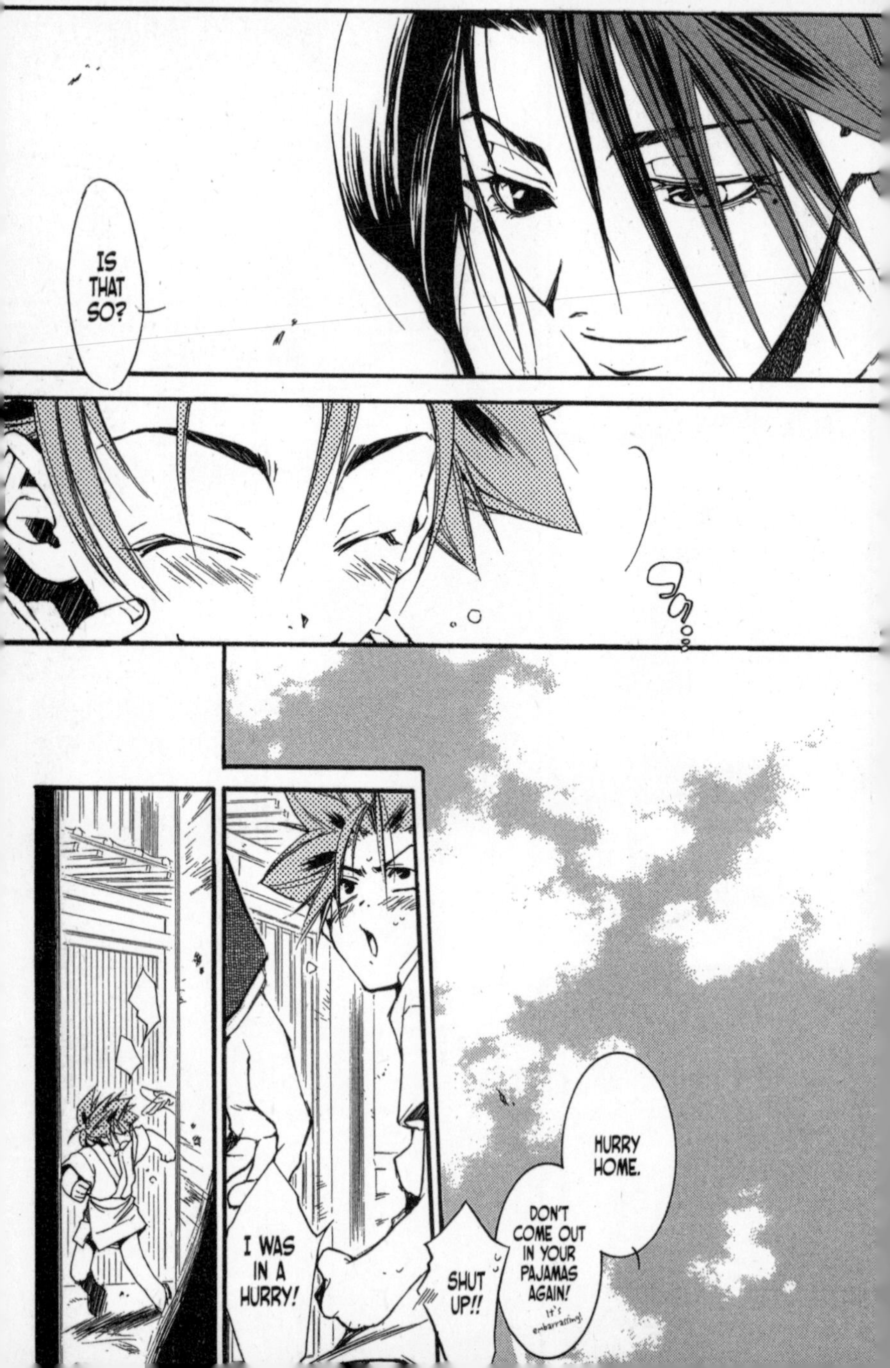
IS THAT SO?
HURRY HOME.
DON'T COME OUT IN YOUR PAJAMAS AGAIN!
It's embarrassing!
SHUT UP!!
I WAS IN A HURRY!

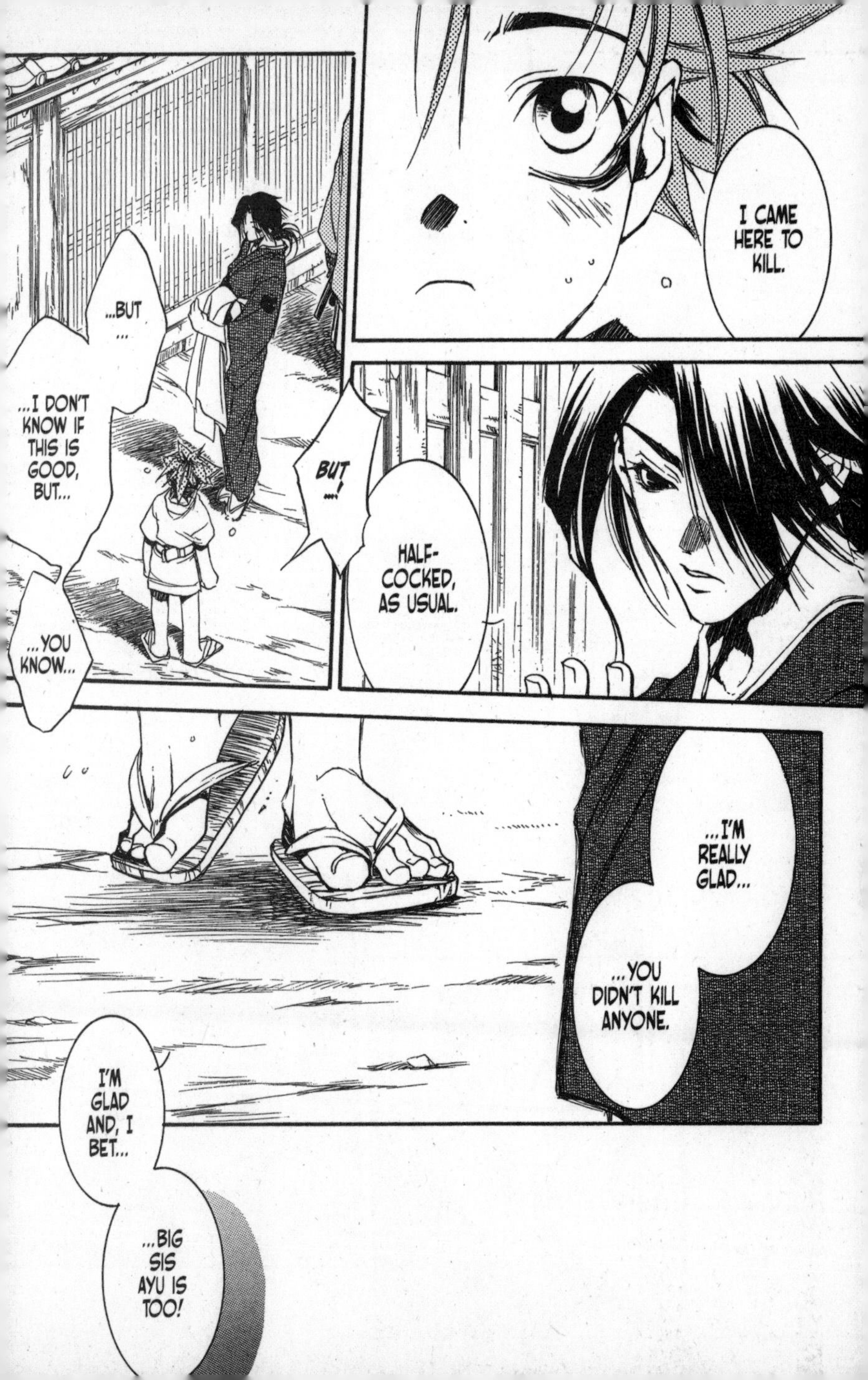

I CAME HERE TO KILL.
BUT ...!
HALF-COCKED, AS USUAL.
...BUT ...
...I DON'T KNOW IF THIS IS GOOD, BUT...
...YOU KNOW...
...I'M REALLY GLAD...
...YOU DIDN'T KILL ANYONE.
I'M GLAD AND, I BET...
...BIG SIS AYU IS TOO!

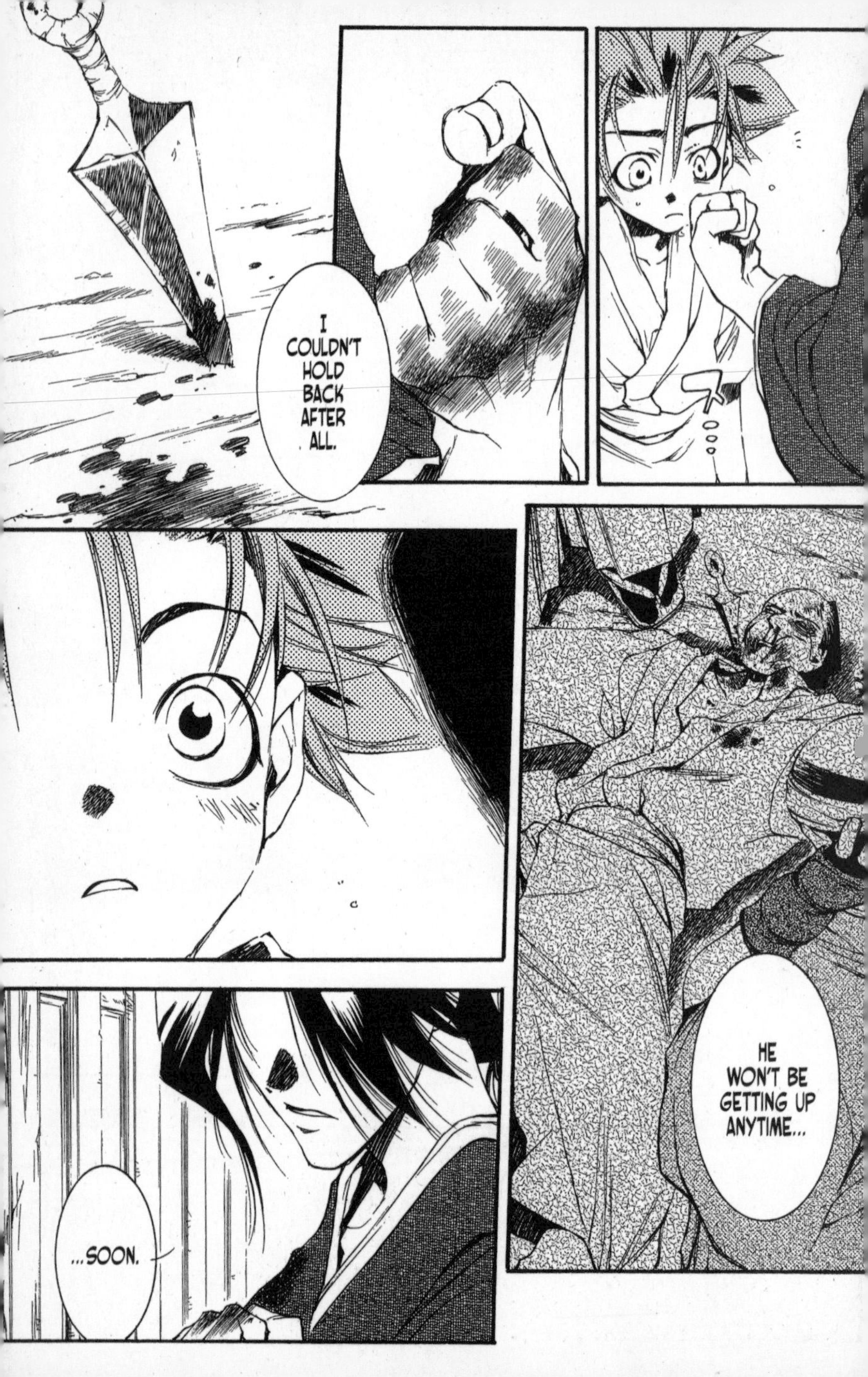
I COULDN'T HOLD BACK AFTER ALL.
HE WON'T BE GETTING UP ANYTIME...
...SOON.

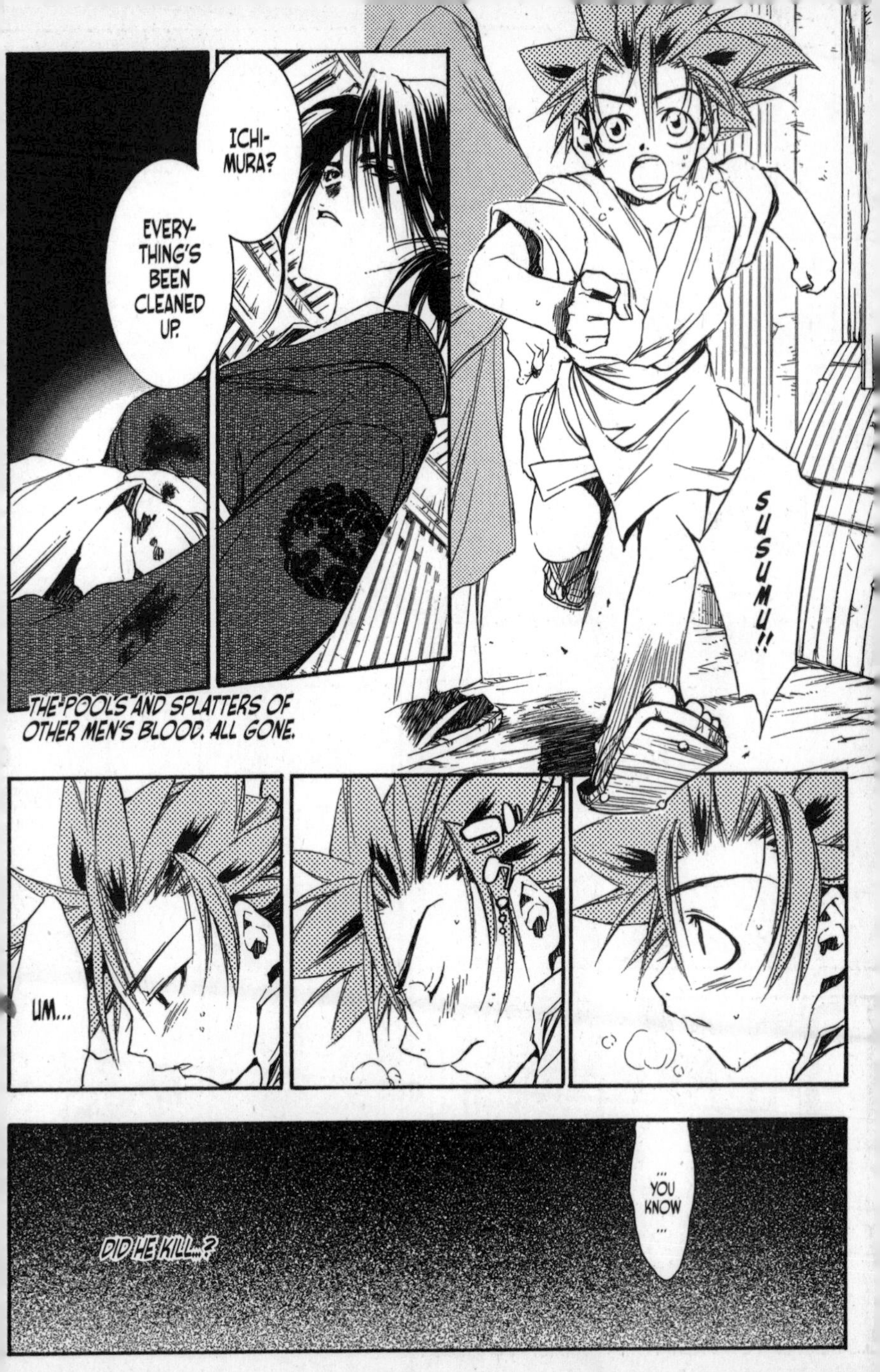
SUSUMU!!
ICHI-MURA?
EVERY-THING'S BEEN CLEANED UP.
THE POOLS AND SPLATTERS OF OTHER MEN'S BLOOD. ALL GONE.
UM...
...YOU KNOW...
DID HE KILL...?

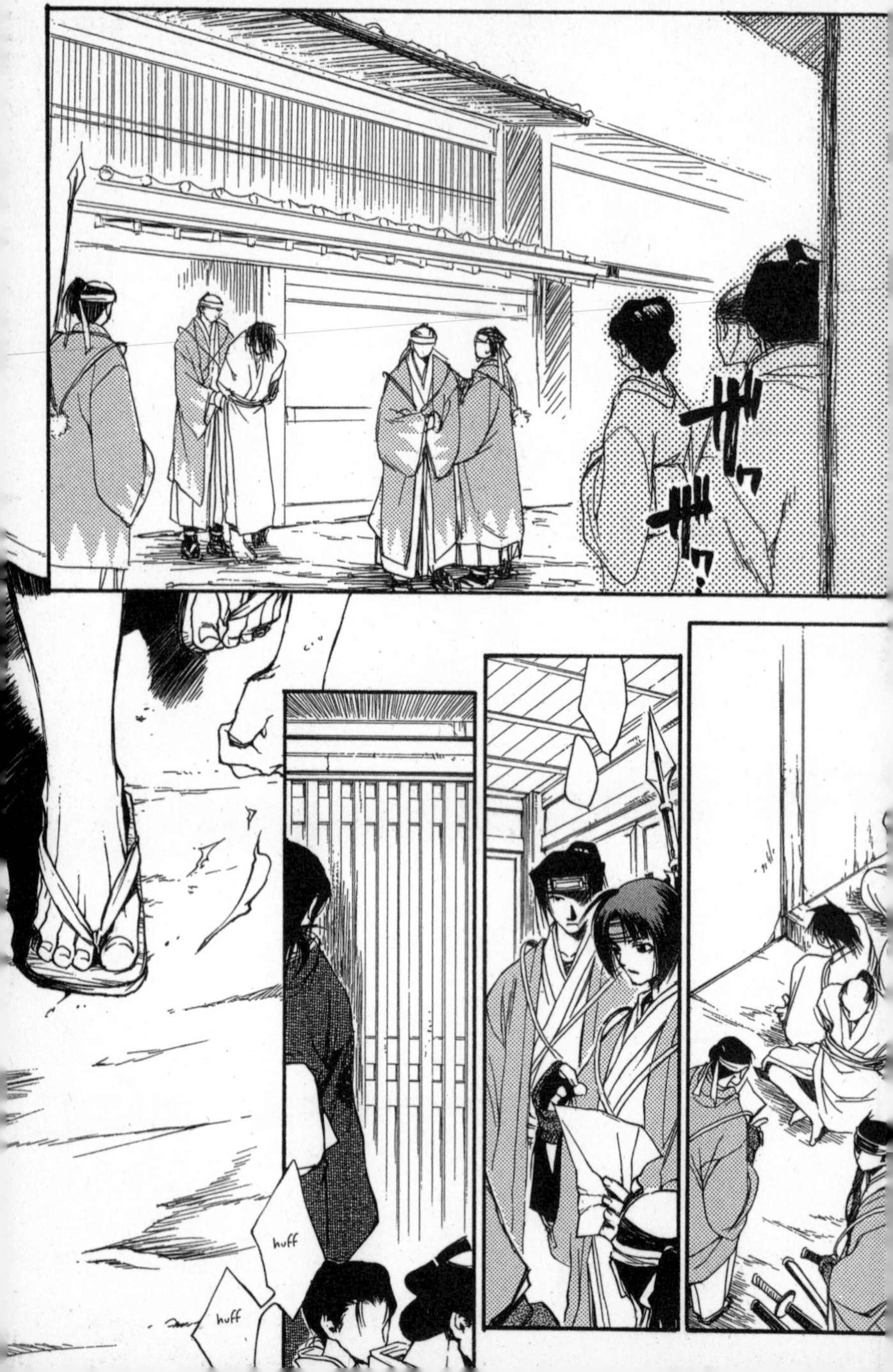
ザワ
ザワ…
huff
huff

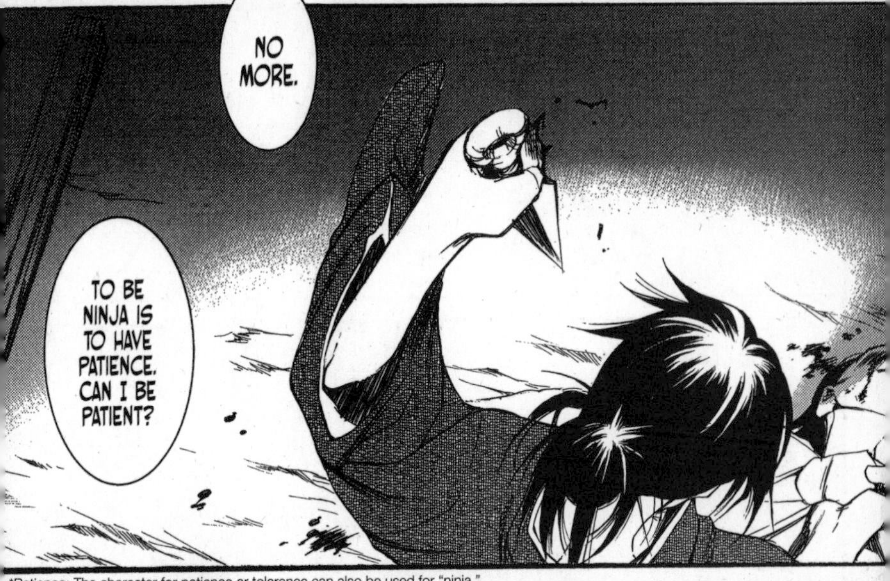
NO MORE.
TO BE NINJA IS TO HAVE PATIENCE. CAN I BE PATIENT?

*Patience: The character for patience or tolerance can also be used for "ninja."

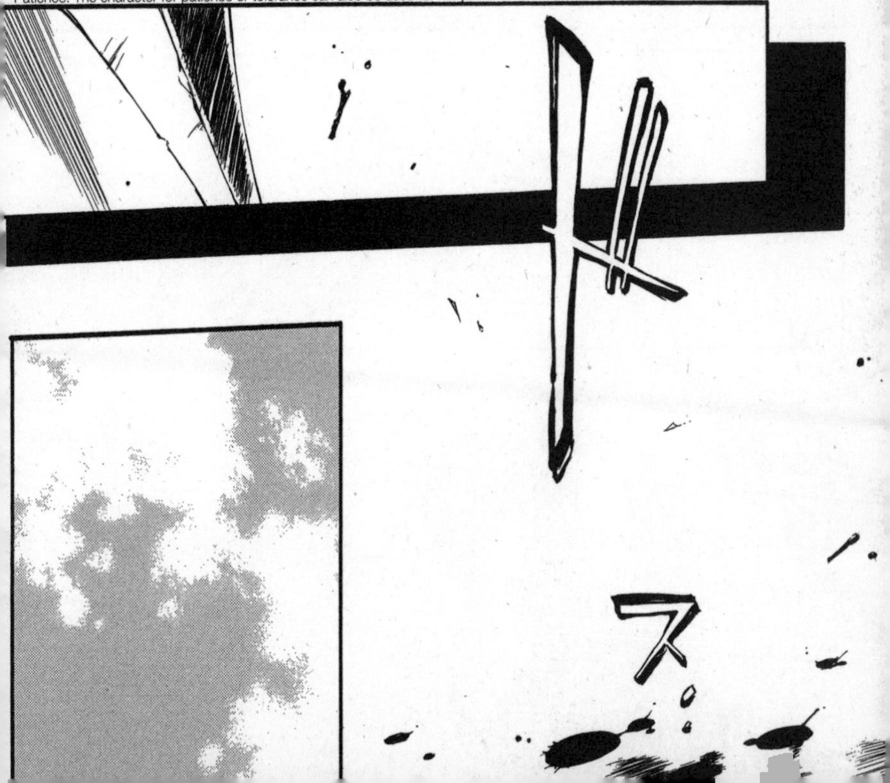

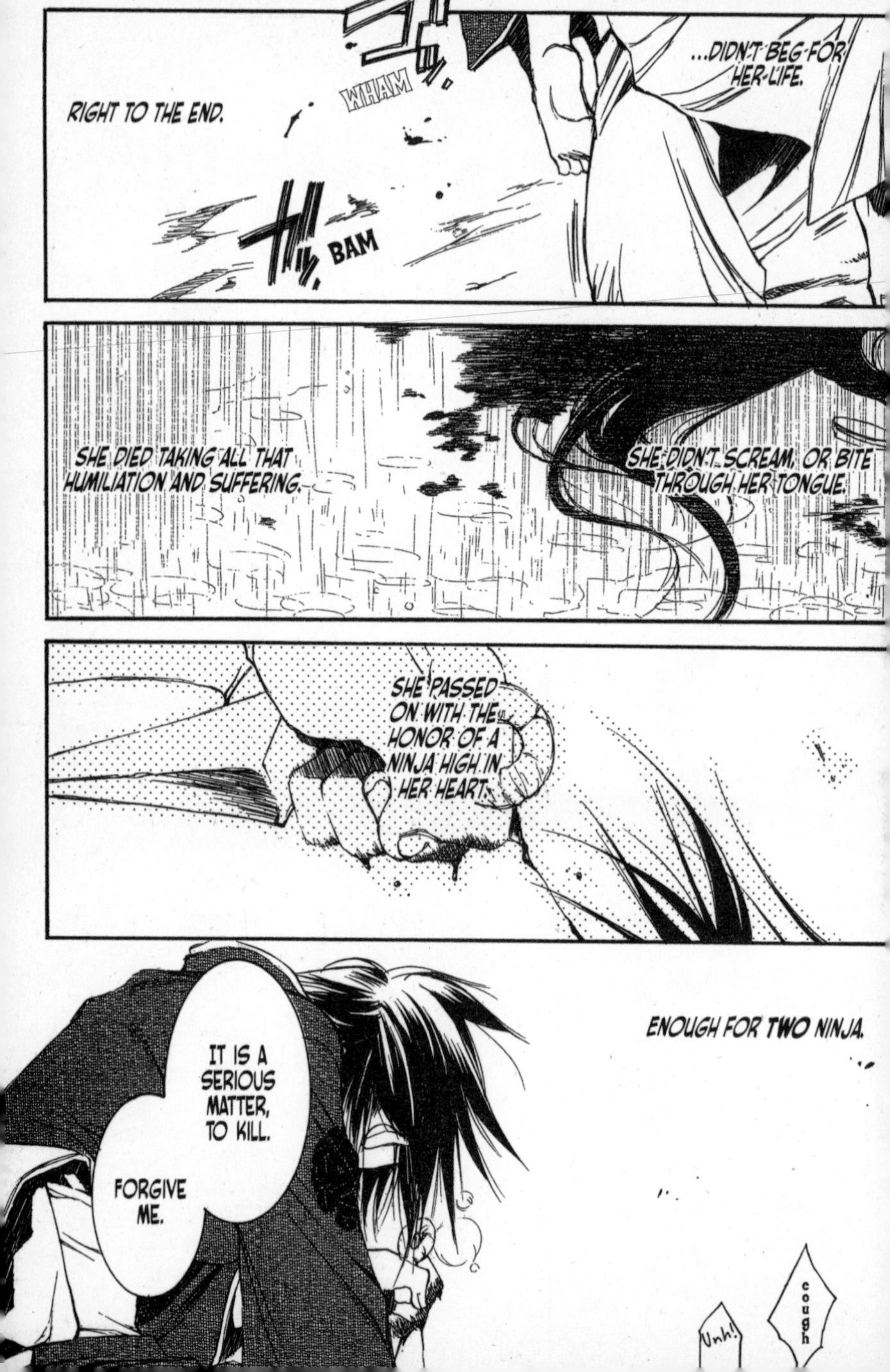
...DIDN'T BEG FOR HER LIFE.
WHAM
RIGHT TO THE END.
BAM
SHE DIDN'T SCREAM, OR BITE THROUGH HER TONGUE.
SHE DIED TAKING ALL THAT HUMILIATION AND SUFFERING.
SHE PASSED ON WITH THE HONOR OF A NINJA HIGH IN HER HEART.
ENOUGH FOR TWO NINJA.
cough
Unh!
IT IS A SERIOUS MATTER, TO KILL.
FORGIVE ME.

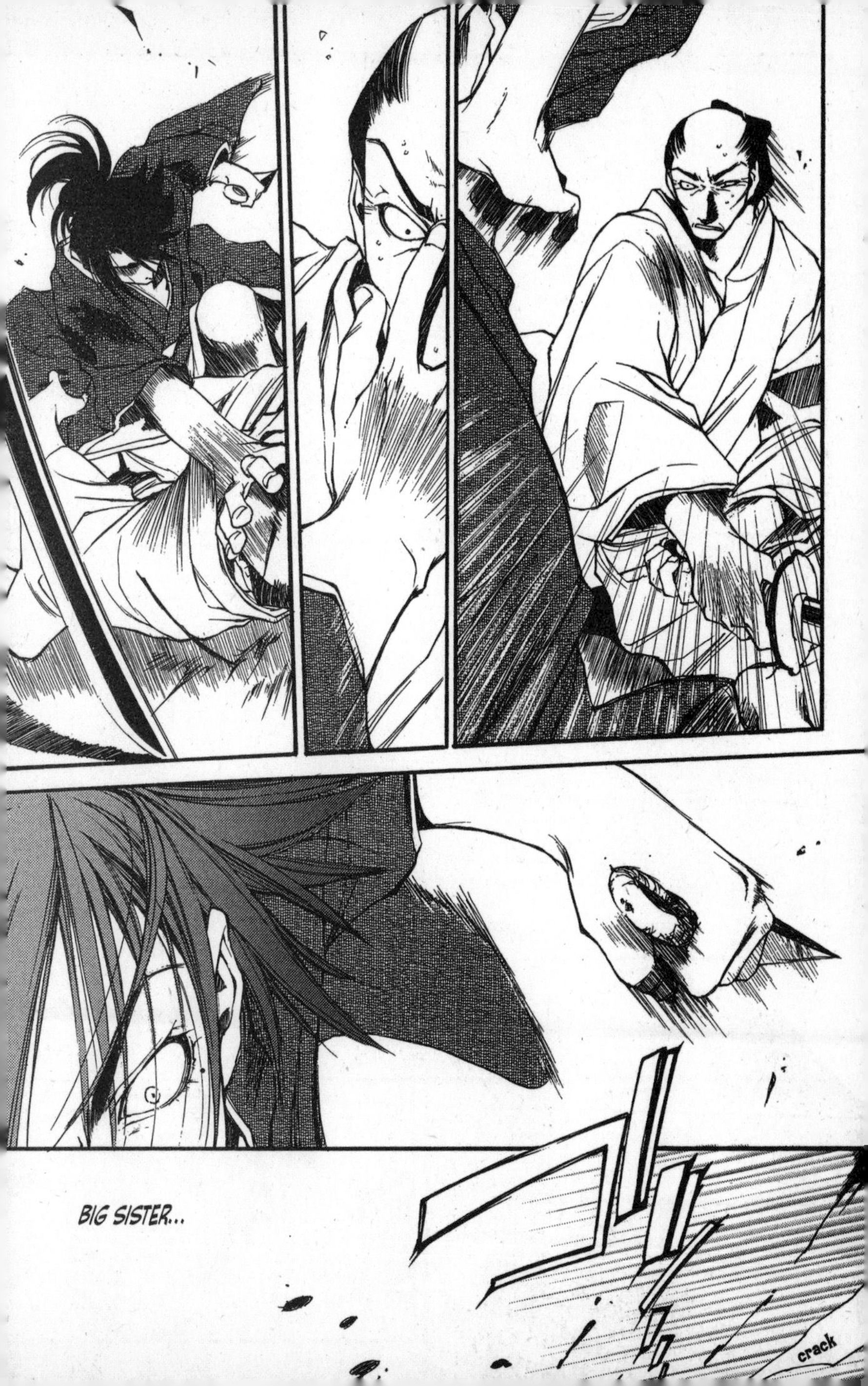
BIG SISTER...
crack

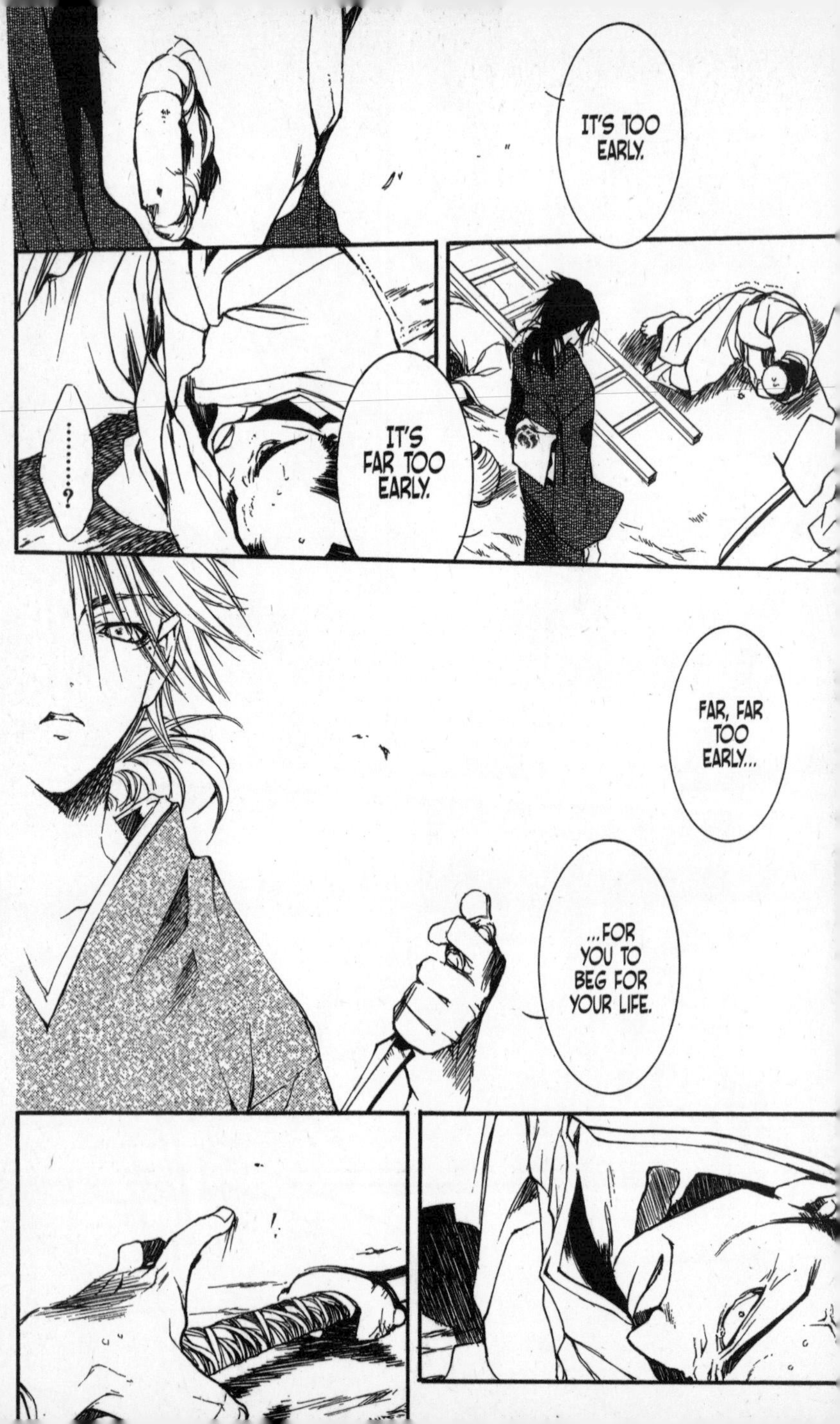
IT'S TOO EARLY.
IT'S FAR TOO EARLY.
......?
FAR, FAR TOO EARLY...
...FOR YOU TO BEG FOR YOUR LIFE.

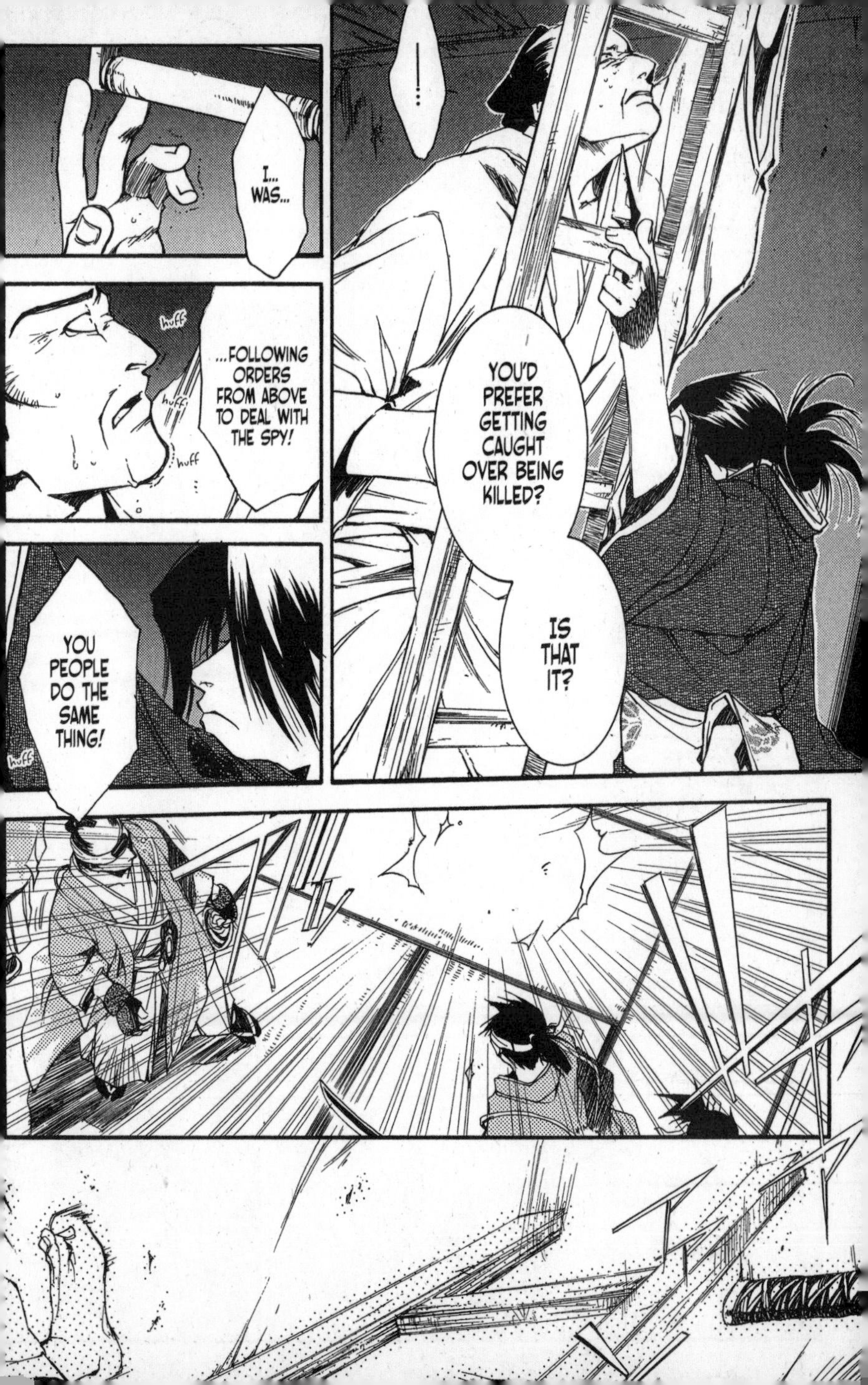

YOU'D PREFER GETTING CAUGHT OVER BEING KILLED?
IS THAT IT?
I... WAS...
huff
...FOLLOWING ORDERS FROM ABOVE TO DEAL WITH THE SPY!
huff
huff
YOU PEOPLE DO THE SAME THING!
huff

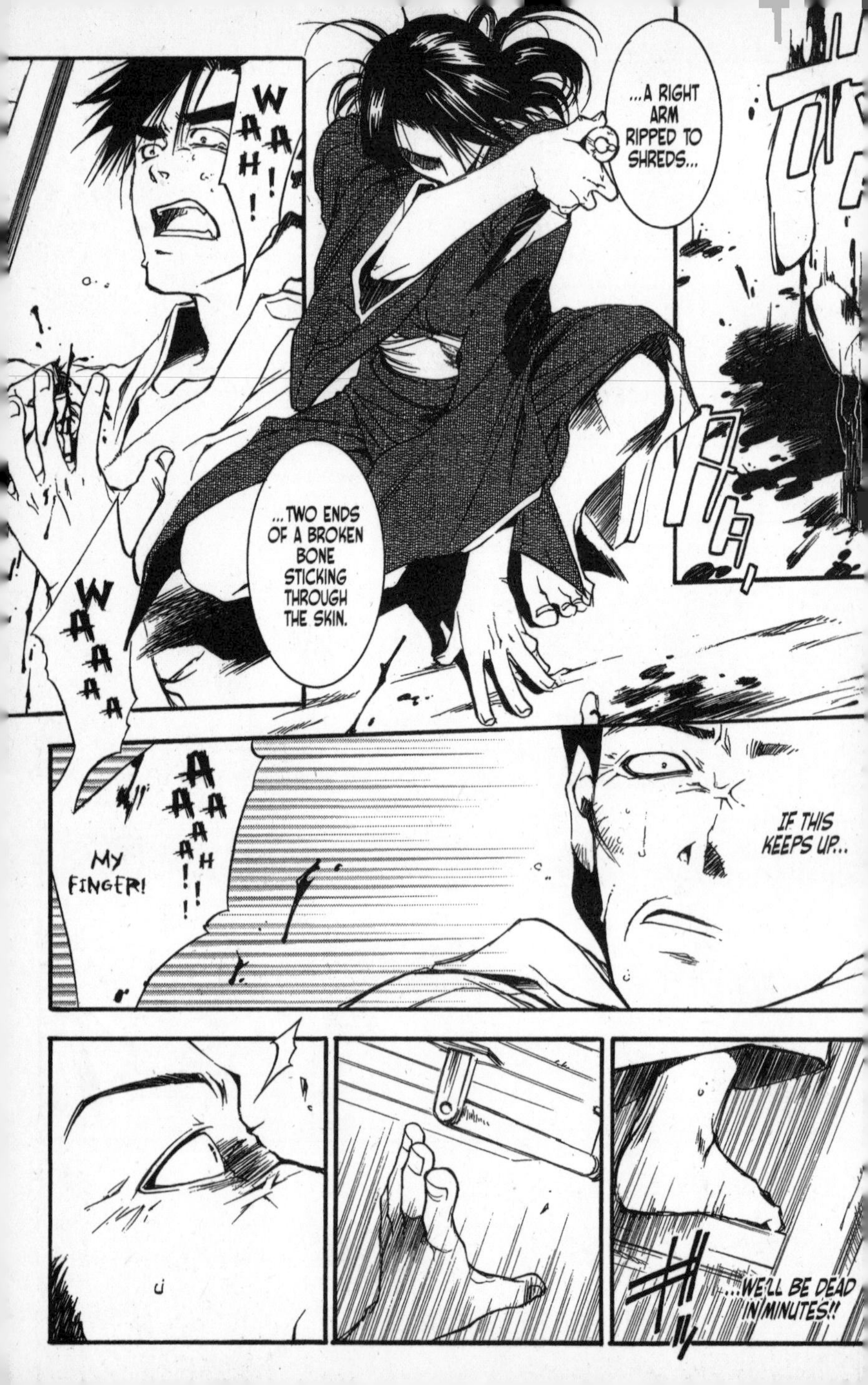
...A RIGHT ARM RIPPED TO SHREDS...
...TWO ENDS OF A BROKEN BONE STICKING THROUGH THE SKIN.
WAAH!
WAAAAA
IF THIS KEEPS UP...
AAAAAH!!!
MY FINGER!
...WE'LL BE DEAD IN MINUTES!!

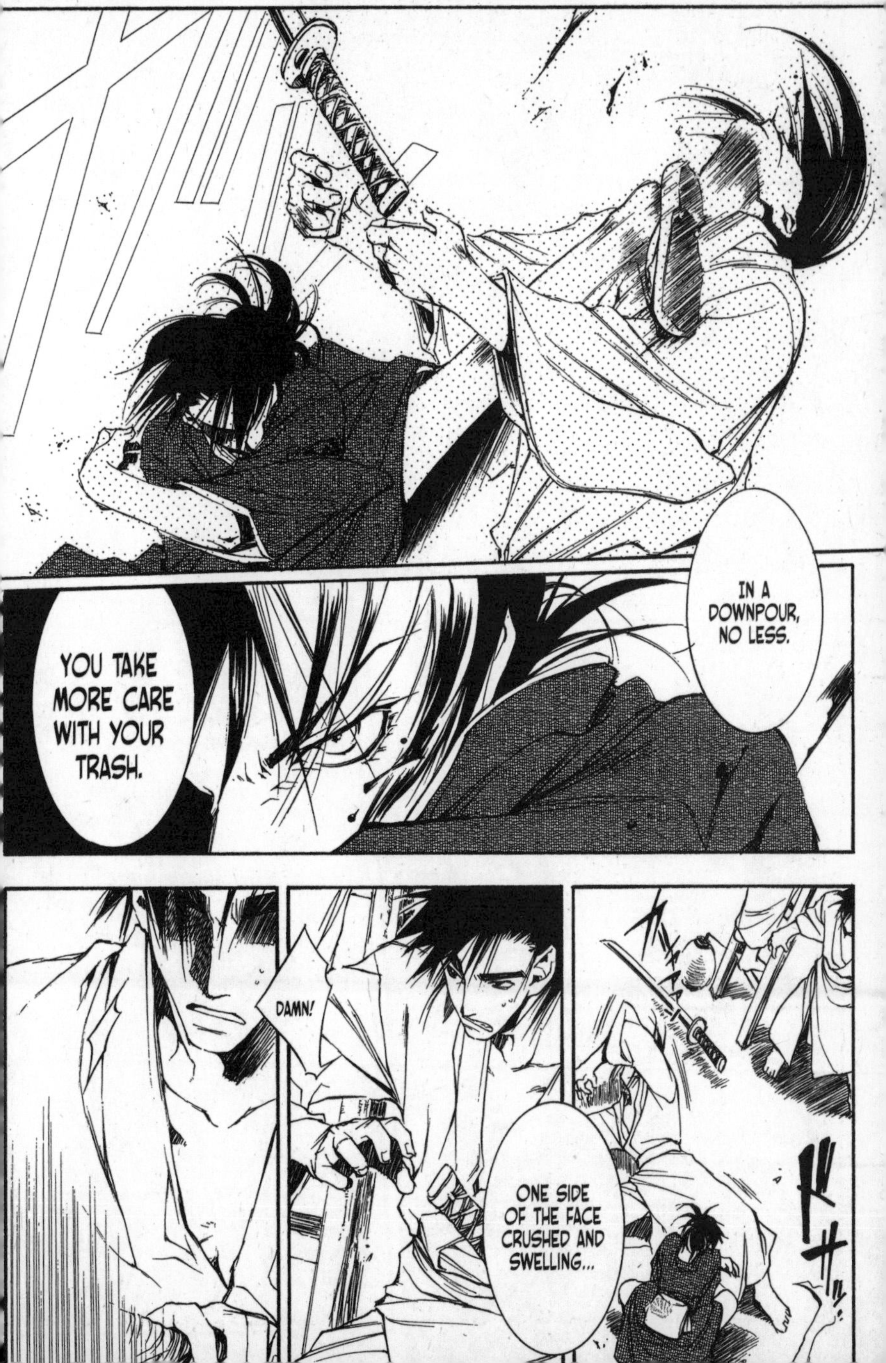
IN A DOWNPOUR, NO LESS.
YOU TAKE MORE CARE WITH YOUR TRASH.
ONE SIDE OF THE FACE CRUSHED AND SWELLING...
DAMN!

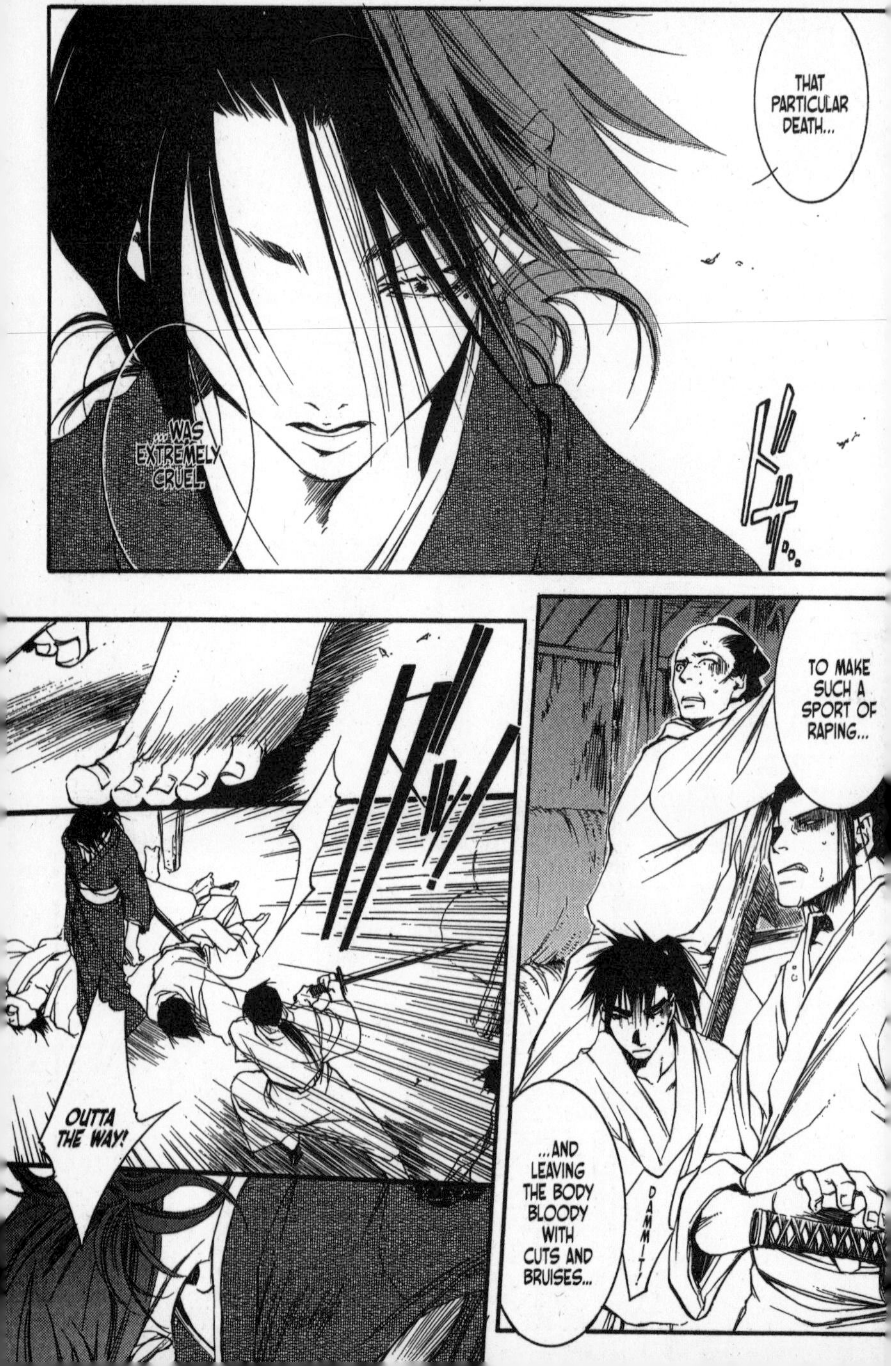
THAT PARTICULAR DEATH...
...WAS EXTREMELY CRUEL.
TO MAKE SUCH A SPORT OF RAPING...
...AND LEAVING THE BODY BLOODY WITH CUTS AND BRUISES...
DAMMIT!
OUTTA THE WAY!

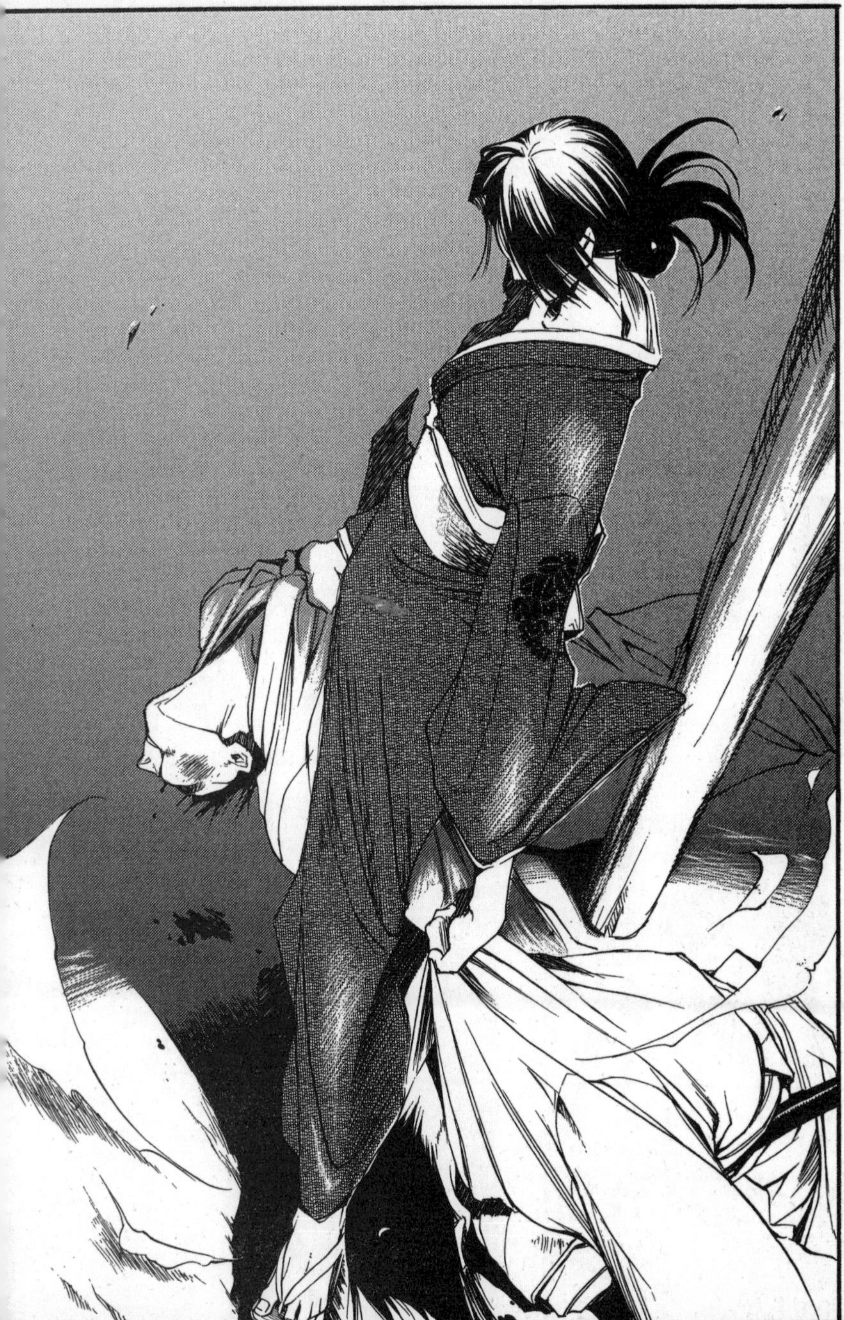

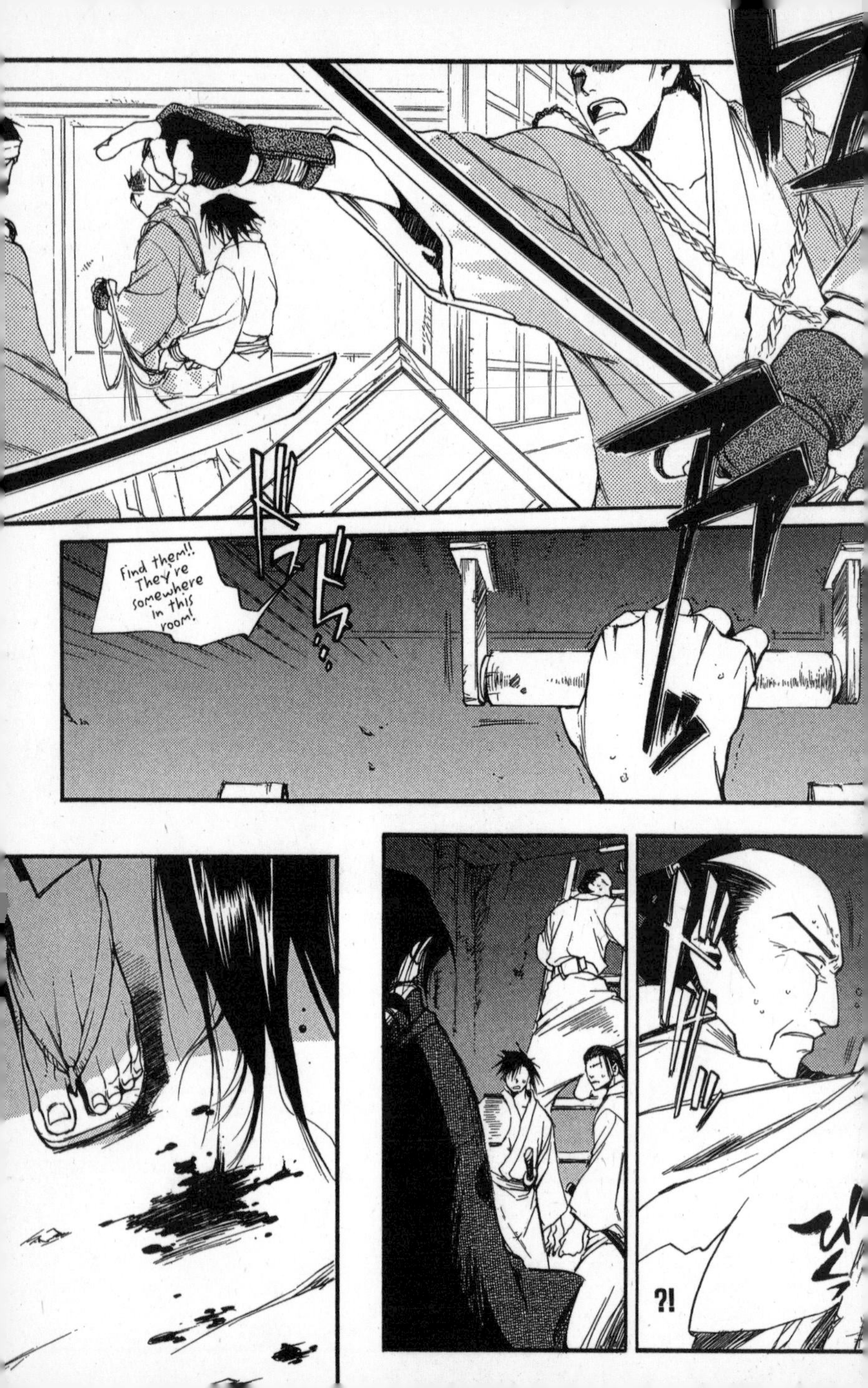
Find them!! They're somewhere in this room!
?!

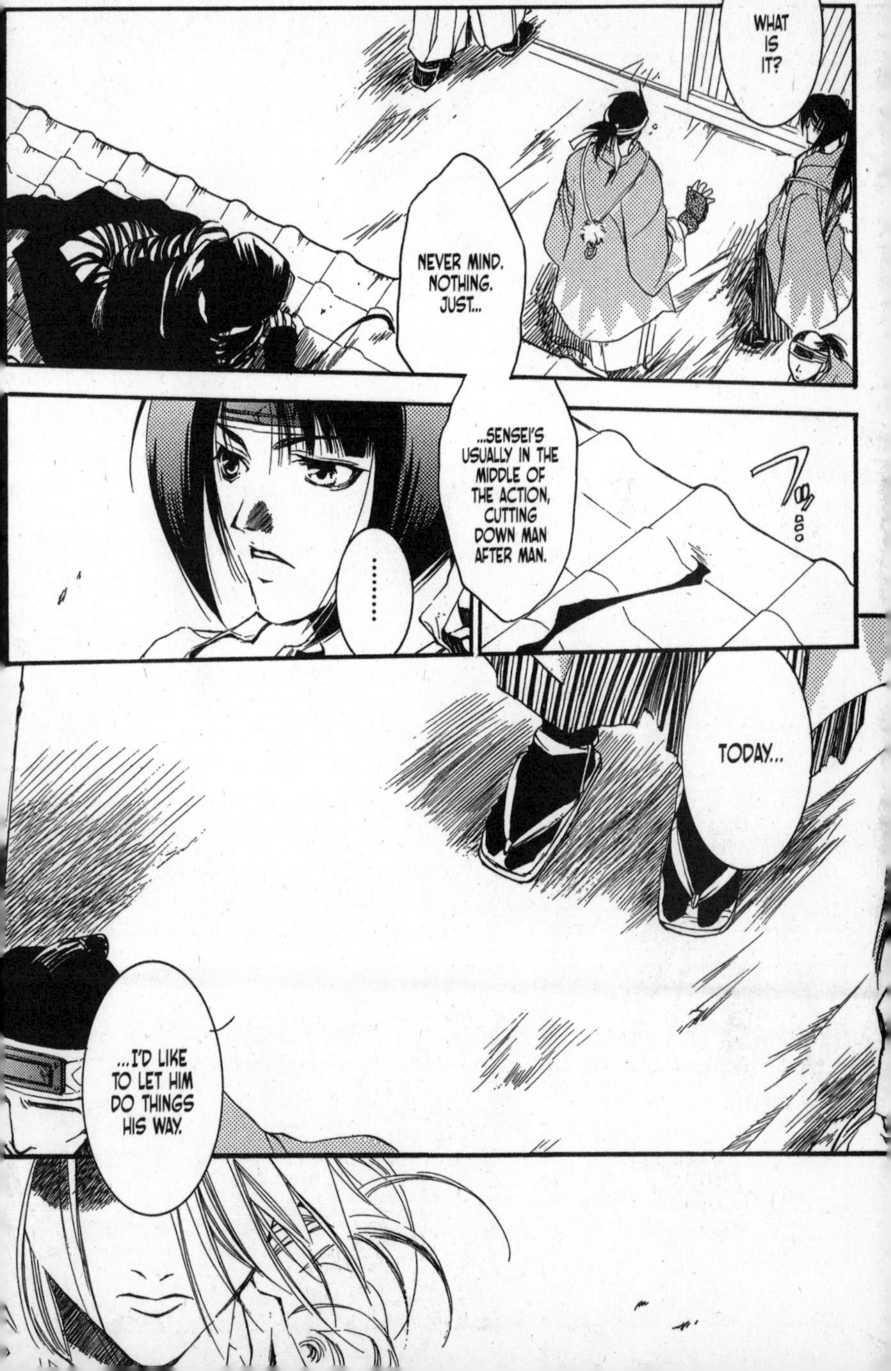
WHAT IS IT?
NEVER MIND. NOTHING. JUST...
...SENSEI'S USUALLY IN THE MIDDLE OF THE ACTION, CUTTING DOWN MAN AFTER MAN.
......
TODAY...
...I'D LIKE TO LET HIM DO THINGS HIS WAY.

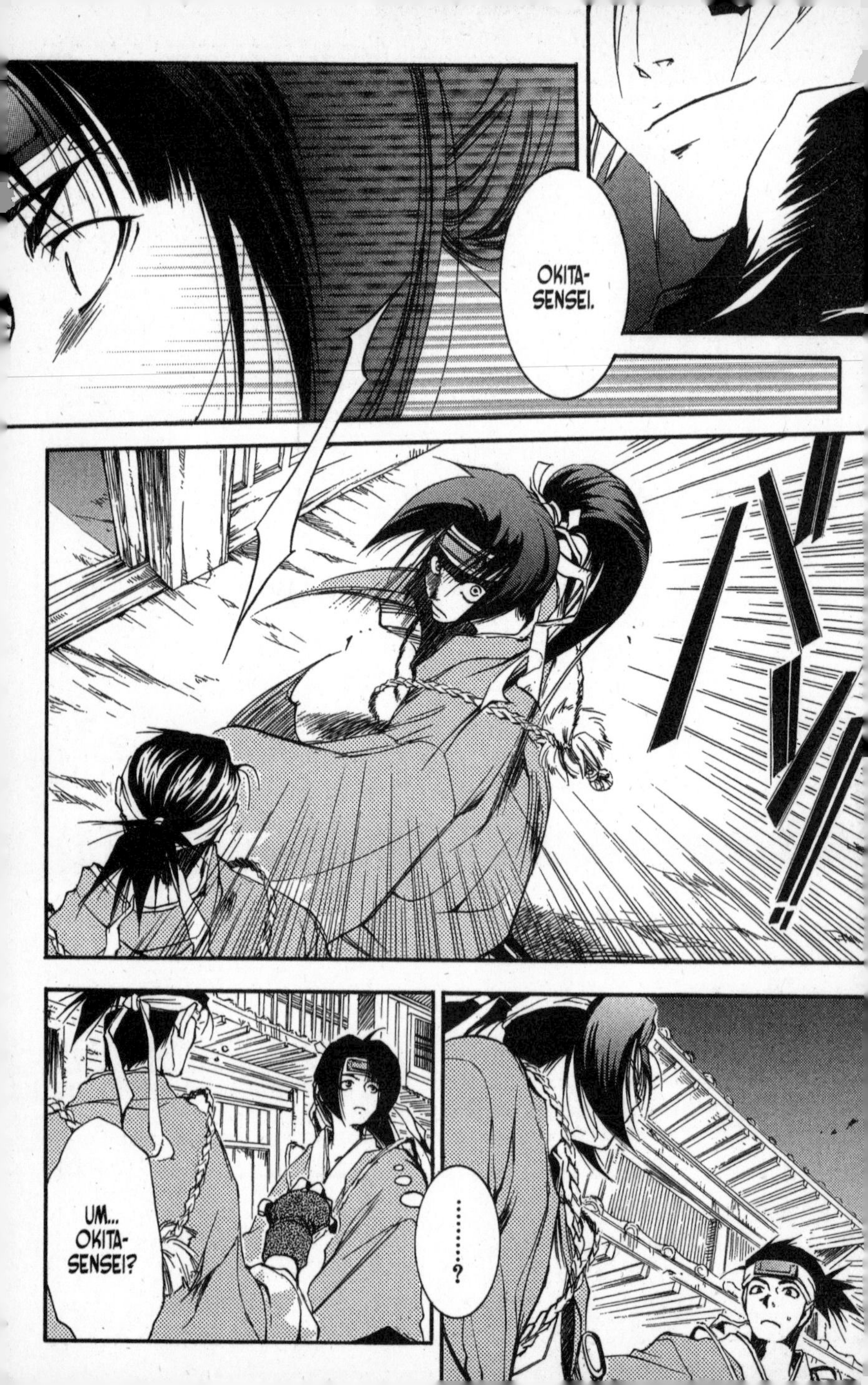
OKITA-SENSEI.
......?
UM... OKITA-SENSEI?

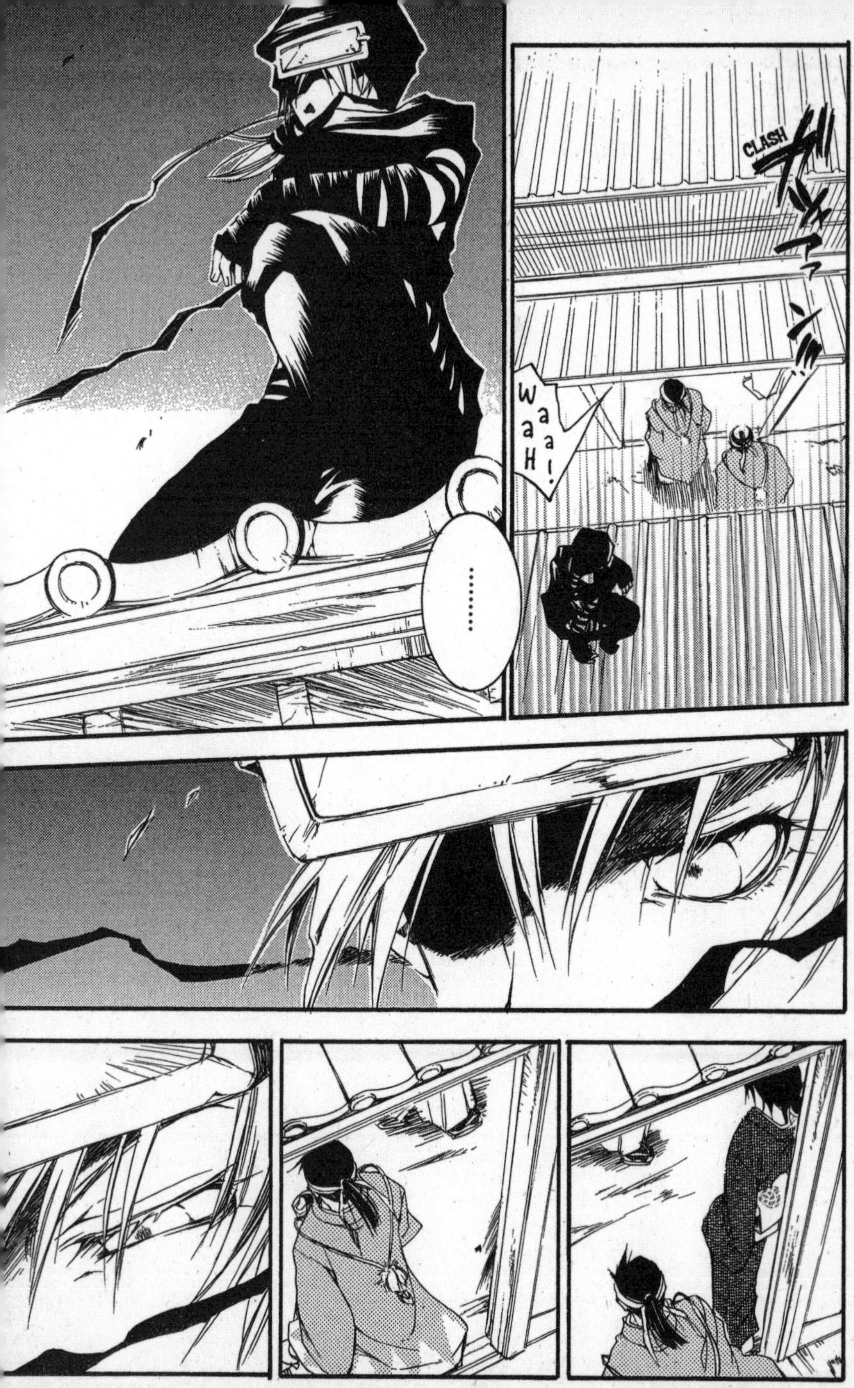
CLASH
WaaaH!
....

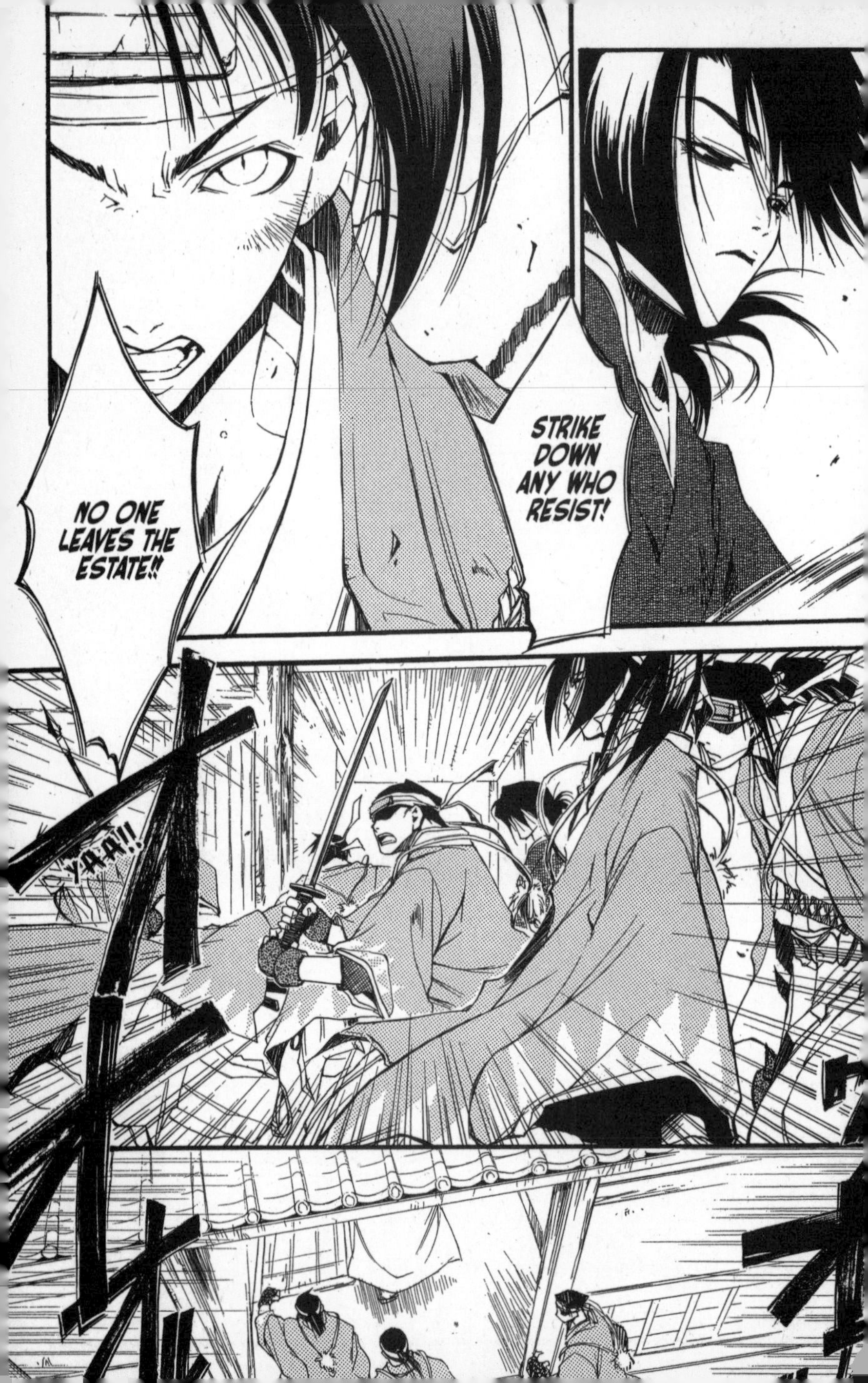
STRIKE DOWN ANY WHO RESIST!
NO ONE LEAVES THE ESTATE!!
YAA!!

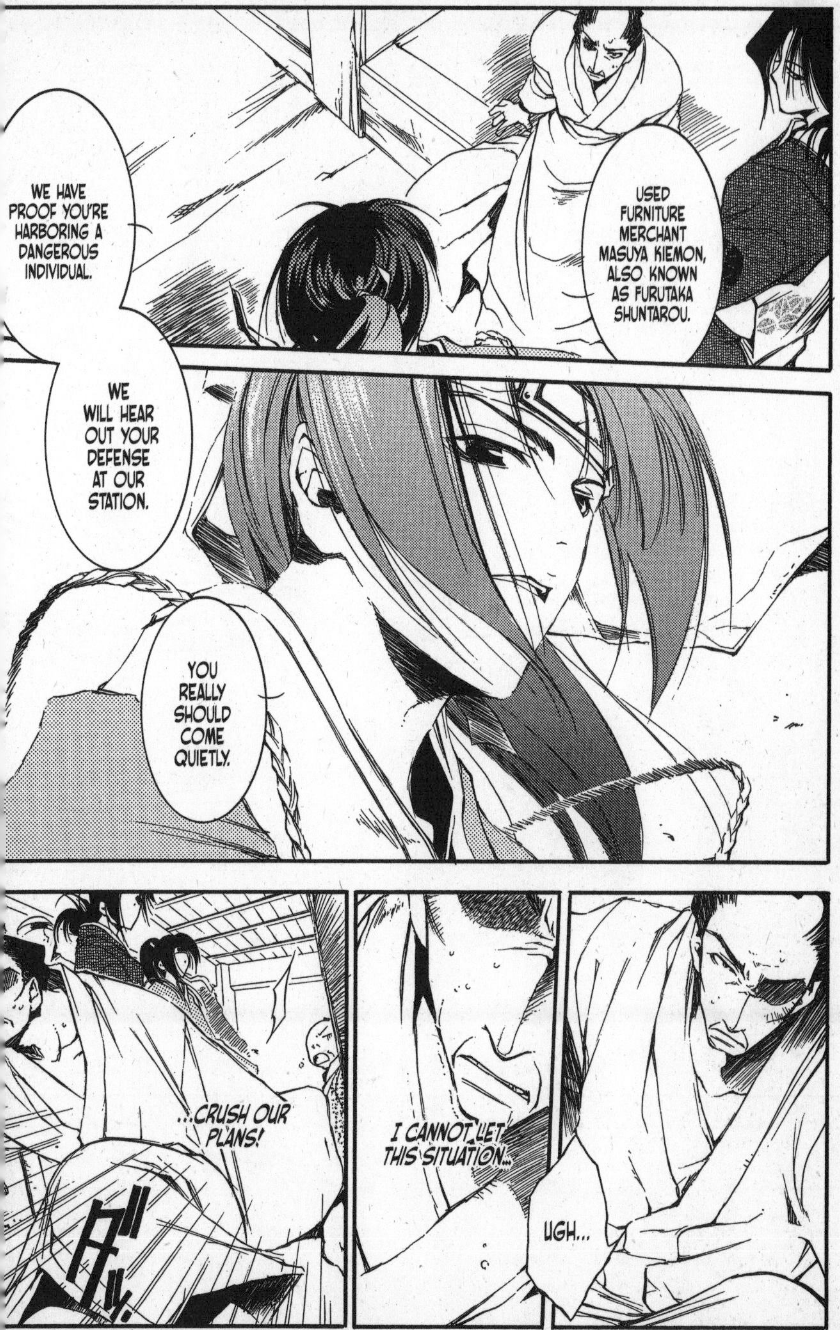
USED FURNITURE MERCHANT MASUYA KIEMON, ALSO KNOWN AS FURUTAKA SHUNTAROU.
WE HAVE PROOF YOU'RE HARBORING A DANGEROUS INDIVIDUAL.
WE WILL HEAR OUT YOUR DEFENSE AT OUR STATION.
YOU REALLY SHOULD COME QUIETLY.
UGH...
I CANNOT LET THIS SITUATION...
...CRUSH OUR PLANS!
ダッ

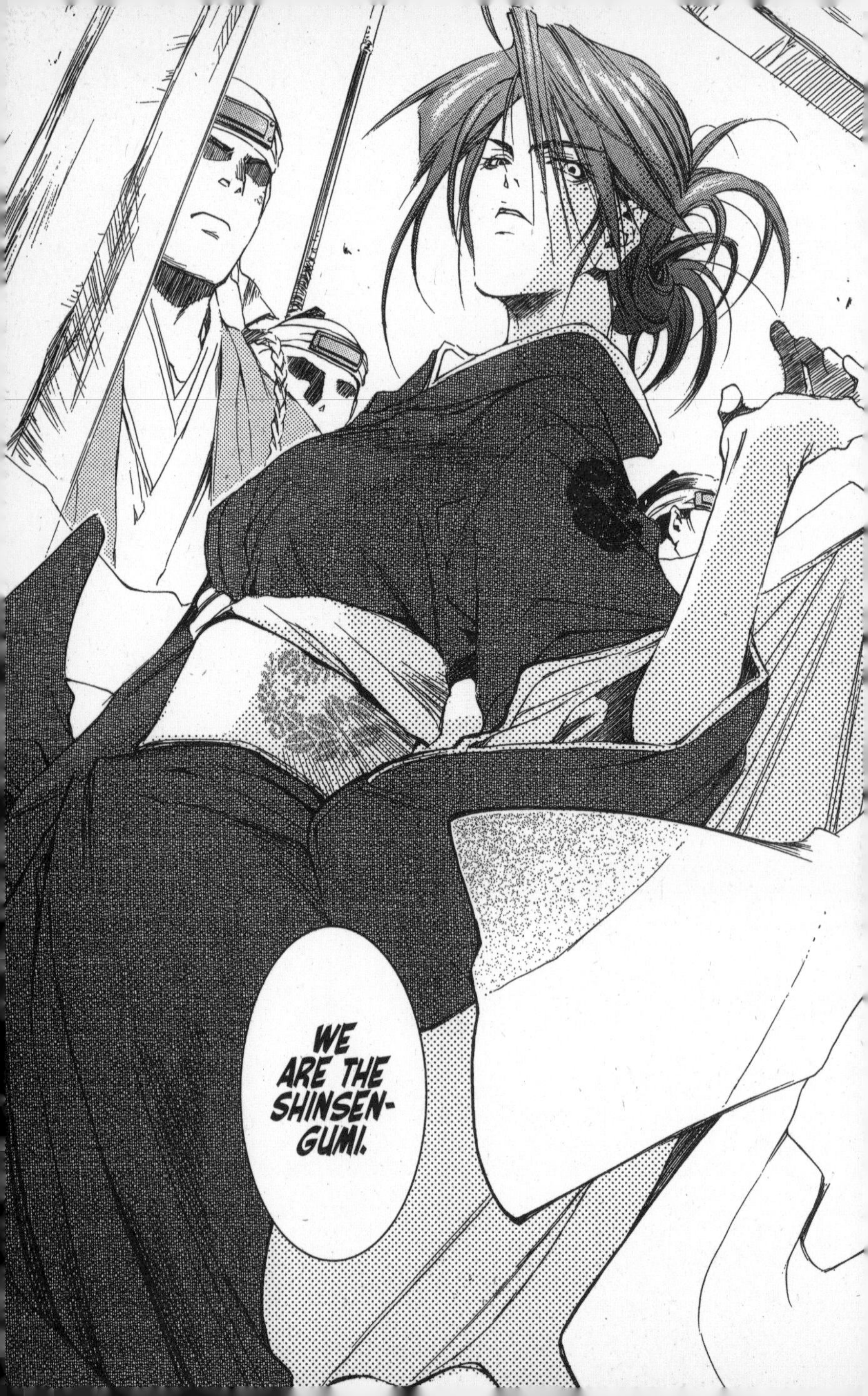
WE ARE THE SHINSEN-GUMI.

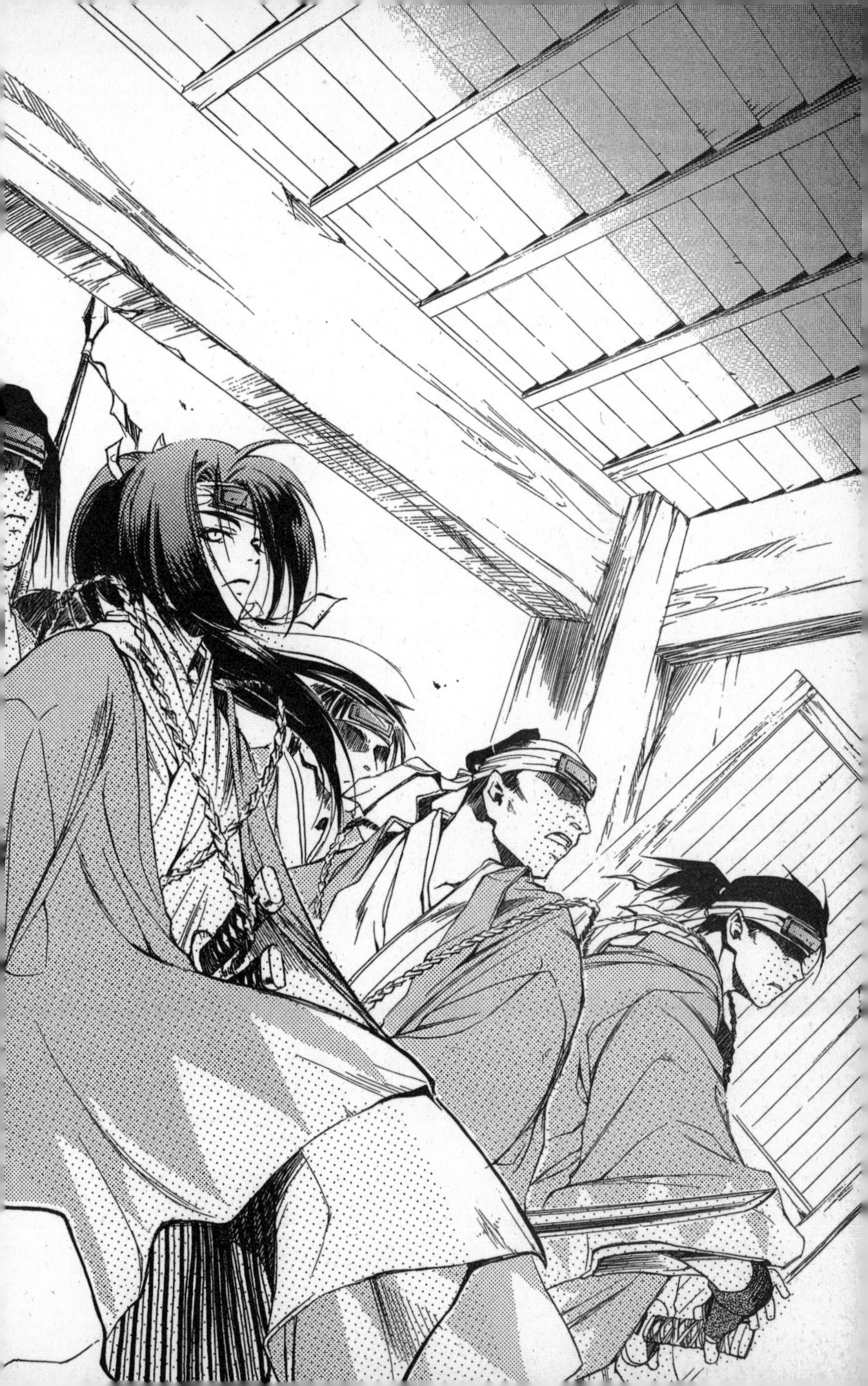

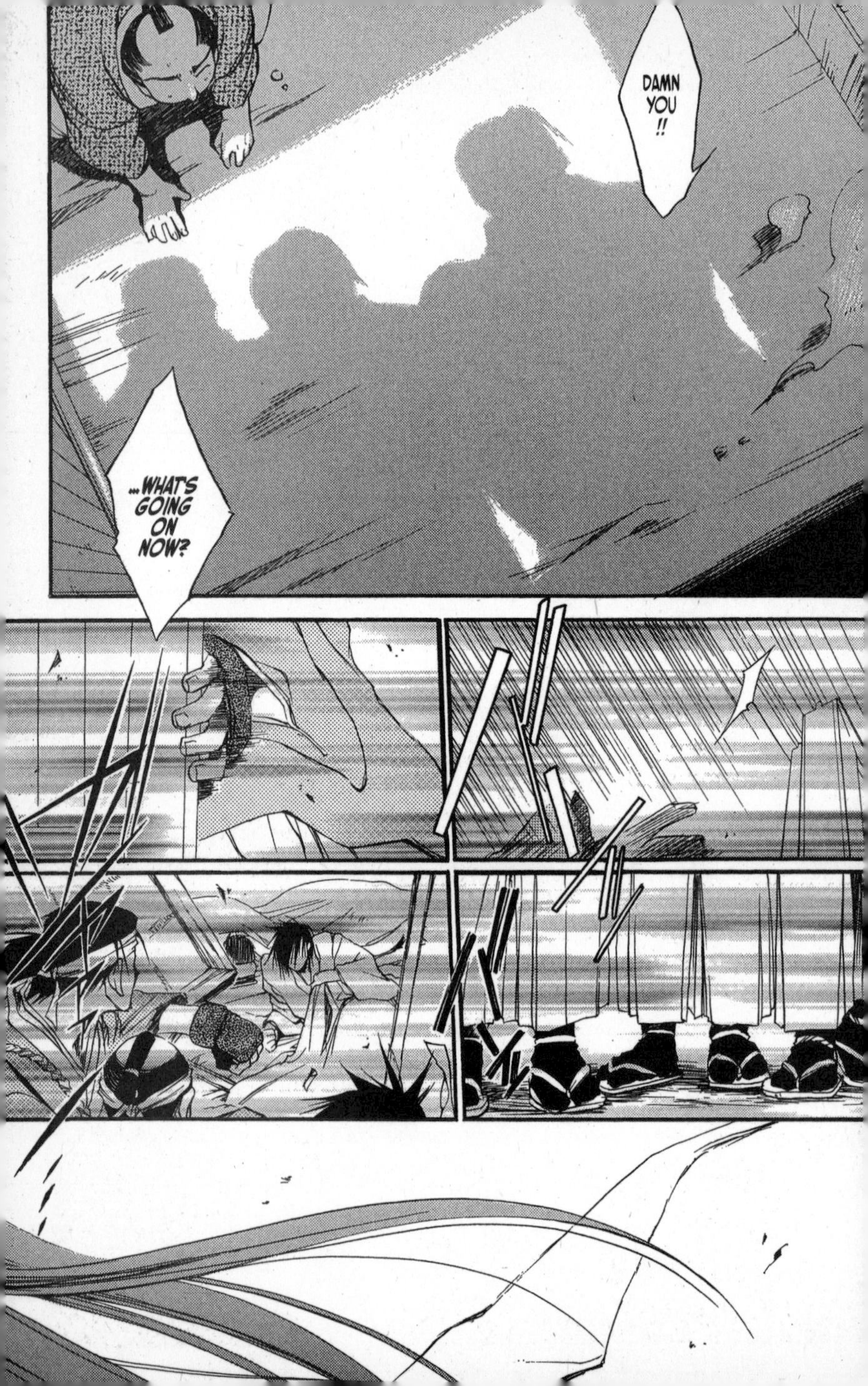
DAMN YOU !!
...WHAT'S GOING ON NOW?

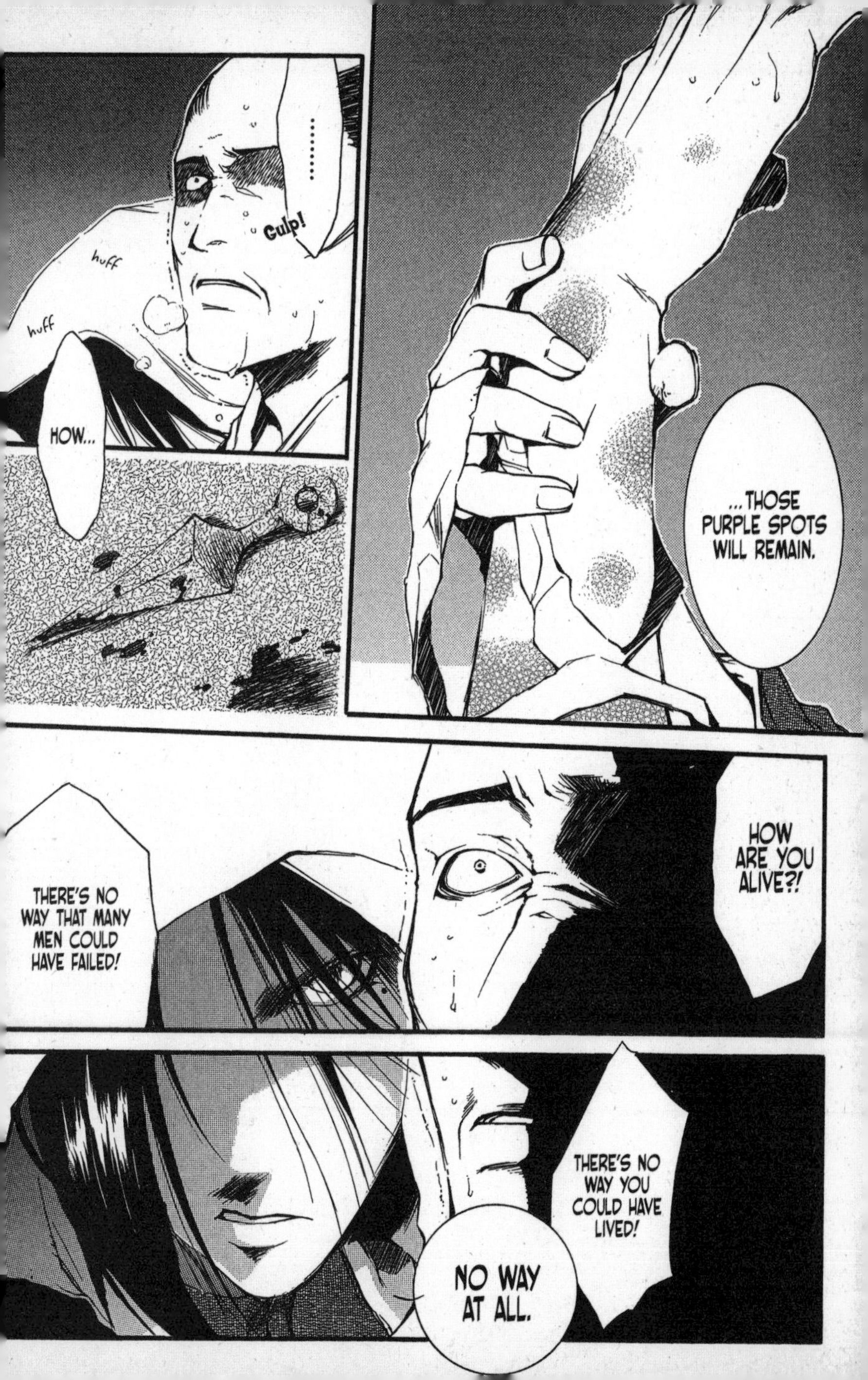
...THOSE PURPLE SPOTS WILL REMAIN.
......
Gulp!
huff
huff
HOW...
HOW ARE YOU ALIVE?!
THERE'S NO WAY THAT MANY MEN COULD HAVE FAILED!
THERE'S NO WAY YOU COULD HAVE LIVED!
NO WAY AT ALL.

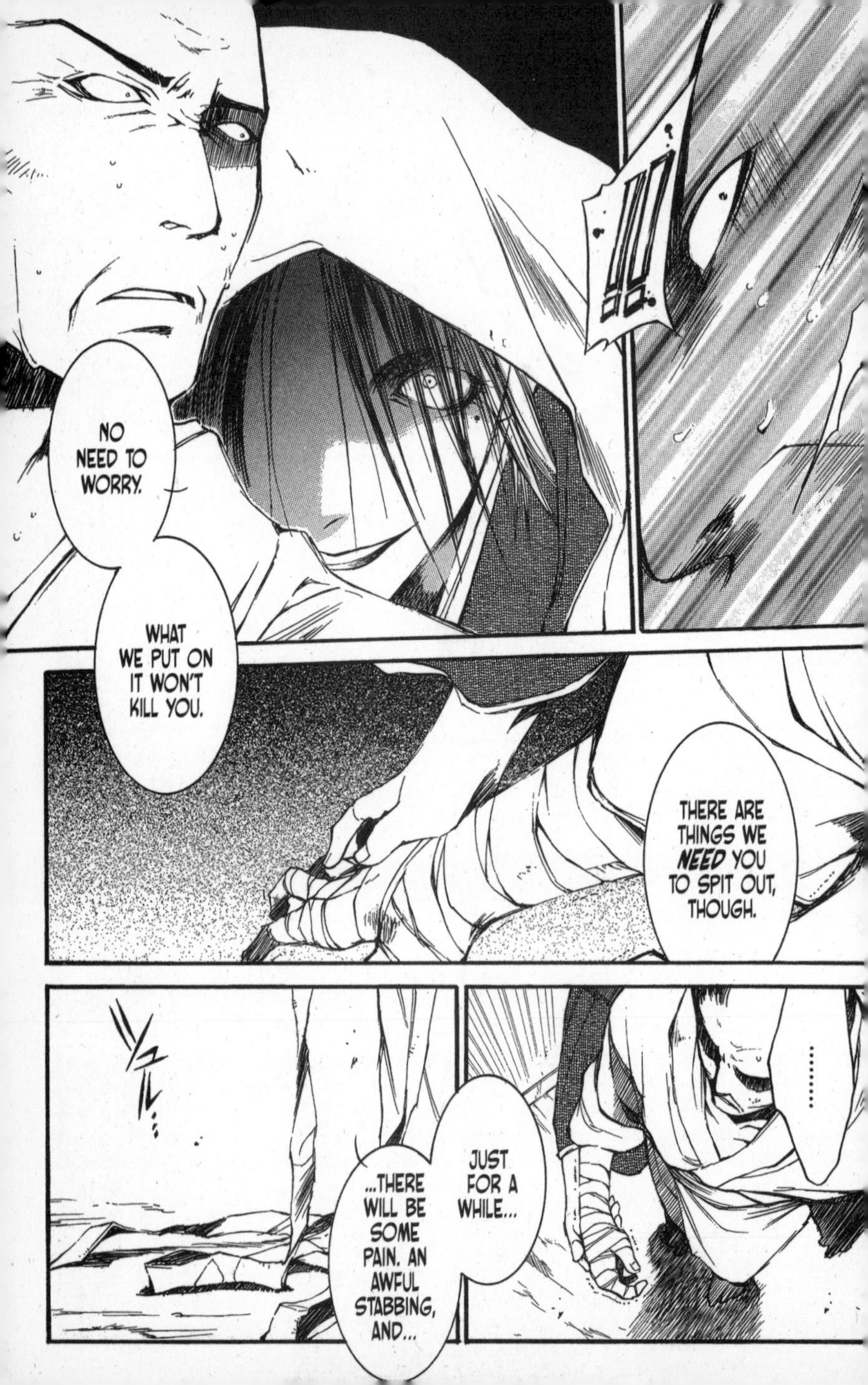
NO NEED TO WORRY.
WHAT WE PUT ON IT WON'T KILL YOU.
THERE ARE THINGS WE ***NEED*** YOU TO SPIT OUT, THOUGH.
......
JUST FOR A WHILE...
...THERE WILL BE SOME PAIN. AN AWFUL STABBING, AND...

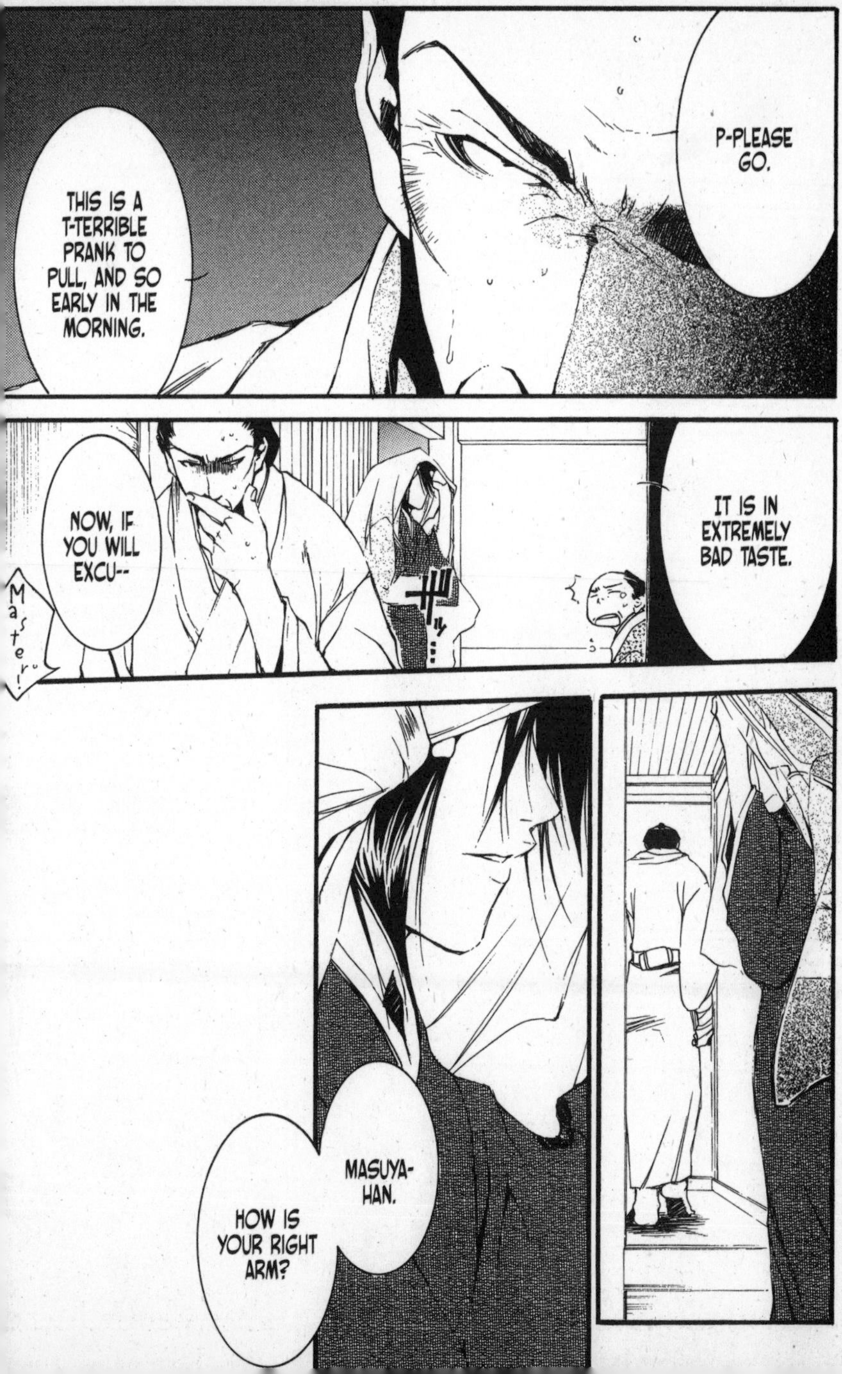
P-PLEASE GO.
THIS IS A T-TERRIBLE PRANK TO PULL, AND SO EARLY IN THE MORNING.
IT IS IN EXTREMELY BAD TASTE.
NOW, IF YOU WILL EXCU--
Master!
MASUYA-HAN.
HOW IS YOUR RIGHT ARM?

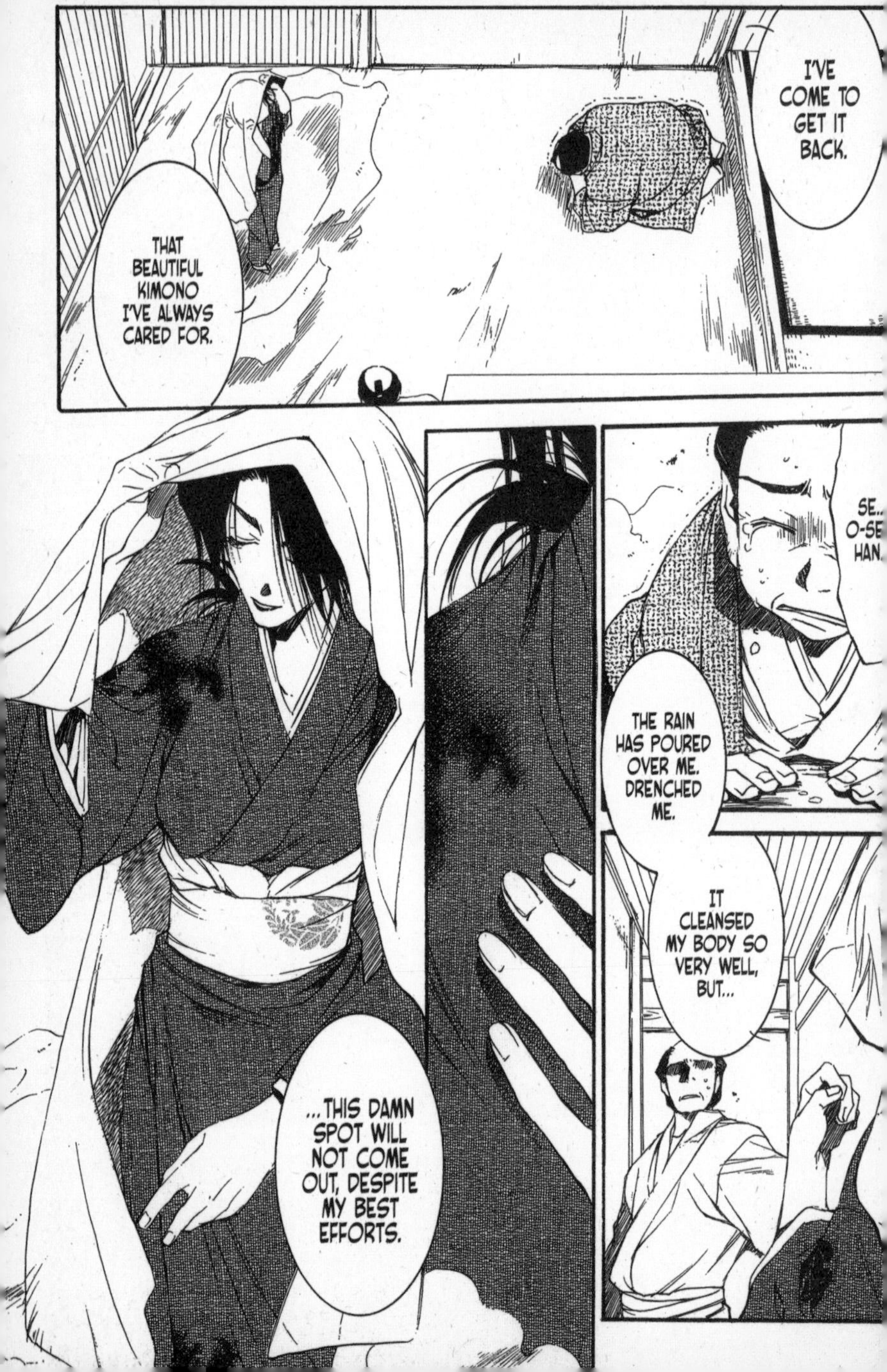
I'VE COME TO GET IT BACK.
THAT BEAUTIFUL KIMONO I'VE ALWAYS CARED FOR.
SE.. O-SE HAN.
THE RAIN HAS POURED OVER ME. DRENCHED ME.
IT CLEANSED MY BODY SO VERY WELL, BUT...
...THIS DAMN SPOT WILL NOT COME OUT, DESPITE MY BEST EFFORTS.

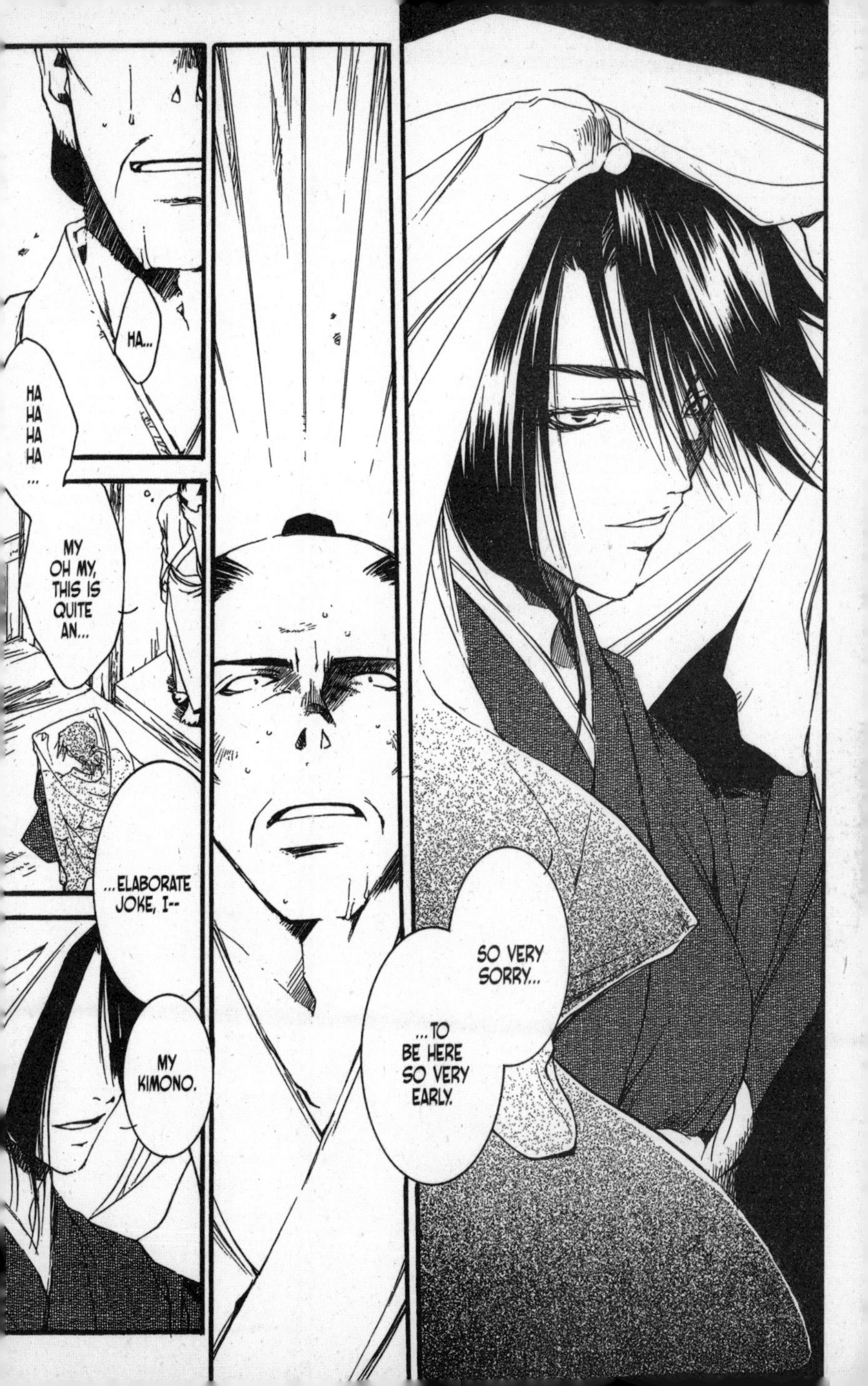

SO VERY SORRY...
...TO BE HERE SO VERY EARLY.
HA...
HA HA HA HA ...
MY OH MY, THIS IS QUITE AN...
...ELABORATE JOKE, I--
MY KIMONO.

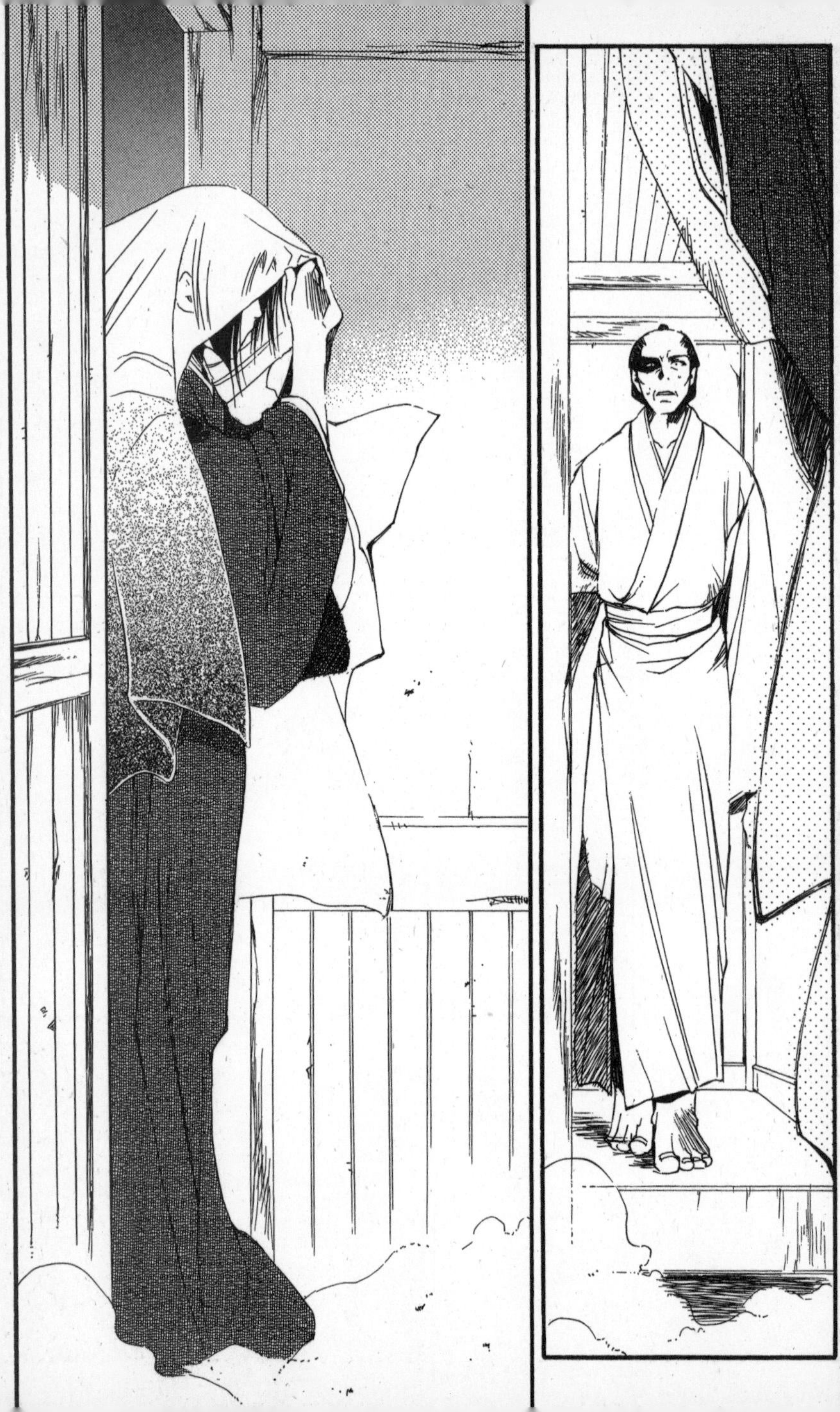

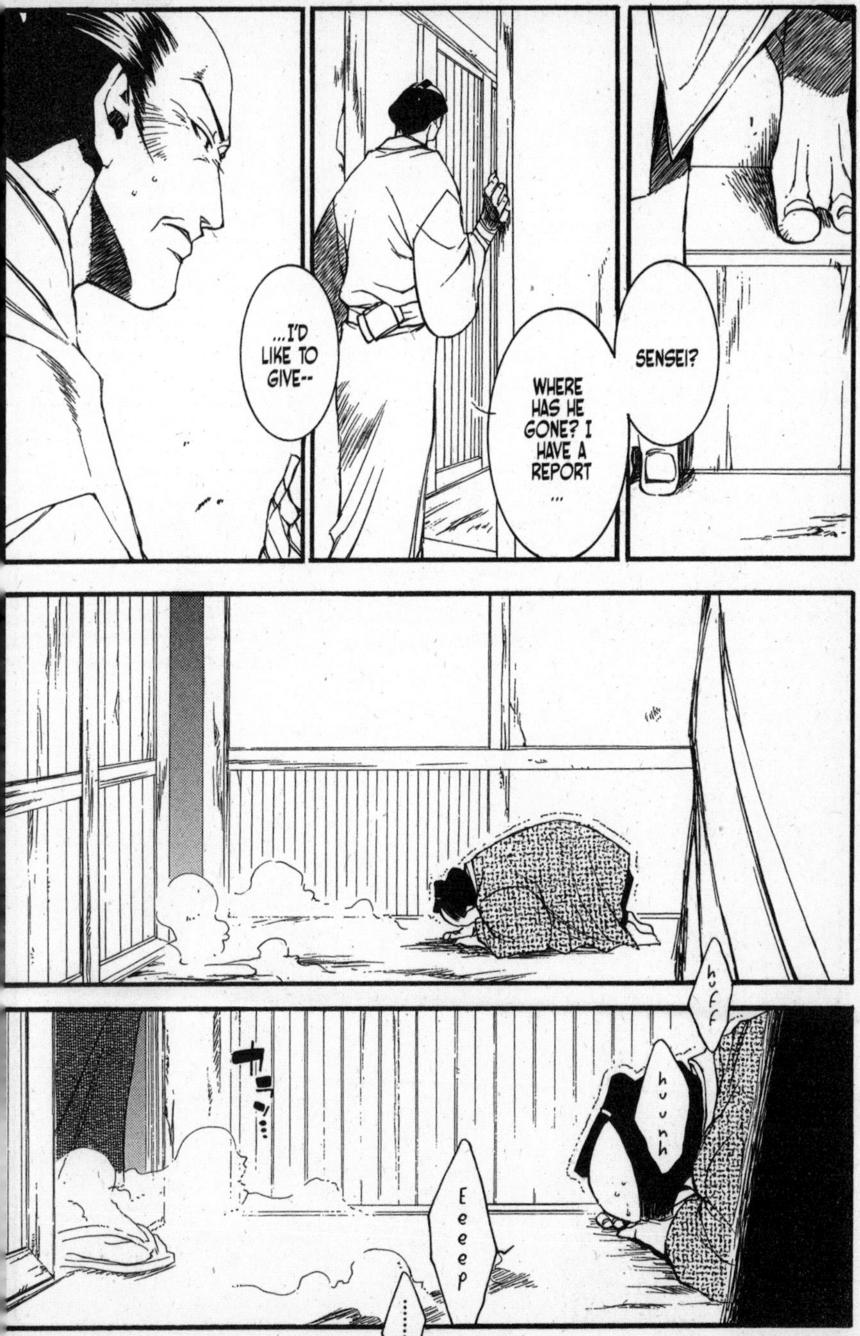
SENSEI?
WHERE HAS HE GONE? I HAVE A REPORT ...
...I'D LIKE TO GIVE--
huff
huunh
Eeeep
....

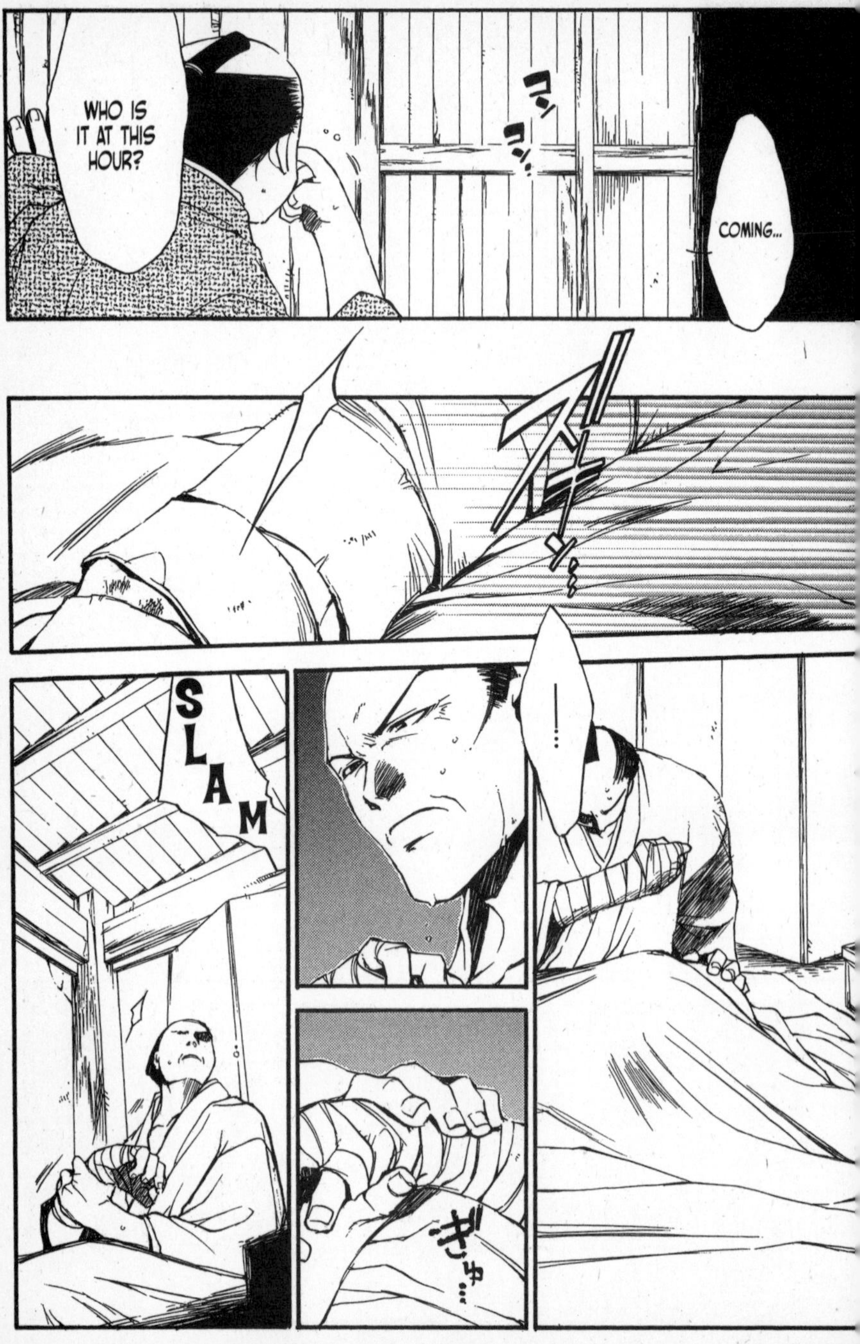
COMING...
コン コン...
WHO IS IT AT THIS HOUR?
ズキッ...
...!
ぎゅ...
SLAM

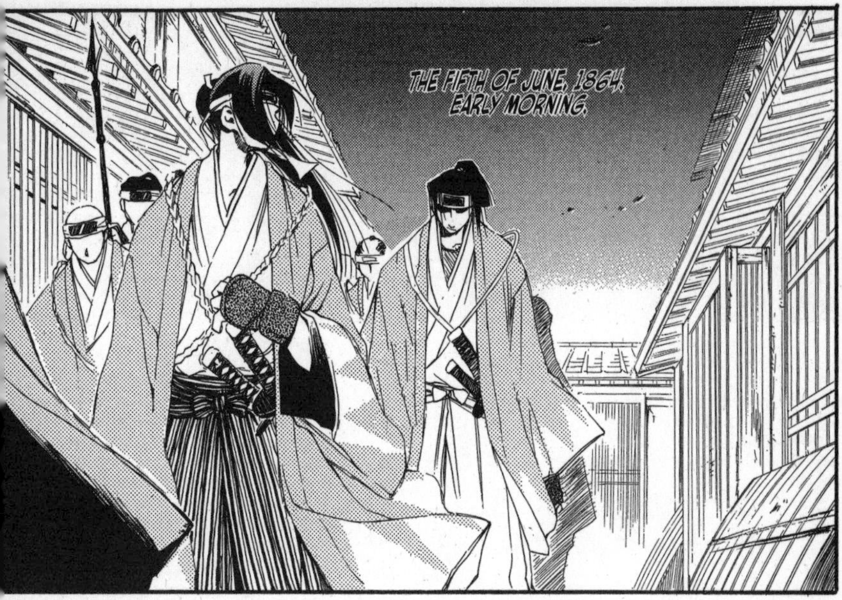
THE FIFTH OF JUNE, 1864, EARLY MORNING.

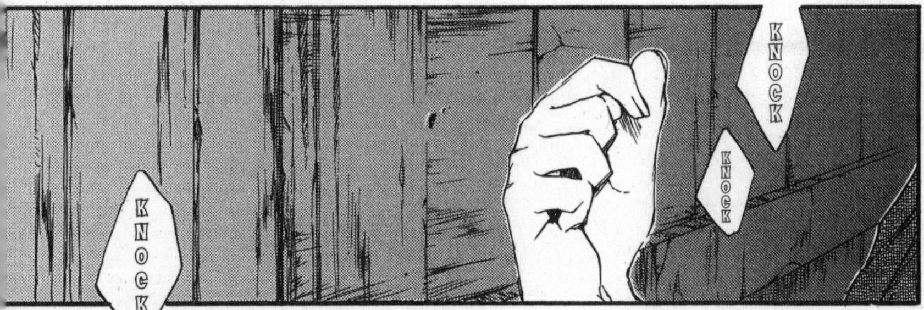
KNOCK
KNOCK
KNOCK

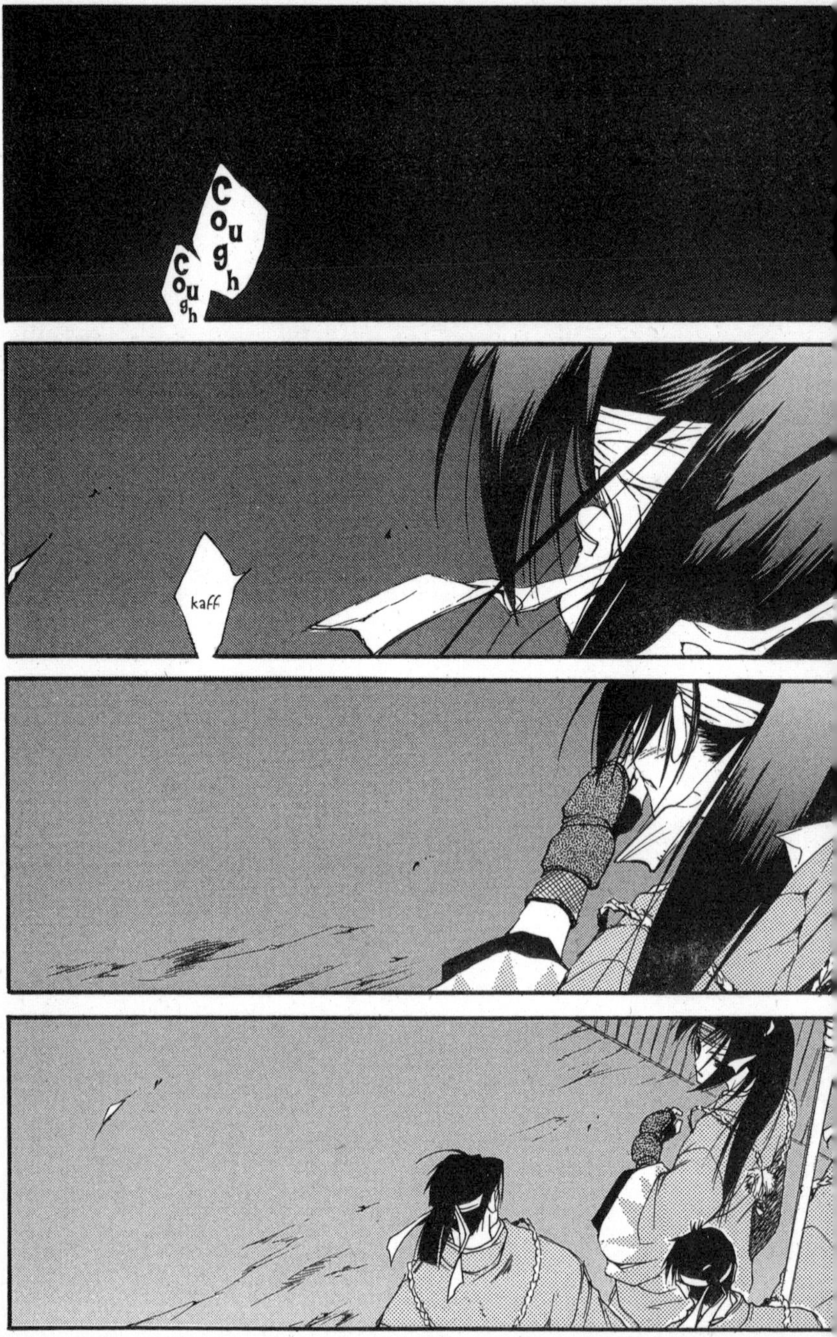
Cough
Cough
kaff

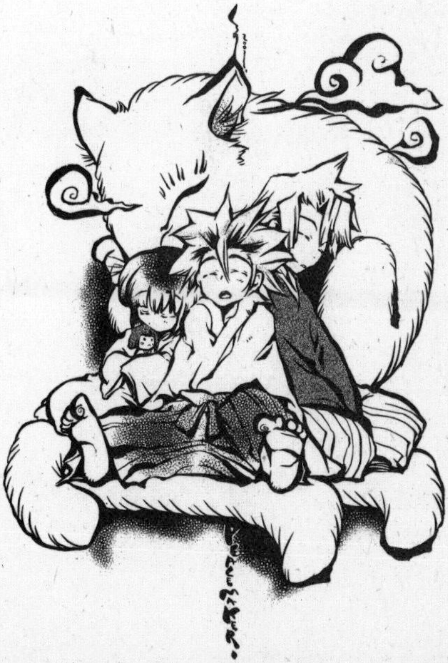
PEACEMAKER.

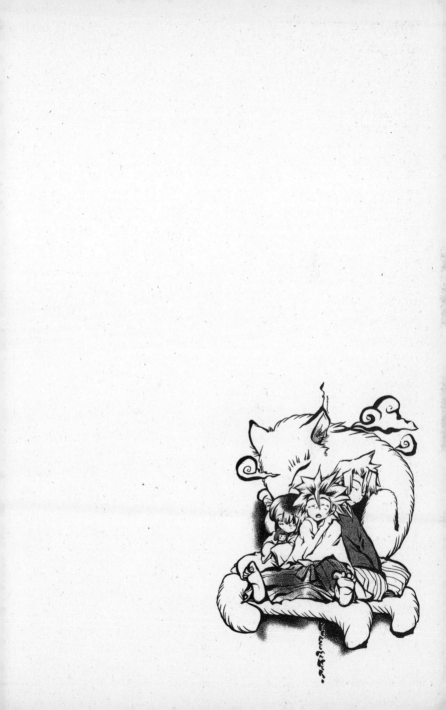

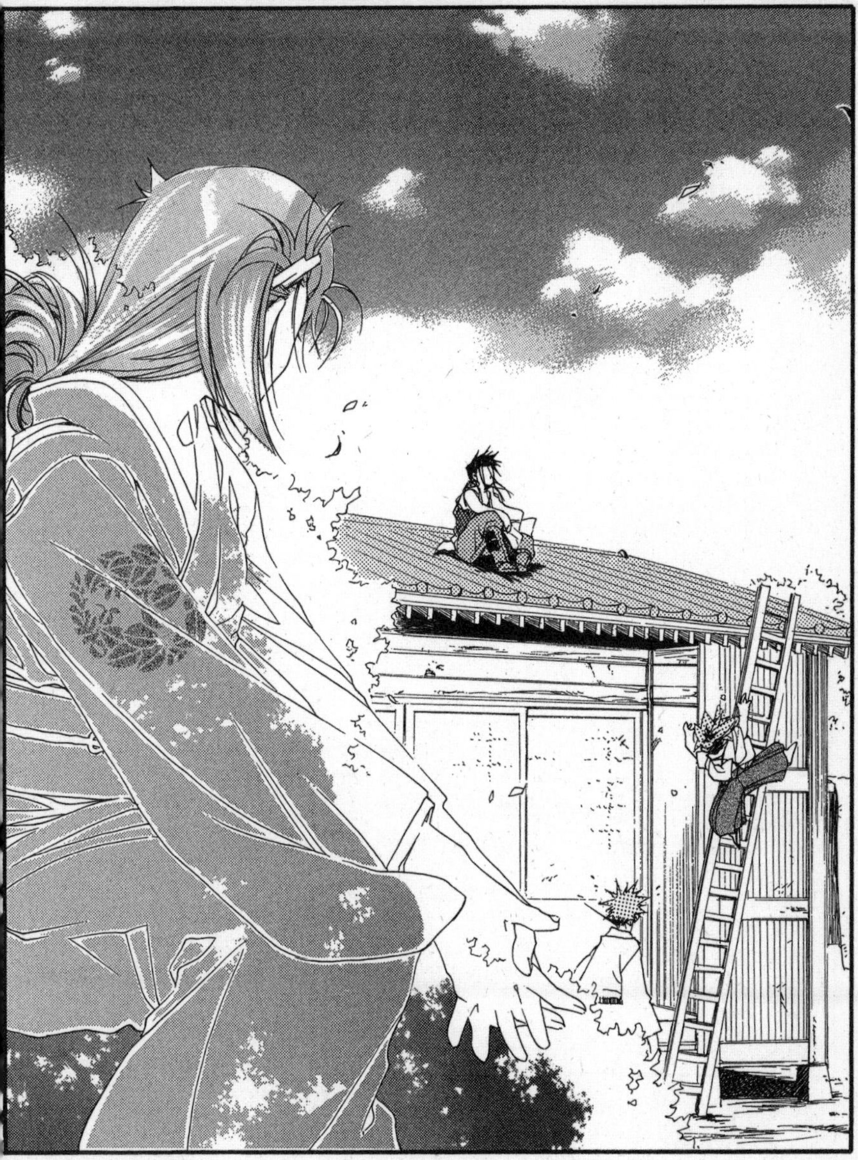

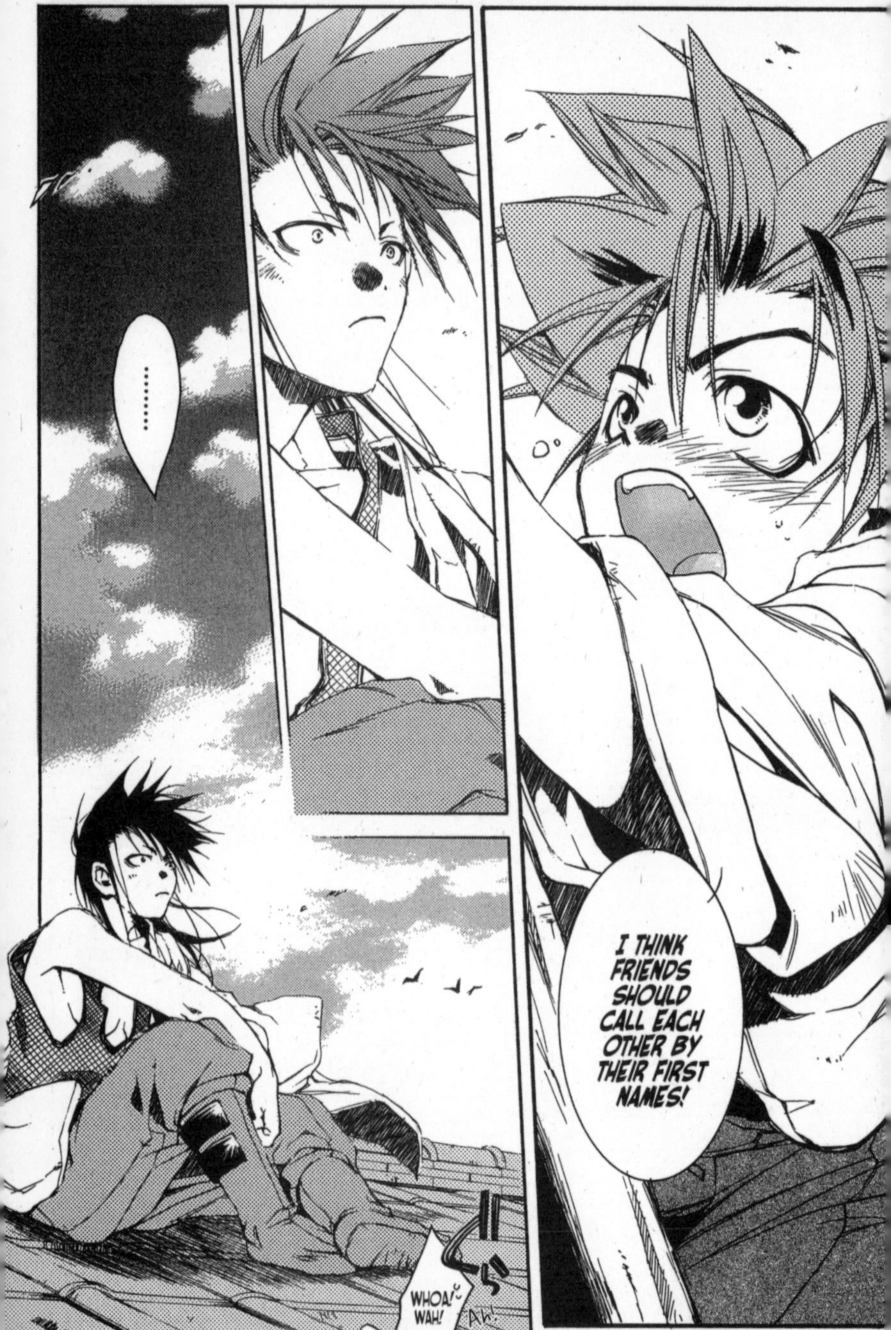
I THINK FRIENDS SHOULD CALL EACH OTHER BY THEIR FIRST NAMES!
......
WHOA! WAH!
Ah!

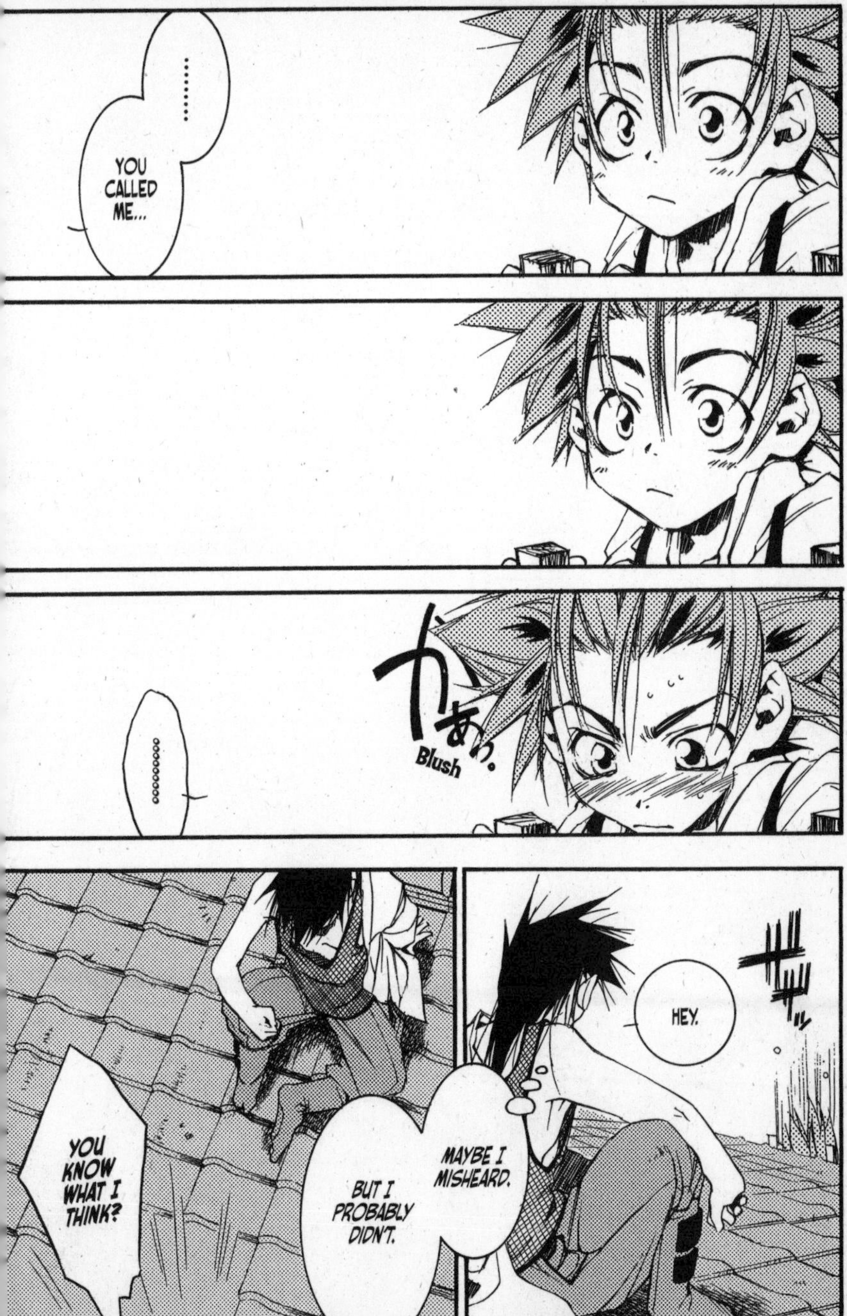
......
YOU CALLED ME...
Blush
......
HEY.
MAYBE I MISHEARD.
BUT I PROBABLY DIDN'T.
YOU KNOW WHAT I THINK?

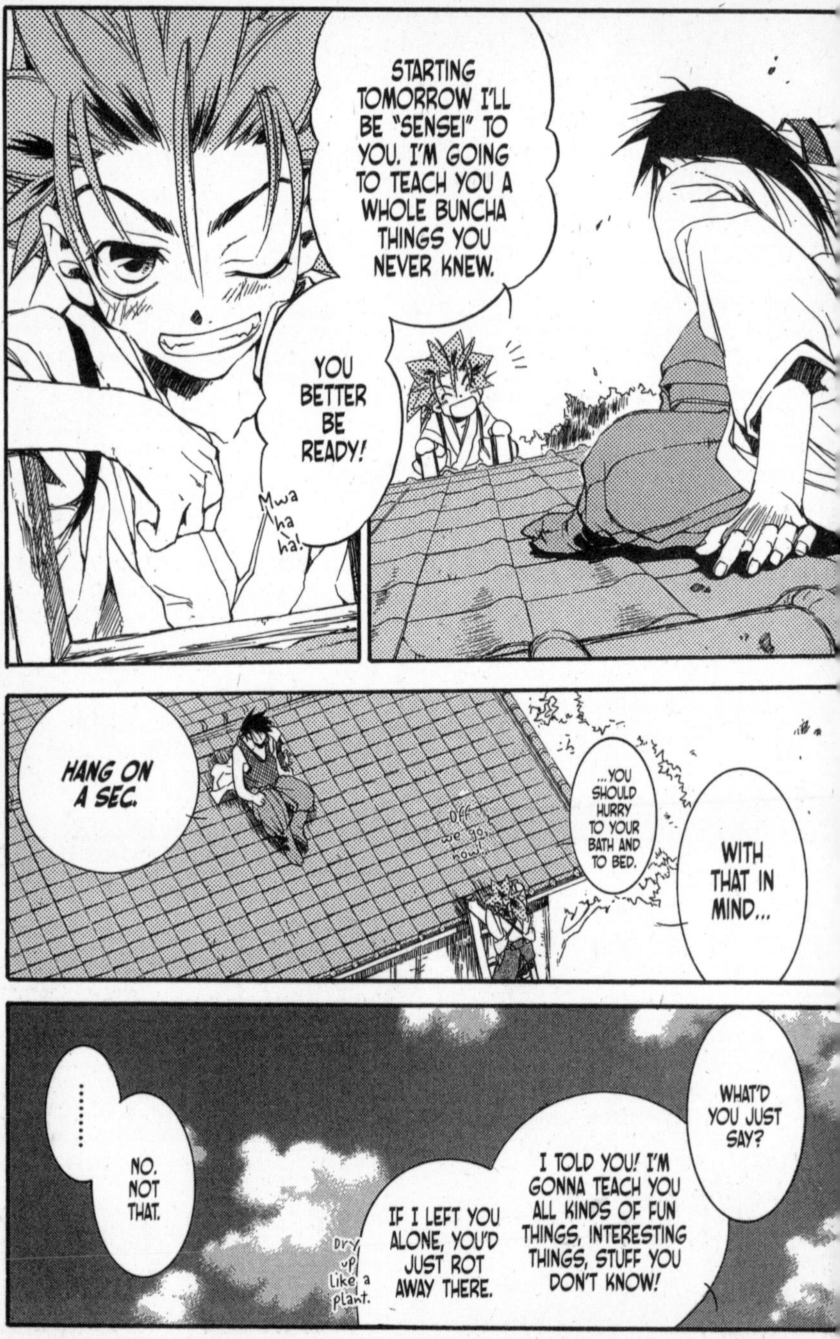
STARTING TOMORROW I'LL BE "SENSEI" TO YOU. I'M GOING TO TEACH YOU A WHOLE BUNCHA THINGS YOU NEVER KNEW.
YOU BETTER BE READY!
Mwa ha ha!
WITH THAT IN MIND...
...YOU SHOULD HURRY TO YOUR BATH AND TO BED.
Off we go, now!
HANG ON A SEC.
WHAT'D YOU JUST SAY?
I TOLD YOU! I'M GONNA TEACH YOU ALL KINDS OF FUN THINGS, INTERESTING THINGS, STUFF YOU DON'T KNOW!
IF I LEFT YOU ALONE, YOU'D JUST ROT AWAY THERE.
Dry up like a plant.
NO. NOT THAT.
......

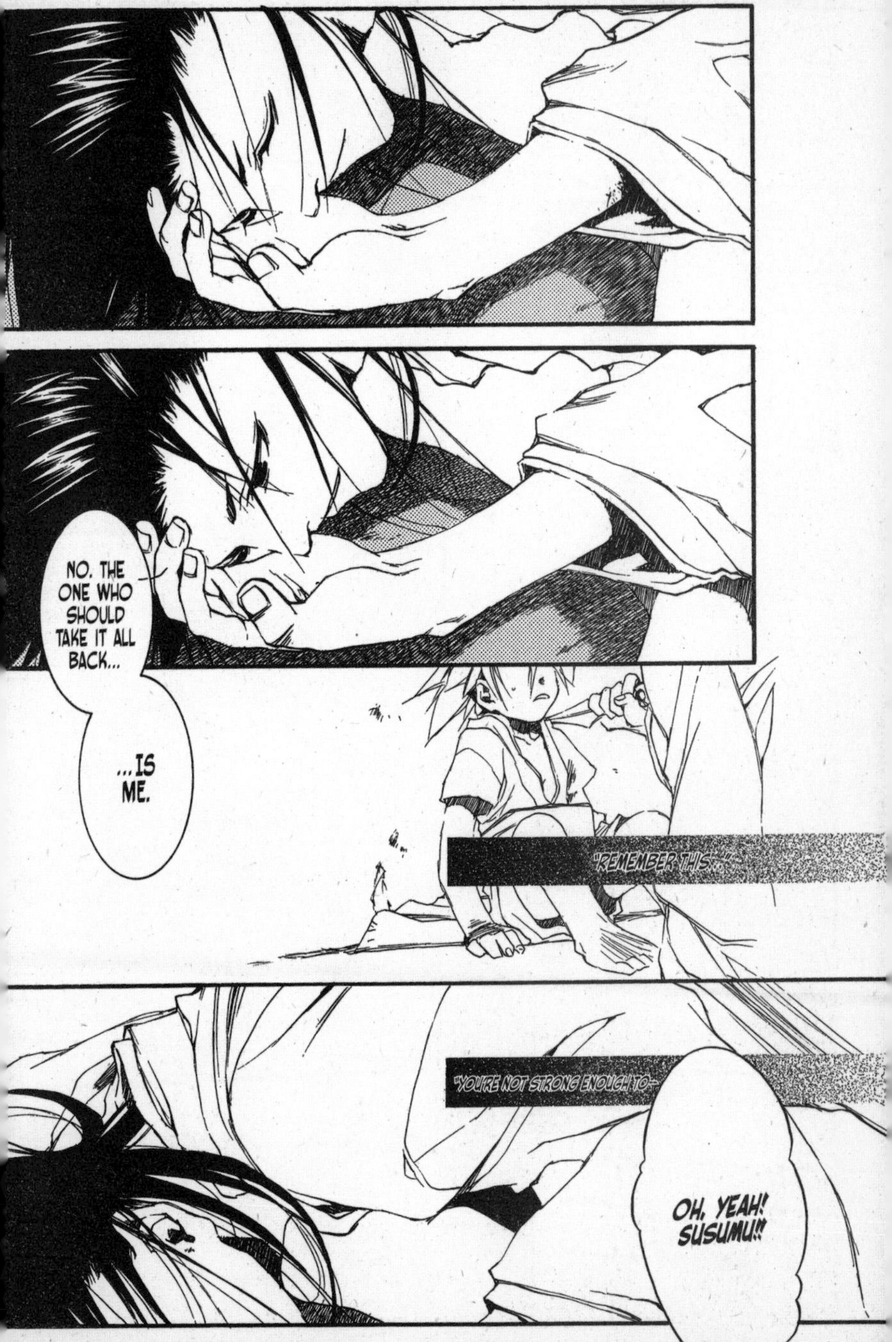
NO. THE ONE WHO SHOULD TAKE IT ALL BACK...
...IS ME.
"REMEMBER THIS..."
"YOU'RE NOT STRONG ENOUGH TO--"
OH, YEAH! SUSUMU!!

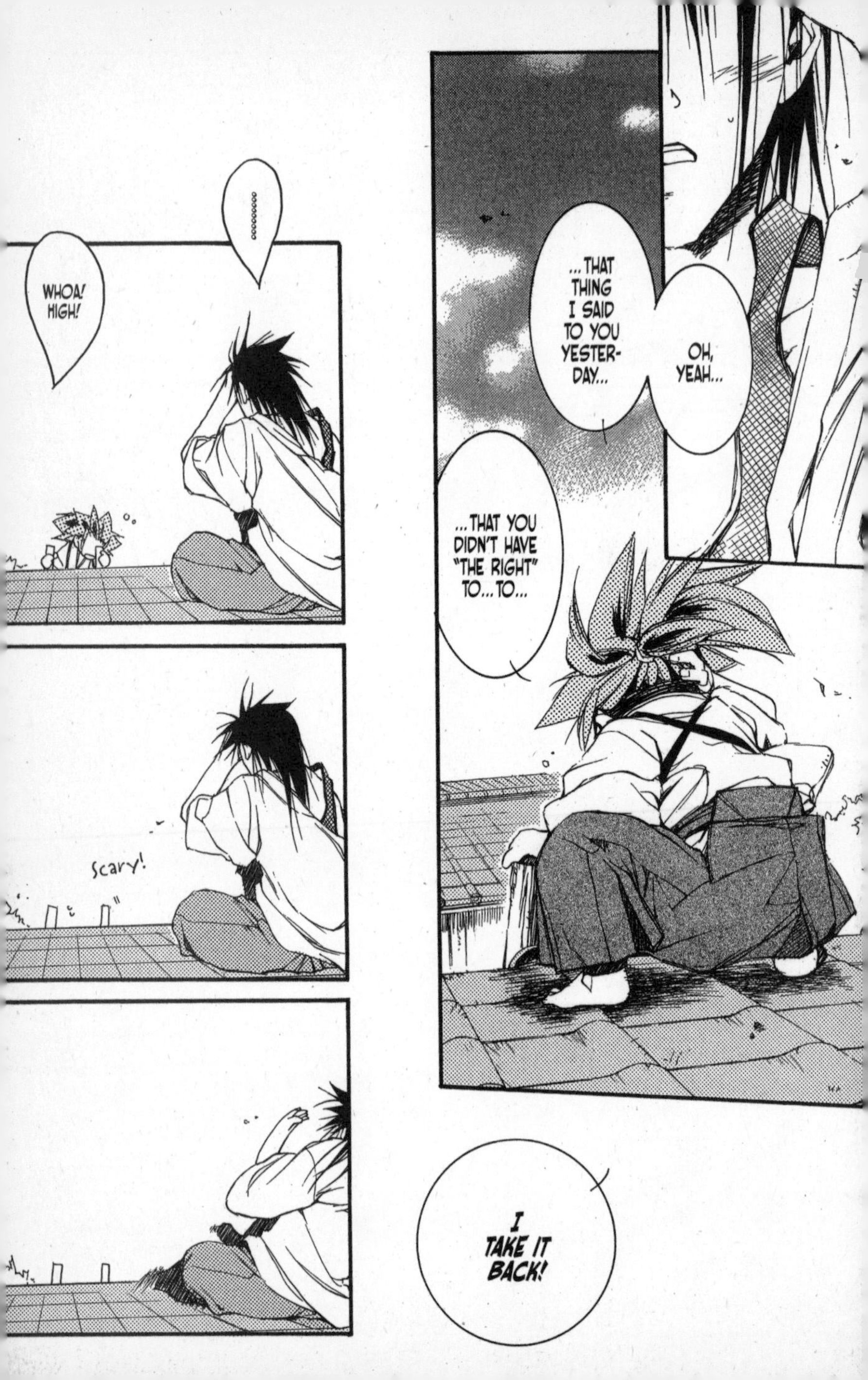

OH, YEAH...
...THAT THING I SAID TO YOU YESTER-DAY...
...THAT YOU DIDN'T HAVE "THE RIGHT" TO...TO...
I TAKE IT BACK!
....
WHOA! HIGH!
Scary!

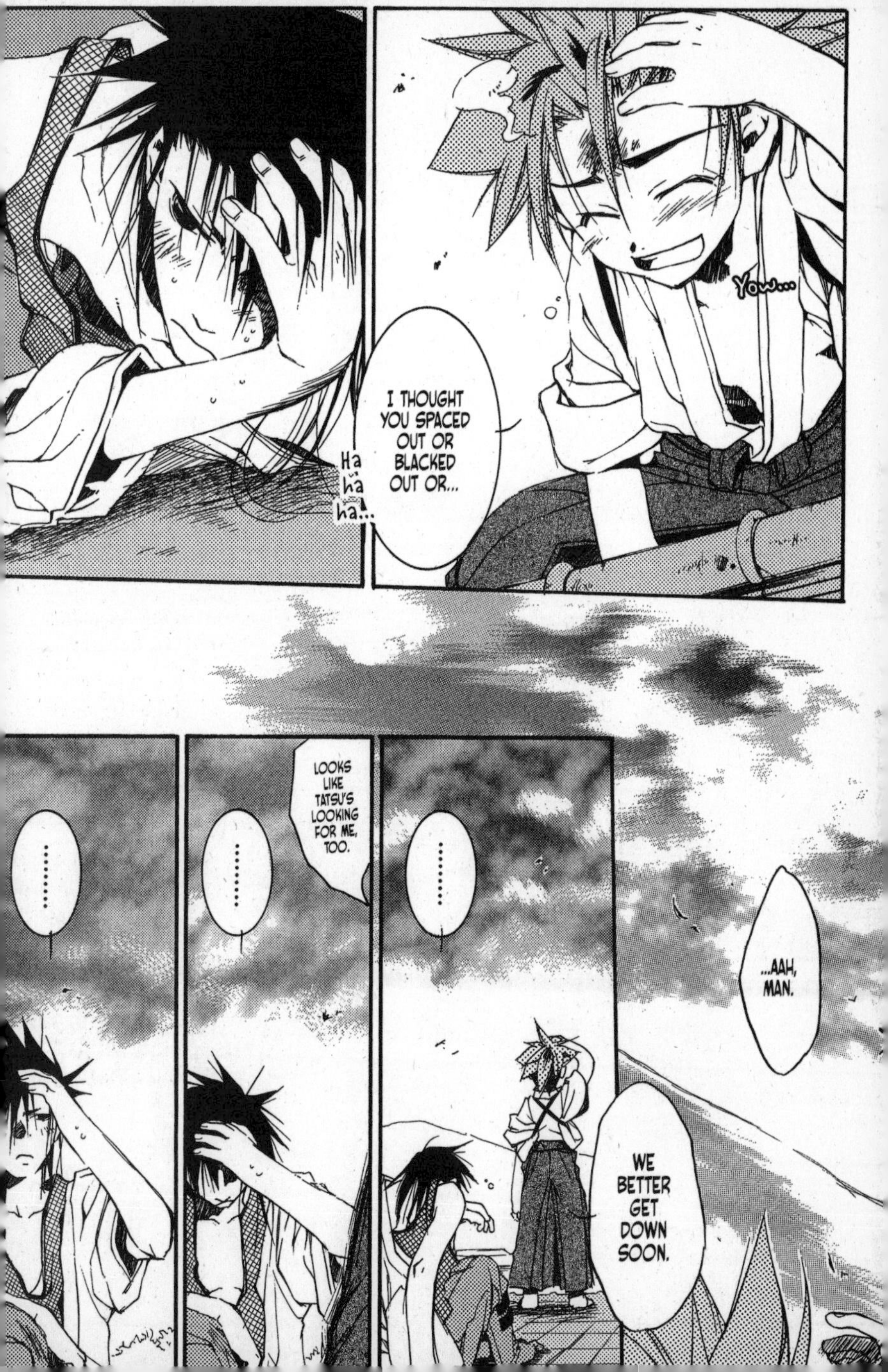
Yow...
I THOUGHT YOU SPACED OUT OR BLACKED OUT OR...
Ha ha ha...
...AAH, MAN.
WE BETTER GET DOWN SOON.
......
LOOKS LIKE TATSU'S LOOKING FOR ME, TOO.
......
......

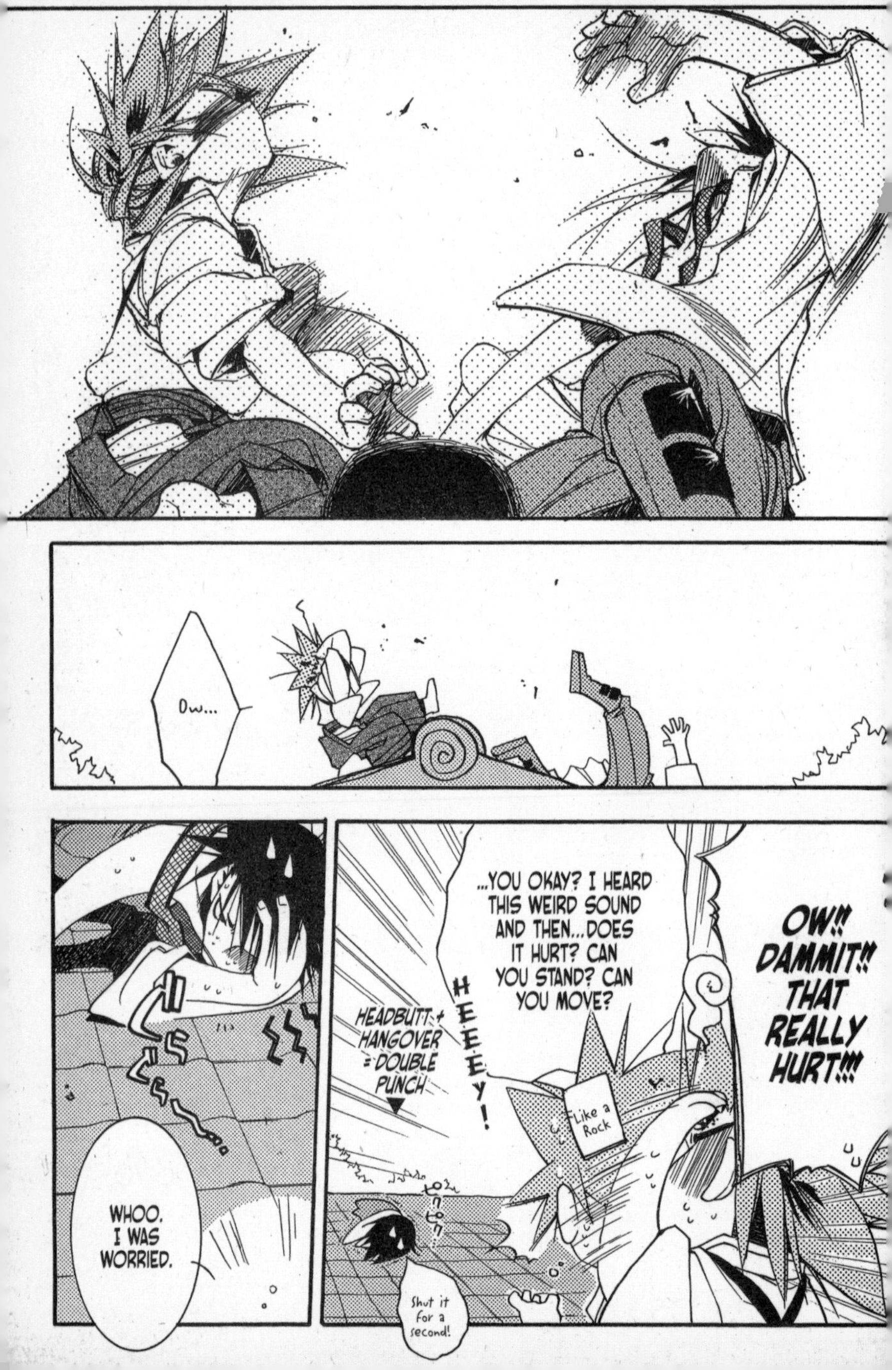
Ow...
OW!! DAMMIT!! THAT REALLY HURT!!!
...YOU OKAY? I HEARD THIS WEIRD SOUND AND THEN...DOES IT HURT? CAN YOU STAND? CAN YOU MOVE?
Like a Rock
HEEEEY!
HEADBUTT + HANGOVER = DOUBLE PUNCH
Shut it for a second!
WHOO. I WAS WORRIED.

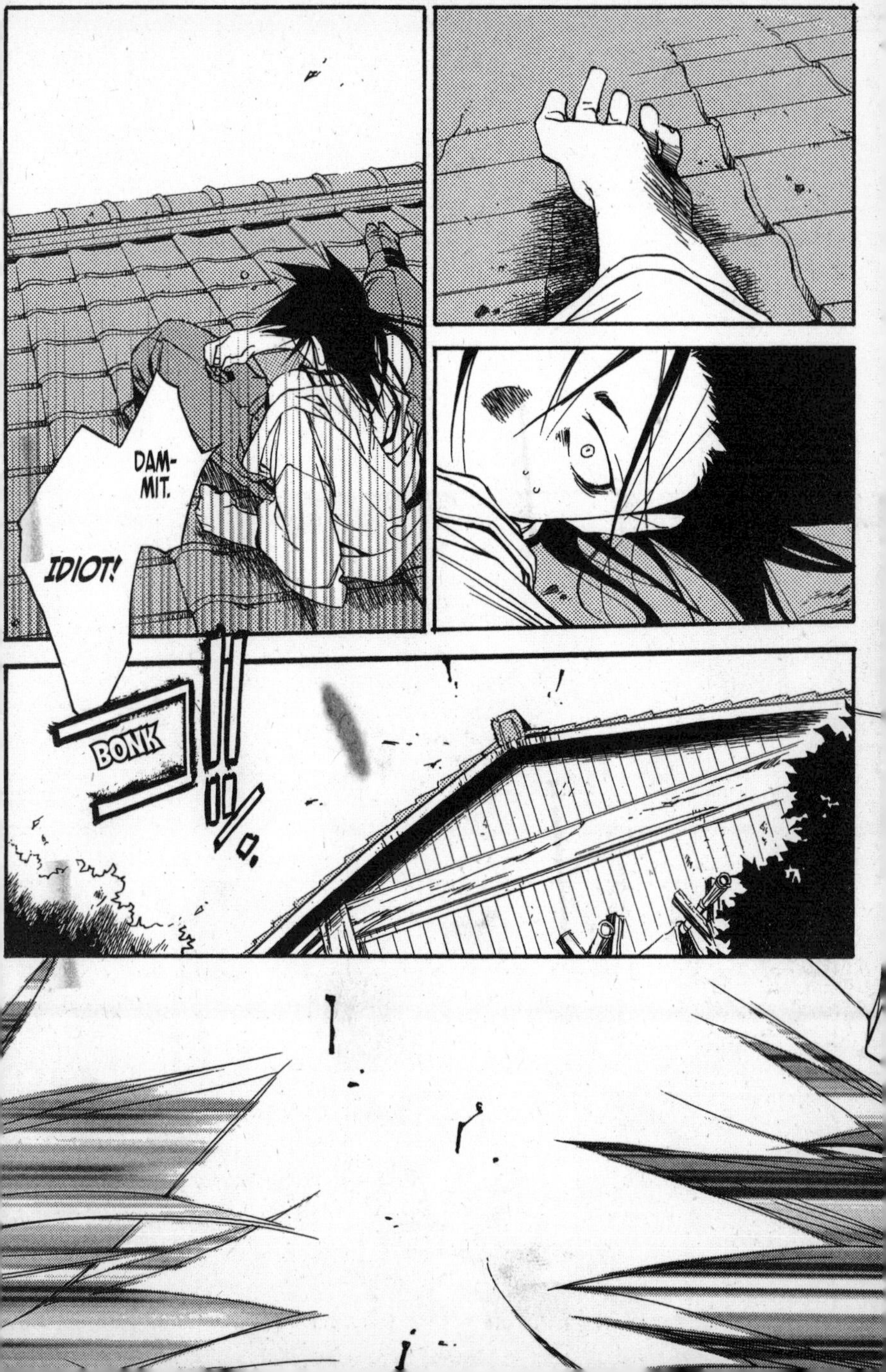
DAM-
MIT.
IDIOT!
BONK

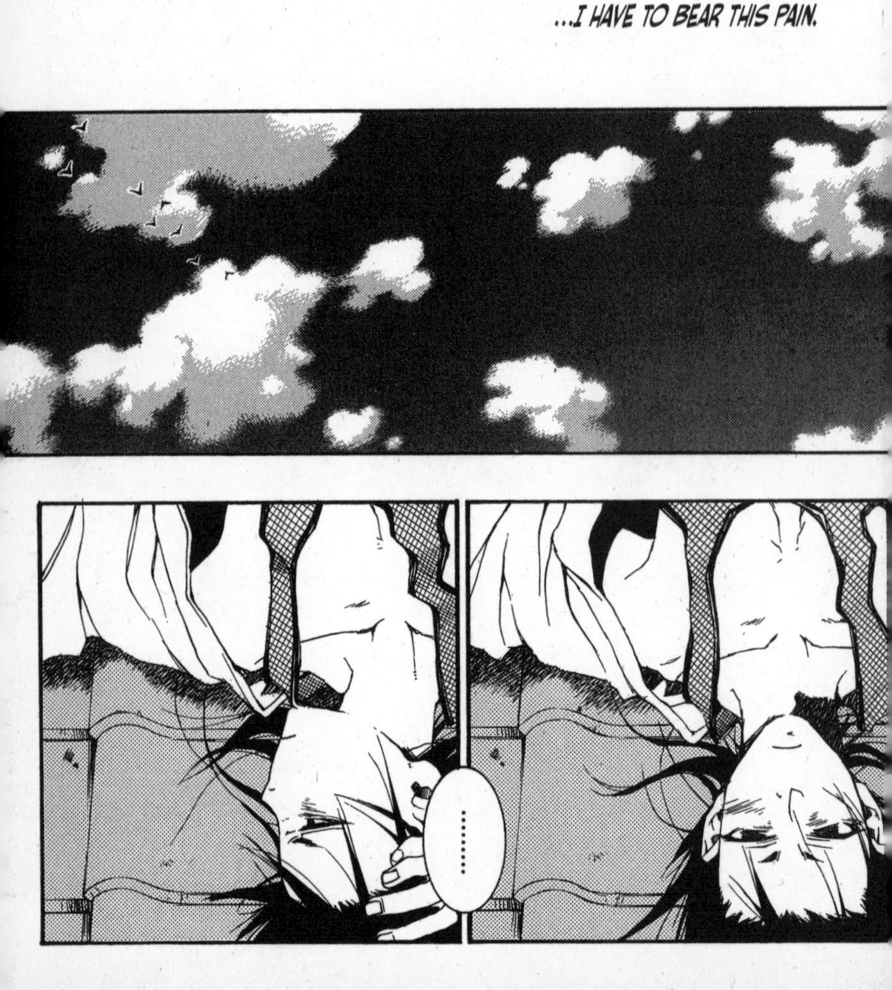
...I HAVE TO BEAR THIS PAIN.
....

AT LEAST UNTIL I STOP CRYING...

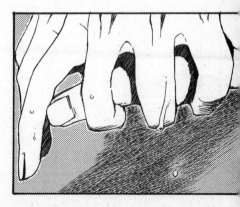

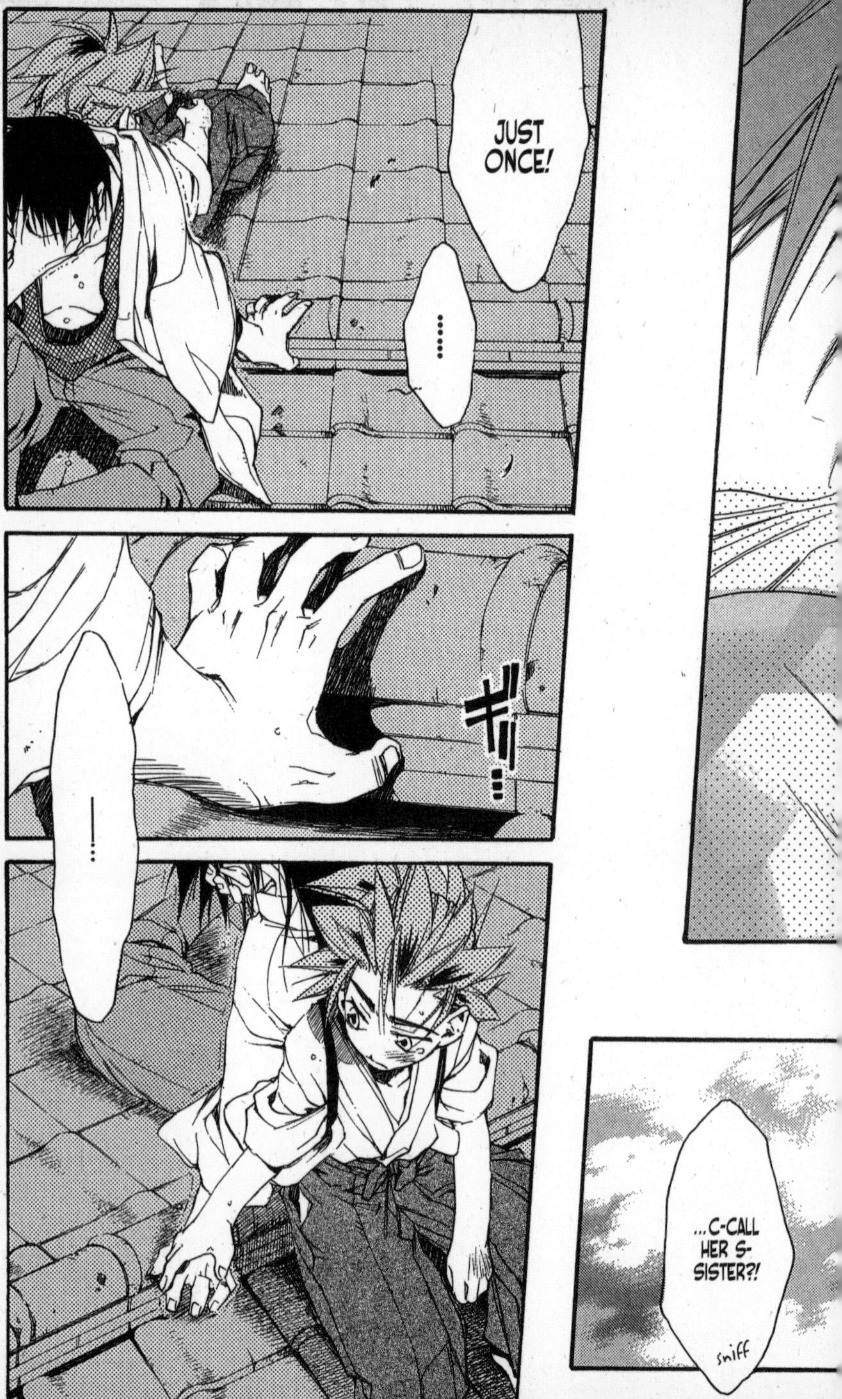
JUST ONCE!
......
ギリ...
......
...C-CALL HER S-SISTER?!
sniff

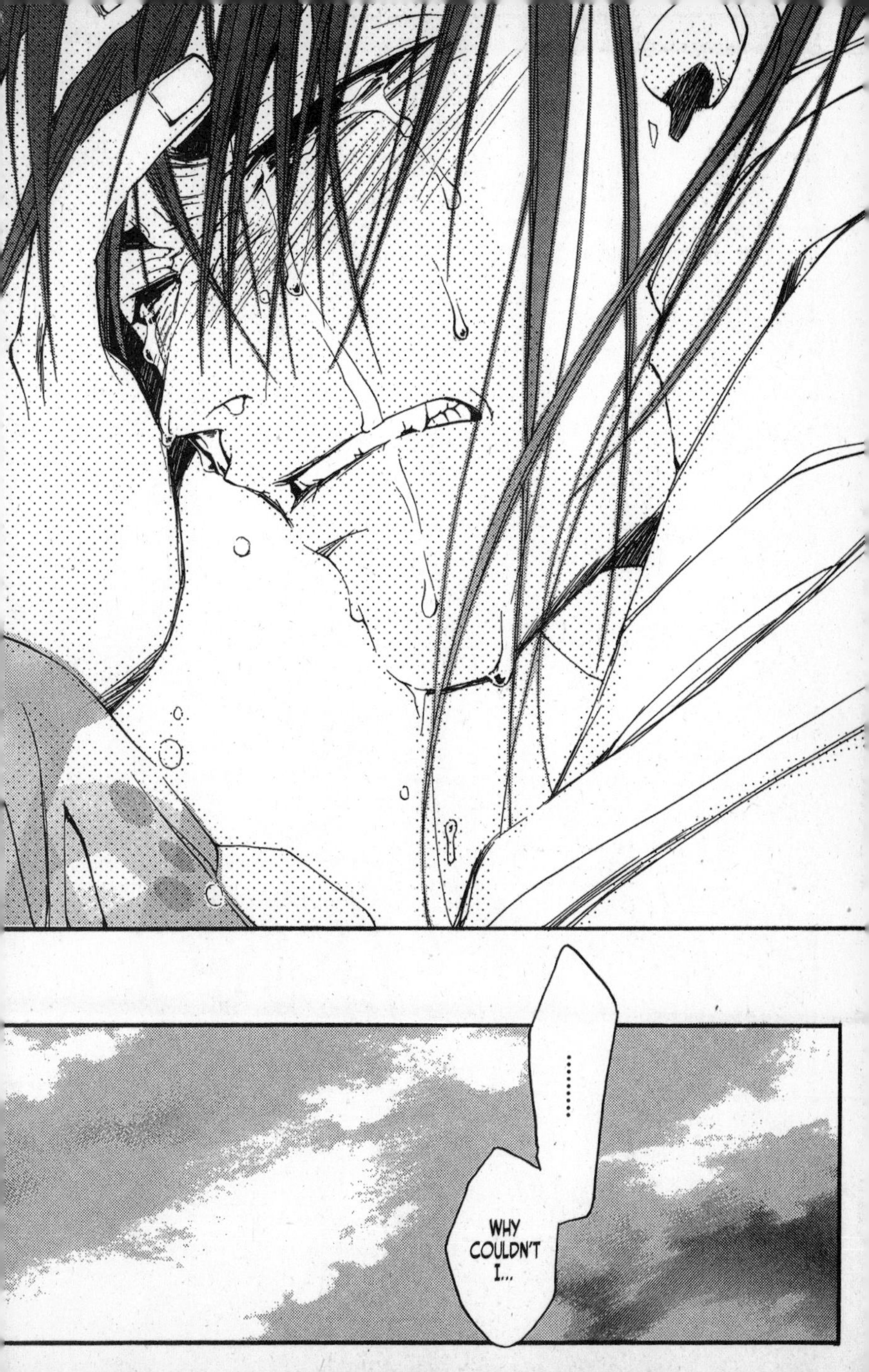
......
WHY COULDN'T I...

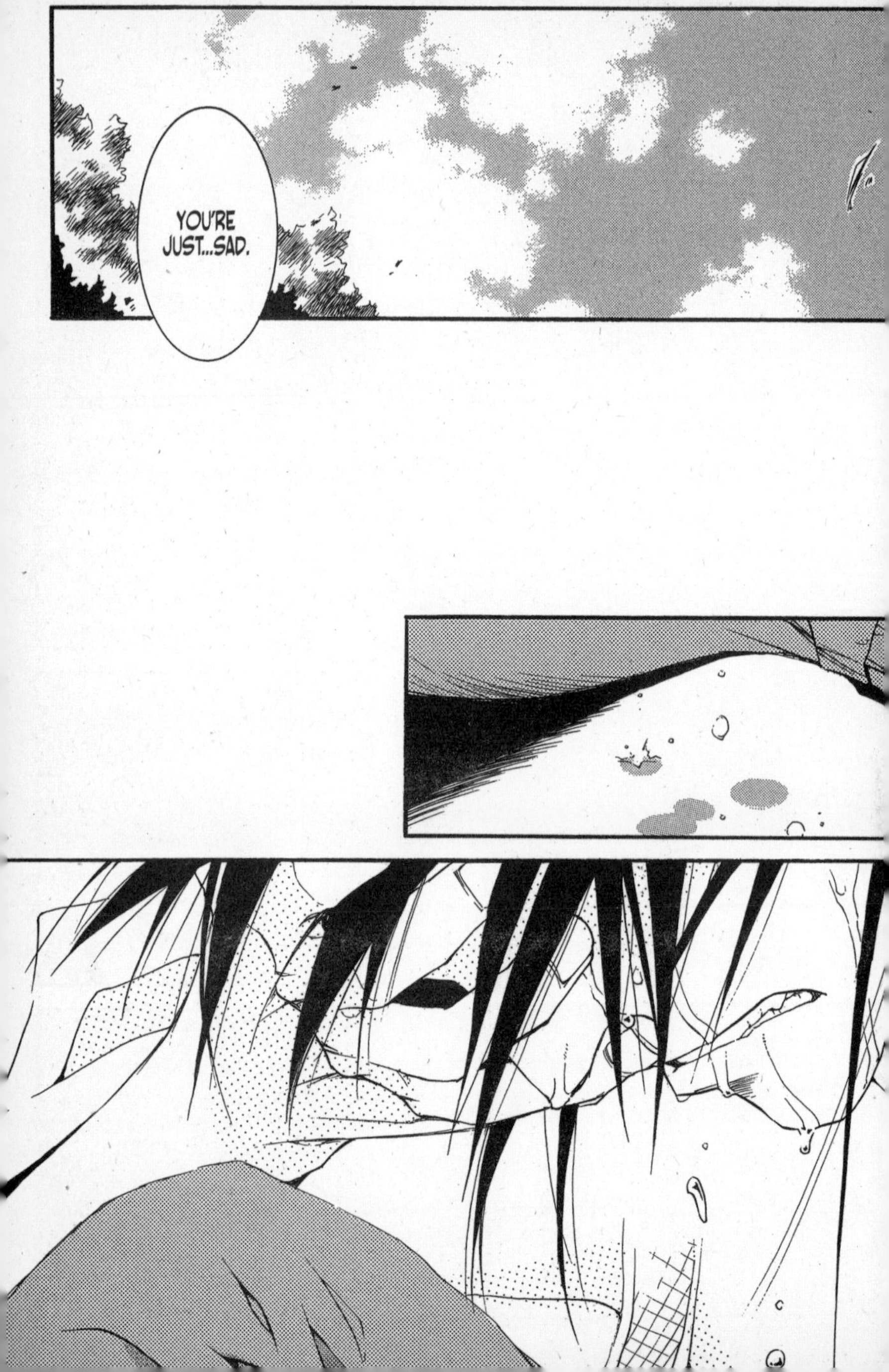
YOU'RE JUST...SAD.

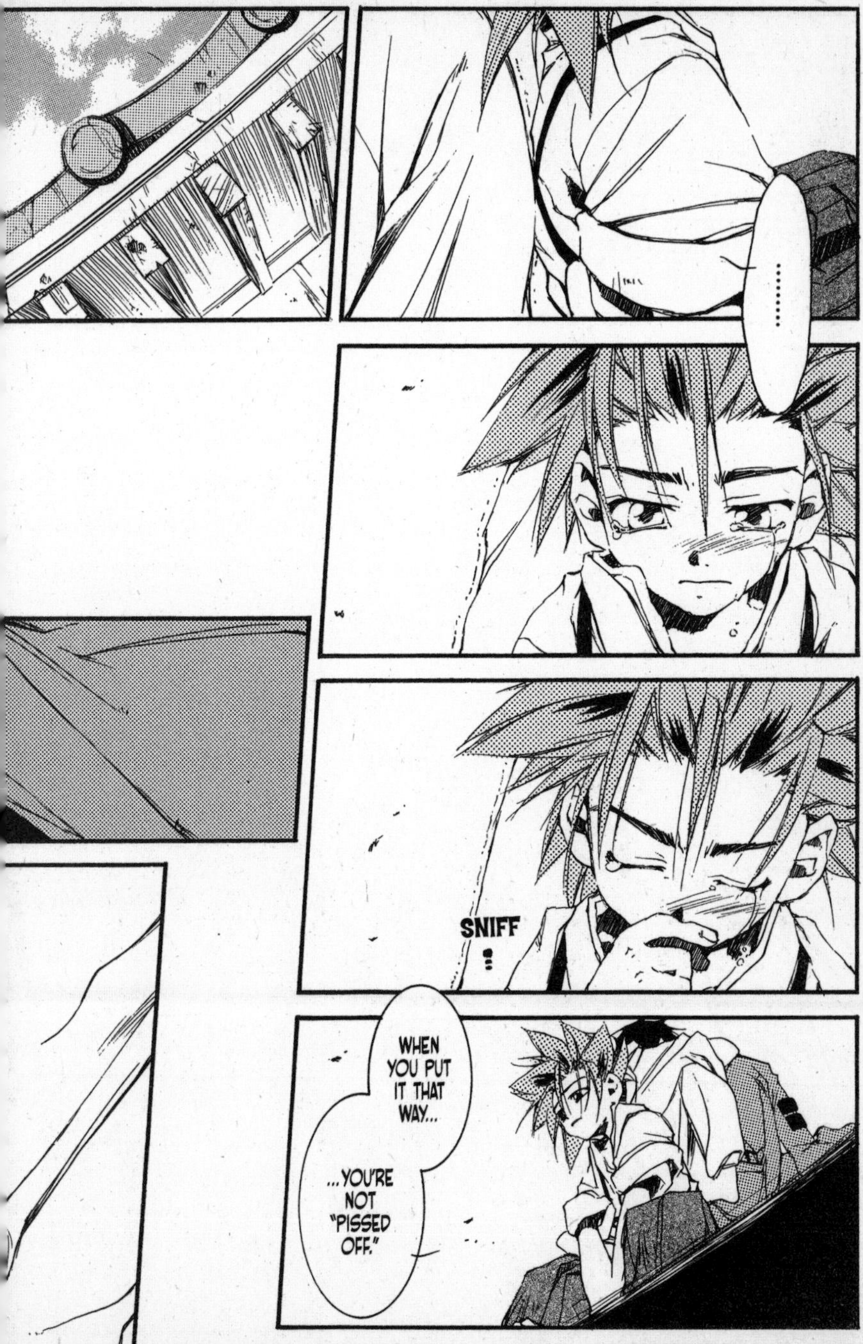
......
SNIFF
WHEN YOU PUT IT THAT WAY...
...YOU'RE NOT "PISSED OFF."

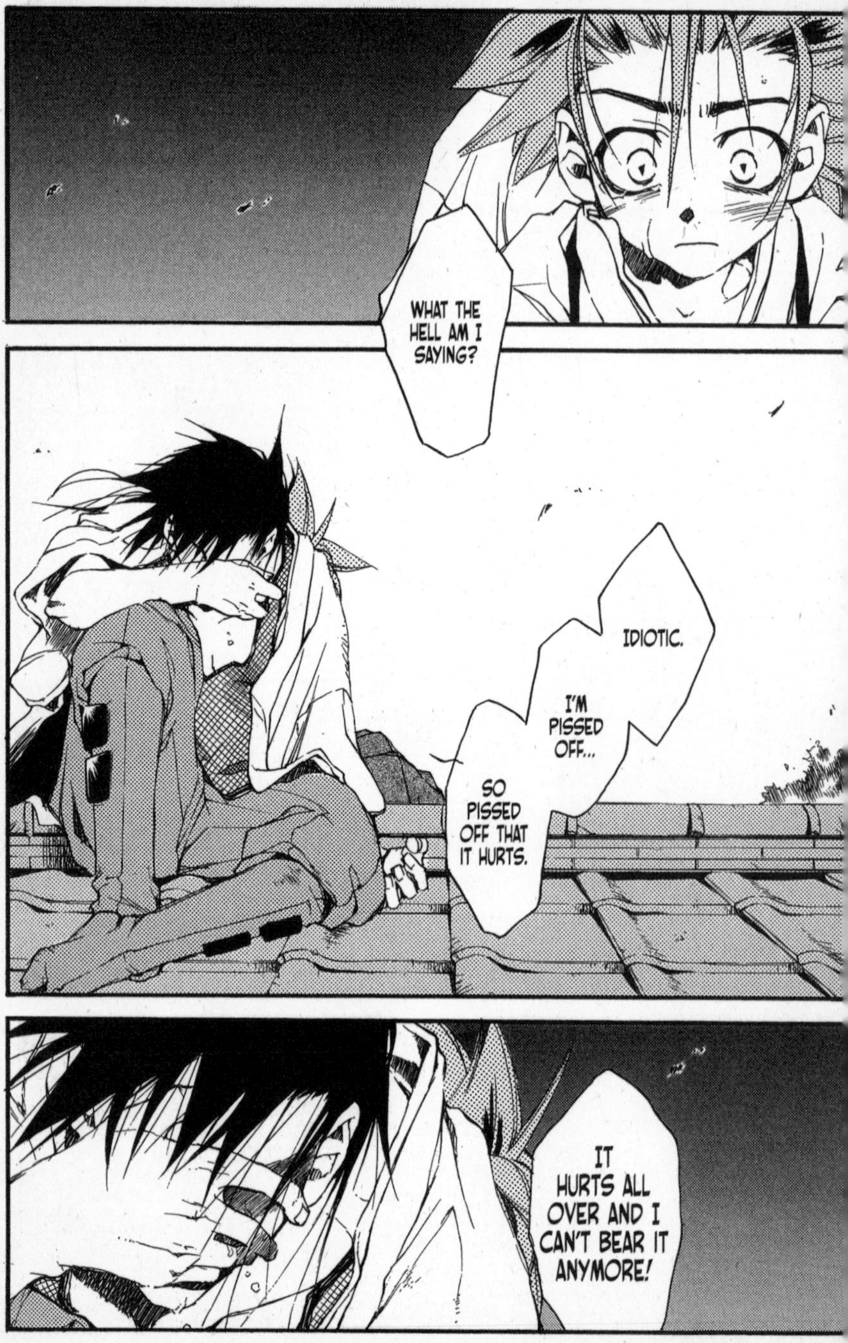
WHAT THE HELL AM I SAYING?
IDIOTIC.
I'M PISSED OFF...
SO PISSED OFF THAT IT HURTS.
IT HURTS ALL OVER AND I CAN'T BEAR IT ANYMORE!

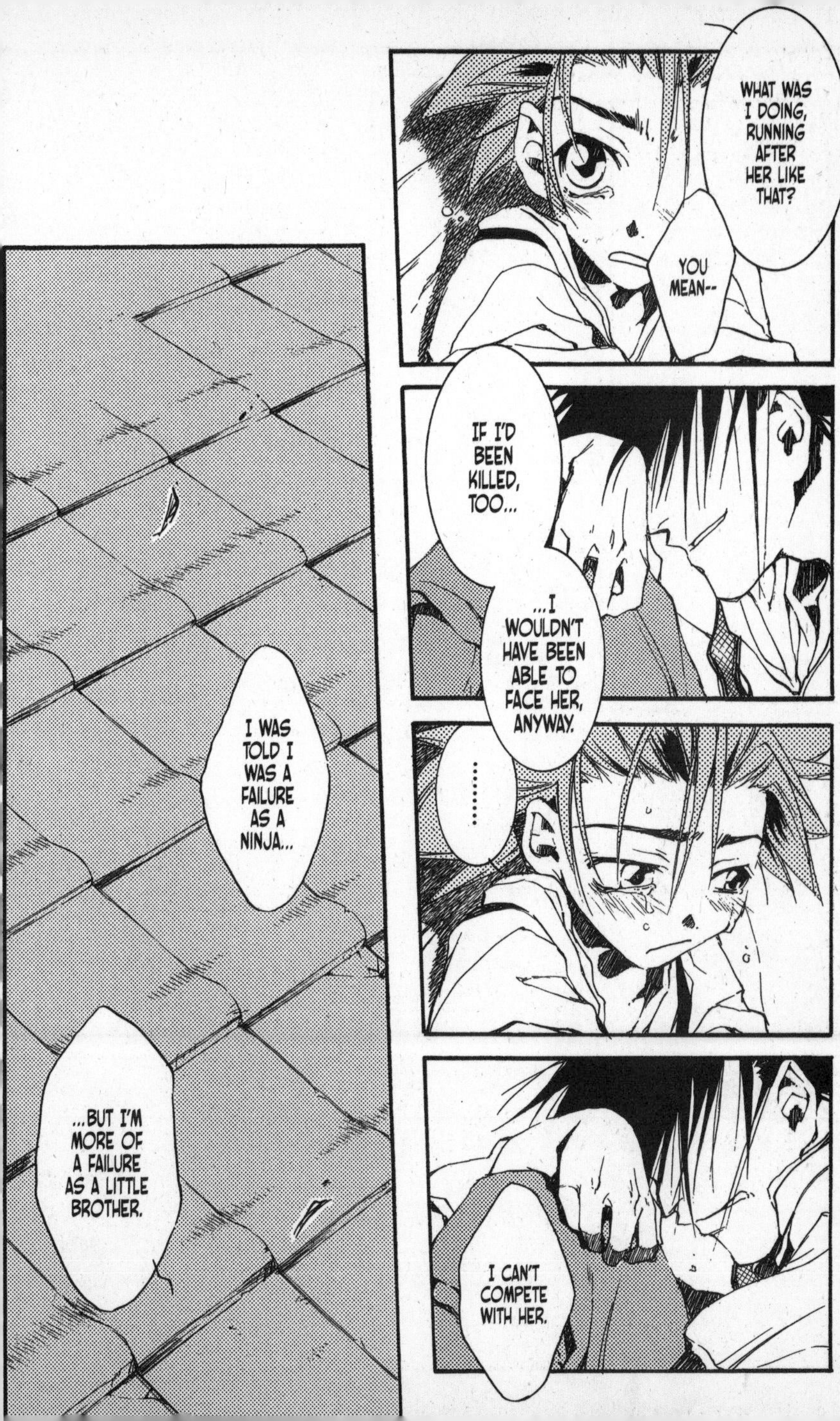
WHAT WAS I DOING, RUNNING AFTER HER LIKE THAT?
YOU MEAN--
IF I'D BEEN KILLED, TOO...
...I WOULDN'T HAVE BEEN ABLE TO FACE HER, ANYWAY.
....
I CAN'T COMPETE WITH HER.
I WAS TOLD I WAS A FAILURE AS A NINJA...
...BUT I'M MORE OF A FAILURE AS A LITTLE BROTHER.

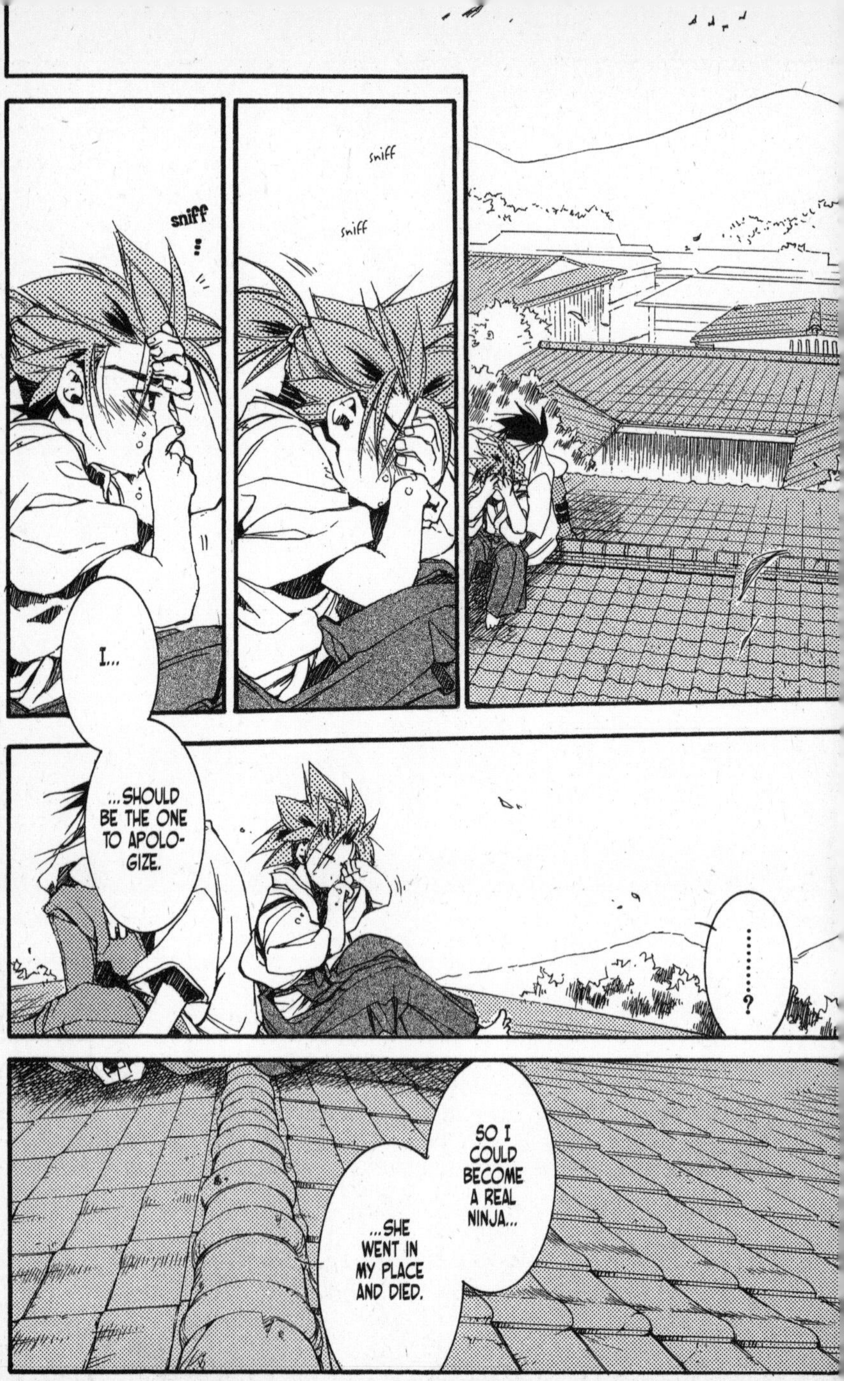
sniff
sniff
sniff
...
I...
......?
...SHOULD BE THE ONE TO APOLOGIZE.
SO I COULD BECOME A REAL NINJA...
...SHE WENT IN MY PLACE AND DIED.

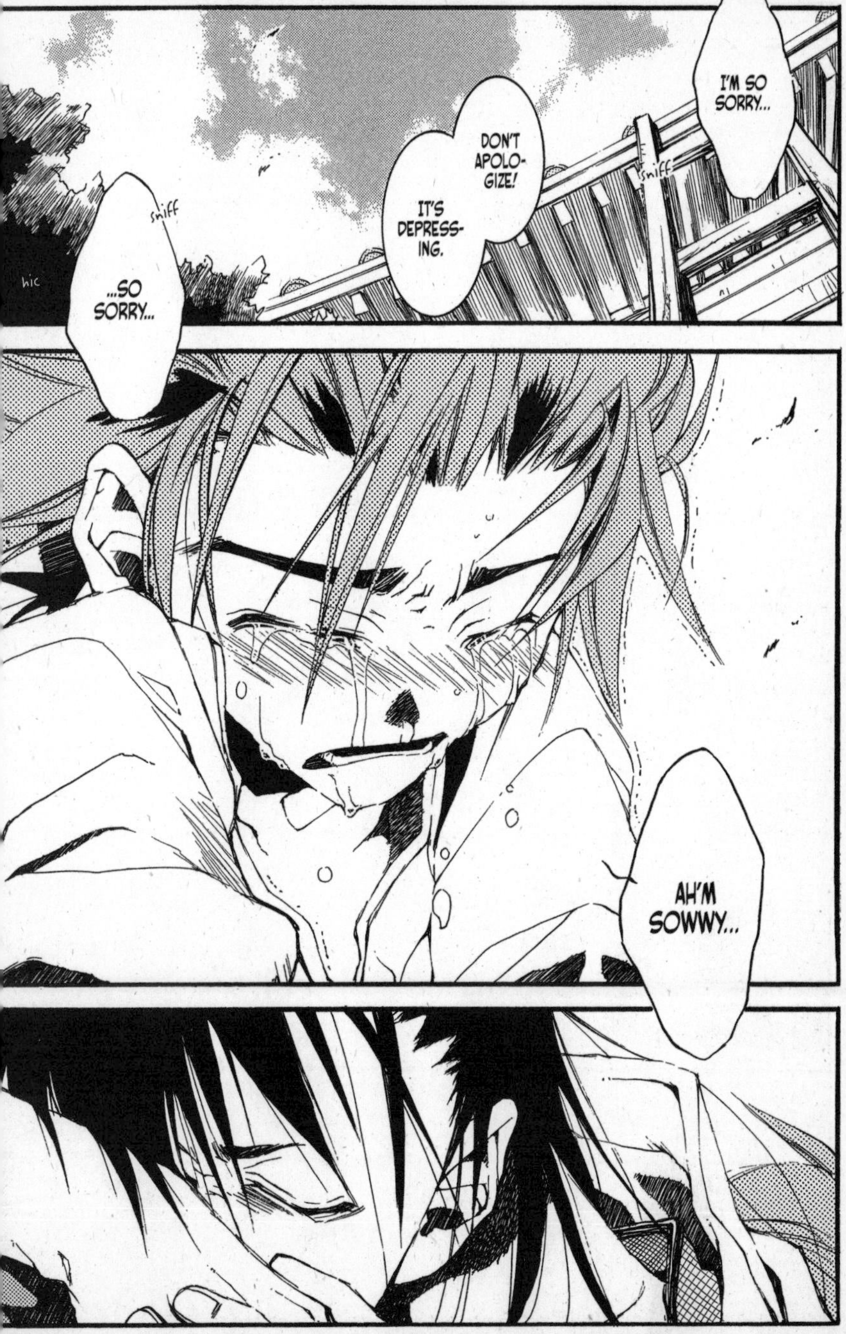
I'M SO SORRY...
sniff
DON'T APOLOGIZE!
IT'S DEPRESSING.
sniff
...SO SORRY...
hic
AH'M SOWWY...

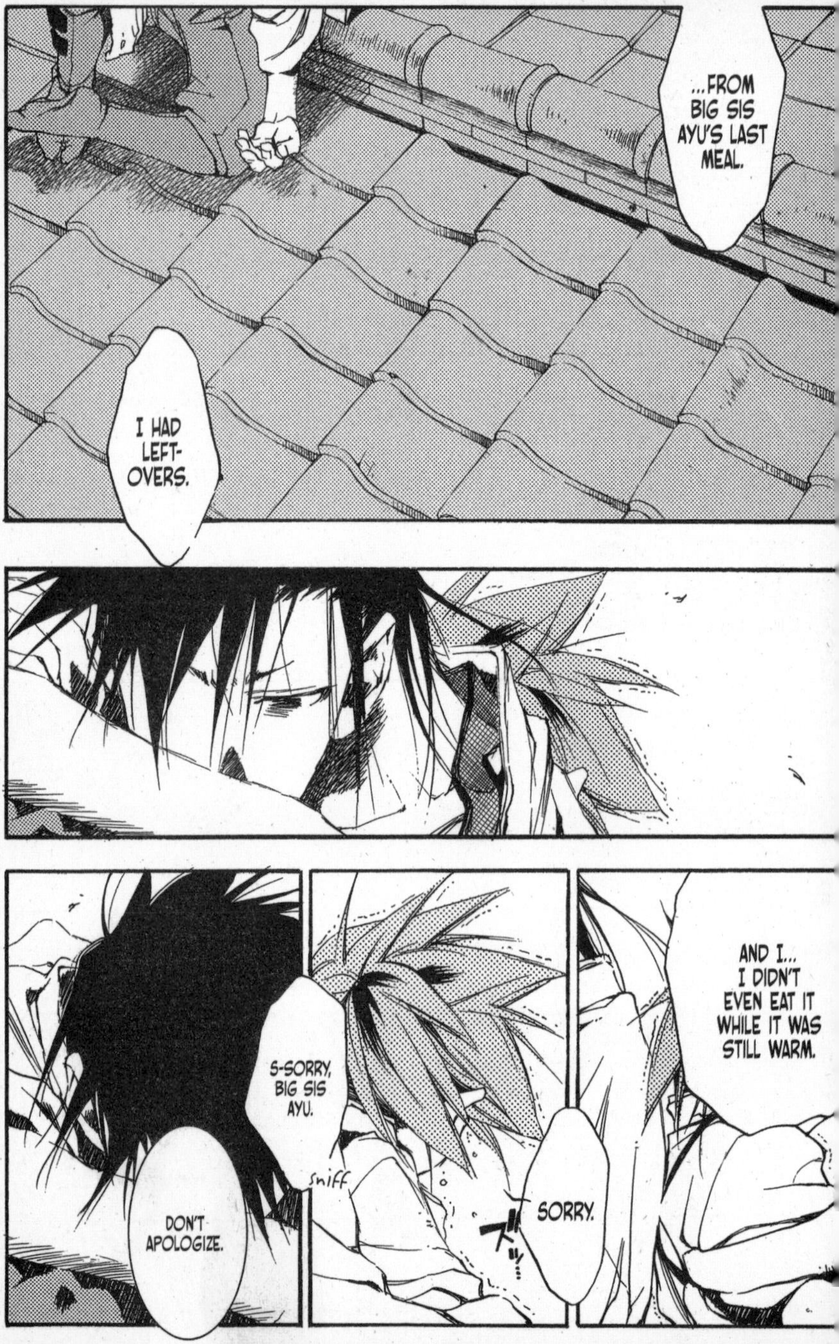
...FROM BIG SIS AYU'S LAST MEAL.
I HAD LEFT-OVERS.
AND I... I DIDN'T EVEN EAT IT WHILE IT WAS STILL WARM.
SORRY.
S-SORRY, BIG SIS AYU.
sniff
DON'T APOLOGIZE.

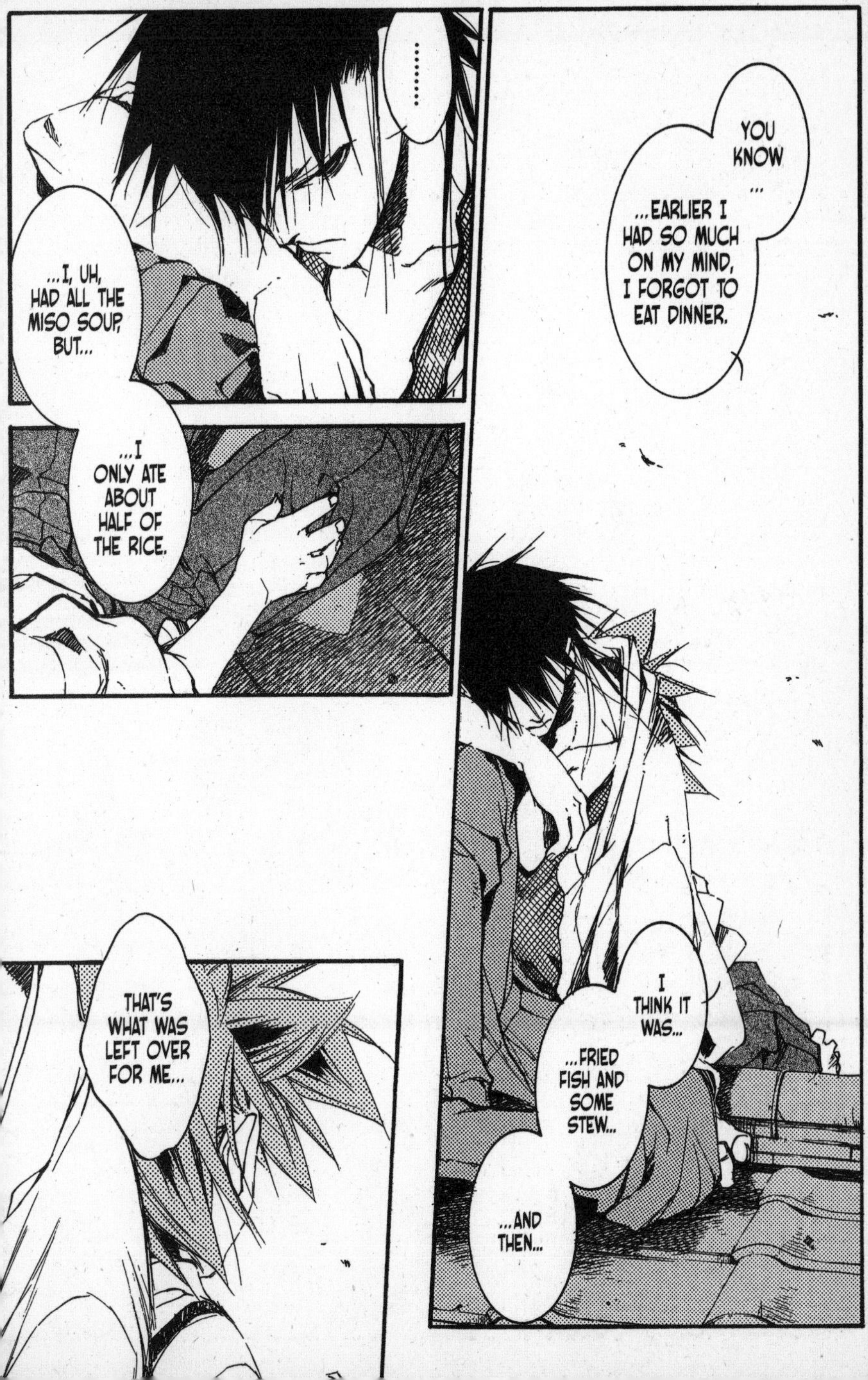
YOU KNOW ...
...EARLIER I HAD SO MUCH ON MY MIND, I FORGOT TO EAT DINNER.
I THINK IT WAS...
...FRIED FISH AND SOME STEW...
...AND THEN...
......
...I, UH, HAD ALL THE MISO SOUP, BUT...
...I ONLY ATE ABOUT HALF OF THE RICE.
THAT'S WHAT WAS LEFT OVER FOR ME...

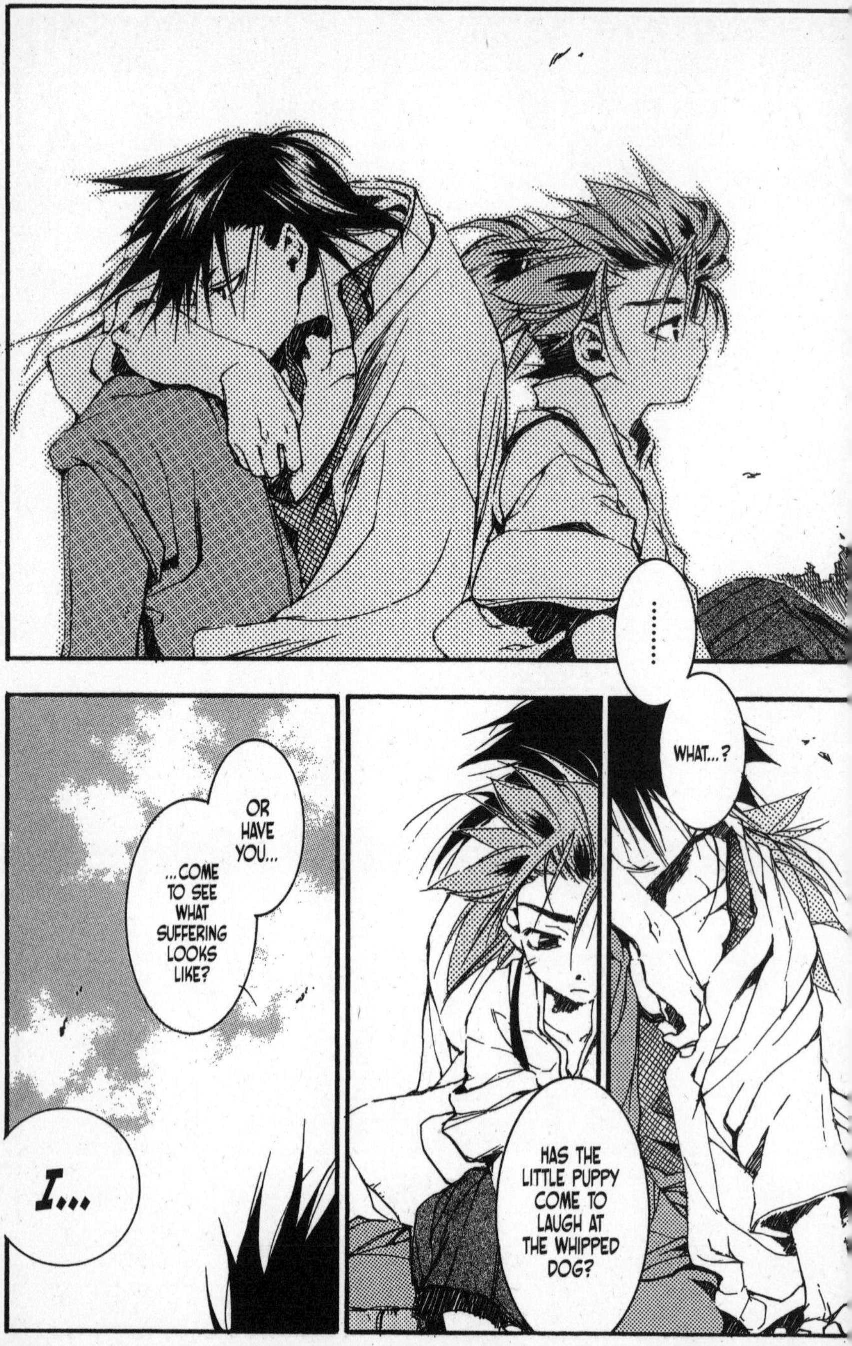
......
WHAT...?
HAS THE LITTLE PUPPY COME TO LAUGH AT THE WHIPPED DOG?
OR HAVE YOU...
...COME TO SEE WHAT SUFFERING LOOKS LIKE?
I...

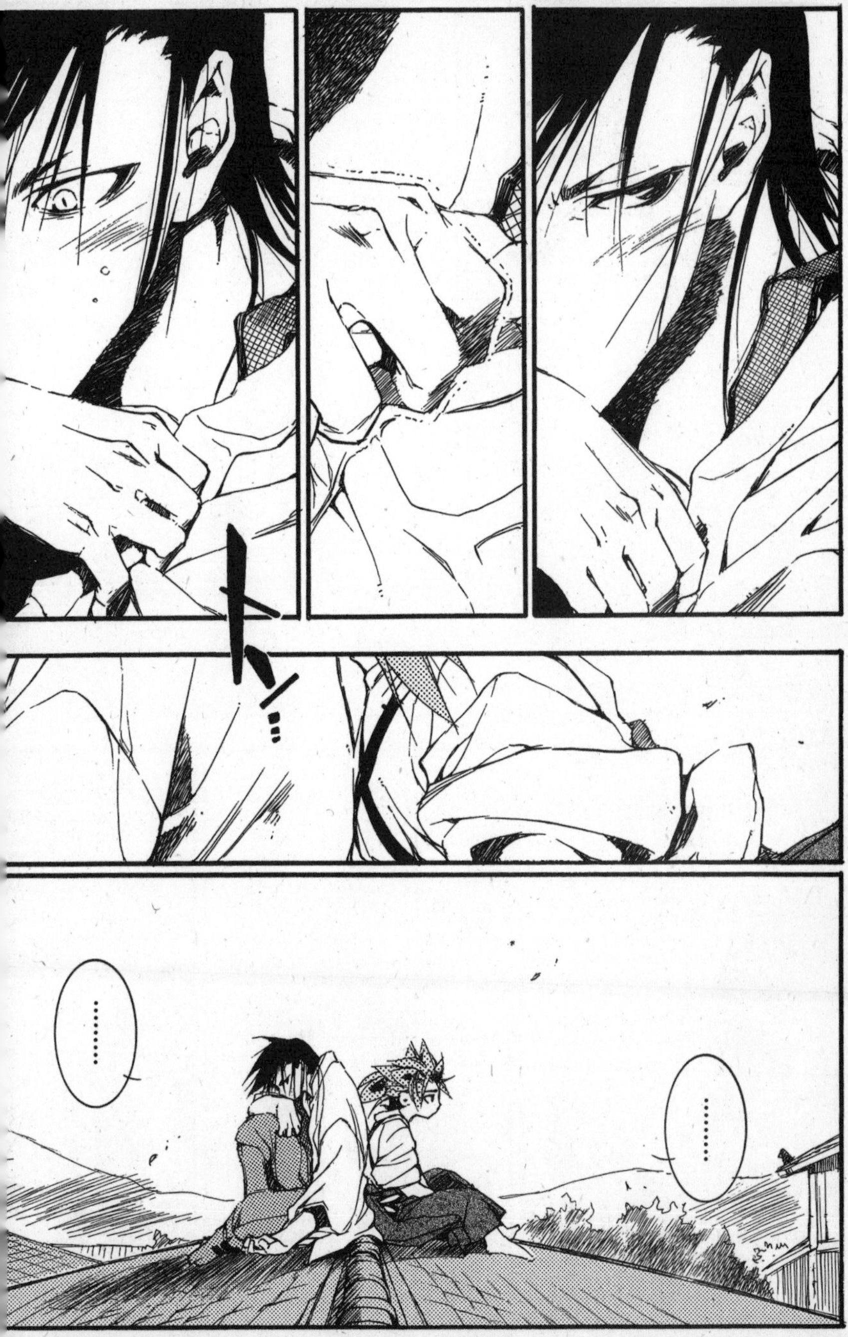
……
……

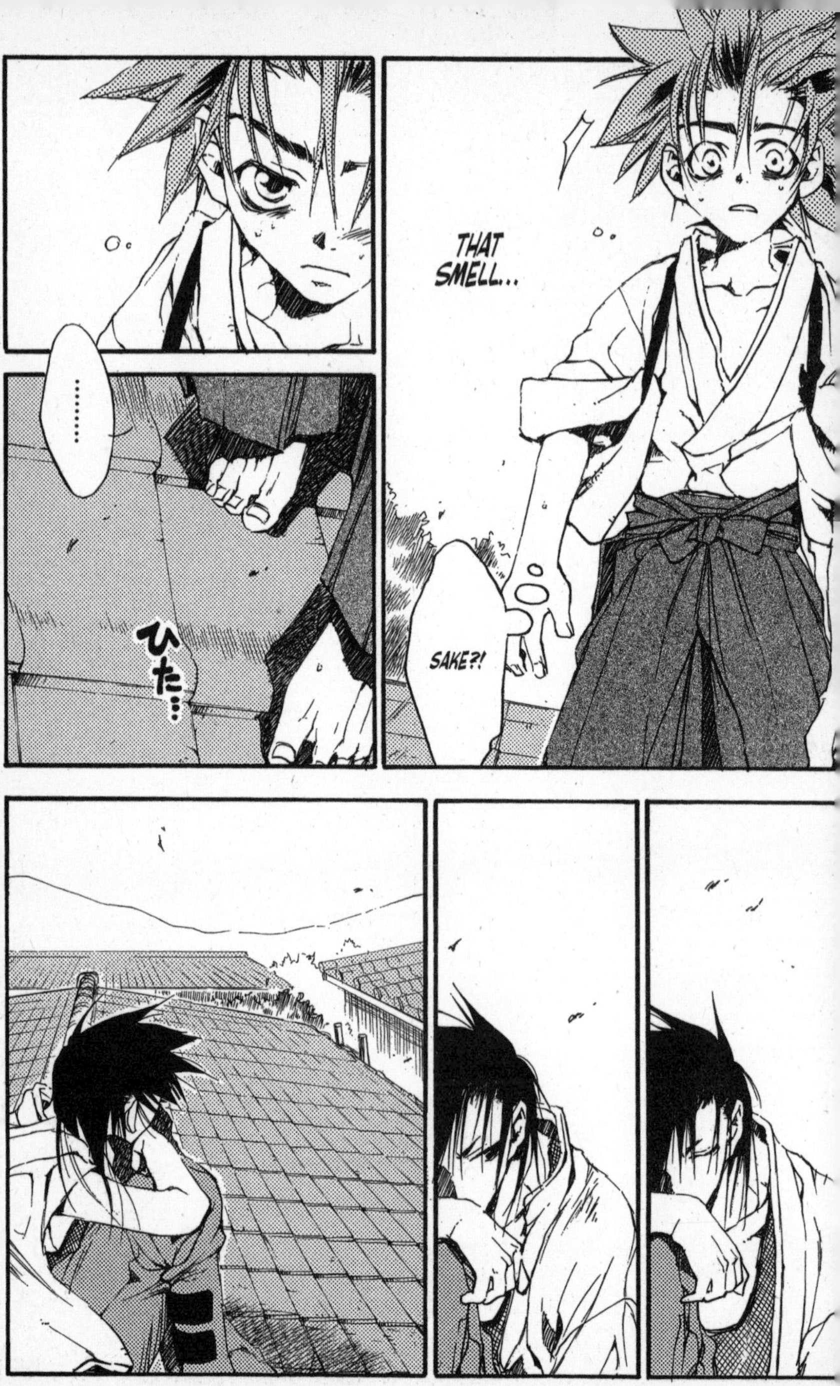
THAT SMELL...
SAKE?!
......
ひた...

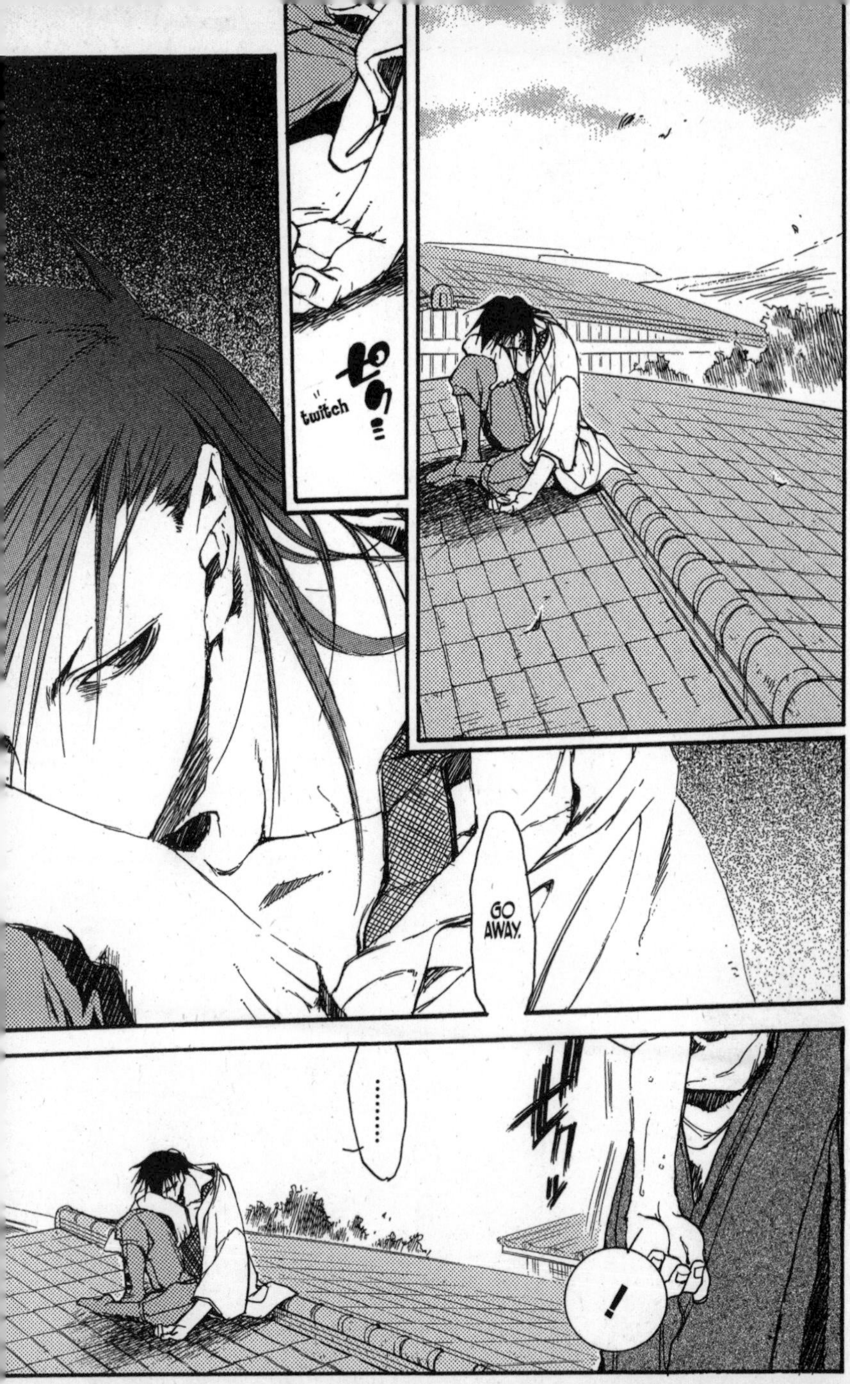
twitch
GO AWAY.
......
!

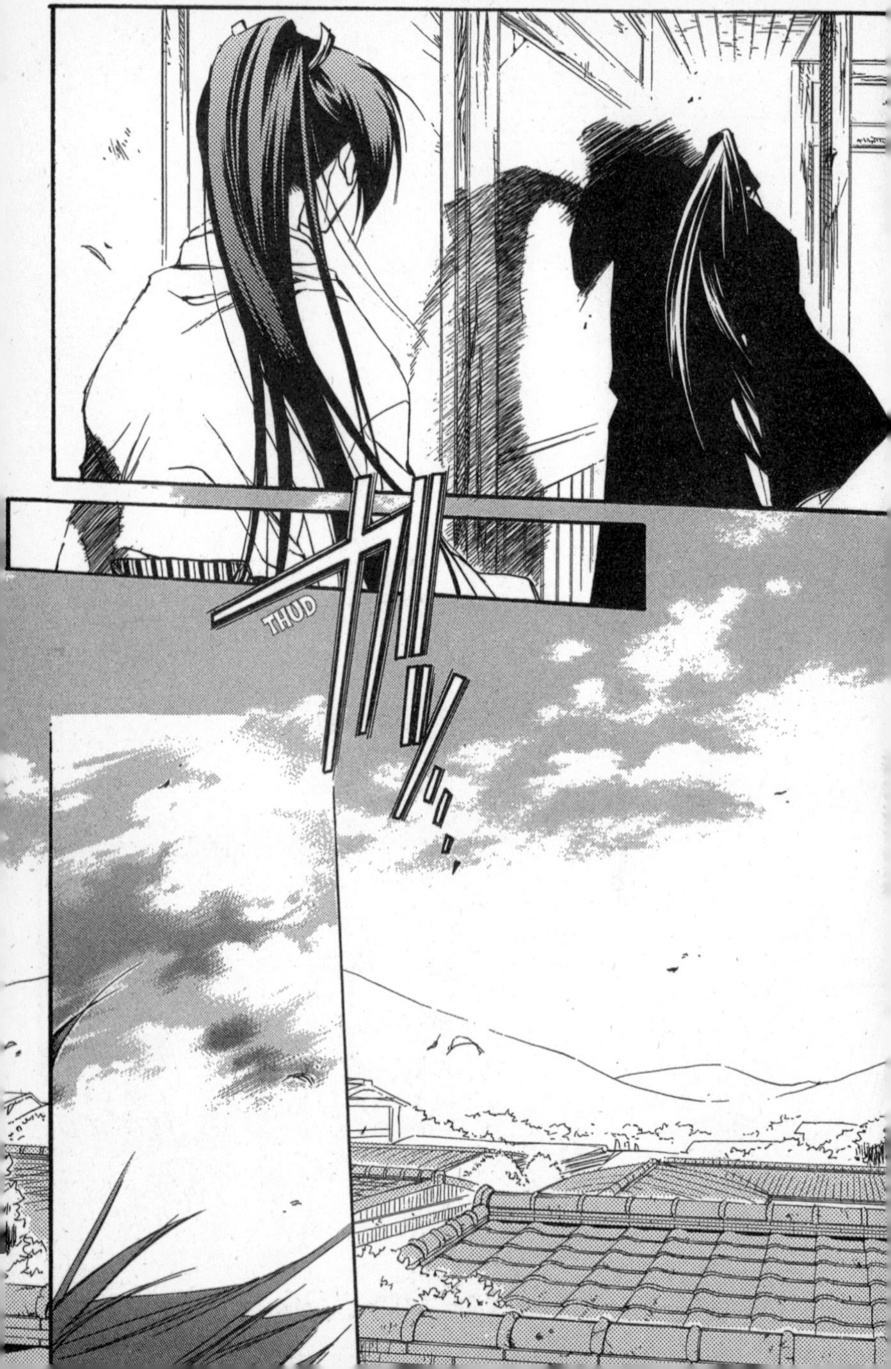
THUD

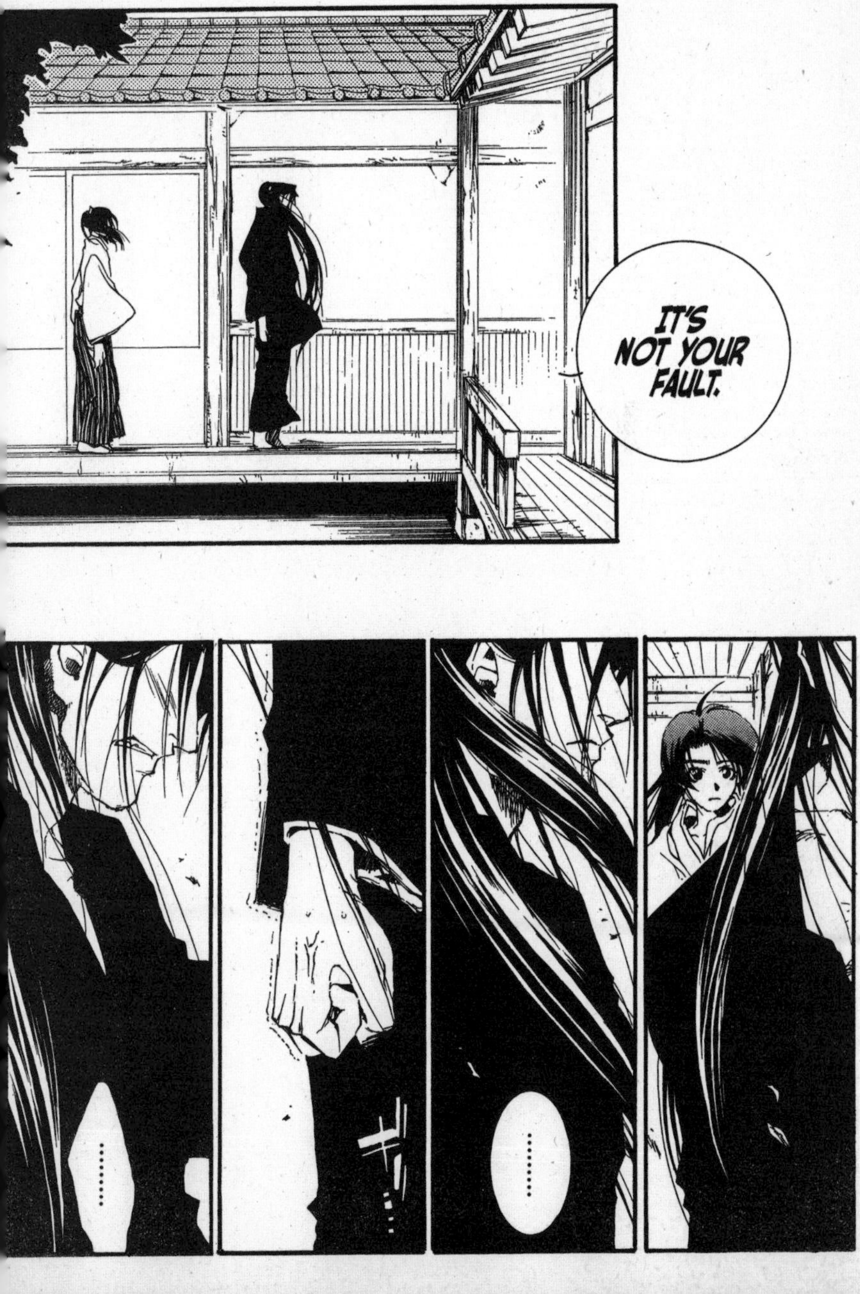
IT'S NOT YOUR FAULT.
....
....

HIJI-KATA-SAN?

BY TAKING OUT MASUYA, WE'LL CRUSH CHOUSHUU.

KEEPING YOSHIDA ALIVE IS NO LONGER NECESSARY.

HIJIKATA-SAN!

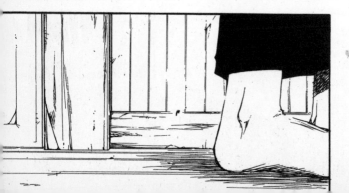

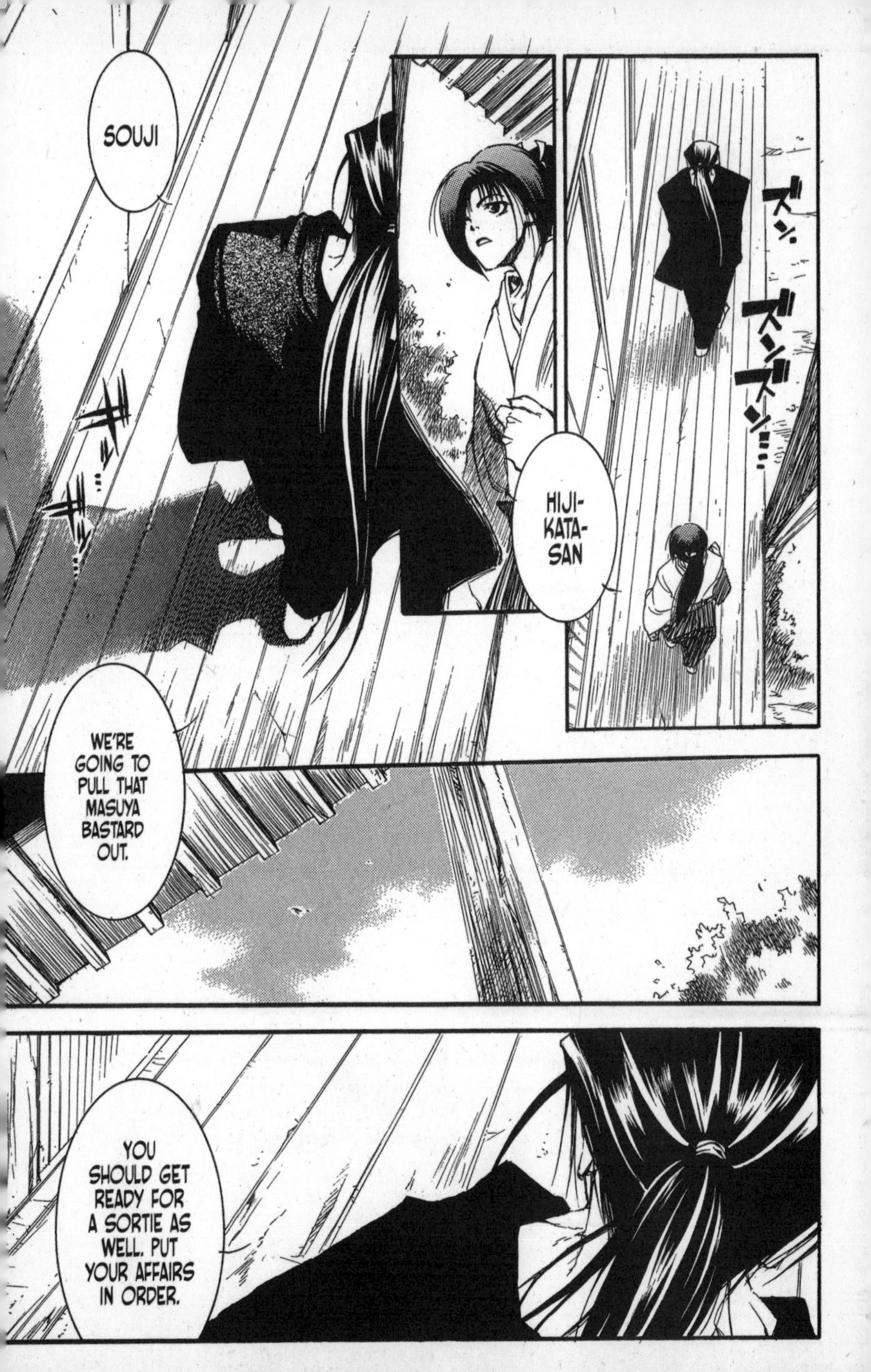
ズンッ
ズンズンッ…
HIJI-KATA-SAN
SOUJI
ザッ…
ザッ…
WE'RE GOING TO PULL THAT MASUYA BASTARD OUT.
YOU SHOULD GET READY FOR A SORTIE AS WELL. PUT YOUR AFFAIRS IN ORDER.

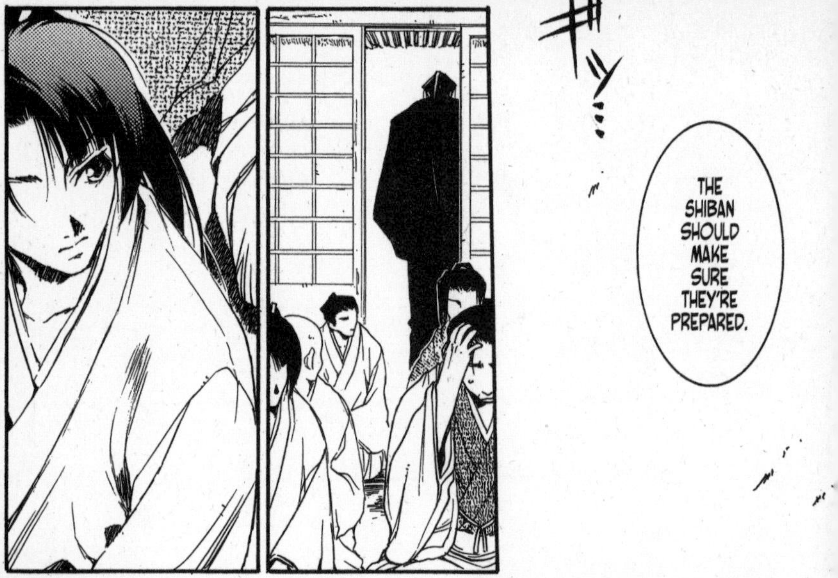
ギッ…
THE SHIBAN SHOULD MAKE SURE THEY'RE PREPARED.

*Shiban: A vanguard of four soldiers.

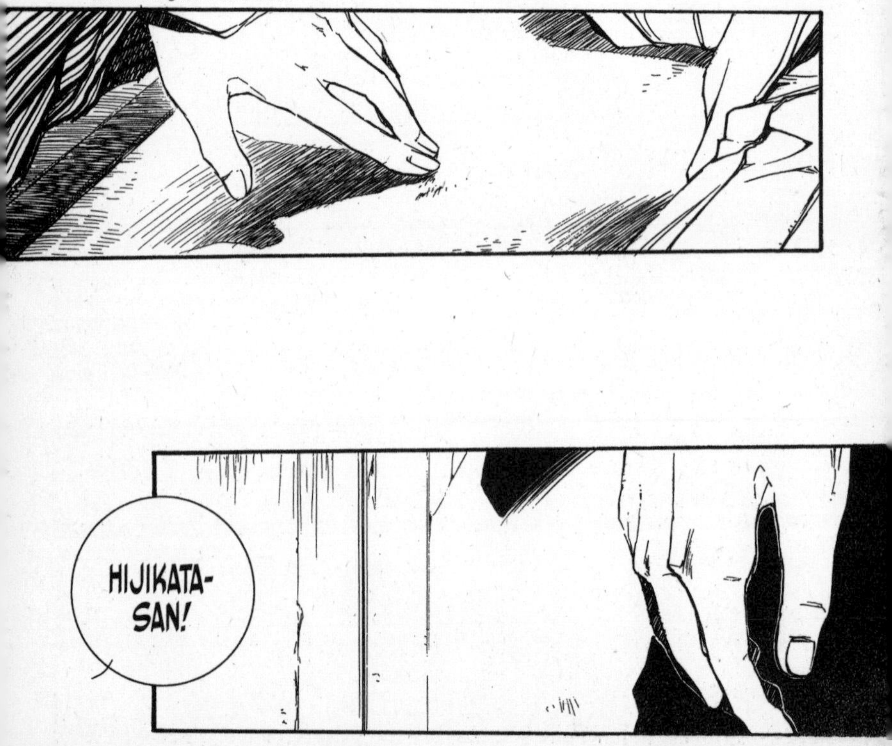
HIJIKATA-SAN!

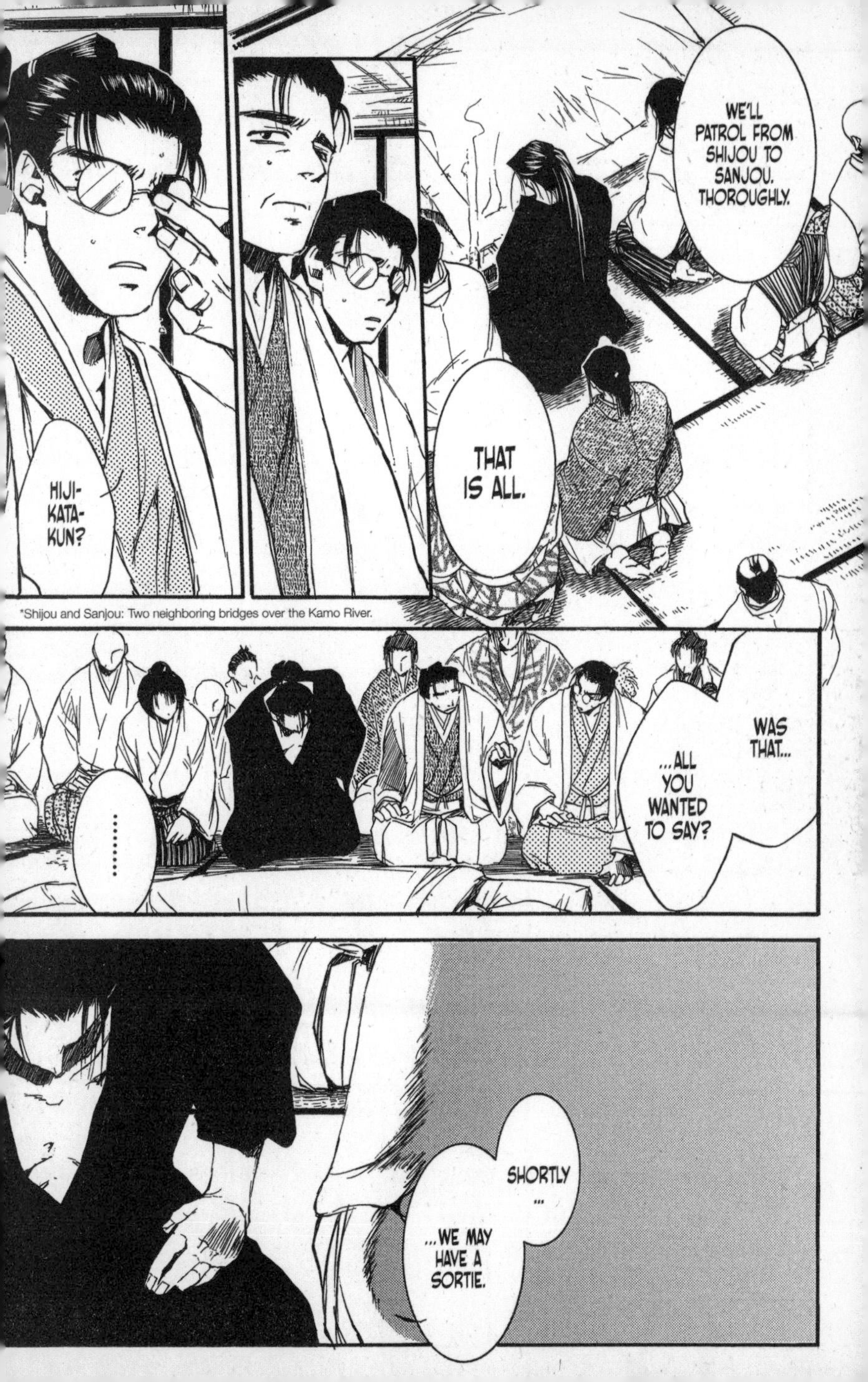
WE'LL PATROL FROM SHIJOU TO SANJOU. THOROUGHLY.
THAT IS ALL.
HIJI-KATA-KUN?
WAS THAT...
...ALL YOU WANTED TO SAY?
....
SHORTLY ...
...WE MAY HAVE A SORTIE.

*Shijou and Sanjou: Two neighboring bridges over the Kamo River.

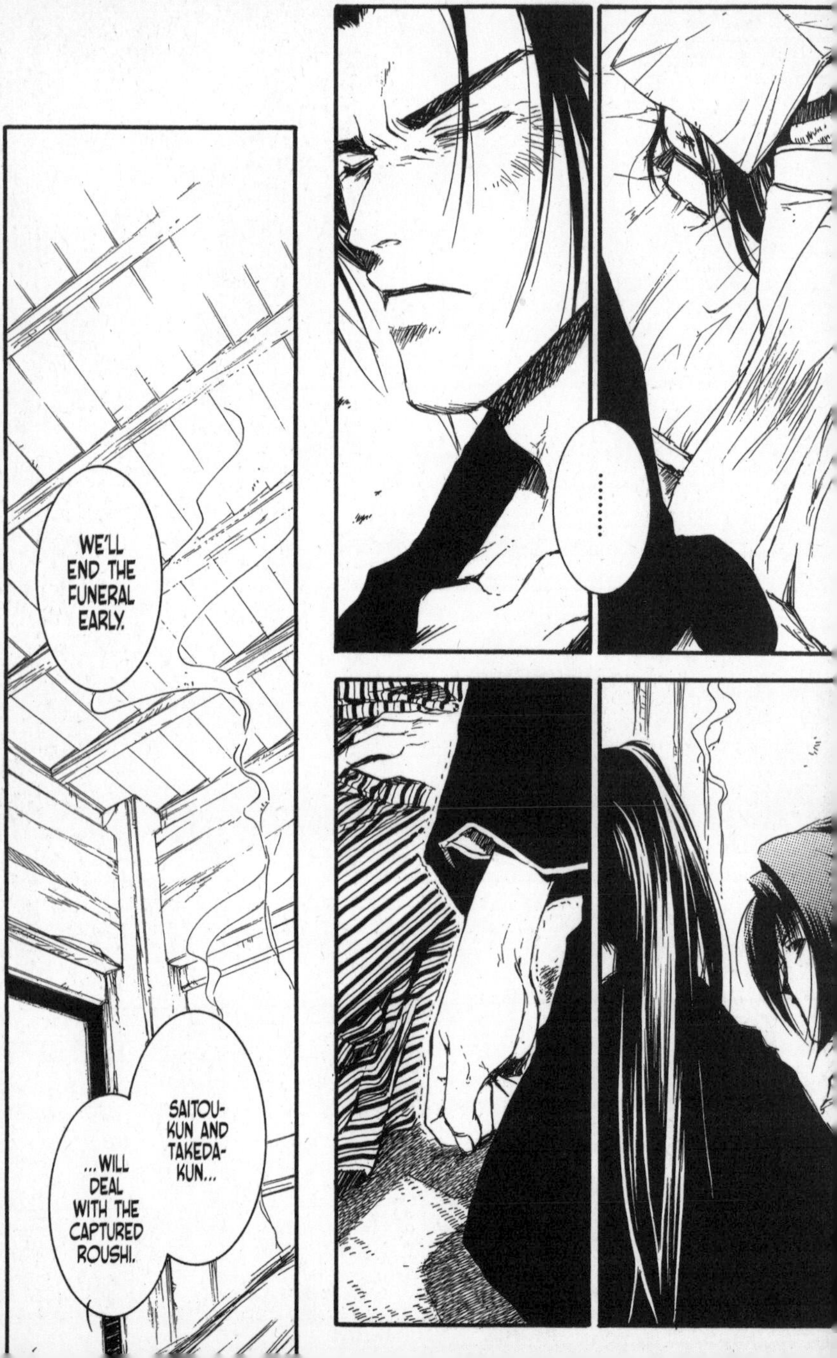
……
WE'LL END THE FUNERAL EARLY.
SAITOU-KUN AND TAKEDA-KUN...
...WILL DEAL WITH THE CAPTURED ROUSHI.

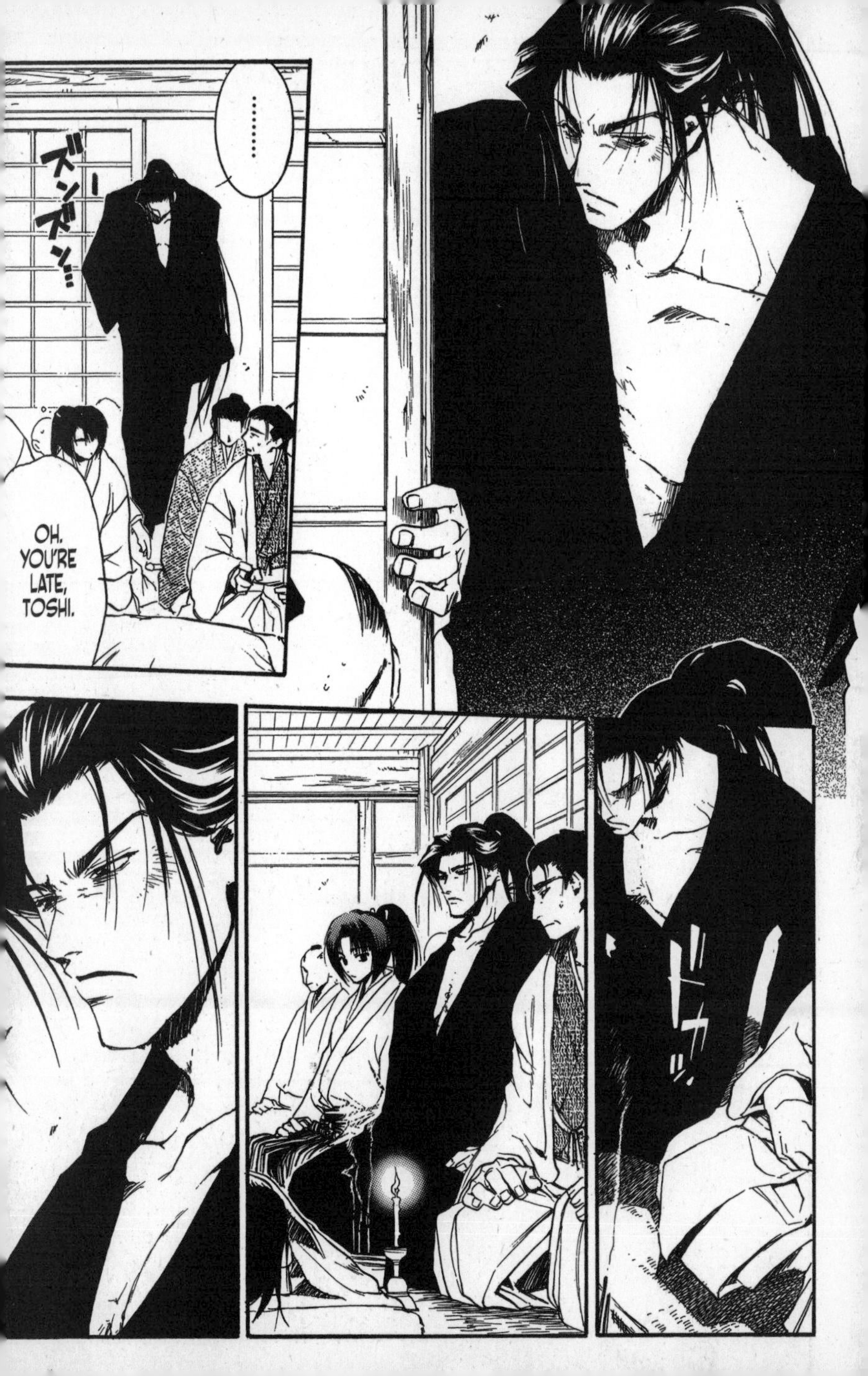
......
ズンズン...
OH. YOU'RE LATE, TOSHI.

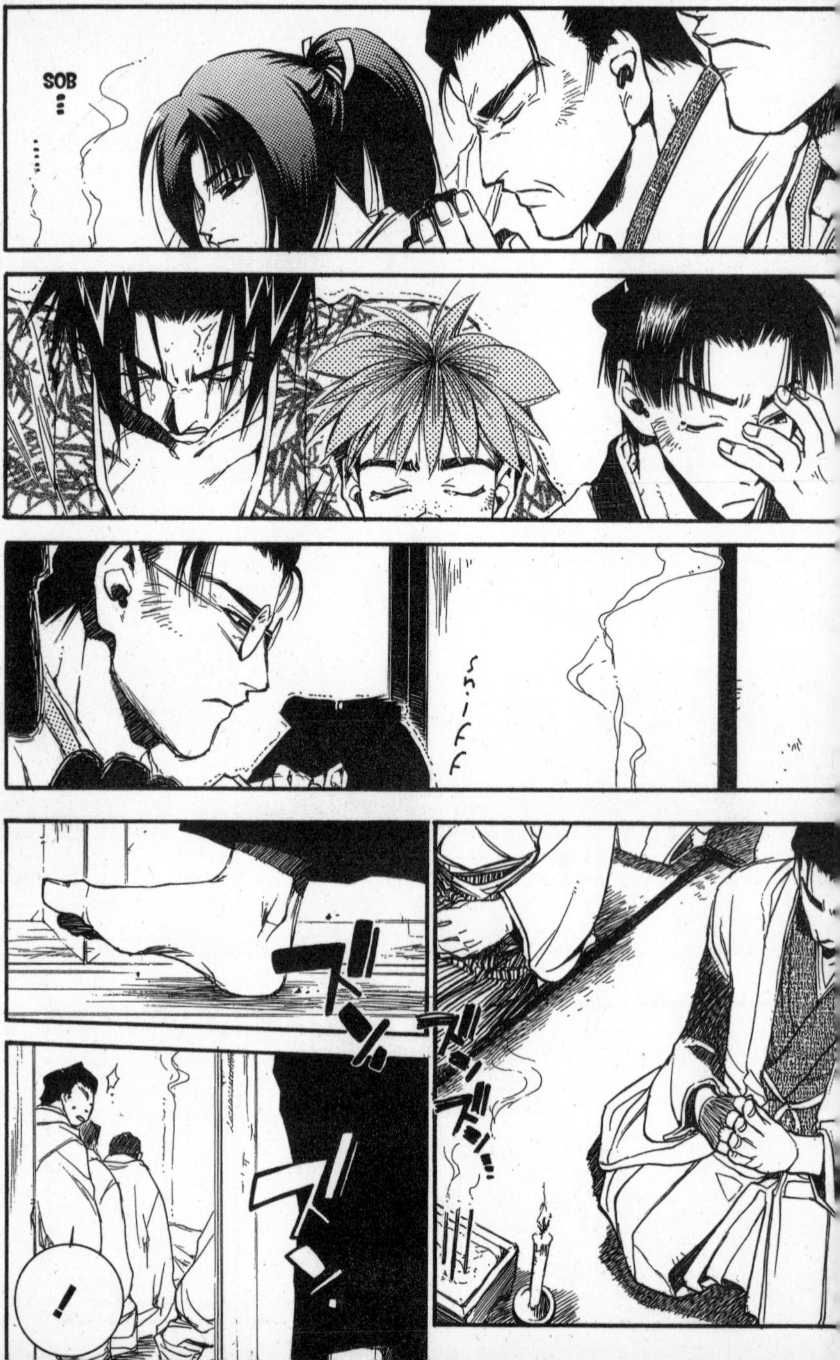
SOB...
.....
sniff
!

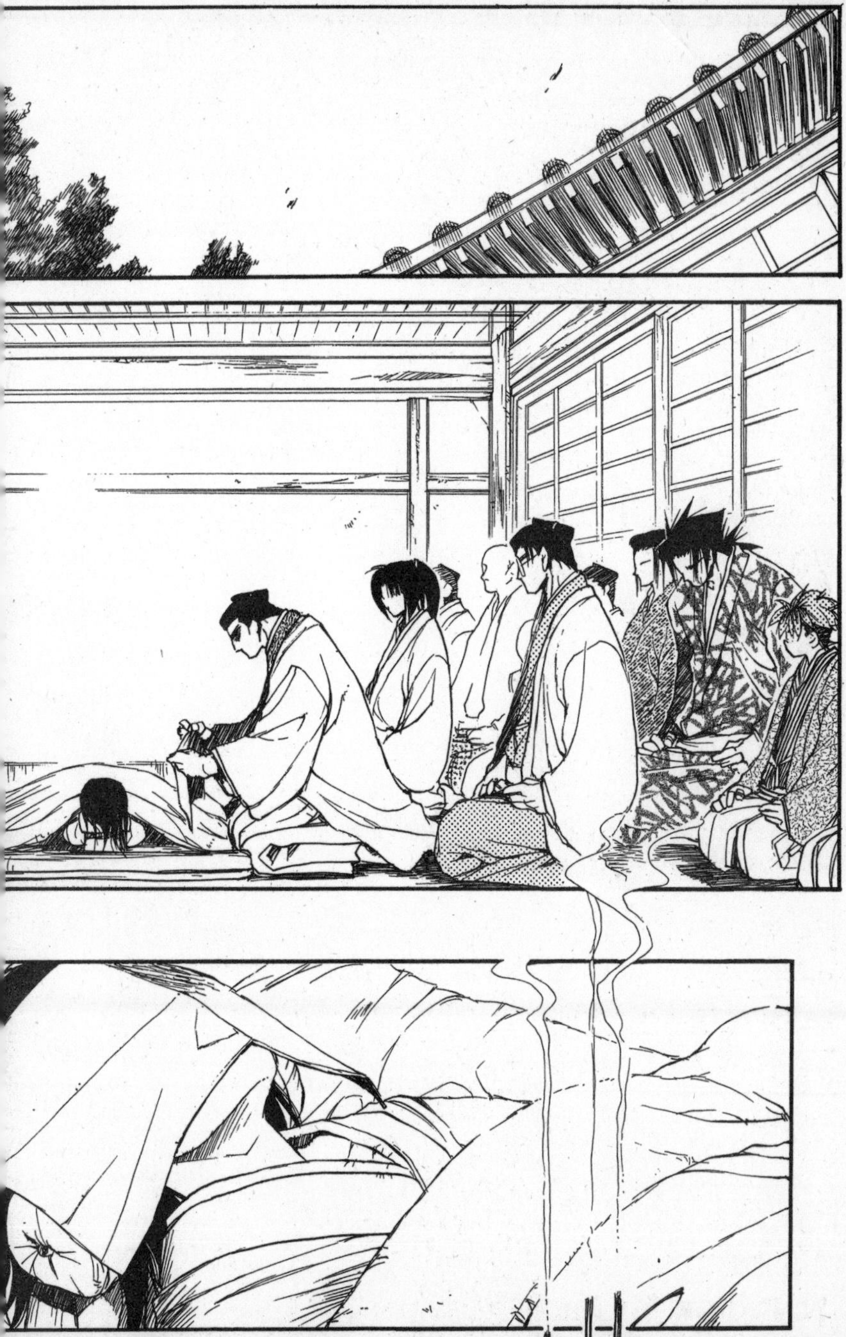

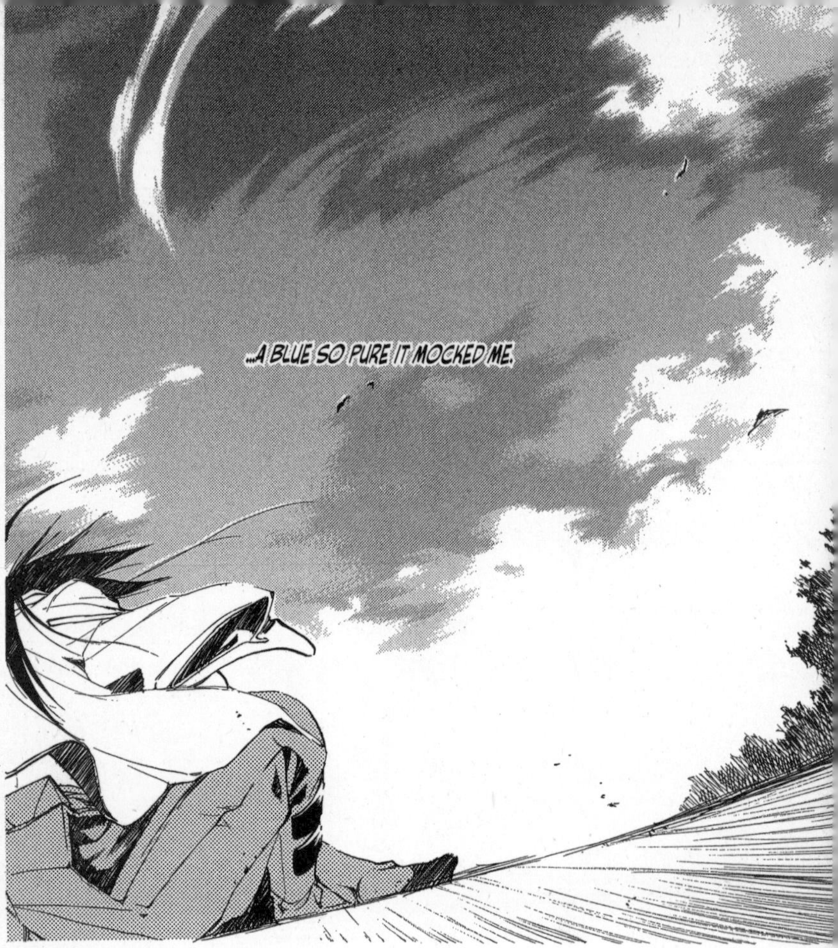
...A BLUE SO PURE IT MOCKED ME.

Act.19
You Know My Name

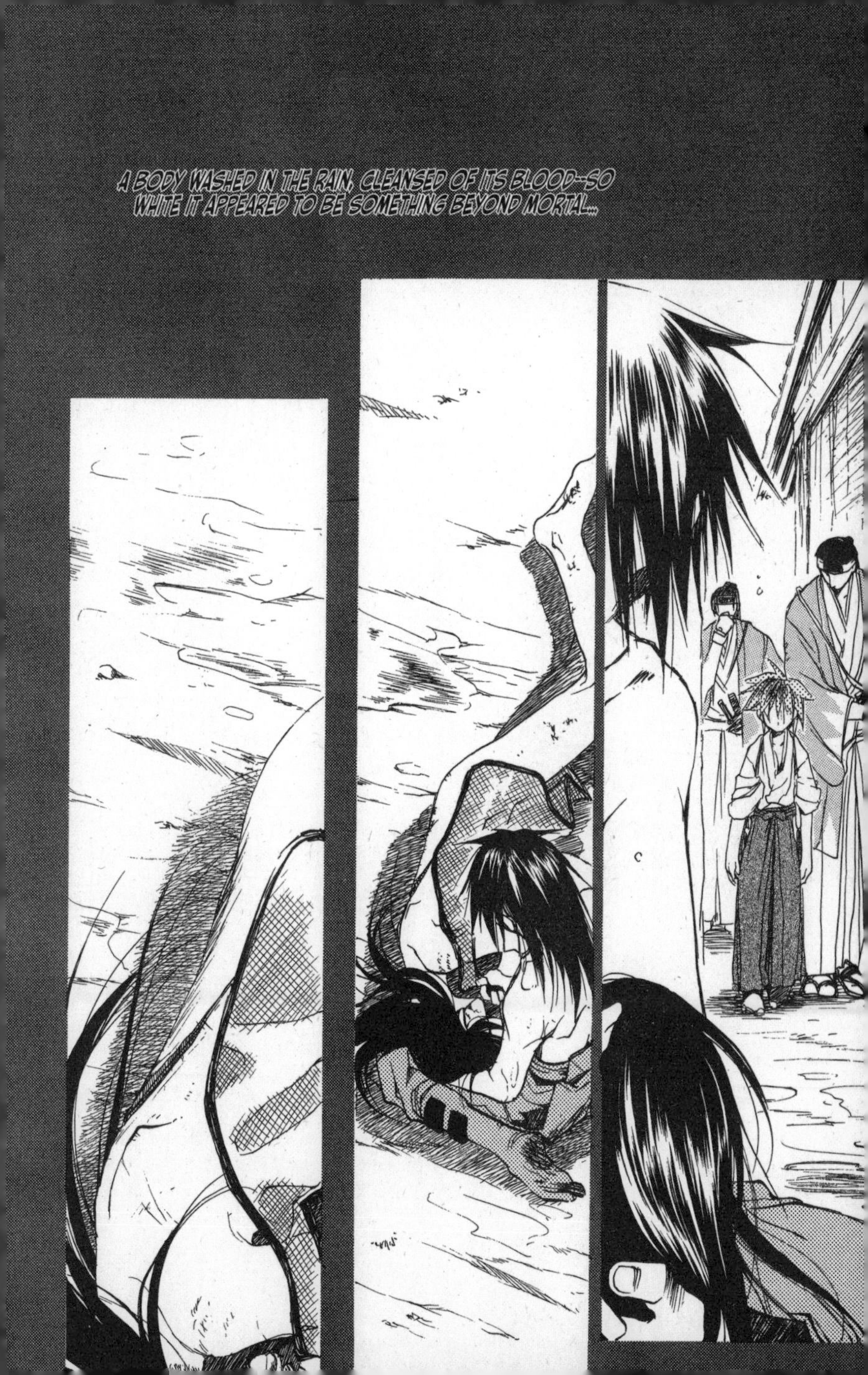
A BODY WASHED IN THE RAIN, CLEANSED OF ITS BLOOD--SO WHITE IT APPEARED TO BE SOMETHING BEYOND MORTAL...

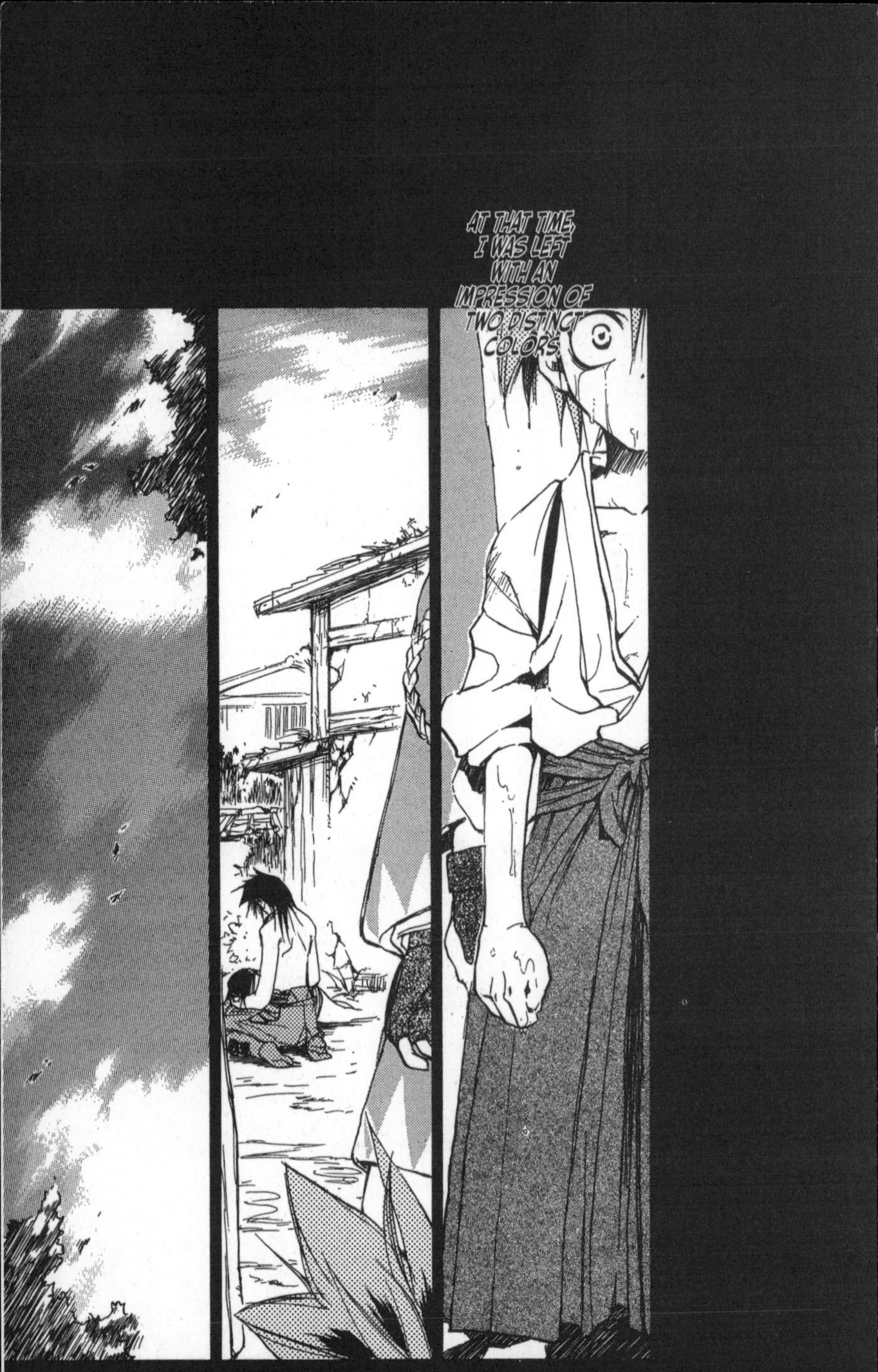
AT THAT TIME, I WAS LEFT WITH AN IMPRESSION OF TWO DISTINCT COLORS.

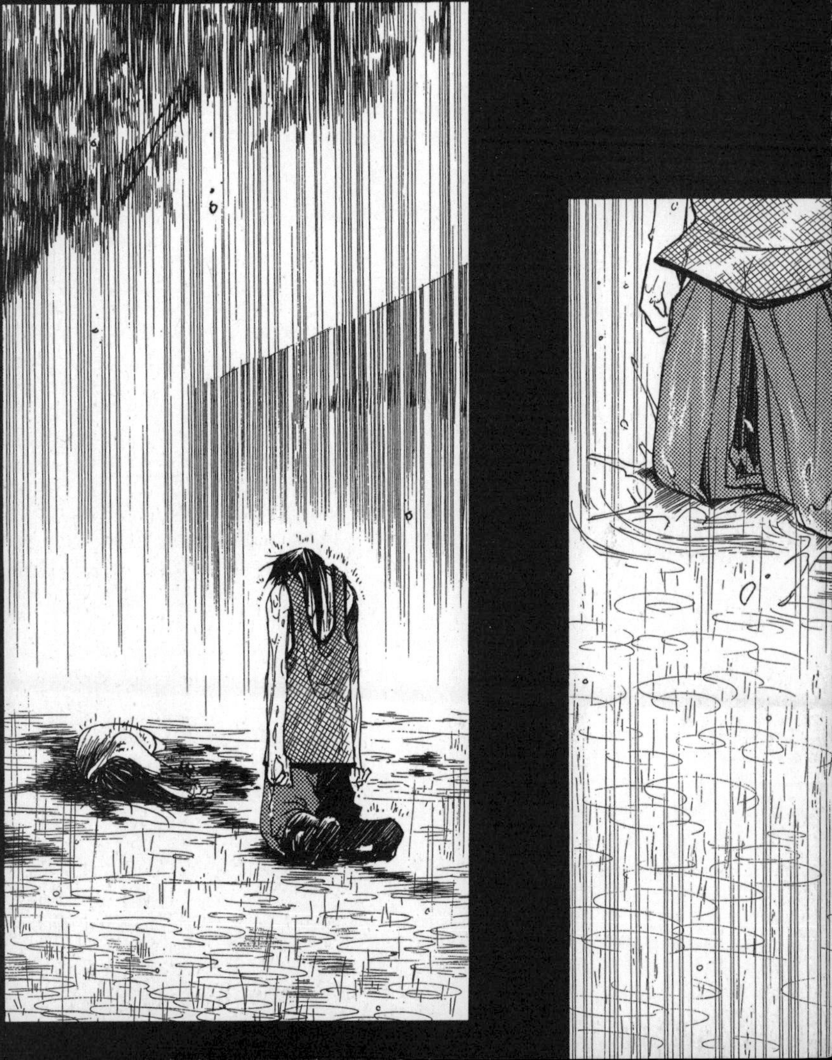

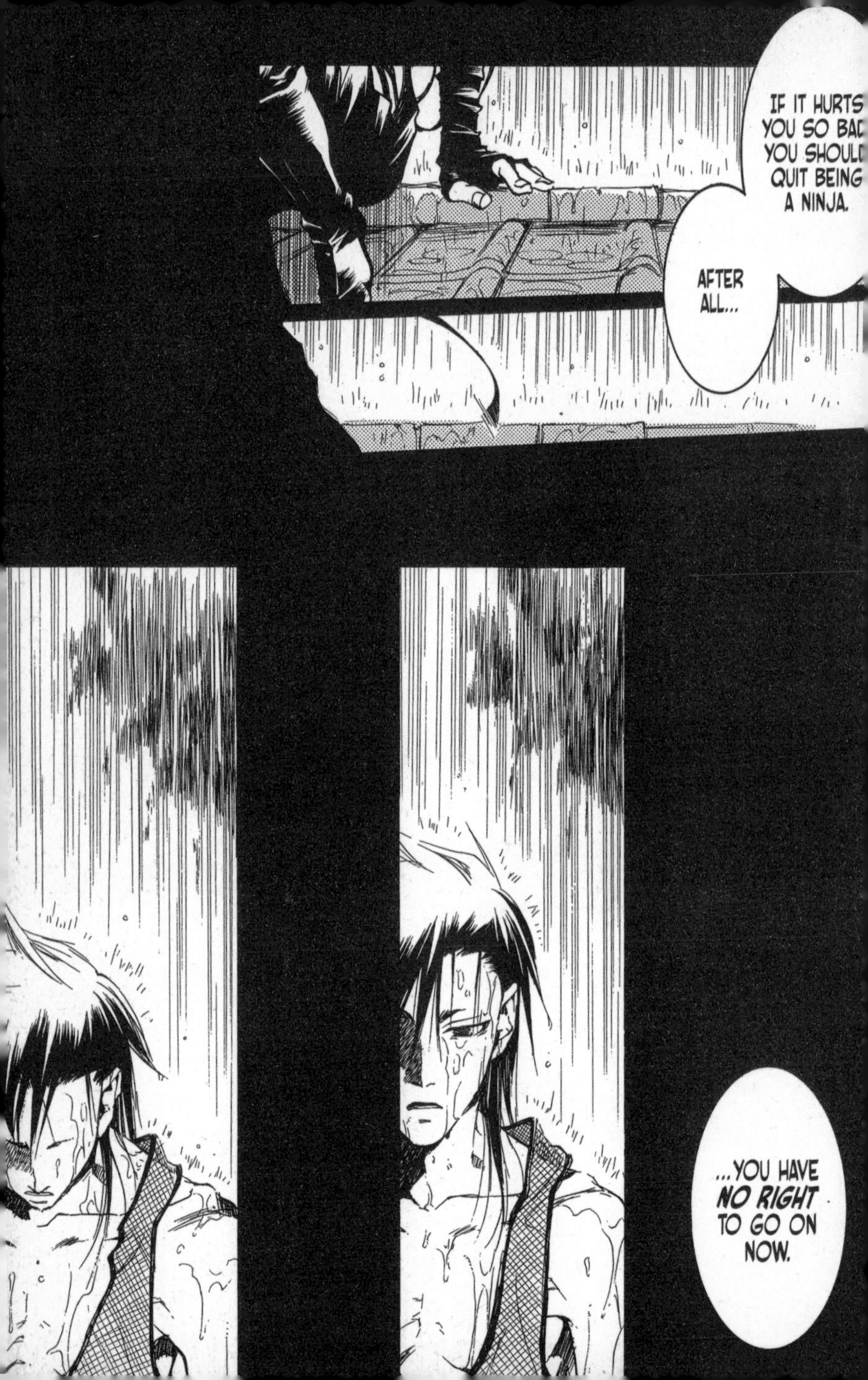
IF IT HURTS YOU SO BAD YOU SHOULD QUIT BEING A NINJA.
AFTER ALL...
...YOU HAVE ***NO RIGHT*** TO GO ON NOW.

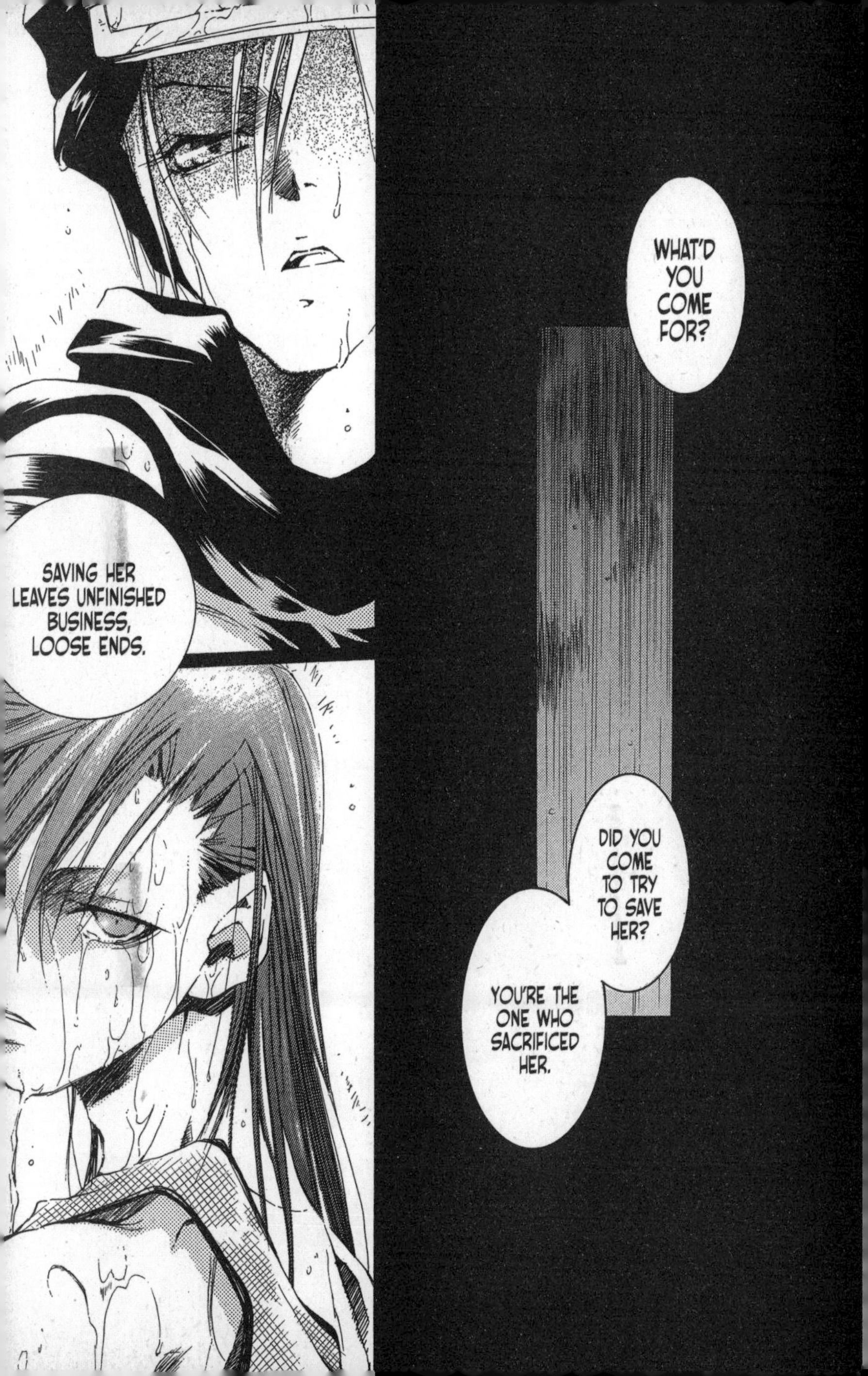
WHAT'D YOU COME FOR?
DID YOU COME TO TRY TO SAVE HER?
YOU'RE THE ONE WHO SACRIFICED HER.
SAVING HER LEAVES UNFINISHED BUSINESS, LOOSE ENDS.

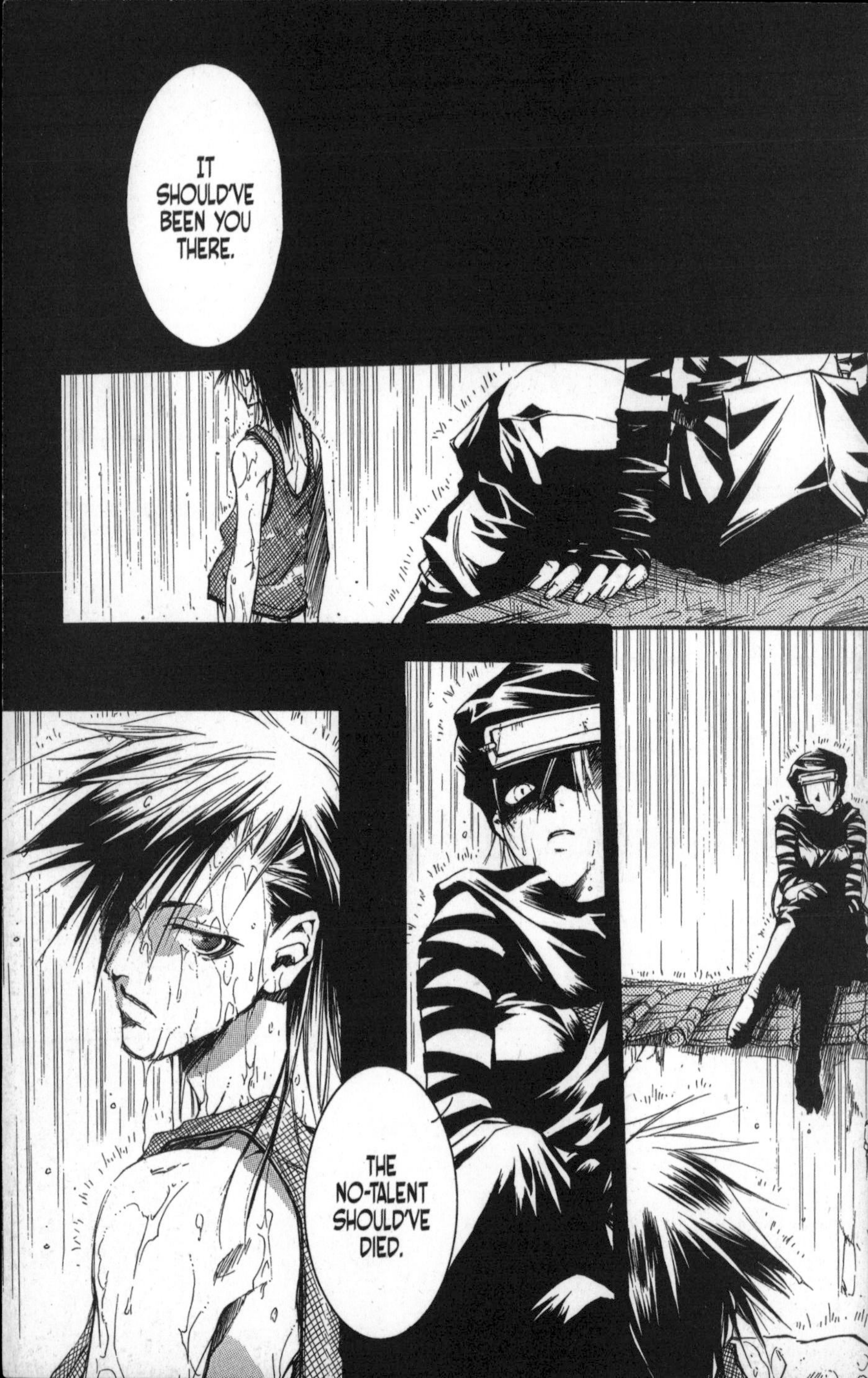
IT SHOULD'VE BEEN YOU THERE.
THE NO-TALENT SHOULD'VE DIED.

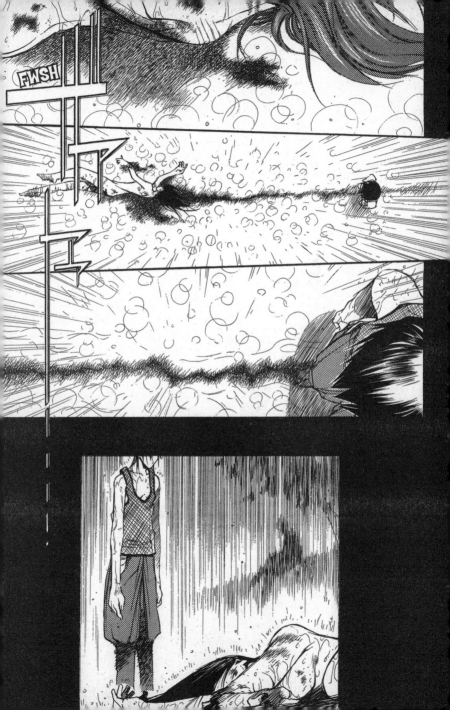
FWSH

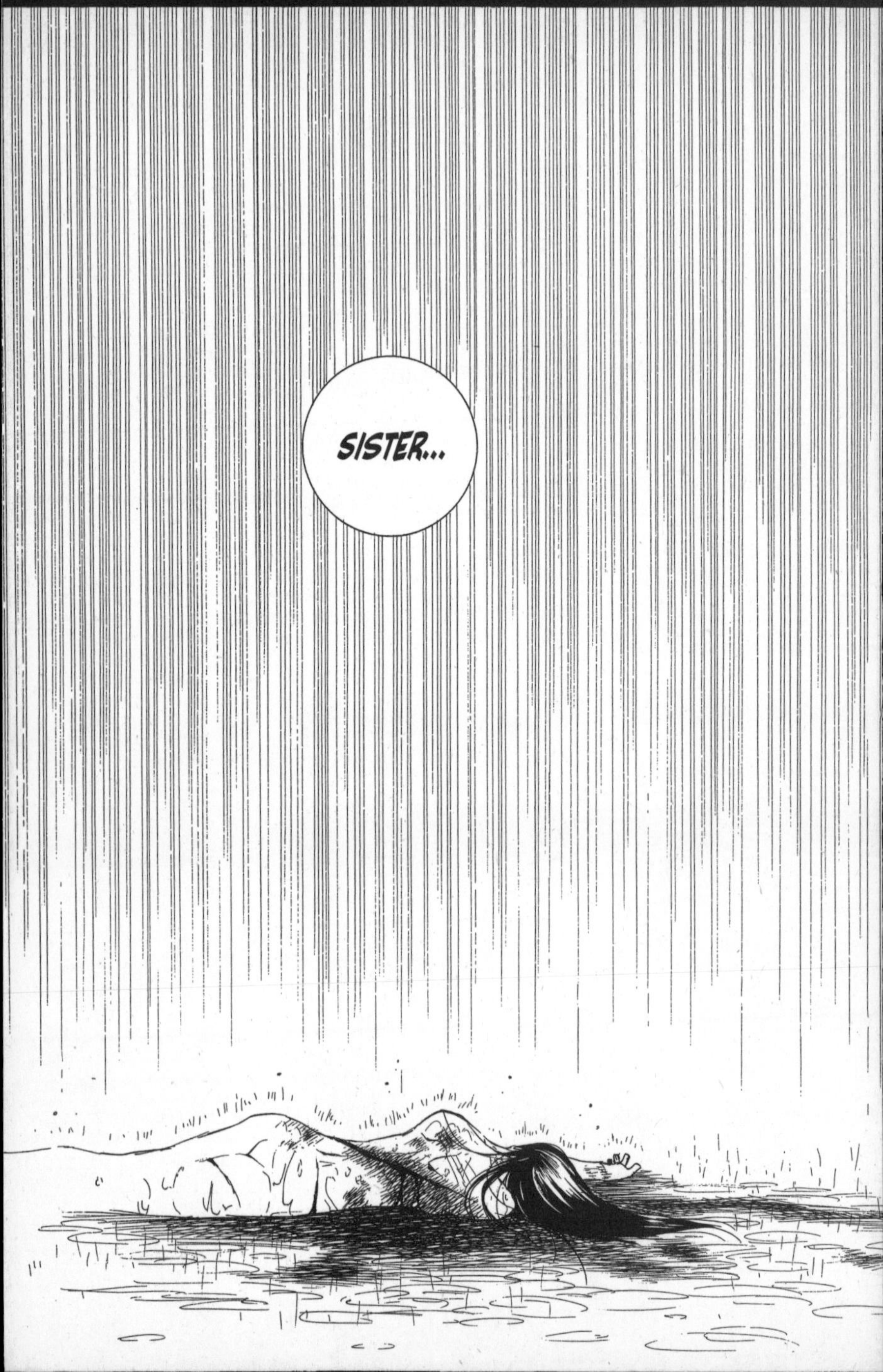
SISTER...

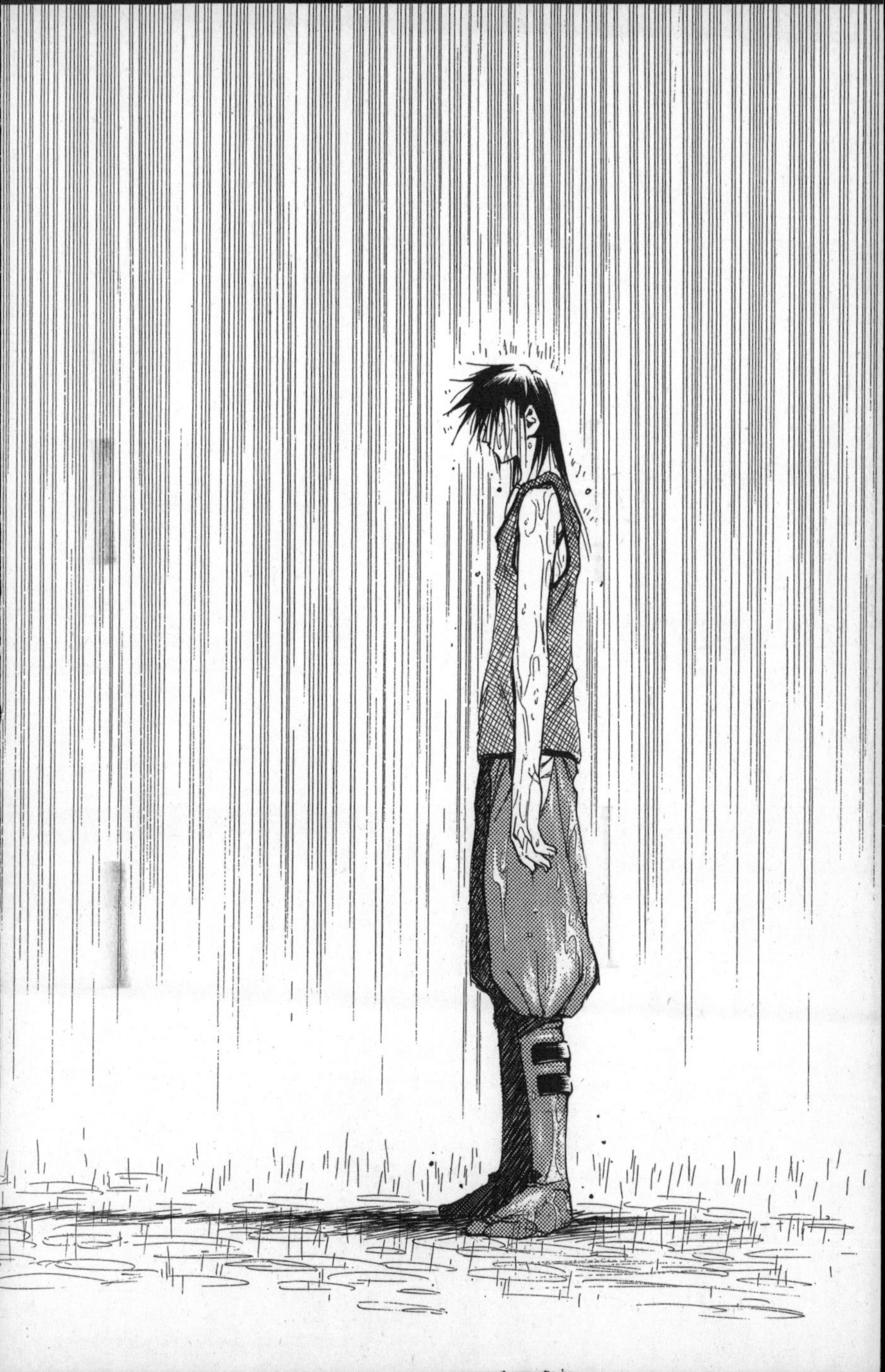

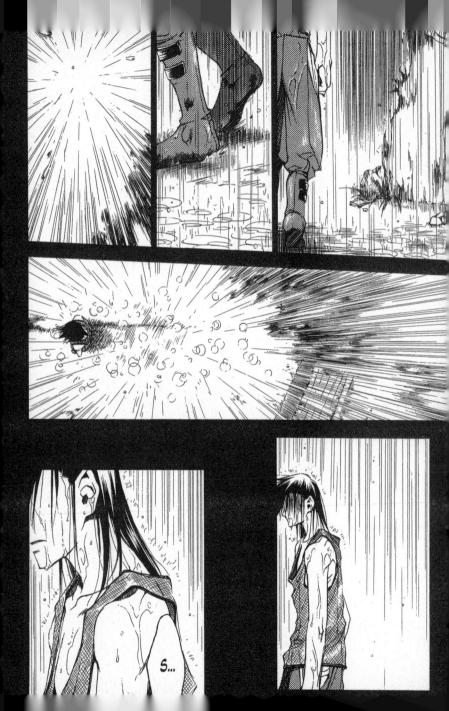

S...

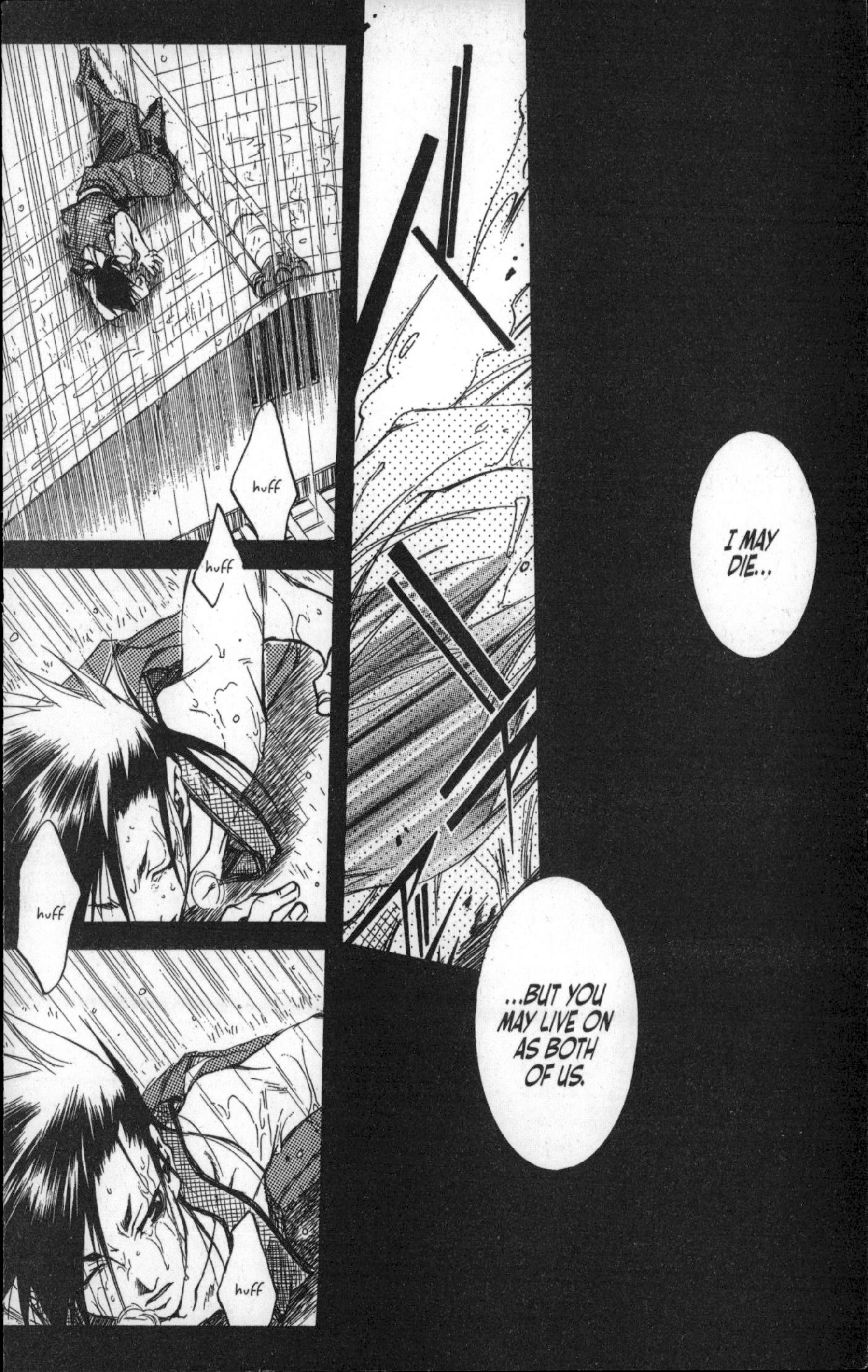
I MAY DIE...
...BUT YOU MAY LIVE ON AS BOTH OF US.
huff
huff
huff
huff

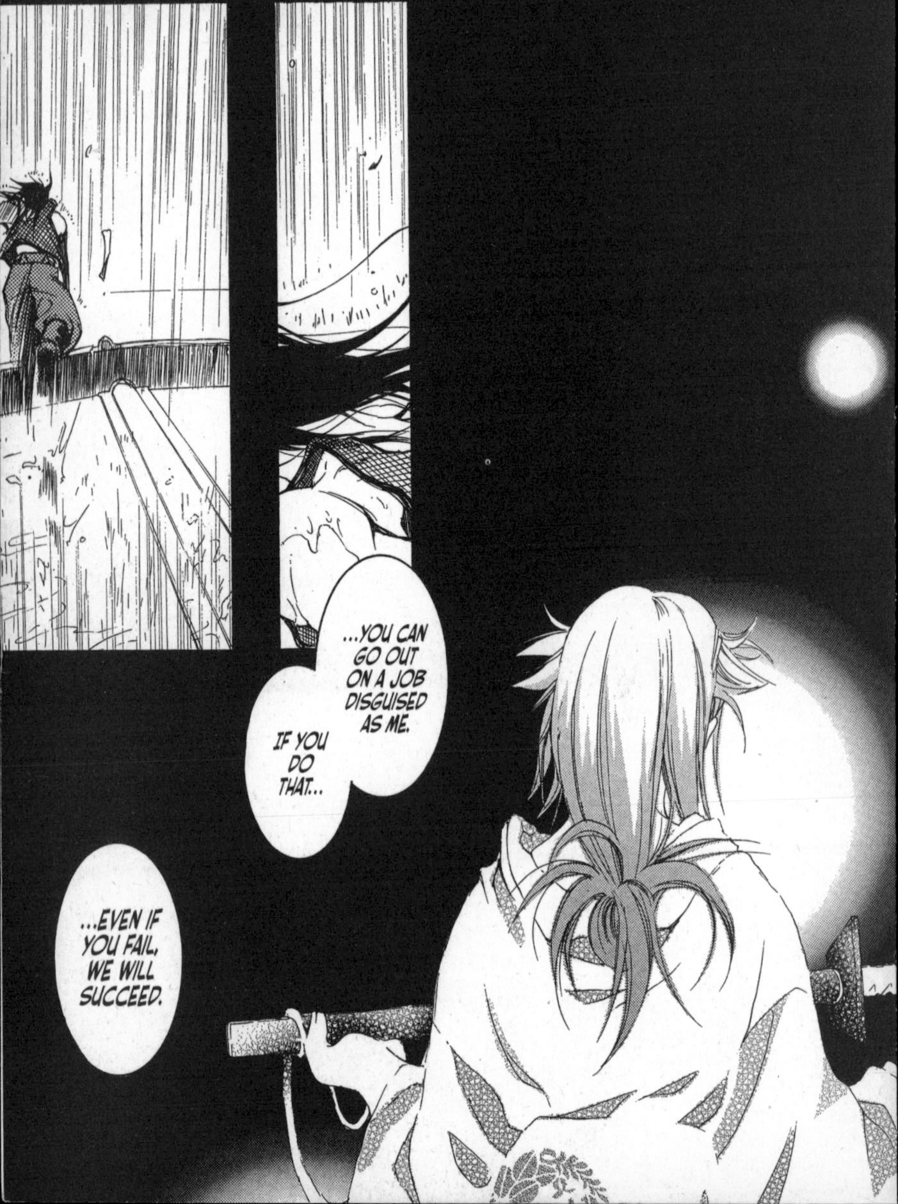
...YOU CAN GO OUT ON A JOB DISGUISED AS ME.
IF YOU DO THAT...
...EVEN IF YOU FAIL, WE WILL SUCCEED.

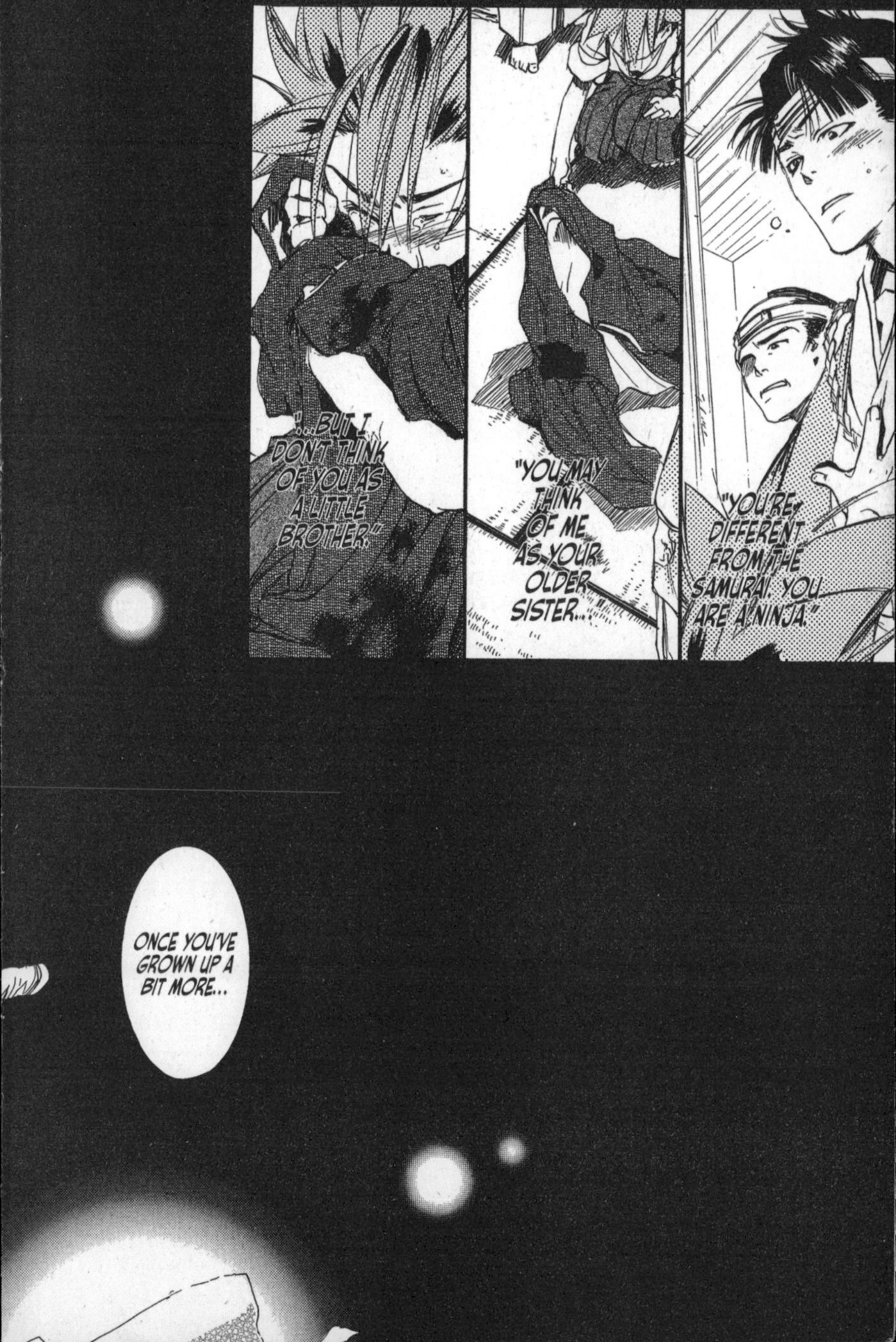
"YOU'RE DIFFERENT FROM THE SAMURAI. YOU ARE A NINJA."
"YOU MAY THINK OF ME AS YOUR OLDER SISTER..."
"...BUT I DON'T THINK OF YOU AS A LITTLE BROTHER."
ONCE YOU'VE GROWN UP A BIT MORE...

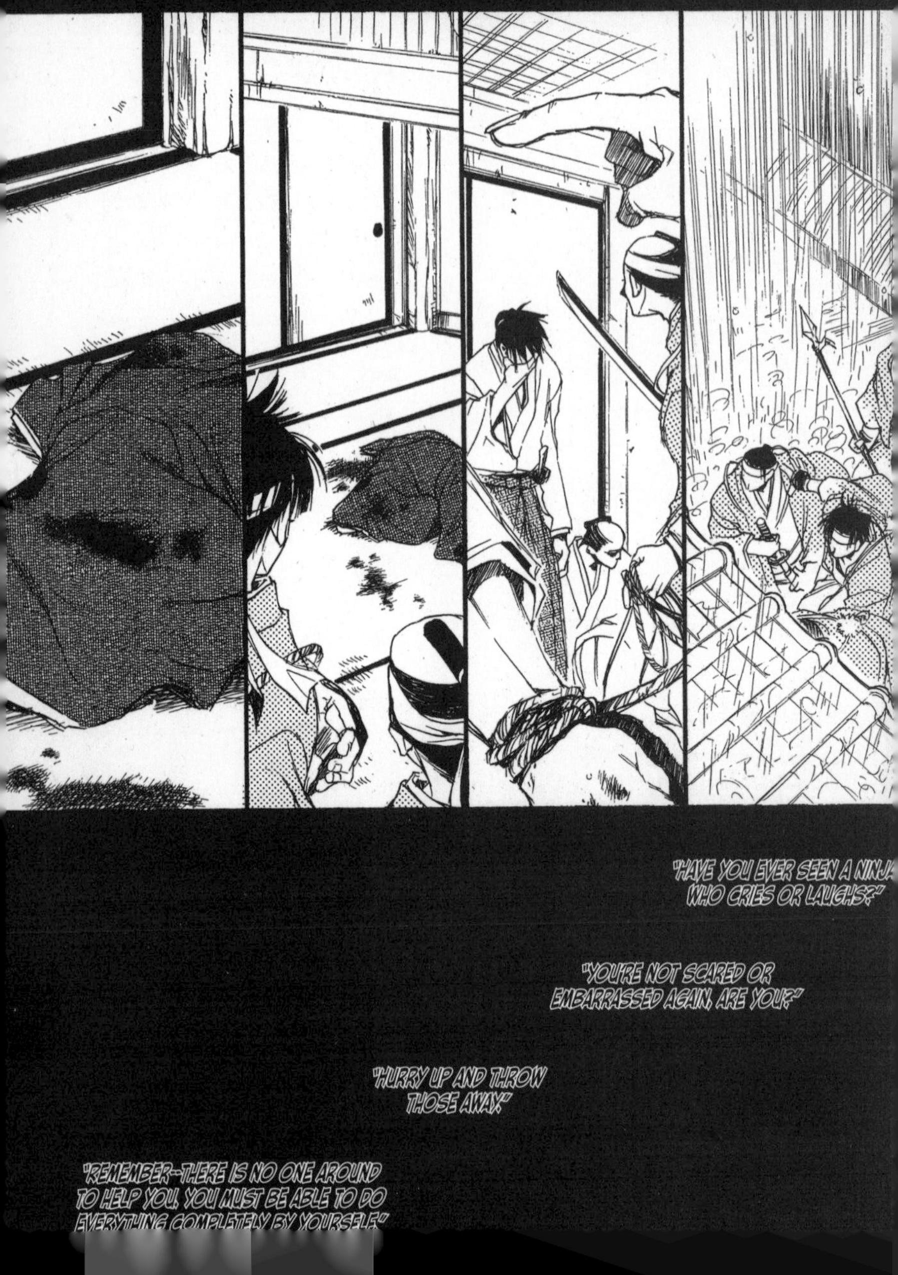
"HAVE YOU EVER SEEN A NINJA WHO CRIES OR LAUGHS?"
"YOU'RE NOT SCARED OR EMBARRASSED AGAIN, ARE YOU?"
"HURRY UP AND THROW THOSE AWAY."
"REMEMBER--THERE IS NO ONE AROUND TO HELP YOU. YOU MUST BE ABLE TO DO EVERYTHING COMPLETELY BY YOURSELF."

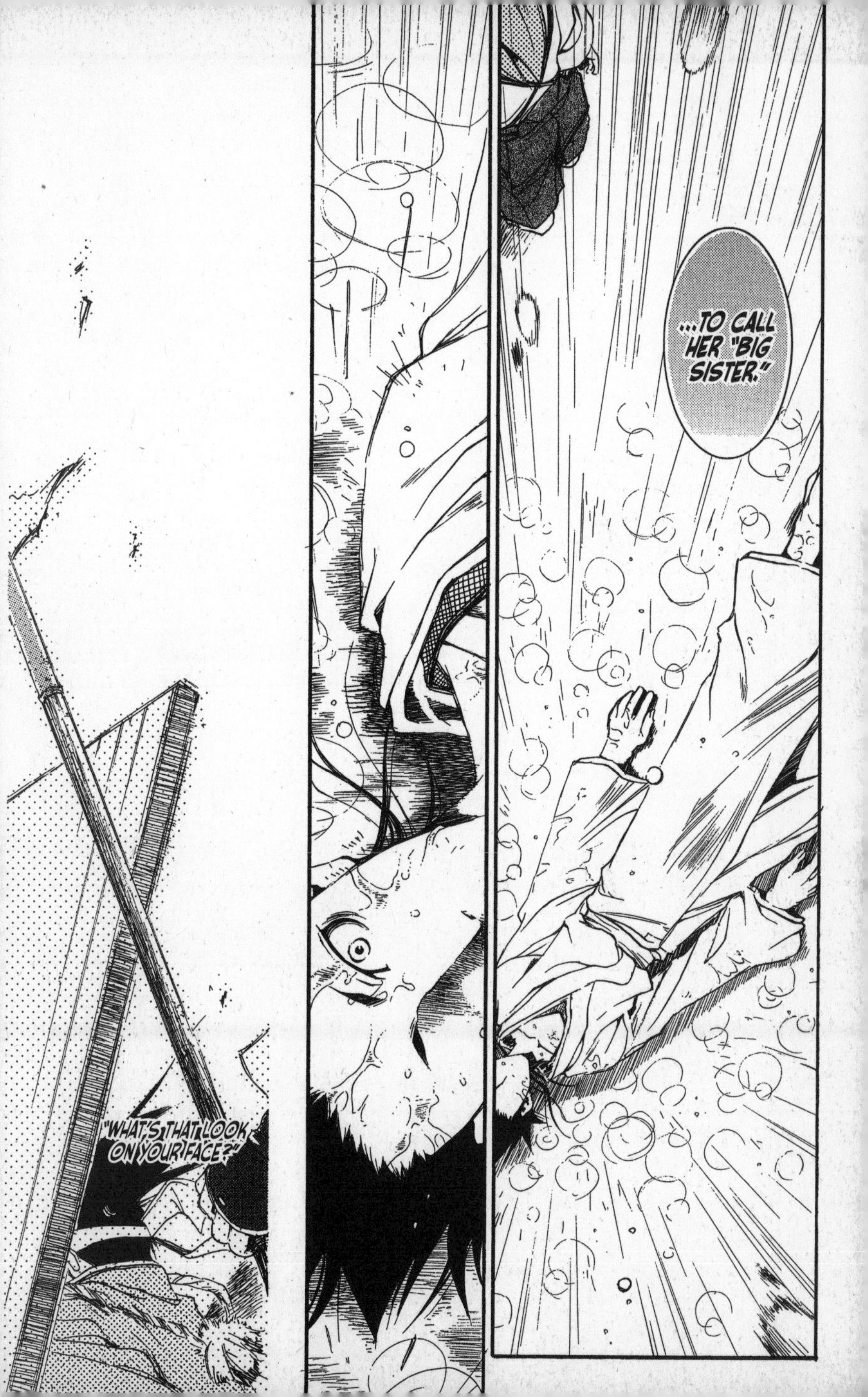
...TO CALL HER "BIG SISTER."
"WHAT'S THAT LOOK ON YOUR FACE?"

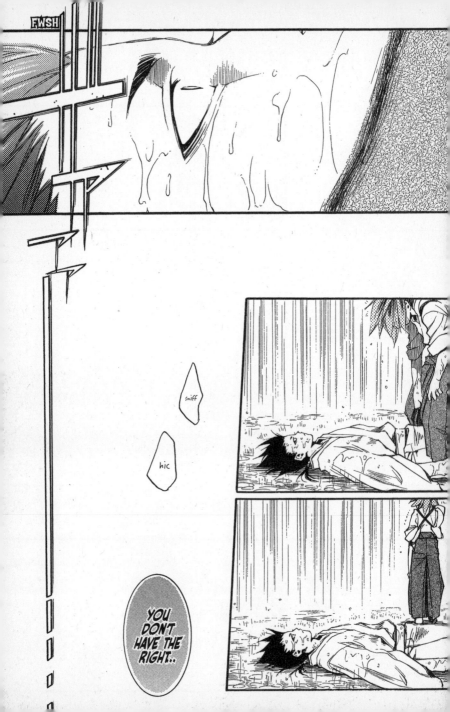

FWSH

sniff

hic

YOU DON'T HAVE THE RIGHT..

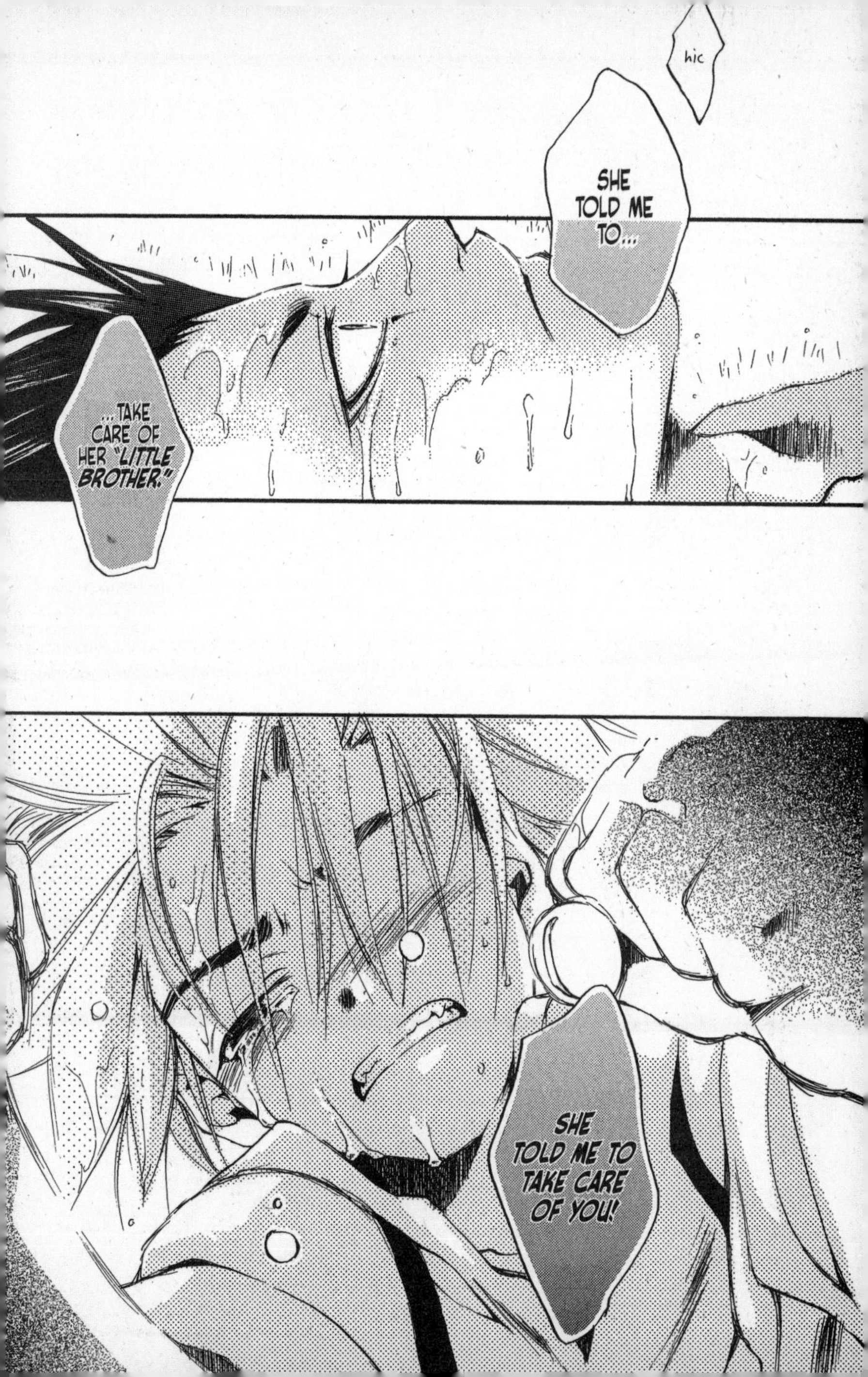
hic
SHE TOLD ME TO...
...TAKE CARE OF HER "LITTLE BROTHER."
SHE TOLD ME TO TAKE CARE OF YOU!

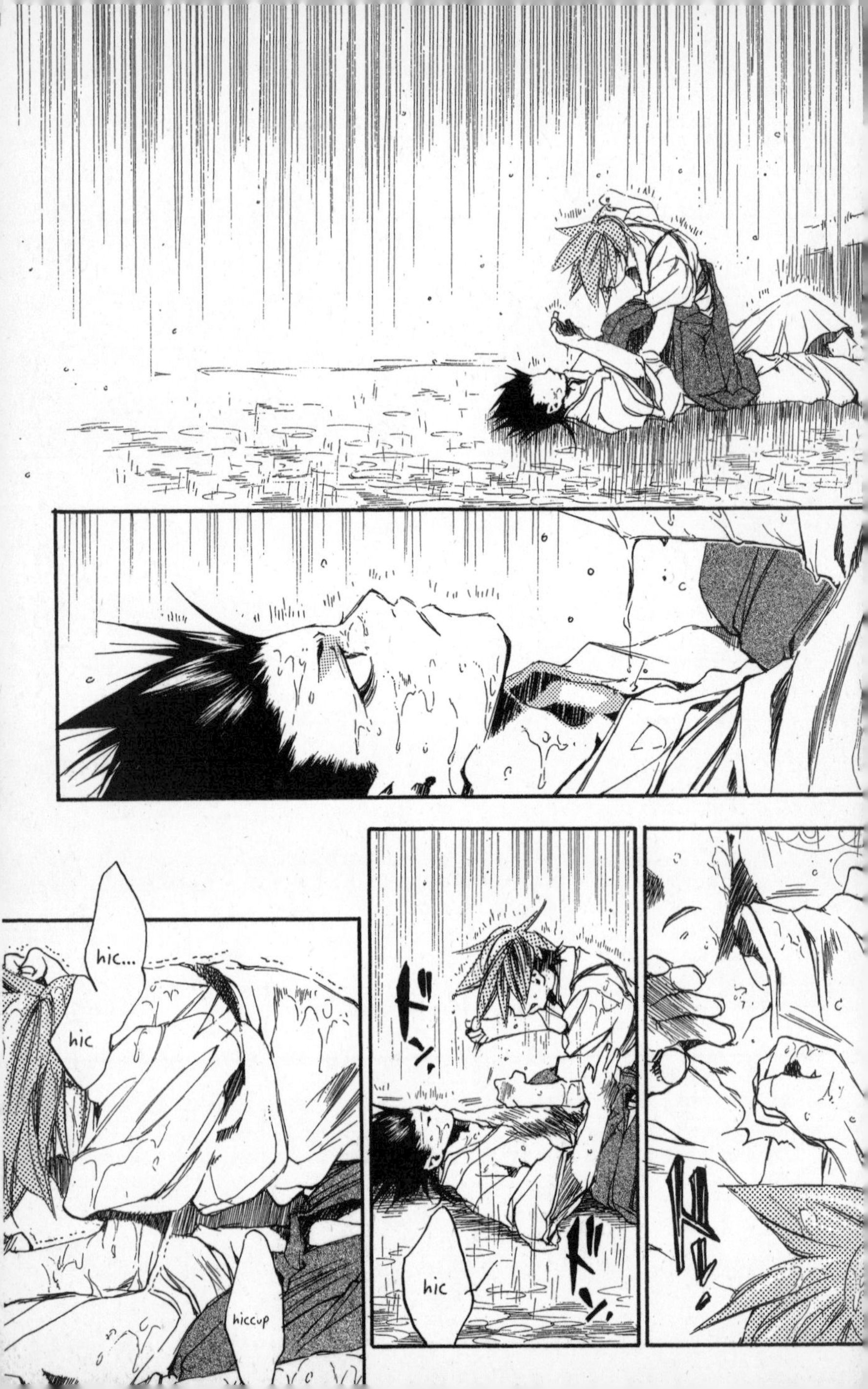
hic
hic...
hic
hiccup

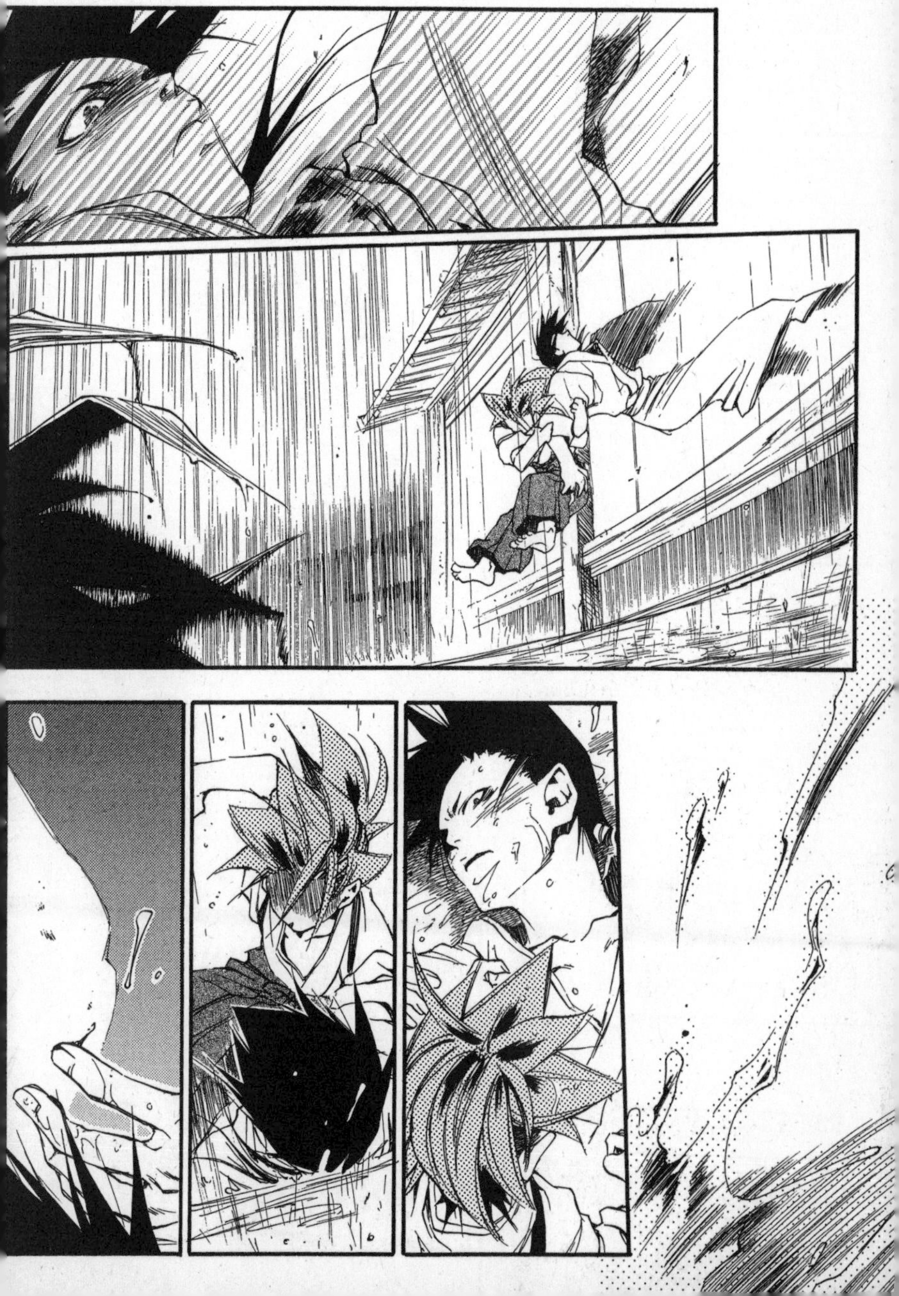

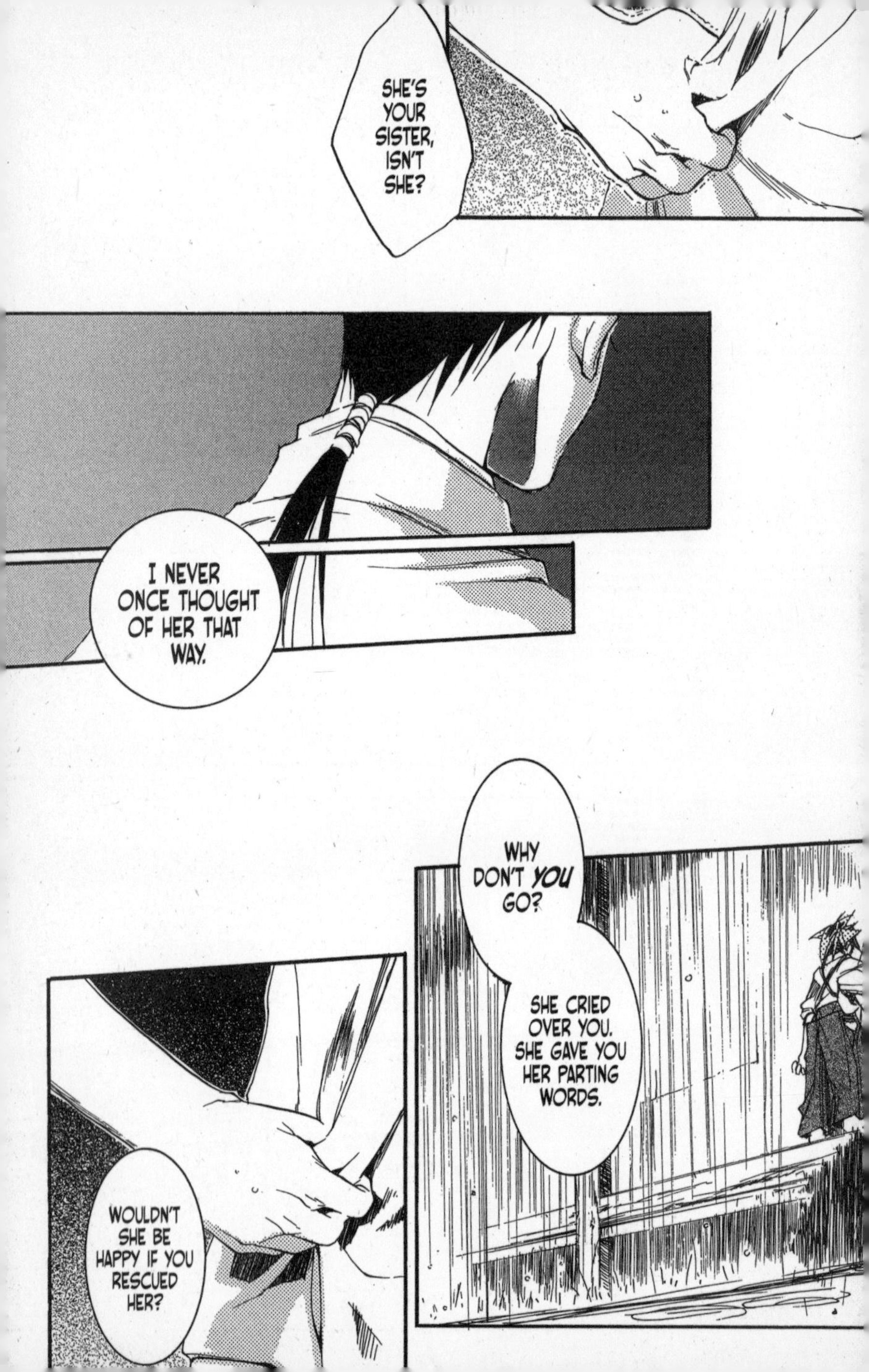
SHE'S YOUR SISTER, ISN'T SHE?
I NEVER ONCE THOUGHT OF HER THAT WAY.
WHY DON'T *YOU* GO?
SHE CRIED OVER YOU. SHE GAVE YOU HER PARTING WORDS.
WOULDN'T SHE BE HAPPY IF YOU RESCUED HER?

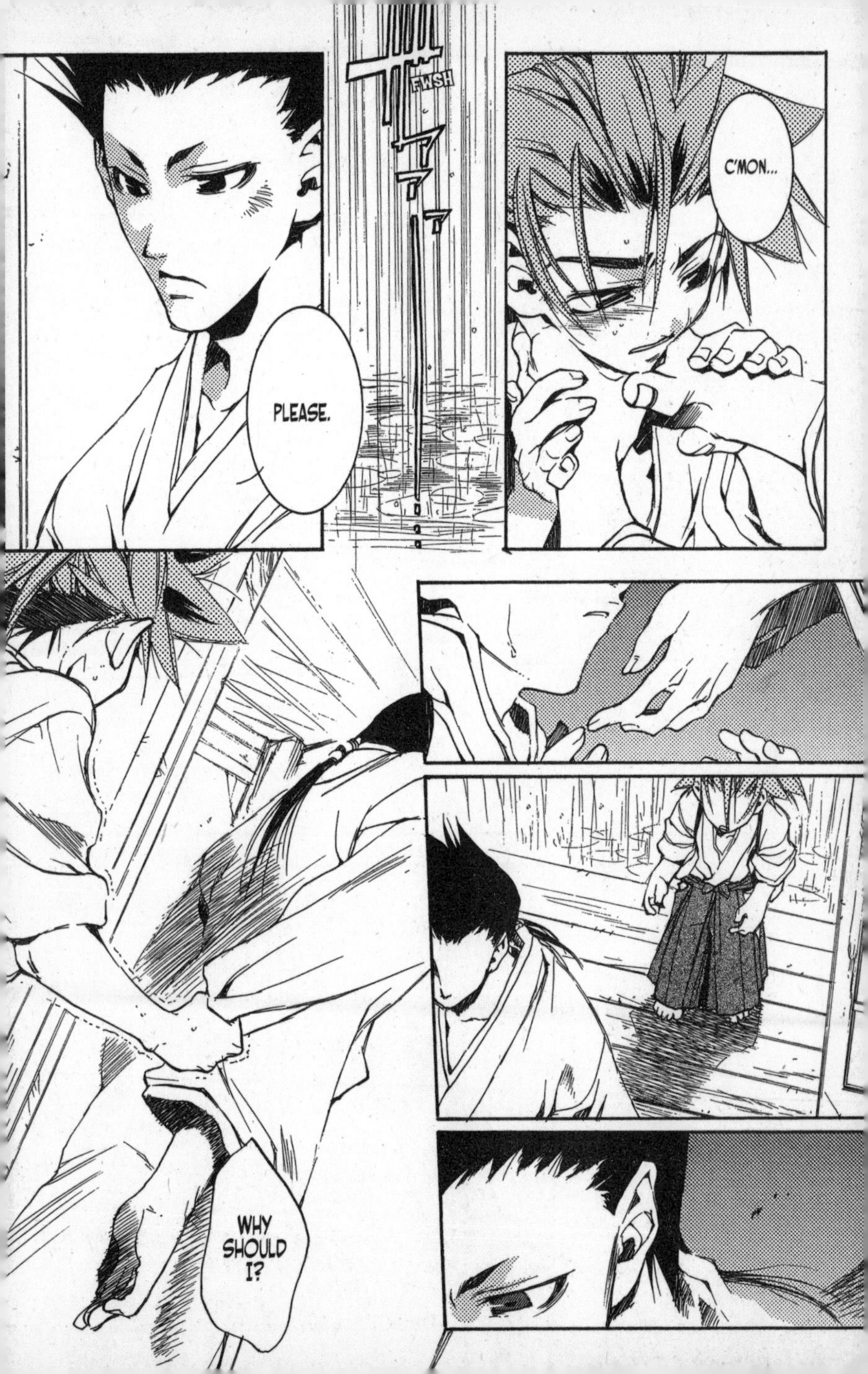
C'MON...
FWSH
PLEASE.
WHY SHOULD I?

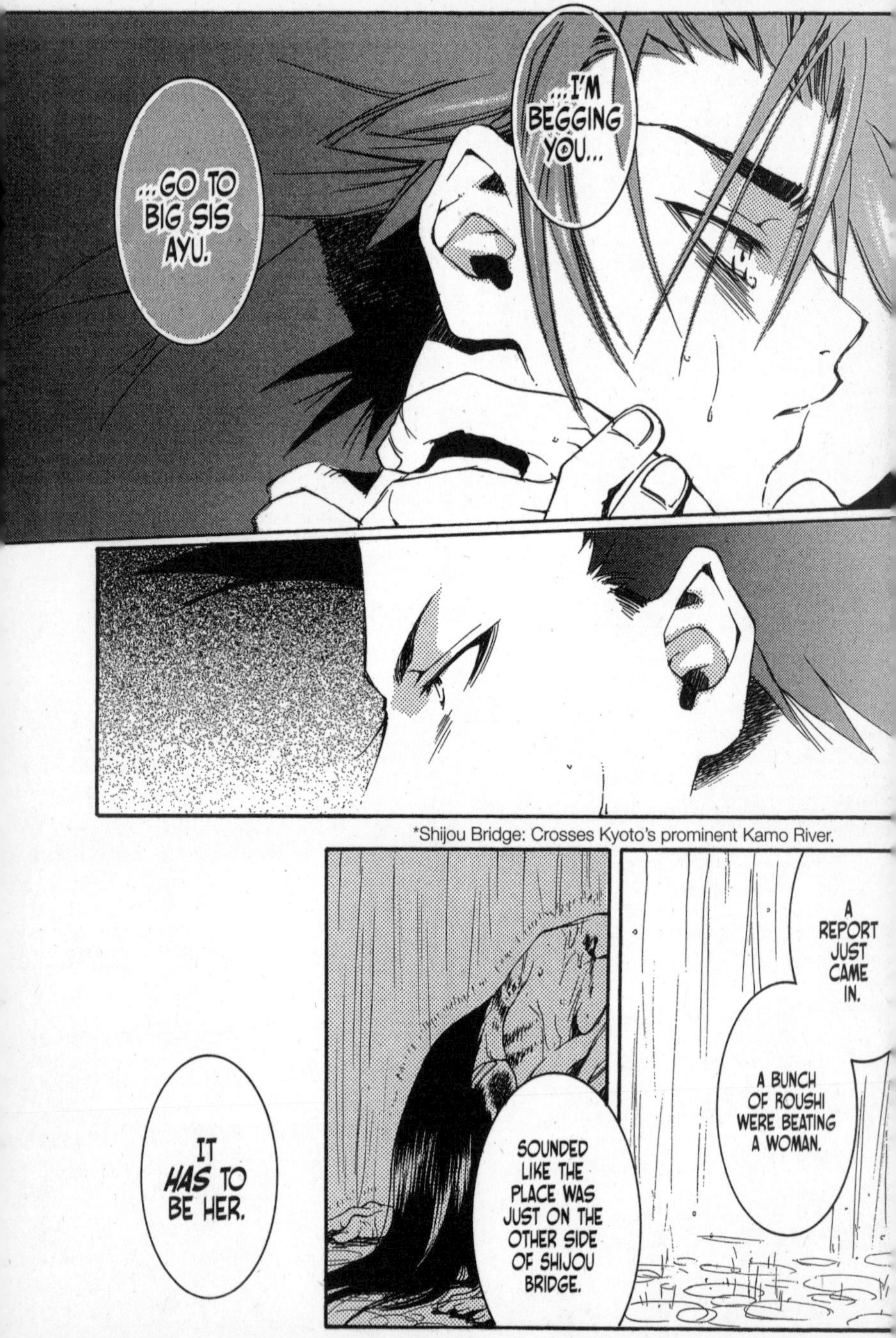
...I'M BEGGING YOU...
...GO TO BIG SIS AYU.
A REPORT JUST CAME IN.
A BUNCH OF ROUSHI WERE BEATING A WOMAN.
SOUNDED LIKE THE PLACE WAS JUST ON THE OTHER SIDE OF SHIJOU BRIDGE.
IT *HAS* TO BE HER.

*Shijou Bridge: Crosses Kyoto's prominent Kamo River.

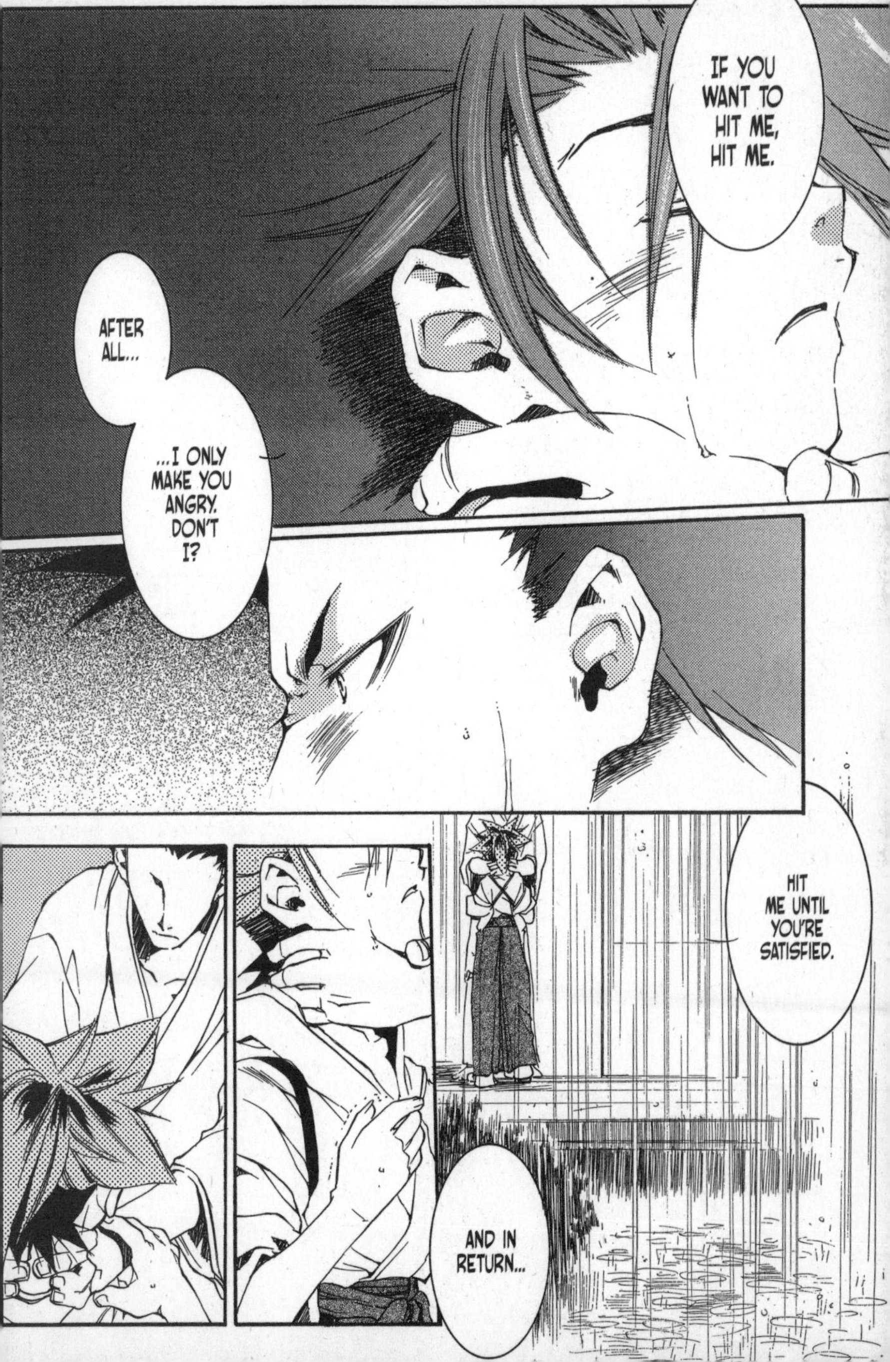
IF YOU WANT TO HIT ME, HIT ME.
AFTER ALL...
...I ONLY MAKE YOU ANGRY. DON'T I?
HIT ME UNTIL YOU'RE SATISFIED.
AND IN RETURN...

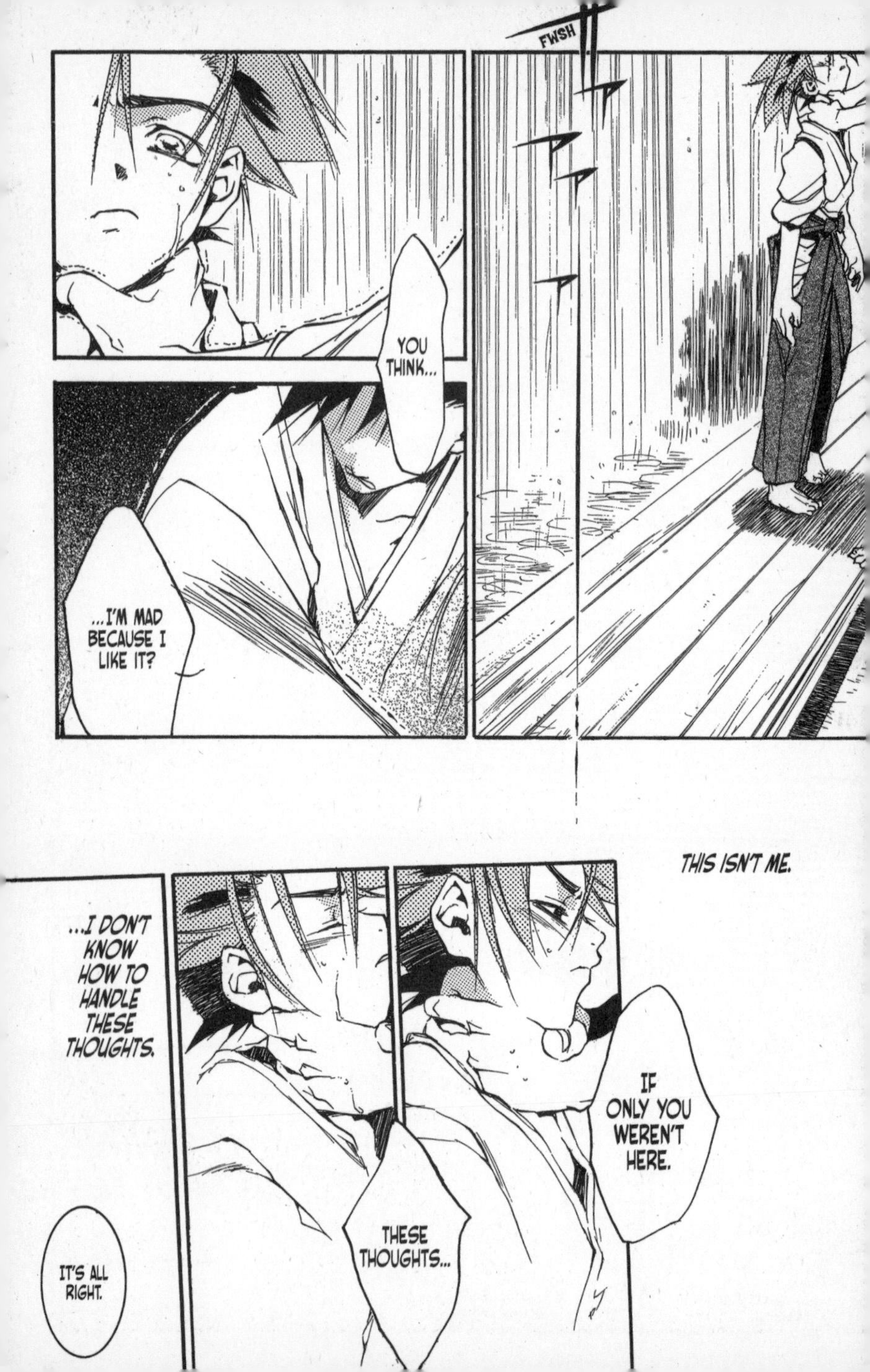
FWSH
YOU THINK...
...I'M MAD BECAUSE I LIKE IT?
THIS ISN'T ME.
IF ONLY YOU WEREN'T HERE.
THESE THOUGHTS...
...I DON'T KNOW HOW TO HANDLE THESE THOUGHTS.
IT'S ALL RIGHT.

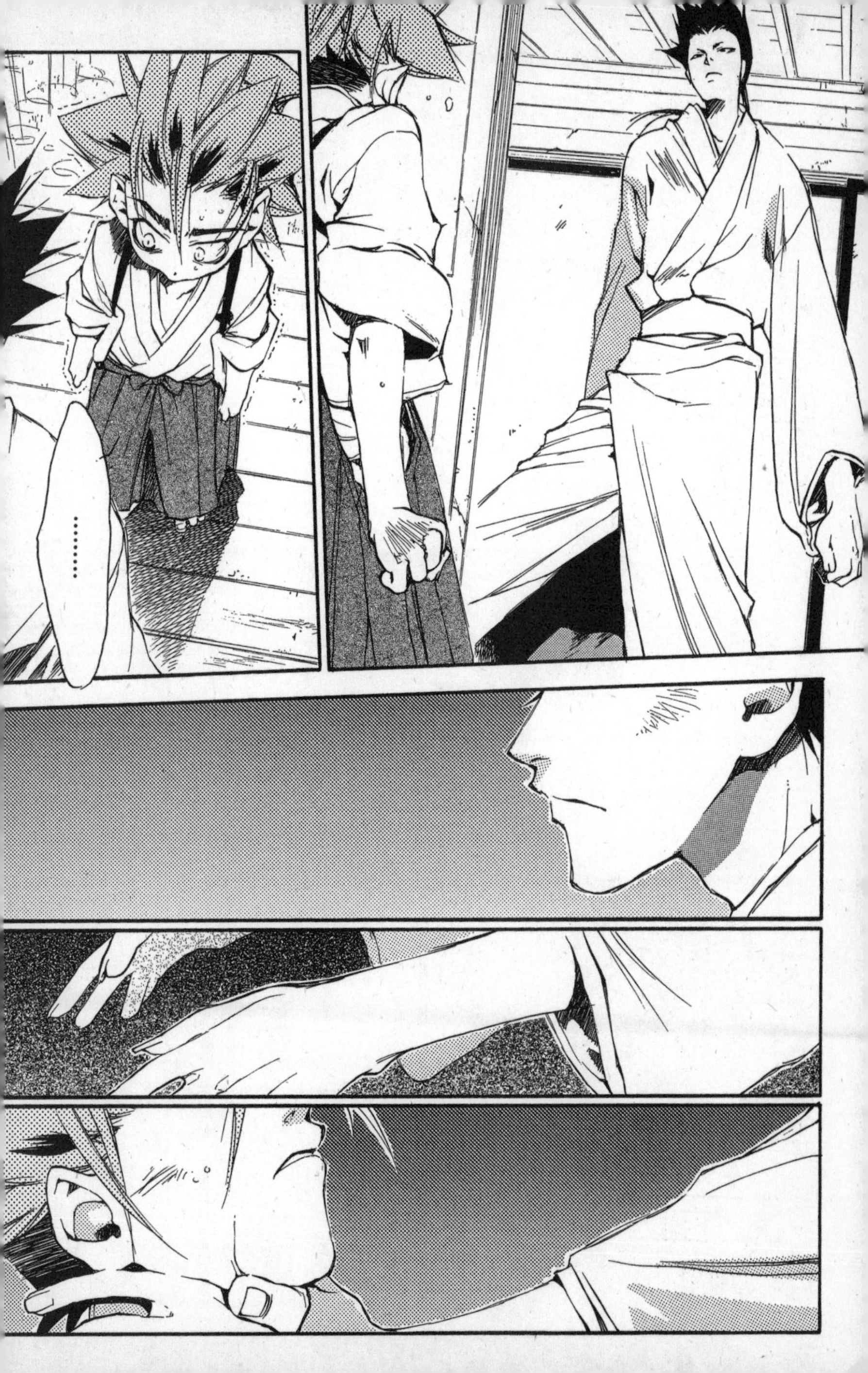
......

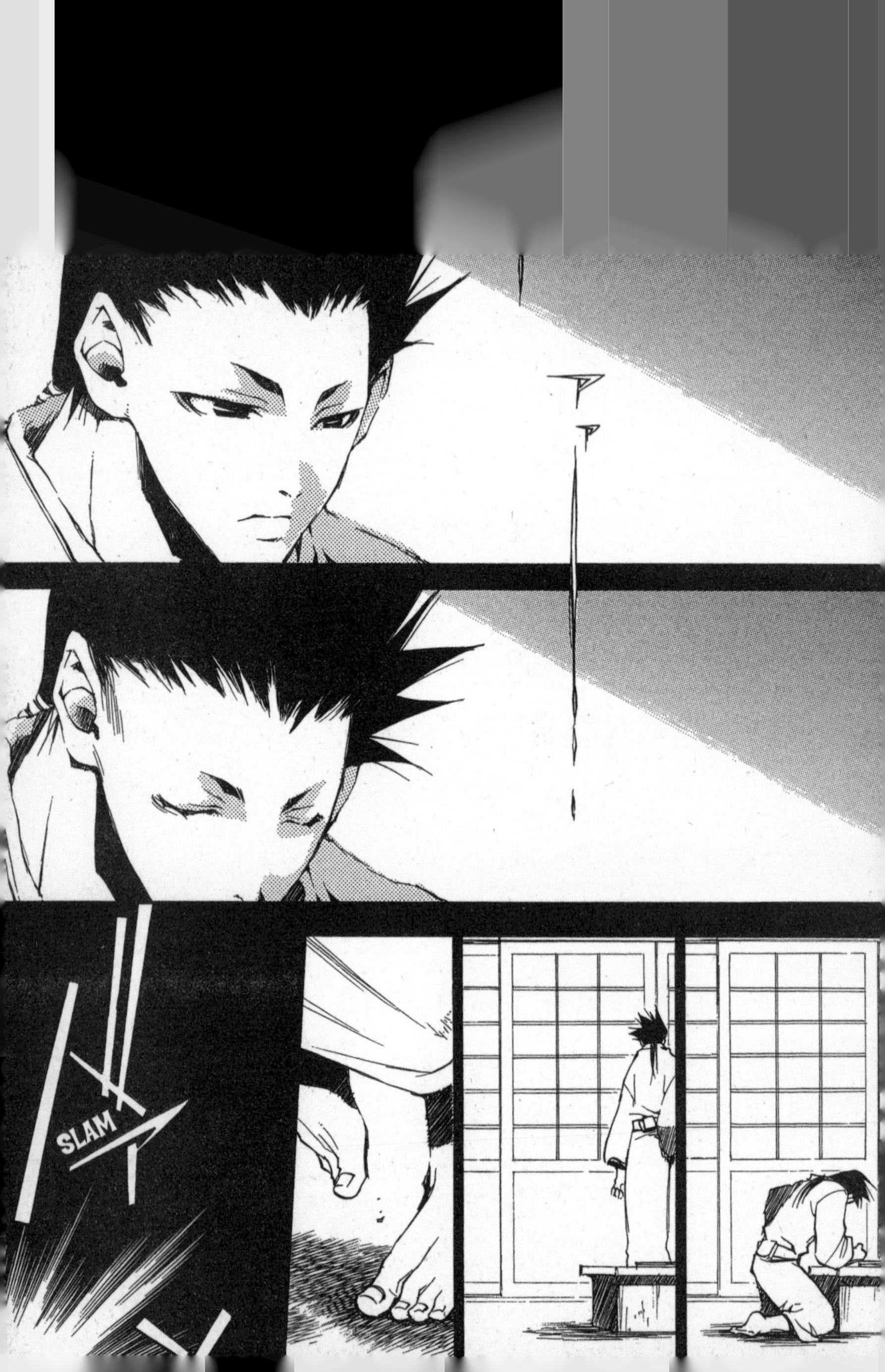
SLAM

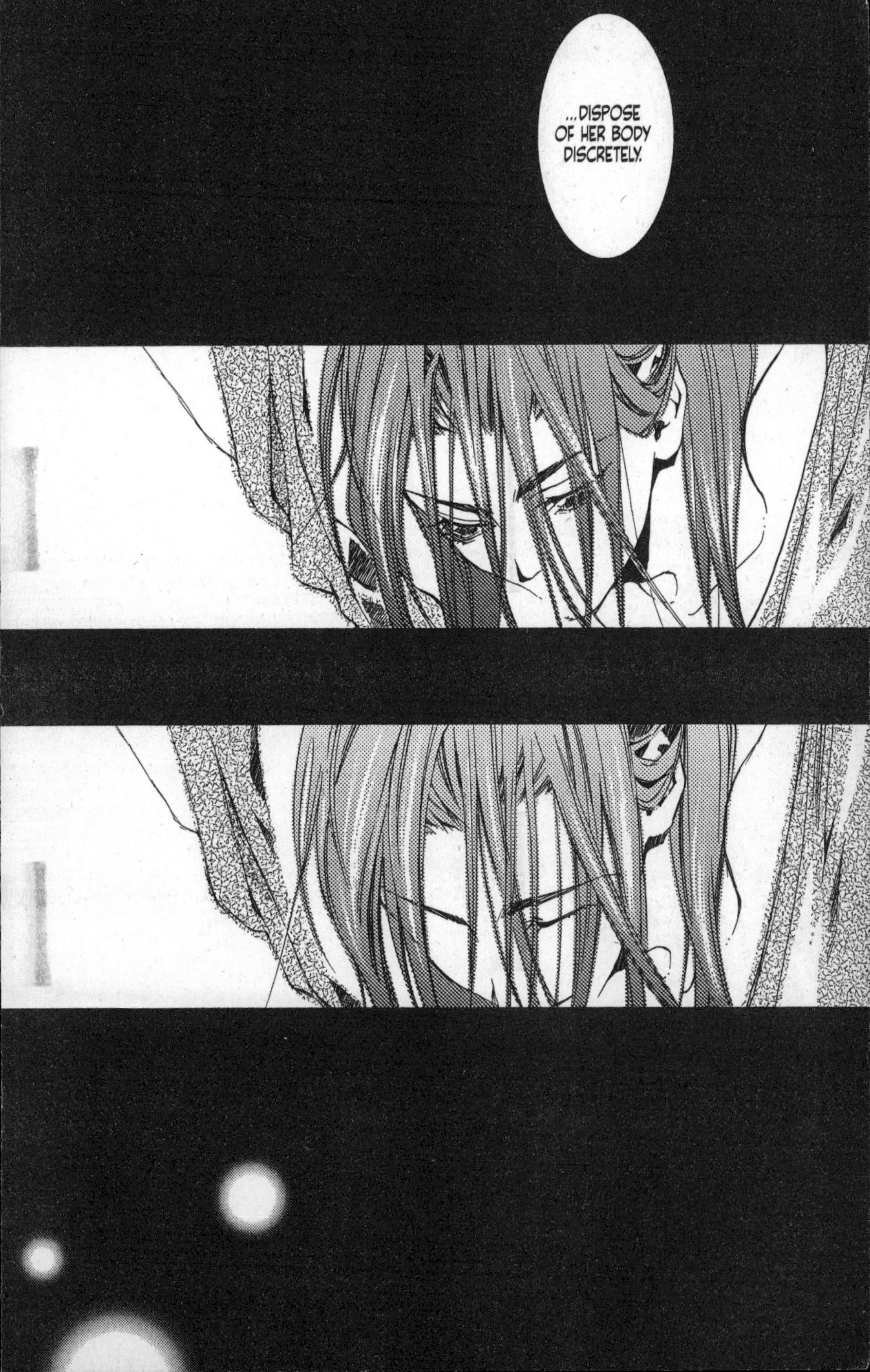
...DISPOSE OF HER BODY DISCRETELY.

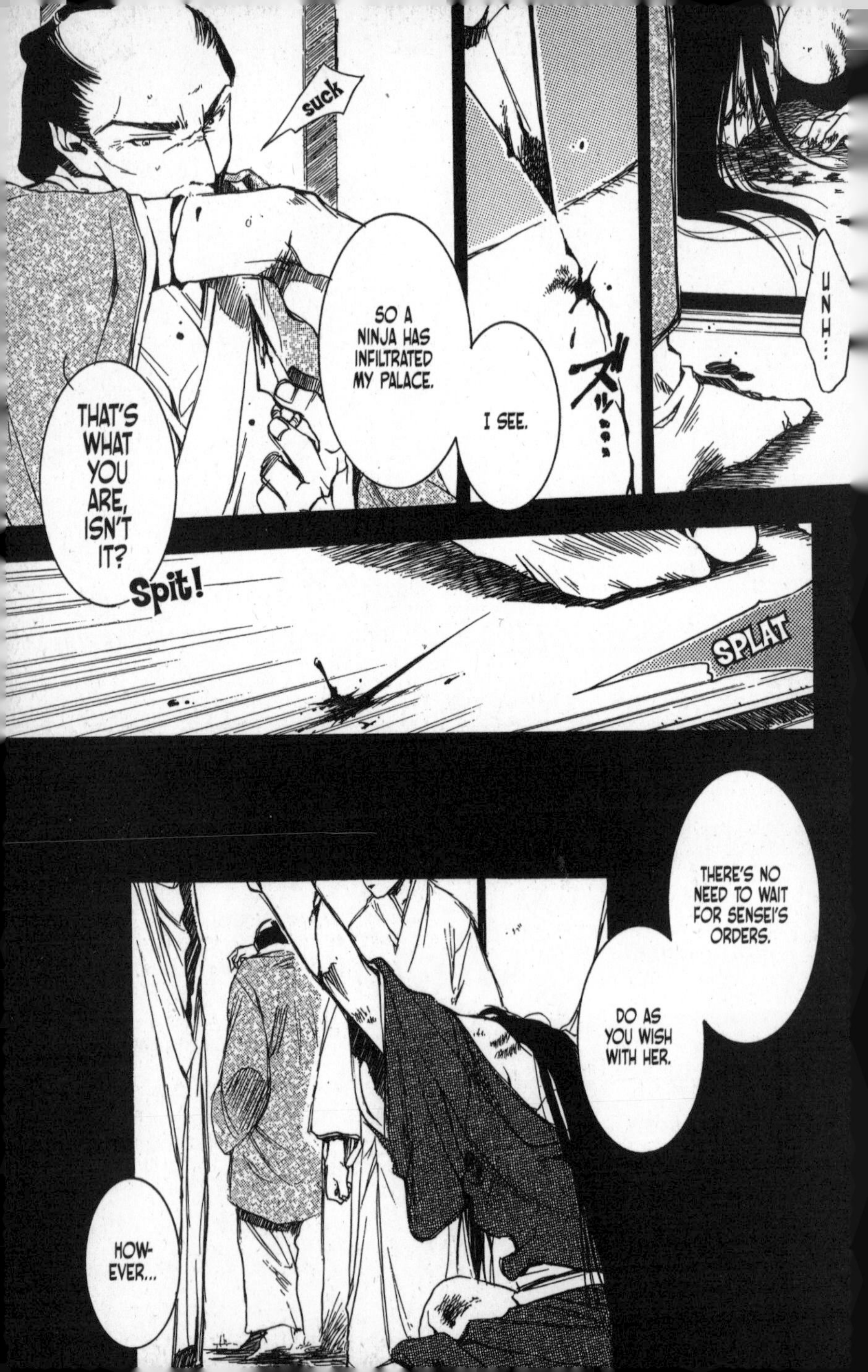

UNH...
ズル
suck
I SEE.
SO A NINJA HAS INFILTRATED MY PALACE.
THAT'S WHAT YOU ARE, ISN'T IT?
Spit!
SPLAT
THERE'S NO NEED TO WAIT FOR SENSEI'S ORDERS.
DO AS YOU WISH WITH HER.
HOW-EVER...

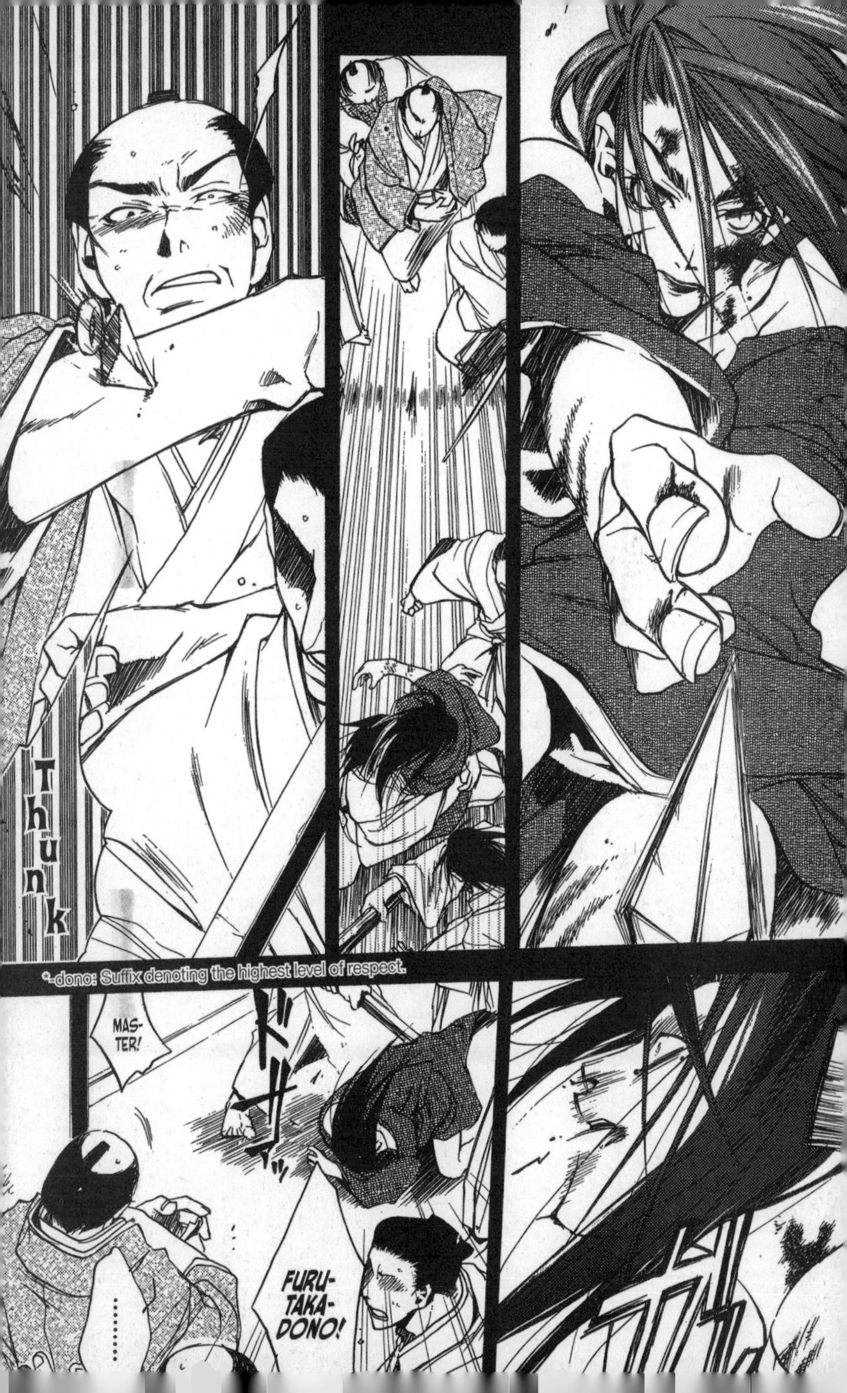
Thunk
MASTER!
FURUTAKA-DONO!
......

*-dono: Suffix denoting the highest level of respect.

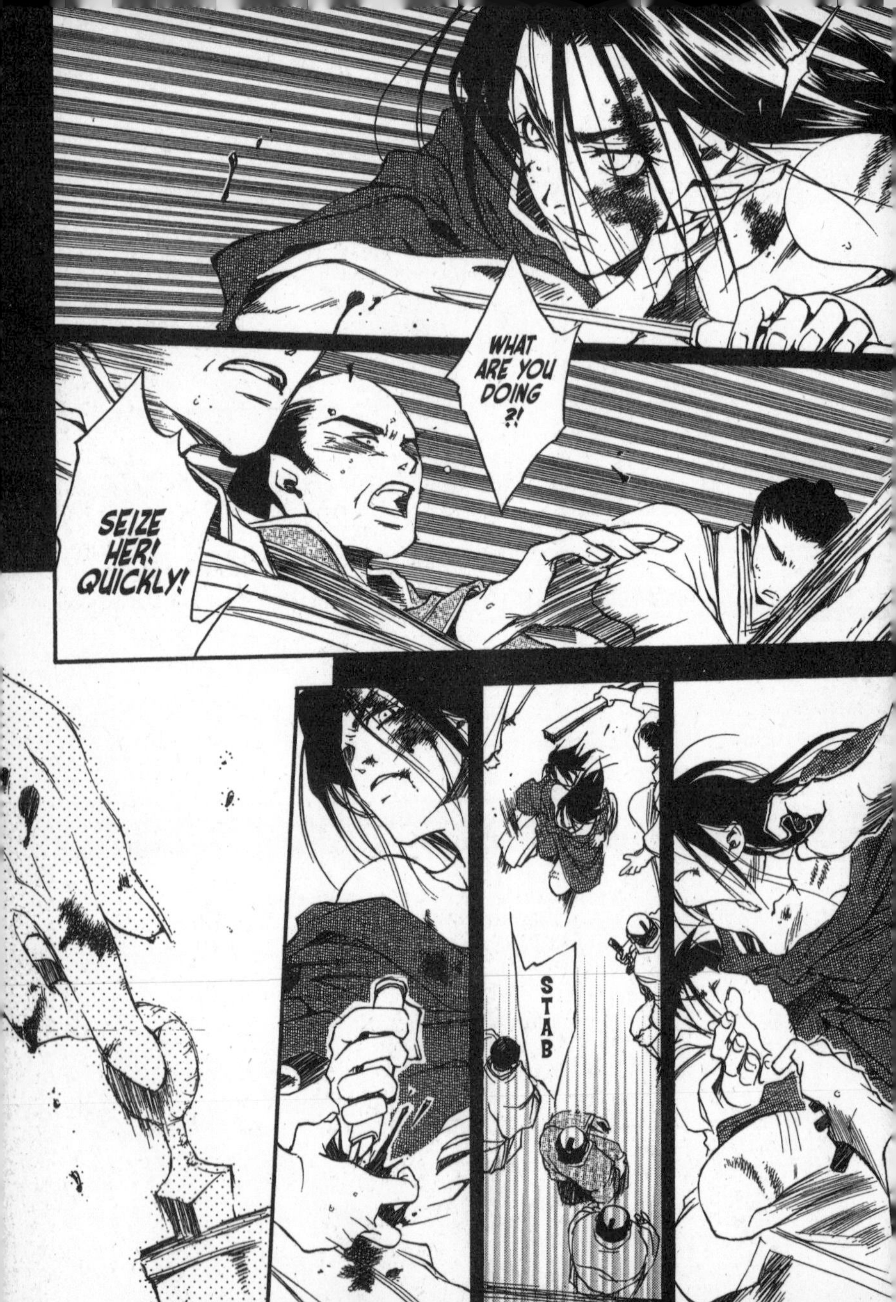
WHAT ARE YOU DOING ?!
SEIZE HER! QUICKLY!
STAB

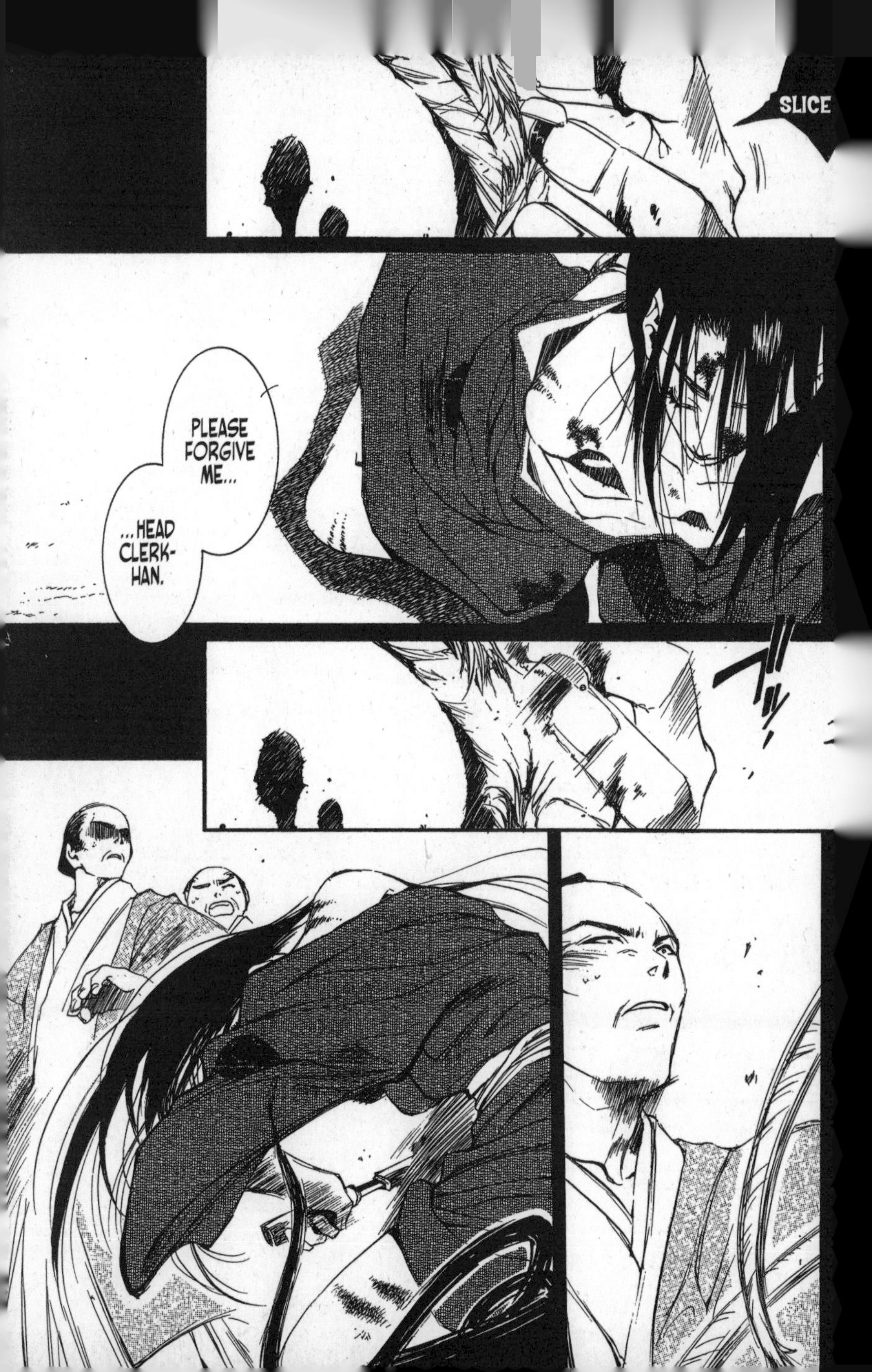
SLICE
PLEASE FORGIVE ME...
...HEAD CLERK-HAN.

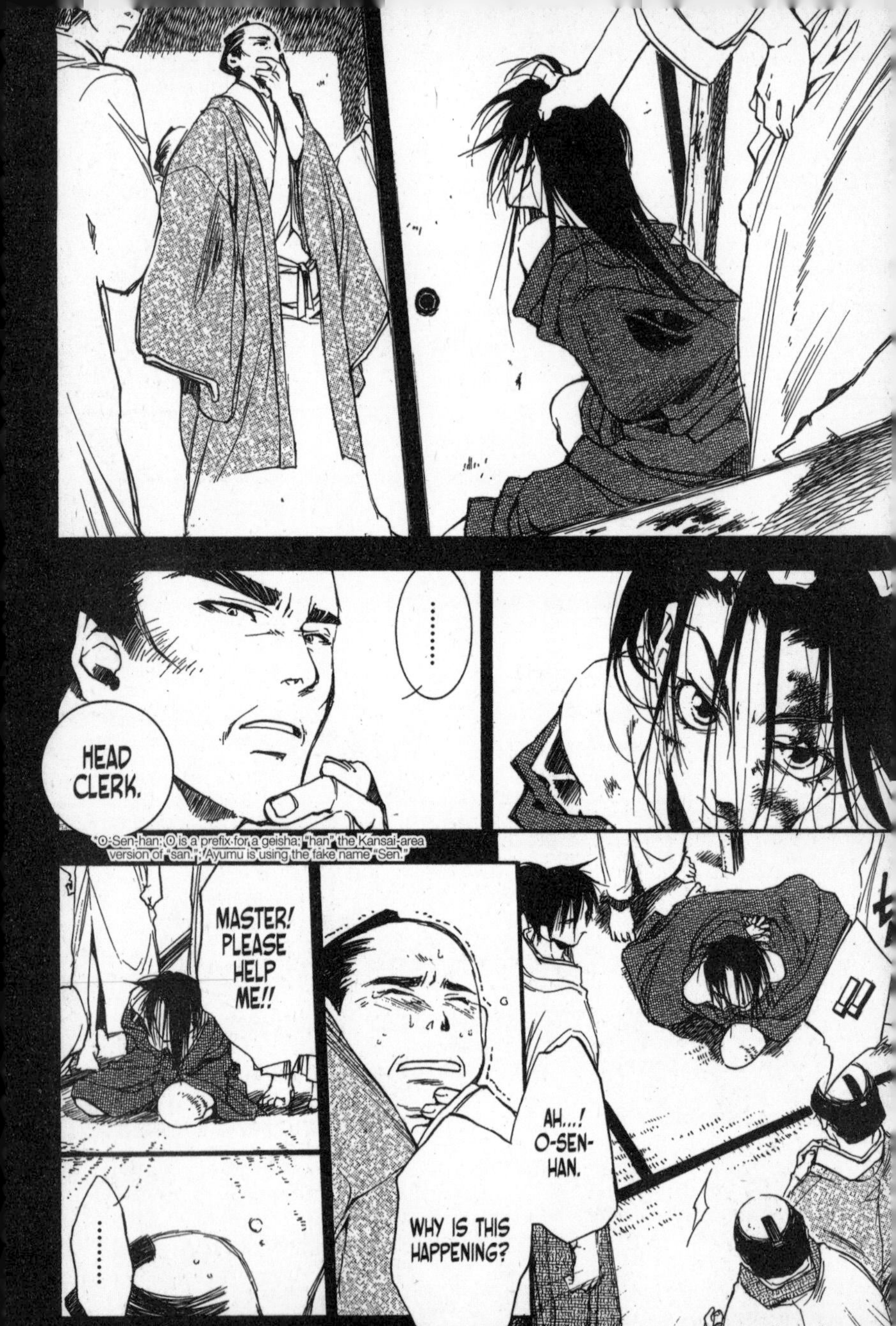
......
HEAD CLERK.
!!
AH...! O-SEN-HAN.
WHY IS THIS HAPPENING?
MASTER! PLEASE HELP ME!!
......

*O-Sen-han: O is a prefix for a geisha; "han" the Kansai-area version of "san."; Ayumu is using the fake name "Sen."

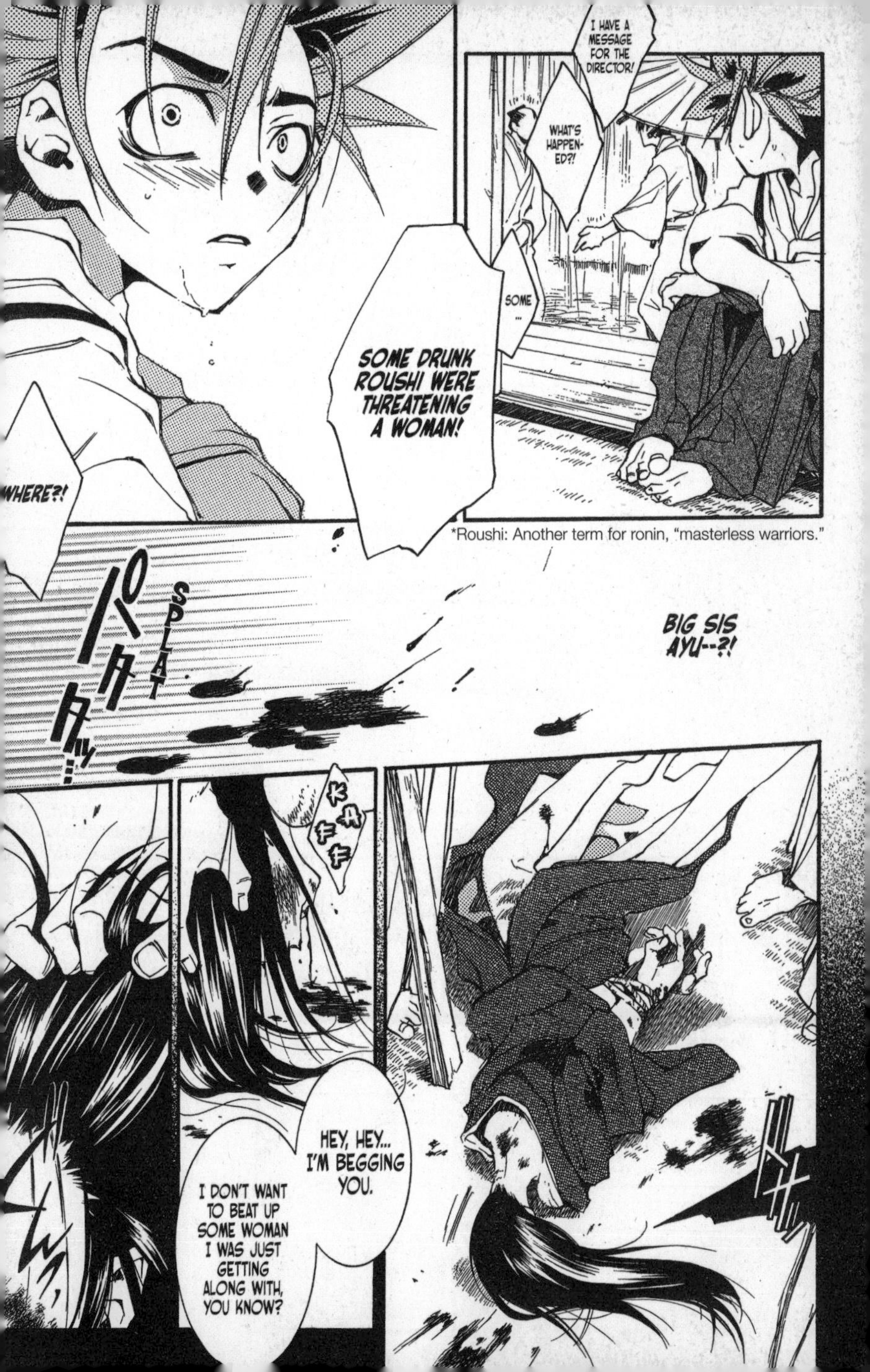
I HAVE A MESSAGE FOR THE DIRECTOR!
WHAT'S HAPPENED?!
SOME ...
SOME DRUNK ROUSHI WERE THREATENING A WOMAN!
WHERE?!
BIG SIS AYU--?!
SPLAT
パタタッ!!
HEY, HEY... I'M BEGGING YOU.
I DON'T WANT TO BEAT UP SOME WOMAN I WAS JUST GETTING ALONG WITH, YOU KNOW?
KAFF
*Roushi: Another term for ronin, "masterless warriors."

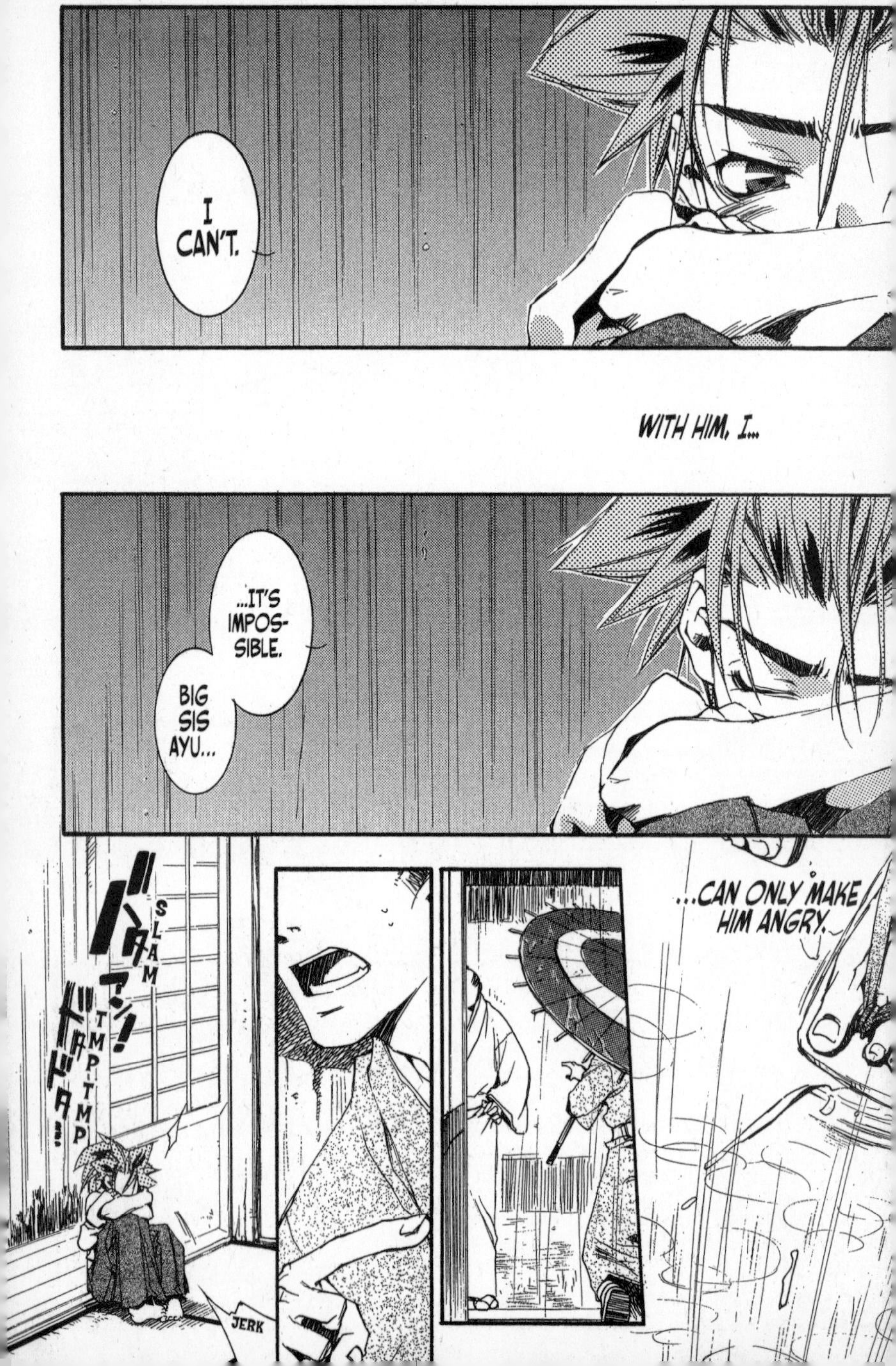
I CAN'T.
WITH HIM, I...
...IT'S IMPOSSIBLE.
BIG SIS AYU...
...CAN ONLY MAKE HIM ANGRY.
JERK
SLAM
TMP-TMP

"EVEN A LITTLE BIT HELPS. GET ALONG WITH HIM."
"YOU CAN FIGHT WITH HIM, AND THEN YOU CAN COMFORT HIM."
"YOU'RE..."
"...THE ONLY ONE WHO CAN."

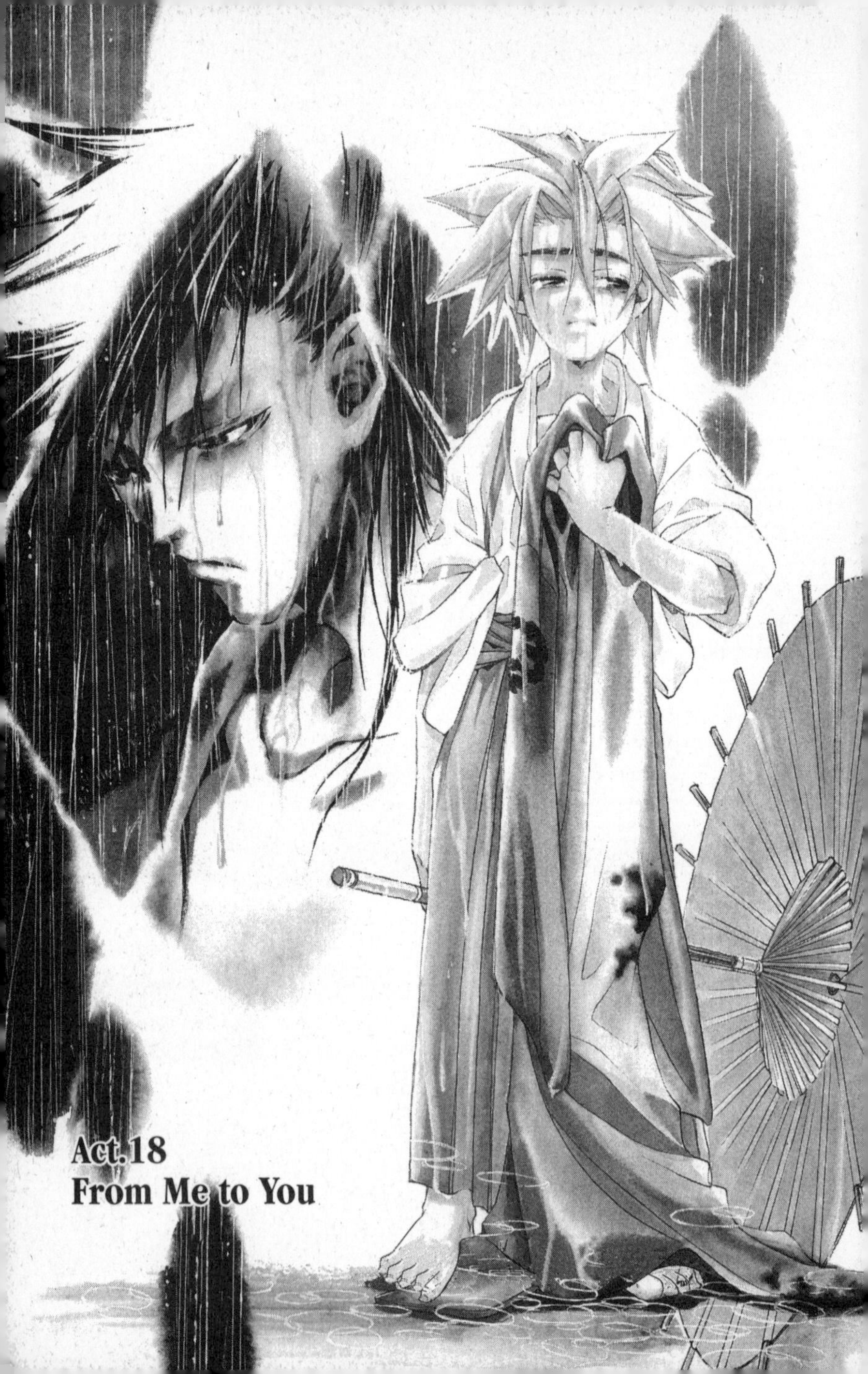
Act. 18
From Me to You

CONTENTS

MAIN CHARACTERS

NAGAKURA SHINPACHI

CAPTAIN OF THE SECOND SQUAD

SMALL BUT STRONG. A SWORDSMAN LIKE OKITA. HE FIGHTS IN THE SHINTO-MUNEN SCHOOL STYLE.

TOUDOU HEISUKE

CAPTAIN OF THE EIGHTH SQUAD

ONE OF THE THREE STOOGES OF THE SHINSENGUMI. HE LIKES CUTE THINGS, INCLUDING TETSU.

HARADA SANOSUKE

CAPTAIN OF THE TENTH SQUAD

A GIANT AMONG MEN, HE'S A MASTER OF THE SPEAR IN THE HOZOIN SCHOOL STYLE. HE'S GOOD FRIENDS WITH SHINPACHI.

ICHIMURA TATSUNOSUKE

TETSU'S OLDER BOTHER AND GUARDIAN. HE'S ALWAYS WORRYING ABOUT TETSU. TATSU WANTS NOTHING TO DO WITH SWORDFIGHTING, AND IS A BOOKKEEPER FOR THE SHINSENGUMI.

YAMAZAKI SUSUMU

SHINSENGUMI NINJA

A SPY FOR THE SHINSENGUMI, HE REPORTS TO HIJIKATA. TACITURN AND COLD, HE HOLDS MANY SECRETS.

SAYA

TETSU SAVED HER FROM SOME RUFFIANS, AND NOW THE TWO ARE FRIENDS. SAYA CANNOT SPEAK, BUT COMMUNICATES THROUGH HAND GESTURES AND WRITING.

 SHINSENGUMI MEMBERS

PERSONS OUTSIDE THE SHINSENGUMI

THE STORY OF PEACE MAKER

IN THE FIRST YEAR OF GENJI, 1864, JAPAN WAS IN GREAT TURMOIL. MILITANT AND XENOPHOBIC FORCES, WHICH HAD LONG OPPOSED THE TOKUGAWA SHOGUNATE, ADVOCATED EXPELLING WESTERN INFLUENCE AND RESTORING THE EMPEROR IN KYOTO TO POWER. TO PROTECT THE SHOGUNATE'S INTEREST IN KYOTO, A LEGENDARY PEACEKEEPING FORCE WAS FORMED FROM TWO HUNDRED-SOME RONIN. THEY WERE THE SHINSENGUMI. THIS IS THE STORY OF ICHIMURA TETSUNOSUKE, WHO SOUGHT TO JOIN THEM.

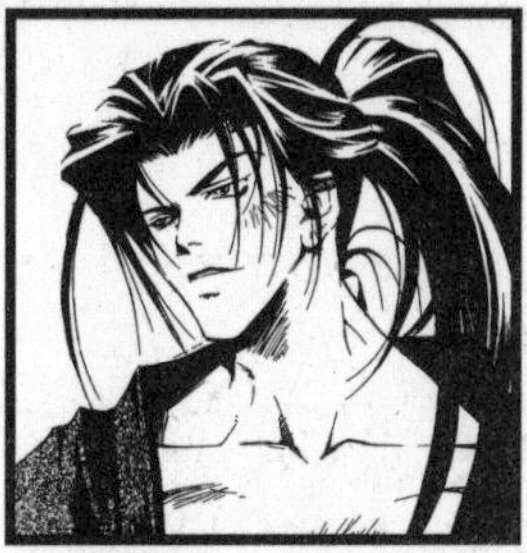

HIJIKATA TOSHIZOU

VICE COMMANDER

BECAUSE OF HIS COLD DEMEANOR AND BRUTALITY, HE IS KNOWN AS THE "DEMON VICE COMMANDER."

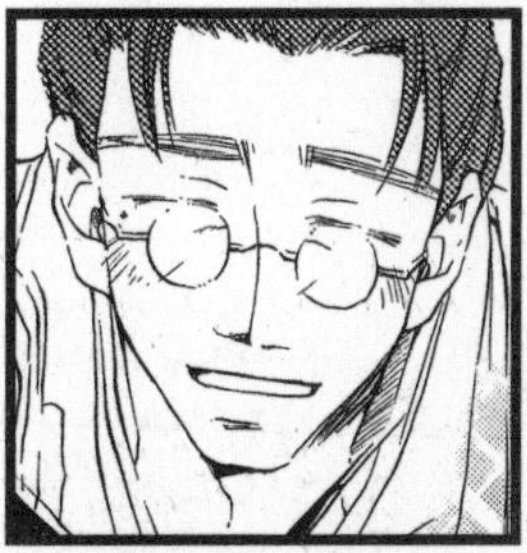

YAMANAMI KEISUKE

VICE COMMANDER

THIS BUDDHA-LIKE VICE COMMANDER COULDN'T BE LESS LIKE HIJIKATA. HE'S OFTEN SEEN CARRYING HIS ABACUS.

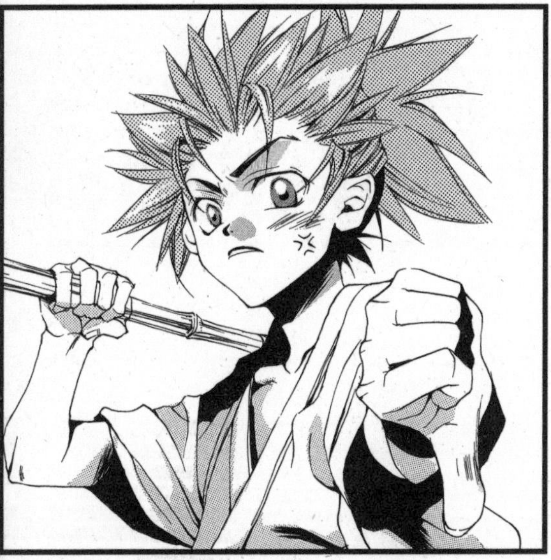

ICHIMURA TETSUNOSUKE

HIJIKATA'S PAGE

BRASH TETSU HAS JOINED THE SHINSENGUMI TO LEARN TO BECOME STRONG. HE WANTS TO GET REVENGE ON HIS PARENTS' MURDERERS, CHOUSHUU REBELS. ALTHOUGH HE JOINED THE SHINSENGUMI WITH ASPIRATIONS OF BECOMING A SWORDSMAN, HE'S BEEN ASSIGNED THE THANKLESS DUTY OF HIJIKATA'S PAGE.

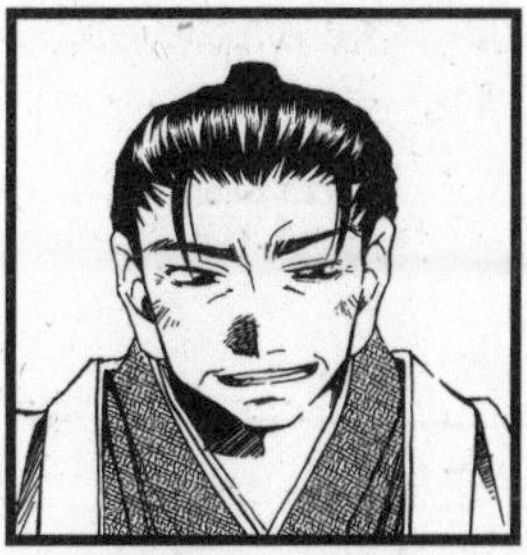

KONDOU ISAMI

DIRECTOR

A FOUNDING MEMBER OF THE SHINSENGUMI AND ALSO A MASTER AT THE SHIEIKAN DOJO IN EDO, THE MAIN DOJO OF THE TENNEN RISHIN STYLE.

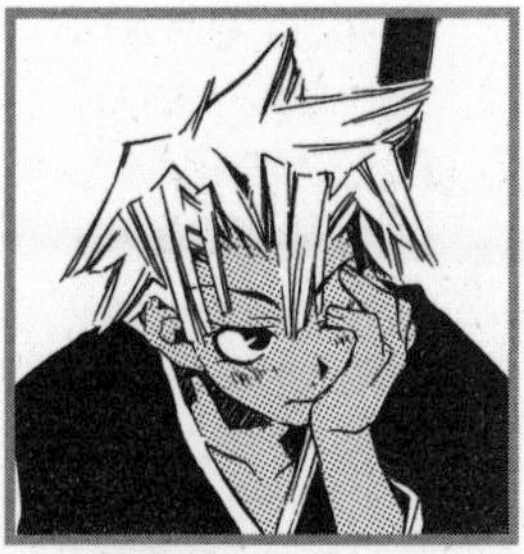

KITAMURA SUZU

A BOY WITH SILVER HAIR. HE HAS NO FAMILY AND LIVES WITH HIS MASTER, YOSHIDA TOSHIMARO. HE AND HIS MASTER OPPOSE THE SHINSENGUMI.

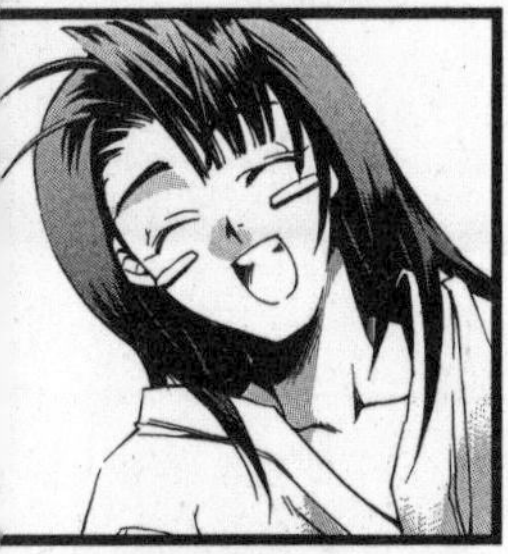

OKITA SOUJI

CAPTAIN OF THE FIRST SQUAD

THE BEST SWORDSMAN IN THE SHINSENGUMI. HE'S GENERALLY CALM AND FRIENDLY, BUT WIELDING A BLADE CAN TRANSFORM HIM INTO A HEARTLESS KILLER.

PEACE MAKER
ピースメーカー

Volume 4
by Nanae Chrono

HAMBURG // LONDON // LOS ANGELES // TOKYO

Peace Maker Volume 4
Created by NANAE CHRONO

Translation - Ryan Flake
English Adaption - Christine Boylan
Retouch and Lettering - Star Print Brokers
Production Artist - Mike Estacio
Graphic Designer - Chelsea Windlinger

Editor - Hope Donovan
Digital Imaging Manager - Chris Buford
Pre-Production Supervisor - Vicente Rivera, Jr.
Production Specialist - Lucas Rivera
Managing Editor - Vy Nguyen
Art Director - Al-Insan Lashley
Editor-in-Chief - Rob Tokar
Publisher - Mike Kiley
President and C.O.O. - John Parker
C.E.O. and Chief Creative Officer - Stu Levy

A **TOKYOPOP** Manga

TOKYOPOP and are trademarks or registered trademarks of TOKYOPOP Inc.

TOKYOPOP Inc.
5900 Wilshire Blvd. Suite 2000
Los Angeles, CA 90036

E-mail: info@TOKYOPOP.com
Come visit us online at www.TOKYOPOP.com

ISBN: 978-1-4278-0078-7

First TOKYOPOP printing: August 2008
10 9 8 7 6 5 4 3 2 1
Printed in the USA

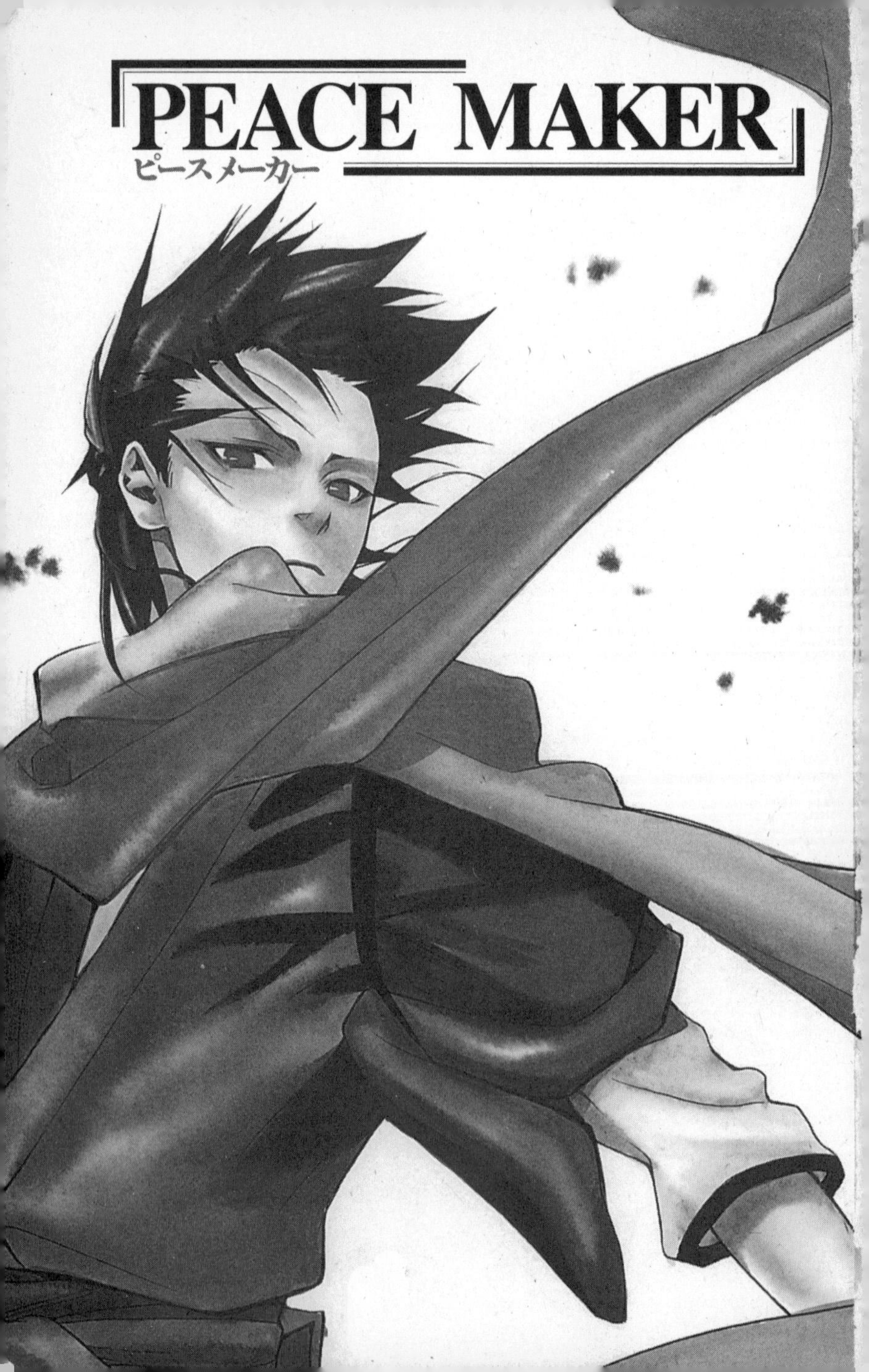
PEACE MAKER
ピースメーカー